WITHDRAWN
FROM THE VPI & SU
LIBRARY COLLECTION

D0567109

New Frontiers in
European Industrial Relations

IB

Industrial Relations in Context

General Editors: Paul Edwards, Richard Hyman and Keith Sisson

New Frontiers in European Industrial Relations

Edited by

Richard Hyman and Anthony Ferner

HD
8376.5
N46
1994
NVTGC

Copyright © Basil Blackwell Ltd. 1994

First published 1994

Blackwell Publishers
108 Cowley Road
Oxford Ox4 1JF
UK

238 Main Street
Cambridge, Massachusetts 02142
USA

All rights reserved. Except for the quotation of short passages for the purposes of criticism and review, no part of this publication may be reproduced, stored in a retrieval system, or transmitted, in any form or by any means, electronic, mechanical, photocopying, recording or otherwise, without the prior permission of the publisher.

Except in the United States of America, this book is sold subject to the condition that it shall not, by way of trade or otherwise, be lent, resold, hired out, or otherwise circulated without the publisher's prior consent in any form of binding or cover other than that in which it is published and without a similar condition including this condition being imposed on the subsequent purchaser.

British Library Cataloguing in Publication Data

A CIP catalogue record for this book is available from the British Library.

Library of Congress Cataloging-in-Publication Data

New frontiers in European industrial relations / edited by Richard
  Hyman and Anthony Ferner.
      p.   cm. — (Industrial relations in context)
   Includes bibliographical references and index.
   ISBN 0-631-18606-9 (alk. paper)
   1. Industrial relations—Europe.   2. Comparative industrial
relations.   I. Hyman, Richard.   II. Ferner, Anthony.   III. Series.
HD8376.5.N46   1994
331'.094—dc20   94-7344
                                                                         CIP

Typeset in 10$^1/_2$ on 12$^1/_2$ pt Palatino by Best-set Typesetter Ltd., Hong Kong
Printed in Great Britain by Hartnolls Ltd., Bodmin, Cornwall

This book is printed on acid-free paper

Contents

List of Figures

List of Tables

Contributors

Simon Clarke, Reader in Sociology, University of Warwick.

Colin Crouch, Fellow and Tutor in Politics at Trinity College, Oxford, and Faculty Lecturer in Sociology.

Paul Edwards, Professor of Industrial Relations and Deputy Director, Industrial Relations Research Unit, University of Warwick.

Colette Fagan, Research Associate for the EC Network on the Situation of Women in the Labour Market, Manchester School of Management, UMIST.

Peter Fairbrother, Senior Lecturer, Department of Sociology, University of Warwick.

Anthony Ferner, Principal Research Fellow, Industrial Relations Research Unit, University of Warwick.

Mark Hall, Senior Research Fellow, Industrial Relations Research Unit, University of Warwick.

Lajos Héthy, Director, Institute of Labour Research, Budapest.

Richard Hyman, Professor of Industrial Relations, School of Industrial and Business Studies, University of Warwick.

Christel Lane, Fellow of St John's College, Cambridge, and Lecturer in Sociology, Faculty of Social and Political Sciences.

Denis MacShane, International Metalworkers Federation, Geneva, and Associate Director, European Policy Institute.

Paul Marginson, Senior Lecturer in Industrial Relations, School of Industrial and Business Studies, University of Warwick.

Jill Rubery, Co-ordinator for the EC Network on the Situation of Women in the Labour Market, and Senior Lecturer in Labour Economics, Manchester School of Management, UMIST.

Keith Sisson, Professor of Industrial Relations and Director, Industrial Relations Research Unit, University of Warwick.

Michael Terry, Reader in Industrial Relations, School of Industrial and Business Studies, University of Warwick.

Jelle Visser, Sociology of Organizations Research Unit (SORU), Sociologisch Instituut, University of Amsterdam.

Foreword

The 'Industrial Relations in Context' series was launched by George Bain in 1983 to complement the established research monographs, 'Warwick Studies in Industrial Relations'. The volumes in the series provide comprehensive, authoritative and up-to-date analysis of current issues and trends in the entire field of employment relations. They are informed by empirical research and scholarship, and by an awareness of the wider social, economic and political contexts.

The series is intended for students doing diploma, undergraduate or postgraduate courses in human resource management and industrial relations at colleges and universities, as well as for those studying industrial sociology, labour economics, labour law and business management. It is also addressed to those in adult education, to those seeking membership of professional bodies like the Institute of Personnel Management, to practitioners in both unions and management, and to the general reader who wants to find out more about employment relations today.

Each volume is composed of original essays that bring together theoretical and empirical knowledge and understanding. Each chapter is stamped with the views of the authors who are experts in their field. Each emphasizes analysis and explanation as well as description. Each focuses on trends over recent decades and says something about likely future developments. And in each volume the text is welded into a coherent whole by editors who combine a distinguished research record with a proven ability to communicate to a wider audience.

The series began with *Industrial Relations in Britain*, edited by George Bain. Subsequent volumes were *Labour Law in Britain*, edited by Roy Lewis, *Employment in Britain*, edited by Duncan Gallie, *Personnel Management in Britain*, edited by Keith Sisson, and *Industrial Relations in the New Europe*, edited by Anthony Ferner and Richard Hyman. *Personnel Management in Britain* has been completely revised for a second edition, as has *Industrial Relations in Britain* under the editorship of Paul Edwards.

Industrial Relations in the New Europe, published in August 1992, reflected the growing attention in the University of Warwick's research and teaching to developments at European level. It brought together experts on 17 western European countries to produce the most comprehensive text on European industrial relations ever written. Already it is established as an indispensable resource for teachers and researchers as well as a valuable guide for practitioners.

New Frontiers in European Industrial Relations complements the previous text in two ways. First, the editors have commissioned a varied and ambitious collection of comparative analyses of key themes in contemporary European industrial relations. Second, three chapters provide soundly based and challenging assessments of current developments in industrial relations in eastern Europe. Together these contributions offer a stimulating and intellectually rigorous overview of the complex changes in European industrial relations today.

Paul Edwards
Richard Hyman
Keith Sisson

Preface

The aims of this book, as we intimated in *Industrial Relations in the New Europe*, are twofold. First, we have sought to exploit the potential for comparative analysis of the 17 national studies of industrial relations in western Europe which were presented in the previous volume. To this end we invited some dozen experts to address specified themes, and encouraged them while focusing primarily on countries with which they were particularly familiar to draw on as wide a range of evidence as possible. The scope for comprehensive coverage inevitably varied according to topic, hence some chapters are more encompassing than others. For all, however, the key criterion on which we insisted from the outset was to provide clear analytical insights of a comparative nature.

In defining the coverage of our previous text, the editorial decisions were straightforward. We included all twelve members countries of the European Union (EU), and also the major western European nations outside the EU. In compiling the present work our choices were far more complex. We wished to combine a focus on the key 'actors' with attention to a number of critical themes and issues. Although our decisions reflect (we trust) an intellectual logic, they are nevertheless the expression of personal preferences (and of the fairly tight constraints on the length of the volume). Hence, for example, in examining the role of employers, we have not included a chapter on employers' associations – which in our view have rarely played a major role in industrial relations initiatives in the past decade; nor on small and medium-sized enterprises (SMEs) which, despite increased importance in the economic structure of many European countries, remain of marginal significance for the transformation of employment relations. A number of important themes – such as new technology, employee participation or 'flexibility' – run through several of the contributions, without having chapters specifically devoted to them.

Our second objective is very different. When we finished work on *Industrial Relations in the New Europe*, it was obvious that the transformation of east and central Europe would provoke radical changes in the world of employment; however, the picture was obscure and unstable, and information available in the west was largely anecdotal. Although serious and informed analysis remains extremely difficult, at least the effort is now worth making. We therefore commissioned three contributions from experts in this field. The first two, on national tripartite institutions and on the transformation of trade unionism, offer wide-ranging comparative evidence and assessments. The third examines emerging industrial relations at company level. Given the paucity of reliable information on the workplace in east/central Europe, detailed comparison remains scarcely possible; the authors thus range only cautiously beyond the evidence of their own research in the former Soviet Union.

As in the previous volume, the editorial process was collaborative and collective. Decisions on overall structure and on the commissioning of authors were made jointly; and though each of us assumed primary responsibility for editorial work on individual chapters, in every case we have both participated in the process of review and revision. In *Industrial Relations in the New Europe* we were listed as editors in alphabetical order; in the present volume the order is reversed. This does not indicate any alteration in our relative contributions.

We have again been highly interventionist editors, and have been fortunate to have had very tolerant authors. We have done our best to sustain a close working relationship with all of them. A workshop in Dublin at the end of 1992 allowed us to keep in contact with our contributors outside Warwick, and it was of great value in allowing us to discuss the preliminary outlines of each chapter and to ensure that our agenda would be covered without serious omissions or overlaps.

Our thanks are due to the authors of *Industrial Relations in the New Europe*, whose body of work provided considerable raw material for most if not all of the contributions in this volume, and who in several cases have provided helpful advice on individual chapters. Without this resource, our aim of adopting a properly comparative approach would have been even more difficult to achieve. Finally we should like to thank our colleagues at the ESRC's Industrial Relations Research

Unit for providing a supportive environment for the whole project, and Norma Griffiths for her secretarial assistance on both this volume and its predecessor.

Richard Hyman
Anthony Ferner

1

Introduction:
Economic Restructuring,
Market Liberalism and the
Future of National Industrial
Relations Systems

Richard Hyman

The Logic of Comparative Industrial Relations

Why present another text on comparative industrial relations? The phrase evokes understandable ennui: so much of what is written under this label consists of either the crude juxtaposition of superficial and ill-digested data (the 'what-I-did-in-my-holidays' approach to analysis), or else a gauche imposition on national experience of preset taxonomies in a manner which suppresses the complex nuances of experience in each country. In other words, comparative industrial relations has often provided an alibi for academic tourism or a pretext for deracinated model-building.

The rationale of this volume combines principle and pragmatism. Recent scholarship – including, we are not too diffident to suggest, the studies in *Industrial Relations in the New Europe* – provide a substantial base of knowledge which may be interrogated theoretically and comparatively. A decade ago there was a dearth of literature on European industrial relations. Most of what was available was restricted to a small number of countries, and was often confined to the description of formal institutions rather than the exploration of actual practice. The information to hand today is immensely richer and more varied. Hence wide-ranging yet solidly grounded comparison is now possible.

The reasons why comparative analysis of industrial relations is necessary stem in part from the increasing internationalization of economic life – a process to which we allude in more detail below – and hence the practical importance of informed awareness of cross-national experience. However, the underlying intellectual rationale has always been part of the more general logic of comparative social research. First, cross-national comparison forces the observer to address critically what is normally accepted as unproblematic within the individual national context: what is otherwise taken for granted is shown to be contingent and perhaps exceptional. Second, and in consequence, comparison forces us to relativize our assumptions about the nature and meanings of the key institutions of industrial relations: companies, trade unions, employers' associations, collective bargaining, labour law. It is a familiar point that shop stewards are not the same as *delegati* and even less similar to *Vertrauensleute*; our very notions of the typical 'actors' in industrial relations are often framed by parochial and particularistic assumptions. This leads in turn to the third argument for comparative analysis: that it offers a more rigorous test of causal explanations developed in individual countries. For example – as Edwards and Hyman point out in chapter 10 – a wide range of cross-national reference contradicts the thesis that an increase in unemployment leads automatically to a decline in the number of strikes. This forces us to consider questions which would not otherwise arise. Do the character and meaning of strikes (or unemployment) differ cross-nationally? Or is the causal linkage mediated by industrial relations institutions (or analogous factors) which are internationally variable? Comparison forces us to refine our explanatory propositions to make them genuinely applicable as general, rather than single-context theories.

There is an intimate relationship between comparative analysis and theory construction. Any choice of comparators – unless totally opportunistic – must reflect some principles of selection derived from theoretically grounded criteria of significance. The process of comparison – unless exclusively descriptive – contributes to the development and refinement of theory by provoking generalization and causal explanation. This is true of both directions of comparative analysis: the focus on similarity (the literal meaning of comparing) and the focus on difference. 'Convergence' theories in the 1950s (Kerr et al. 1960), for example, diagnosed common trends in diverse societies which they attributed to an underlying 'logic of industrialism': common economic forces, in their view, overrode cultural and institutional diversity. Conversely, contrasting economic performance in countries with many structural and institutional similarities has been attributed by Maurice et al. to national specificities which were not previously assigned much explanatory significance; in their words, the differences they document 'can be interpreted only in terms of the complex, multifarious interaction between socialization and organization' (1986: 120). The reciprocity between these two modes of analysis: one which explores similarity and convergence, the other difference and divergence – provides the potential for the advance and refinement of theory in industrial relations.

Our subject is notoriously one in which explicit theorization is poorly developed, so it is worth expressing our view of the role of theory in industrial relations. (We do not say 'industrial relations theory', for we do not regard industrial relations as a distinct discipline with its own conceptual and theoretical apparatus, but rather as a field of study in which a variety of disciplinary perspectives can be applied, integrated and tested.) Theoretically informed comparison is an art rather than a science. As Przeworski and Teune (1970) have argued, explanatory theories comprise a trade-off between generality, parsimony and accuracy. They insist, indeed, that accuracy should not be seen as the overriding priority: explanation (and prediction) in social analysis is a matter of probabilities, not certainties. Moreover, any theory can be 'saved' in the face of seeming falsification by the addition of sufficient qualifications and *ceteris paribus* clauses; hence the importance of parsimony as a criterion of useful theorizing. The narrower the empirical frame of reference, the easier it is to construct simpler theories which fit (most of) the facts; hence the particular challenge contained in cross-national comparison.

Humans, Resources and Management

Comparative analysis offers potentially new insights into the perennial disjuncture between social action and social structure. People make their own history, but they do not make it just as they choose. . . . As the old millennium draws to a close, industrial relations analysts have become fluent in the discourse of strategic choice; but the choices appear increasingly bounded by the constraints of global competitive forces. The Weberian nightmare seems realized as the options narrow; freedom consists in adapting to external coercive laws. Does social and economic progress – supposedly the multiplication of resources – in fact entail the ever firmer subordination of humans to a system of management which is itself increasingly subordinated to market forces? Several decades ago, convergence theorists answered a similar question to depressing effect. First, social practice was driven by a structural, economic logic; second, where choice remained it was exercised by elites rather than by wider collectivities. As we argued in introducing our previous volume, the diversity of recent experience in European industrial relations refutes any simple notion of convergence. But does continued differentiation merely demonstrate the immovable weight of tradition: the recalcitrance of inherited national 'industrial orders', as Lane describes them in chapter 7, which inhibit choice as effectively as any transnational structural logic? If so, Weber was wrong only in failing to emphasize the national variability of the iron cage.

If the conclusion is that real choices indeed remain, we have still to establish *who* is free to choose. The 'managerial demiurge', proclaimed by Wright Mills (1951) almost half a century ago, has now come firmly into his (rather infrequently her) own. If the products of a thousand MBA-factories are now the key strategic actors, what scope is there for other social agents? It is now commonplace to argue that management sets the industrial relations agenda; the implication of the rise of the giant Euro-company, imply Marginson and Sisson, is that the driving-force for the reshaping of European industrial relations is to be found in a handful of corporate boardrooms. We make no excuse for concentrating, in the remainder of this Introduction, on the possible scope for alternative types of agency. To do so, we must review schematically the post-war history of national European industrial relations systems.

Different kinds of post-war settlement

In the Introduction to *Industrial Relations in the New Europe* we emphasized the differential institutional robustness of national industrial relations systems. This theme is developed by many of the present contributors. Yet every social institution is the outcome of a process of social creativity – whether at a distinct historical moment (for example, by legal enactment) or through a protracted evolution. And as many social analysts would insist, the very facticity and persistence of social institutions depend on their constant reaffirmation by powerful actors. In this manner, structure and action interconnect.

Continuity and change are always reciprocally conditioning: total transformation and total stasis are equally impossible. Yet the relative importance of change and continuity can alter; and it is for this reason that historical analysis can plausibly speak of turning-points and hence periodize the record of the past.

For western Europe, the 1940s were obviously such a turning-point. All continental nations except Sweden and Switzerland experienced war, enemy occupation or dictatorship – often in combination. The post-war reconstitution of national identities and political systems, and the painful process of economic reconstruction, opened unprecedented space for institutional creativity. In no country were inherited traditions liquidated: but their grip was everywhere relaxed. The onset of the cold war created new fault lines which, at least in the countries with strong communist movements, imposed a further process of societal realignment.

It has become common to speak of 'post-war political–economic settlements' (Lange et al. 1982: 209): national institutional arrangements, and implicit or explicit procedural norms, created a new regulatory framework for class relations, which in most countries was to remain effective for several decades. There have been a number of attempts to categorize national variants in patterns of post-war settlement. For Regini (1984: 124–5) the key distinction is between systems based on national concertation, the political isolation of labour and pluralistic fragmentation. To elaborate his analysis: in the former (notably Scandinavia, The Netherlands, Austria and – from the 1960s – Germany), trade unions became integrated within a tripartite system of national economic and social policy formation; while the principles of social partnership were reflected also in company industrial relations. In the second group, comprising the Mediterranean countries, governments intervened in the economy in a one-sided alliance with capital. Here, labour's exclusion from national policy-making was replicated in hard-line anti-unionism within individual companies. Britain came closest to the third model, with well-entrenched collective bargaining subject to only minimal political or juridical regulation.

Crouch has proposed a somewhat different developmental model which takes account of both the strength of trade union organization, and the degree of strategic co-ordination of both capital and labour. In his analysis, the 1940s constituted a major watershed in terms of the societal impact of unionization: before the second world war, those countries with the strongest unions tended to experience the highest levels of conflict; with the post-war formation of new structures of industrial relations, conflict was highest in countries with weaker unions (1993: 204). His analysis is consistent with familiar accounts of European industrial relations in terms of virtuous and vicious circles. Hence one cluster of countries can be characterised by stronger unions acquiring a recognized public status which enhanced both their internal and external authority; in another, the marginalization of weak unions encouraged internal division and continued lack of representative capacity. In some countries, however, there was less fit between union membership and public status: the stronger unions in the United Kingdom inhibited from an active role in macro-economic concertation by a low degree of structural cohesion and an ideological commitment to voluntarism; numerically weaker unions in Switzerland and The Netherlands whose status was enhanced by policies of 'social promotion' of labour organizations (Katzenstein 1984).

The cross-national differences between institutional regimes of industrial relations constructed after 1945 are of evident importance for the understanding of more recent trends. Nevertheless, some common themes deserve emphasis. Almost universally, post-war settlements were the outcome of strategic interventions and accommodations by governments, employers and labour movements, in which the last were commonly strengthened by their record as components of national resistance movements and by a prevailing populist mood which often included the commitment to escape the deprivations resulting from inter-war mass unemployment. In some countries, labour's achievements were short-lived: the cold war resulted in the reimposition of capitalist discipline in both the polity and the workplace. Nevertheless, even here there were typically important residues of the moment of advance – in terms, for example, of individual and collective statutory rights for employees. Such gains, it has become common to argue, were a direct reflection of the economic context of the mid-twentieth century.

Fordism, Keynesianism and national industrial relations regimes

For the purpose of this discussion it is necessary to present only a simplified sketch of an analysis which is often complex and convoluted: the proposition that changing systems of capital accumulation engender complementary institutional arrangements, including patterns of industrial relations. The argument – which it is unnecessary to review critically here – appears in many versions (for example, Gordon et al. 1982; Piore and Sabel 1984; Lipietz 1985; Boyer 1988).

Common to all variants is the thesis that the first half of the twentieth century saw the emergence of a dominant system of production and capital accumulation for which the motor vehicle industry is the archetype, and which accordingly is identified as Fordism. The rise of Fordism rested on the principle of economies of scale: the production of standardized commodities for mass markets, in large factories using dedicated machinery, and with a largely semi-skilled work-force. This dominant economic model encouraged two sets of institutional developments which for 'regulation' theorists are interconnected.

At the level of the company, the principle of standardization in production was mirrored by bureaucratic systems of personnel administration, which were in turn compatible with formalized machinery of collective bargaining. Large-scale industrialization assisted the rise of mass trade unionism, based on a work-force with collective strength but little or no individual labour market power. Although unionization was initially resisted forcefully by major employers – including, of course, Ford – most came eventually to accept that institutionalized industrial relations could actually assist in providing regularity and predictability in the employment relationship.

At societal level, the viability of mass production became underwritten by government policies of demand management and other forms of macroeconomic intervention, including the development of state welfare provision. As suggested above, in many countries the enhanced strength and status of labour movements made them important participants in constructing national post-war settlements, and the Keynesian welfare state owed much to their initiatives. Elsewhere – particularly in the southern European societies, which in the 1940s were still largely agricultural – the impact of labour movements was weaker, but state socio-economic intervention was central to a politically driven strategy of industrialization. Here too, aspects of the Keynesian welfare state could be adopted for their contribution to social stability, their role in the structuring of a 'modern' labour force, and their value in ensuring a secure framework for the expansion of private industrial capital (factors which also increased the acceptability of such state intervention in northern Europe).

It is unnecessary to embrace all the elements of 'regulation theory' in order to recognize the value of such an account for making sense of the relative stabilization of mid-century industrial relations. While the 'Fordist regime of accumulation' was nowhere as encompassing or uncontradictory as such analyses suggest, it is nevertheless plausible to interpret large-scale industry as the dynamo of many key sociopolitical developments in the western world. When mid-century authors celebrated the consolidation of 'mature' industrial relations – symbolized by the mutual recognition by unions and employers of their counterparts' rights and status, the institutionalization of employees' grievances, and the containment and ritualization of strikes – the tendencies they identified were neither unilinear nor irreversible. On the contrary, they can now be seen as historically conditioned and contingent concomitants of a distinct phase of economic evolution.

Challenges from above, below and beyond

It is possible to identify a series of developments, both endogenous and exogenous, which eroded the basis of stable national systems of industrial relations.

Two endogenous developments – both stemming from the consolidation of the Keynesian welfare state – seem crucial. The first is the general weakening of collective bargaining as a vehicle of restraint. In the early post-war years, most union leaders (or after 1948, non-communist ones) were committed to policies of national reconstruction which seemed to require self-restraint by labour. Workers themselves, as well as their representatives, were still affected by a 'depression mentality' (Cronin 1979) and did not seek to exploit the stronger labour market position which relatively full employment had brought them (Flanagan et al. 1983: 649). The shocks to so many centralized systems of collective bargaining at the end of the 1960s marked the end of this inherited restraining effect. The national dynamics of breakdown clearly varied (Crouch and Pizzorno 1978): in some countries involving wage grievances as price inflation and a slowdown in economic growth made pay bargaining increasingly conflictual; in others, accumulated discontent over working conditions as large employers pursued rationalization strategies, the impact of which fell outside the agenda of collective bargaining. The upsurge of conflict a quarter-century after the end of the war is also consistent with the thesis of a generation shift: an industrial work-force with higher aspirations and expectations than their parents, who took employment security increasingly for granted and perceived regular improvements in real income as an automatic right.

The second challenge derived from the growing social role of the state. Increased expenditure generated macroeconomic tensions, leading commentators to speak of a 'fiscal crisis of the state' (O'Connor 1973; Offe 1984). Public sector employees and their unions, who formerly had played a subsidiary role in most national industrial relations systems, became important actors in their own right. In Sweden – discussed by many of the contributors to this volume as the archetype of a once robust industrial relations model – could be seen most starkly the tensions between a manufacturing sector constrained by the need to compete in international markets which had traditionally set the pace in collective bargaining, and a 'sheltered' public sector whose unions developed the force and will to press their own distinctive agenda.

The key endogenous factor was increased competitiveness in a global economy in which institutions of inter-governmental co-ordination and regulation proved ineffectual. The post-war reconstruction or consolidation of national industrial relations systems occurred when a buoyant US economy was internationally dominant, and when the international monetary regime agreed at Bretton Woods in 1944 ensured a stable environment for cross-national trade. Economic stability in western countries – the foundation of stable industrial relations – was also assisted by a trend in terms of trade to their advantage and to the disadvantage of primary producer nations.

In the 1960s and 1970s, it is generally agreed, the international economy became an engine of instability. The American economy stagnated, with recessionary effects overseas, while the costs of the Vietnam war generated world-wide inflationary pressures. The post-war international monetary regime disintegrated. The 'oil shocks' of the 1970s marked a new volatility in terms of trade and reinforced price inflation. At the same time, 'newly industrializing' economies began to present a serious competitive challenge in sectors of manufacturing where western European and North American producers had long dominated.

In most western European countries, the disruptive effects of these changes on industrial relations were temporarily dampened by tightening the integration of trade unions in macroeconomic management. The process widely analysed as neo-corporatism (for example, Schmitter and Lehmbruch 1979) had at its core the shoring up of centralised union discipline in collective bargaining – different forms of explicit or implicit incomes policies – in exchange for enhanced trade unions status and in many cases the consolidation of social benefits and statutory employment rights.

Such 'Keynes-plus' institutional arrangements (Ross 1981) proved only temporarily effective. Where they were more successful in containing the inflationary potential of collective bargaining, intra- and inter-union tensions built up; the resulting challenges from below either undermined central disciplines, or forced national leaders to adopt a more ambitious stance. A worsening of labour market conditions imposed new demands on state budgets to support the growing numbers of unemployed, further aggravating the problem of fiscal crisis. One common response, examined in Ferner's chapter 3, has been the attempt to 'roll back' and redefine the limits of state economic activity. Controversies over such initiatives as privatization exemplify the disintegration of the political consensus on which post-war settlements and their later revisions depended.

Coinciding with these trends was what many writers have interpreted as the end (or at least the crisis) of Fordism. Although analyses differ, all variants treat as interconnected a series of transformations in production: an increased differentiation and segmentation of product markets; exploitation of microprocessor-based technological innovation to achieve rapid change in product lines; more decentralized production, often based in far smaller units than under Fordist systems; a more differentiated labour force, some key groups possessing new technical skills, but many others marginalized from the central productive process. As part of this process of segmentation and 'flexibilization', in most European countries there has been a substantial increase in female participation in the labour force: an often ambiguous development, as Rubery and Fagan demonstrate in chapter 6. For theories of post-Fordism, growing differentiation within the arena of production and accumulation tore apart the institutions of 'Fordist' collective bargaining, driving the process of decentralization of industrial relations practices and encouraging systems of company- and plant-specific regulation.

Overshadowing all these developments has been the eclipse of the nation-state as an effective economic agent. As Marginson and Sisson document, the transnational corporation – already important several decades ago – today dominates European industrial relations. Currency and stock markets, linked by increasingly sophisticated global technologies, exert decisive influence on industrial relations developments within single countries: financial institutions are able 'to "vote with their feet" – or better, their computers – against currencies suspect of inflationary tendencies' (Streeck 1992: 305). Suspicion in this regard falls on any government attempting to pursue non-deflationary policies as a defence against rising unemployment. As Mitterrand discovered in 1982, Keynesianism in one country is no longer possible. The completion of the single European market, sweeping away many institutional restraints on the impact of transnational economic forces, further undermines the capacity of nation-states to pursue autarchic policies.

Towards Keynesianism in one continent?

No national industrial relations system has escaped the operation of these forces, although the impact has differed substantially: a consequence, as we argued in the Introduction to our previous volume, in part of variations in national economic circumstances, in part of the contrasting robustness and adaptability of national institutional frameworks. Many of these variations are explored systematically and in detail in the chapters which follow.

What general scenarios emerge from these accounts? One, probably the most realistic, is highly depressing. The industrial relations systems in each European country reflect different forms of inter- and intra-class compromises rooted in an era when 'the political capacities of European nation-states' (Streeck 1992: 304) were considerable. The largely anarchic vagaries of international finance, and the far more calculative interventions of giant transnational firms, spell the exhaustion of these inherited regulatory regimes. Whether deregulation and fragmentation occur explosively or by a more gradual process of attrition can be affected by the underlying strength or weakness of national systems: but the inevitability of the eclipse of even robust models of industrial relations is inescapable. On this reading, the question asked of Sweden in the previous volume – can the model survive? – invites an unambiguous negative; while the challenges to institutional stability in Germany, despite the relatively sanguine assessment offered by Lane in chapter 7, can be interpreted as the beginning of the end.

Yet is such a view unduly pessimistic? We may return to the structure–actor relationship mentioned above. As one of us has argued previously (Hyman 1987: 30), structural determinism entails the interplay of contradictory forces: 'strategic choice exists, not because of the absence or weakness of structural determinations, but because these determinations are themselves contradictory'. This is certainly true of the current workings of the global economy: hence the popularity of notions of 'disorganized capitalism' (Lash and Urry 1987).

Within the space for strategic choice, as suggested above, large companies have seized a hegemonic role, and their advantage will be enhanced by the liberal market regime now enshrined across the European Community[1] and poised to embrace the whole continent. Centralization of capital poses particular challenges in industrial relations systems where cohesive workplace union organization formerly exerted a powerful and largely autonomous influence; as Terry shows in chapter 9, trade unions across Europe are still grappling uncertainly with the consequences. Meanwhile, among employers themselves – as Crouch explores in chapter 8 – responses to intensified competition, including the readiness to challenge established institutional arrangements, vary according to the detailed options available in each country.

If employers enjoy the most obvious options to initiate change, is there none the less scope for alternative strategic choices pursued by different actors? From distinctive perspectives, both Visser and Hyman in chapters 4 and 5 respectively examine the options available to trade unions in Europe; though the assessment of each is sombre, they agree that room for manoeuvre still exists, and that outcomes can vary considerably according to unions' differential organizational capacity and the vision and sophistication of their aims and methods.

Nevertheless, market liberalism itself constrains the available options. As Streeck (1992) has powerfully demonstrated, a 'level playing field' for competition among firms reinforces the power of all firms in their relations with unions and with governments. The notion of 'social dumping', though often deployed simplistically and insensitively, accurately captures the probability that transnational deregulation of labour and product markets will engender a process of 'regime competition', in which the achievements of labour movements and of governments committed to the social regulation of economic relations will be competitively devalued. 'Being less mobile, the only way in which both governments and labor can respond to regime competition is by offering capital positive inducements not to emigrate, which are likely to include assurances of friendly (that is, less demanding) behavior' (1992: 326).

Streeck's conclusion is that the incremental erosion of socially regulated employment regimes is inevitable within a voluntarist international order. Collective regulation, to remain viable in current circumstances, must become international in application. Here, the question of a 'social dimension' to the EC single market becomes of central relevance. Experience to date is less than encouraging. As Hall demonstrates in chapter 11, the institutional obstacles to far from ambitious regulatory proposals have so far been imposing.

Nevertheless, there are some signs that the log-jam created by institutional inertia and the veto power of individual governments and organized capital may be breakable. Unregulated regime competition – by imposing severe restraints on national decisions on taxation, public expenditure and employment protection – has helped encourage high and rising levels of unemployment in virtually every European country. Yet, as suggested above, this has the almost inevitable effect (despite near-universal efforts to reduce levels of unemployment compensation and restrict eligibility) of imposing additional strains on public budgets, quite apart from the costs in terms of social damage and political disenchantment. The suggestion of the EC Commission in its 1993 report on employment (1993: 18) that 'unemployment is the major economic and social challenge facing the Community in the 1990s' is not merely rhetorical. With varying nuances, demands for the reconstitution at European level of procedures for social regulation of market forces seem to be gathering momentum.

Is Keynesianism in one continent possible or desirable? There is a risk that internal reregulation within the EC may have as its corollary the strengthening of external boundaries: the 'Fortress Europe' scenario. We may have doubts how far even an enlarged EC can withstand the wider dynamics of a global economy. Likewise, the very notion of a socially regulated internal market may be questioned: once released, can the genie of economic liberalism really be forced back into the bottle?

These are serious issues, though far beyond our present brief. Keynesianism in one continent may be unattainable; or if achieved, may prove ineffectual; but at the time of writing – late 1993 – there is no evident alternative. For industrial relations, as we understand the term, to persist, it is essential to impose some form of deliberate social control on the arbitrary dynamics of global capital flows and the often disruptive decisions of the transnational giants. Such a goal requires precise analysis and effective organization on the part of those – the great majority of industrial relations actors – who will be the losers if current deregulatory trends cannot be halted. It is our hope that the discussions in this volume may contribute to this end. If western Europe, with its long and diverse traditions of imposing social control over market anarchy, cannot collectively reconstruct such mechanisms to meet the challenges of the approaching millennium, the prospects for the eastern and central European economies examined in our three concluding chapters are bleak indeed.

Note

1   While this volume was in press, the official title of the European Community was changed to European Union. In general we have retained in the text what is still the more familiar name.

References

Boyer, R. (ed.) 1988: *The Search for Labour Market Flexibility*. Oxford: Clarendon Press.

Cronin, J.E. 1979: *Industrial Conflict in Modern Britain*. London: Croom Helm.

Crouch, C. 1993: *Industrial Relations and European State Traditions*. Oxford: Clarendon Press.

Crouch, C. and Pizzorno, A. (eds) 1978: *The Resurgence of Class Conflict in Western Europe*. London: Macmillan.

European Communities Commission, 1993: *Employment in Europe – 1993*. Luxemburg: Office for Official Publications.

Flanagan, R.J., Soskice, D.W. and Ulman, L. 1983: *Unionism, Economic Stabilization and Incomes Policies: the European experience*. Washington: Brookings Institute.

Gordon, D.M., Edwards, R. and Reich, M. 1982: *Segmented Work, Divided Workers*. Cambridge: Cambridge University Press.

Hyman, R. 1987: Strategy or structure? Capital, labour and control. *Work, Employment and Society*, 1(1) 25–55.

Katzenstein, P. 1984: *Corporatism and Change: Austria, Switzerland and the politics of industry*. Ithaca: Cornell University Press.

Kerr, C., Dunlop, J.T., Harbison, F.H. and Myers, C.A. 1960: *Industrialism and Industrial Man*. Cambridge: Harvard University Press.

Lange, P., Ross, G. and Vanicelli, M. 1982: *Unions, Change and Crisis: French and Italian union strategy and the political economy*. London: Allen and Unwin.

Lash, S. and Urry, J. 1987: *The End of Organised Capitalism*. Oxford: Polity Press.

Lipietz, A. 1985: *The Enchanted World*. London: Verso.

Maurice, M., Sellier, F. and Silvestre, J.-J. 1986: *The Social Foundations of Industrial Power: a comparison of France and Germany*. Cambridge, Mass.: MIT Press.

O'Connor, J. 1973: *The Fiscal Crisis of the State*. New York: St Martin's Press.

Offe, C. 1984: *Contradictions of the Welfare State*. London: Hutchinson.

Piore, M. and Sabel, C. 1984: *The Second Industrial Divide: possibilities for prosperity*. New York: Basic Books.

Przeworski, A. and Teune, H. 1970: *The Logic of Comparative Social Inquiry*. New York: John Wiley.

Regini, M. 1984: The conditions for political exchange: how concertation emerged and collapsed in Italy and Great Britain. In J.H. Goldthorpe (ed.), *Order and Conflict in Contemporary Capitalism*, Oxford: Clarendon Press, 124–42.

Ross, G. 1981: What is progressive about unions? *Theory and Society*, 10(5) 609–43.

Schmitter, P.C. and Lehmbruch, G. (eds) 1979: *Trends Towards Corporatist Intermediation*. London: Sage Publications.

Streeck, W. 1992: National diversity, regime competition and institutional deadlock: problems in forming a European industrial relations system. *Journal of Public Policy*, 12(4) 301–30.

Wright Mills, C. 1951: *White Collar: the American Middle Classes*. New York: Oxford University Press.

2

The Structure of Transnational Capital in Europe: the Emerging Euro-company and its Implications for Industrial Relations

Paul Marginson and Keith Sisson

Introduction

The impact of multinational companies on employment and industrial relations practice has been a focus of concern for more than two decades. In the 1960s growing recognition of the bargaining power advantages possessed by multinationals over local work-forces, communities and nation-states – exemplified by their potential ability to switch production between countries – generated pressure to regulate their activities. In part this was reflected in the attempt by international agencies such as the ILO, OECD and UN to draw up codes of conduct, covering industrial relations practice as well as other matters, during the 1970s. It also led to calls from trade unions for transnational collective bargaining and the formation of the first international company councils. Within Europe, concern primarily focused on the activities of overseas, largely North American-owned multinationals: vividly captured in Servain-Schreiber's *Le Défi américain* (1967). Controversy surrounded the nature of employment brought by North American companies – how permanent was it, and would its semi-skilled nature undermine the local skills base – and the extent to which North American multinationals brought new industrial relations practices to Europe.

Recognition of the employment and industrial relations consequences of decisions by European-based multinationals came with the growing recession of the late 1970s and associated concerns over de-industrialization. Home-based multinationals were said to be relocating certain kinds of activity abroad, to locations with plentiful supplies of cheap, unprotected labour. Debate crystallized around theories of a 'new international division of labour' shaped not by colonialist states but by multinationals – which were regarded as the principal economic force of neo-colonialism. These concerns were paralleled by the growing importance of western Europe as a source of, as well as a destination for, overseas investment.

Ultimately, theories of a new international division of labour foundered on their inability to account for two key features of international investment flows: that they continue to occur predominantly between advanced industrialized countries; and that their two-way character now makes western European multinational activity in North America as important as the earlier flow in reverse. Recent debate has increasingly focused on the role of multinational companies in the globalization of economic activity. Multinationals have surpassed international trade flows as the most important single source of international economic exchange (UN 1993). Profound changes are under way in the organization and management structures of multinational companies, as they transform themselves from a collection of related but distinct national subsidiaries into organizations with integrated activities across borders. The organization of production and the servicing of an increasing range of national markets is becoming transnational in nature: headquarters functions are being spread across different countries, and formally independent suppliers are being brought within the strategic ambit of the corporation. Transnational companies, as they are increasingly called, are a new force.

Nowhere is this transformation more evident than in western Europe, where the breaking down of economic frontiers resulting from the creation of the single European market within the European Community and the European Economic Area (EEA) of 18 countries, has encouraged large companies to reposition themselves on a Europe-wide footing. This has been accompanied by a wave of acquisitions, mergers, demergers, divestments, joint ventures and strategic alliances across the continent. Forms of strategic control over formally independent organizations have also increased; they include licensing, franchising and subcontracting arrangements as well as financial holdings. Internally, this process has resulted in widespread corporate restructuring and rationalization, reflected in the creation or strengthening of European-level management structures able to integrate production, distribution and marketing across Europe, and conversely in the devolution of operational responsibility and financial accountability to individual business units within organizations.

Although relatively few in number, these Euro-companies are of considerable significance in economic and employment terms. Their actions, as chapter 11 illustrates, also have broader policy implications. Their emergence has been accompanied by some tentative developments towards new industrial relations arrangements at the European-level such as voluntary European works councils (EWCs) (Gold and Hall 1992). But powerful influences have also been working in the opposite direction, reflecting the devolution of responsibility for day-to-day management to individual businesses within the enterprise. Moreover, intensified international competitive pressures, in part a result of the creation of common European markets, have stimulated moves by large companies to shape their employment systems according to their own business requirements. This has resulted in a widespread, if uneven, decentralization across European countries as companies shift the locus of industrial relations regulation away from sector level towards 'organization-based' arrangements. The future of multi-employer bargaining, which forms the primary framework for determining employees' pay and conditions in the majority of European states, is one key area in which the decisions of these large companies will be crucial for many small and medium-sized employers.

The activities of Euro-companies, and their significance for management's conduct of industrial relations, are the central subjects of this chapter, which opens with a profile of the companies. Their numbers and influence are growing, primarily as a result of recent mergers and acquisitions. However, they remain unevenly spread across countries, in both outward and inward investment activity. The challenges that these Euro-companies represent to essentially nationally-based systems of industrial relations are examined in the second section. Three kinds of challenge are identified: that posed by management decisions taken beyond the jurisdiction of particular national systems; those arising from the centralization of management structures at European level; and those stemming from management decentralization.

We argue that the impact of this threefold challenge will depend on both the management approaches of different Euro-companies, and the ways in which company approaches continue to be constrained and shaped by the institutional arrangements of different national and regional systems of industrial relations. Accordingly, the third section considers the implications of 'insider' and 'outsider' systems of corporate governance, and corporate strategy, structure and style for management approaches to industrial relations. The fourth section addresses the ways in which different national systems of industrial relations facilitate or preclude particular management approaches, thereby leading companies to segment and stratify their activities across different locations. The fifth section considers possible responses of Euro-companies to the social policy initiatives that may accompany further economic and monetary integration in Europe. In closing the chapter, we comment on some of the broader implications of the development of a transnational economy.

European Companies in Profile

Comprehensive data on large employers within the European Community indicate that there are almost 8,500 organizations which employ one thousand or more employees. This total includes public sector organizations, both service and trading, and those whose business activities are confined to one country. Applying the closest possible criterion to the draft EWC directive, Sisson et al. (1992) identified about 1,000 organizations of this size which have subsidiaries in at least two EC member states. These Euro-companies comprise roughly 880 groups based within the EC, and more than 50 headquartered elsewhere in the world (including elsewhere in Europe). These figures provide a conservative estimate of the numbers of Euro-companies, for they exclude the growing number of medium-sized companies which are becoming transnational in scope (*Economist* 1993; Windolf 1993); transnationals where control is exercised through indirect forms of ownership, which are also of growing importance; and companies based in the six EFTA countries.

None the less, the importance of Euro-companies in employment terms is graphically illustrated by these data. The 880 companies with their headquarters in the EC employed a total of 13.6 million worldwide. However, their importance to different countries varies both in the location of parent headquarters and as recipients of inward investment. Among the four largest EC member states, 332 companies employing 6.1 million are based in the United Kingdom, 257 employing 3.4 million in Germany, and 117 employing 1.9 million in France, while there are just 32 companies based in Italy employing a total of 0.67 million. Of the other eight member states, The Netherlands is pro–minent with 89 European-scale companies employing 1.1 million. At the other extreme, only two of the companies are based in Greece and one in Portugal (Sisson et al. 1992).

'Non-manufacturing' activities (including services, construction, energy and water, together with the activities of 'holding' companies) are more strongly represented than manufacturing among these Euro-companies; manufacturing groups are outnumbered by about two to one. Again there are differences between countries. For example, 'non-manufacturing' accounts for the largest number of UK-based companies, whilst a majority of the German-based companies are in manufacturing. France too has more Euro-companies in manufacturing than does Britain.

Similar patterns are evident amongst the largest 100 employers in Europe listed in table 2.1. The importance of Swedish-, Swiss- and US-based companies is also indicated: these accounted for nine of the 100 largest companies identified.

Table 2.1 The 100 largest international companies operating in the EC (with subsidiaries in at least two EC member states)

Company	Country	Sector	Employees
IRI	It	Holding Company	416,193
Daimler Benz	Ger	Automobiles	368,226*
Siemens	Ger	Electrical Equipment	365,000
BAT Industries	UK	Diversified Holding Co.	311,917
Philips	Neth	Electrical Equipment	304,800
Unilever PLC/NV	N/UK	Food Processor	296,000
Fiat	It	Automobiles	286,294
Volkswagen	Ger	Automobiles	250,616*
British Telecom	UK	Telephone Co.	247,912
SNCF	Fr	Railways	214,035
CGE	Fr	Communications Equipment	210,300
Nestlé	Swi	Food Processor	196,940*
ABB	Swe/Swi	Electrical Equipment	189,493*
Bayer	Ger	Chemicals (Diversified)	170,200*
Hoechst	Ger	Chemicals (Diversified)	169,295*
Peugeot	Fr	Automobiles	159,100
Générale des Eaux	Fr	Electric Utilities/ Waterworks & Supply	153,901*
Electrolux	Swe	Household Durables	152,900
Grand Metropolitan	UK	Beverages – Brewers	137,379
BET	UK	Diversified Holding Co	137,101
BASF	Ger	Chemicals (Diversified)	136,990
Thyssen	Ger	Iron & Steel	136,091
Royal Dutch Shell	N/UK	Oil (International)	135,000
Lonrho	UK	Diversified Holding Co	134,488
I.C.I	UK	Chemicals (Diversified)	133,800
British Aerospace	UK	Aircraft Manufactures	127,500†
Ford	US	Automobiles	126,300
Mannesmann	Ger	Machinery	125,785†

Table 2.1   *Continued*

Company	Country	Sector	Employees
Michelin	Fr	Tyre & Rubber Goods	124,408
Electricité de France	Fr	Electricity Services	121,600
British Petroleum	UK	Oil (International)	119,850
Barclays	UK	Commercial & Other Banks	116,500
BTR	UK	Diversified (Industrial)	109,501
General Electric	UK	Electrical Equipment	107,435
IBM	US	Office Equipment	100,000
National Westminster	UK	Commercial & Other Banks	96,000
Veba	Ger	Diversified Holding Co.	94,514
Trusthouse Forte	UK	Restaurants & Hotels	92,900
Bass	UK	Beverages – Brewers	90,138
General Motors	US	Automobiles	90,000
Hanson	UK	Diversified Holding Co.	89,000
Saint Gobain	Fr	Building Materials	87,816*
Lloyds Bank	UK	Commerical & Other Banks	84,679
Schneider	Fr	Electrical Equipment	80,658
British Gas	UK	Natural Gas Utilities	80,481
Ahold	Neth	Retail – Grocer Chain	80,284
Volvo	Swe	Automobiles	78,700
Boots	UK	Retail – General Merchandise	78,648
RWE	Ger	Non-Ferrous Metals	78,162
Marks & Spencer	UK	Retail – Department Stores	75,144
Robert Bosch	Ger	Electrical Equipment	74,199
Elf Aquitaine	Fr	Oil International	72,700*
Renault	Fr	Automobiles	71,898*
Akzo	Neth	Chemicals (Diversified)	70,900
Bouygues	Fr	Construction	69,609
Pirelli Spa	It	Tyre & Rubber Goods	69,329
Ericsson LM	Swe	Office Equipment	69,229
BMW	Ger	Automobiles	66,267
Karstadt	Ger	Retail – Department Stores	66,122
Preussag	Ger	Non – Ferrous Metals	65,705
Krupps	Ger	Holding Company	64,432
P & O	UK	Sea Transport	64,423
Coats Viyella	UK	Textiles Products	63,598
Smithkline Beecham	UK	Drugs	62,800
Man	Ger	Machinery – Industrial/ Speciality	62,048
Crédit Lyonnais	Fr	Commercial & Other Banks	61,508
Thorn EMI	UK	Entertainment & Leisure	61,124

Table 2.1   *Continued*

Company	Country	Sector	Employees
Banque Nationale de Paris	Fr	Commercial & Other Banks	60,332
Pilkington	UK	Building Materials	60,300
Midland Bank	UK	Commercial & Other Banks	60,237
Kingfisher	UK	Retail – General Merchandise	58,796
RTZ	UK	Non – Ferrous Metals	57,653
Olivetti	It	Office Equipment	56,937
Deutsche Bank	Ger	Commercial & Other Banks	56,580
Lucas Industries	UK	Auto Parts – Original Equipment	55,957
Rolls – Royce	UK	Aerospace/Defence	55,475
Delhaize	Bel	Retail – General Merchandise	55,000
British Steel	UK	Iron & Steel	54,400
Macdonalds	US	Restaurants	54,000
Sears	UK	Retail – General Merchandise	52,306
British Airways	UK	Air Transport	52,054
Ladbroke Group	UK	Entertainment & Leisure	51,015
BSN Groupe	Fr	Food Processor	49,693*
Courtaulds	UK	Chemicals (Diversified)	47,500
United Biscuits	UK	Food Processor	46,958
Continental	Ger	Tyre & Rubber Goods	46,849*
Inchcape	UK	Diversified Holding Co	46,831
Whitbread	UK	Beverages – Brewers	46,819
Carrefour	Fr	Retail – Grocery Chain	46,600
BICC	UK	Electrical Equipment	46,035
Accor Int	Fr	Restaurants & Hotels	45,630
Solvay et Cie.	Bel	Chemicals (Diversified)	45,011
Ferruzzi Finanziaria	It	Diversified Holding Co	44,500
Air France	Fr	Air Transport	44,335
Lufthansa	Ger	Air Transport	43,845
TSB	UK	Commercial & Other Banks	43,640
Bull	Fr	Holding Company	43,617*
Bertelsmann	Ger	Holding Company	43,509
Allianz Holding	Ger	Insurance – Multiline	43,117*
Hawker Siddley	UK	Diversified – Industrial	42,600

* Known to have a European Works Council within the group.
† British Aerospace and Mannesman participate in consortia, Airbus Industrie and Europipe, which have a European Works Council.

Source: adapted from Sisson et al. (1992)

A full account of the differing economic and employment significance of Euro-companies across countries needs to consider inward investment patterns as well. The best data available, albeit approximate, are those which measure the share of domestic employment accounted for by overseas-owned companies. This ranges from 5 per cent or less in Denmark, Italy, The Netherlands and Sweden to 10 per cent or more in Austria, France, Germany, and, on the basis of estimates for manufacturing only, the United Kingdom too (Dunning 1993: 354). Overseas-based transnationals have a significant employment presence in Greece, Spain and Portugal. France, Germany and, above all, the United Kingdom emerge as the countries which are both important bases for, and recipients of, transnational economic activity.

The numbers of Euro-companies have swelled since the mid-1980s with the acceleration in cross-border mergers, acquisitions and strategic alliances. Mergers and acquisitions by the 1,000 largest European industrial enterprises rose steadily from 208 per year in 1984–5 to 492 per year in 1988–9. Over the same period the proportion of those mergers which were cross-border rose from just under 40 per cent to some 55 per cent. Joint ventures, which are most frequently cross-border in nature, increased from 82 in 1984–5 to 129 in 1988–9 (Buiges et al. 1990: 57–63). The pattern is uneven across countries: during 1989 and 1990 two-thirds of all cross-border acquisitions within the EC were made by companies based in five countries: France, Germany, Sweden, the United Kingdom and the United States. And almost one-half of all companies acquired were UK-owned (Hamill 1992: 138–9). Examples of these processes within the EEA are the merger of Swedish-based Asea with Swiss-based Brown Boveri to form ABB; Nestlé's acquisitions of British-based Rowntree and, in alliance with BSN, of French-based Perrier; and the GEC-Alsthom and Siemens-GEC joint ventures. Companies based outside Europe have been active too: for example, General Motors' acquisition of Saab and Fujitsu's purchase of an 80 per cent stake in ICL. Some cross-border realignments have foundered, such as Pirelli's failed bid for Continental, the merger of their car operations proposed by Renault and Volvo and the break-up of DAF-Leyland following the bankruptcy of the Dutch parent.

Two points are worth emphasizing in concluding this profile. First, the growth in the numbers and reach of Euro-companies is affecting not only the traditionally more open economies within Europe, such as The Netherlands, Sweden and the United Kingdom. An increasing number of companies based in France and Germany are becoming transnational; this is also the case in the hitherto relatively closed Norwegian economy. Spain too has become an important location for companies based elsewhere in Europe and overseas. Overall, the European-based multinational is much more widespread than in the 1970s, when the major industrial relations issues arose from the activities of mainly North American-owned companies.

Second, the emergence of a growing number of transnational companies organized on a European scale has major economic and political implications. The spread of their operations and the international nature of their management structures, discussed in the next section, signify the arrival of a new force within the European economy with its own distinct interests. Euro-companies have already begun to develop their own form of interest representation: the European Round Table and the Multinational Business Forum, which comprises some 50 transnationals based in eleven different countries. Whether they will develop a distinct 'European' management style is considered later. Of immediate concern is the challenge they pose to national systems of industrial relations.

Challenges to National Systems of Industrial Relations

The growing number of Euro-companies poses three main challenges to national systems of industrial relations and in particular to forms of worker representation, which remain essentially based on national trade union organization. First, Euro-companies are able to co-ordinate and control industrial relations outcomes from one country to another. Second, they possess the capacity to develop pan-European policies and practices and to create new structures of industrial relations at Euro-company level. Third, the growth of 'organization-based' employment systems threatens the sectoral multi-employer bargaining which is the dominant system in most countries.

Co-ordination and control

The devolution of operational responsibility and financial accountability to strategic business units, as described later, does not mean that control from company or divisional headquarters is any less. Instead its form is changing, as management by task has been replaced with management by performance. As the information-processing capacities of company and divisional headquarters have been steadily enhanced, mainly by developments in computer technology and communications systems, intensive monitoring of a range of financial and other performance indicators has become increasingly possible. Corporate offices now routinely monitor data on labour performance, such as unit labour costs, productivity, conflict and numbers employed (Marginson et al. 1988).

Such information gives headquarters managers in transnational companies the ability to compare performance between sites within and across borders, to reward and punish individual sites with capital investment decisions, and, by threatening so to do, to extract concessions on working practices and on terms and conditions from work-forces in different localities (Mueller and Purcell 1992). This power is most evident during a phase of corporate restructuring and rationalization. One vivid example was Hoover's decision in early 1993 to concentrate its production facilities in one line of business in Scotland, at the expense of one of its French plants. The company's decision was explicitly conditional on securing a series of concessions from the Scottish work-force (EIRR 1993c).

Such actions draw attention to the fact that strategic management decisions affecting the working lives and employment of thousands of employees are increasingly being taken beyond national jurisdictions (Windolf 1993). Employees and their representatives, faced with the scaling down or closure of their plant by an overseas parent, have at present few rights to be informed or consulted about the cross-border dimensions of such corporate restructuring. Neither, save for a small number of Euro-companies with their own voluntary arrangements for employee information and consultation (see below), do they have rights of representation at the European (or international) level of management where such strategic decisions are taken. Hence the pressure for some form of EWC from the European Trade Union Confederation, the international trade union secretariats and many individual unions.

Euro-company industrial relations systems in the making?

It is not just a question of co-ordination and control, however. The second challenge stems from the centralization of management organization occurring within Euro-companies: the creation of unified management structures at European level in place of, or with precedence over, nationally based subsidiaries. In companies such as Ford and General Motors, highly integrated production and marketing are part of a single structure of European management. In other cases, such as Nestlé and Unilever, the primary axis of management decision-making and control has shifted from national subsidiaries, responsible for all business activities in a particular territory, to international business divisions, responsible for the production, distribution and marketing of particular products and services across territories. This development has provided Euro-companies with the strategic potential to establish a pan-European approach to employee and industrial relations management, a potential that shows increasing signs of being realized as companies move to develop organization-specific employment systems.

A Europe-wide approach to employee management may find expression in the explicit or implicit pursuit of common policy objectives in different countries. For example, a company may wish its subsidiaries to adopt a common approach because it is concerned to project a particular image in the market-place: many companies – a long-standing example is Philips – have pursued 'total quality' strategies to improve their customer service image. It may also do so because it has developed an overriding philosophy for the management of human resources – Digital and IBM would be examples – or because similarity amongst its operations in different countries gives rise to similar kinds of problems. One instance of an explicit policy to deal with a similar problem is the introduction by Ford of employee involvement programmes in several European countries.

A pan-European approach is clearly evident in the creation of new European-level industrial relations structures: to date upwards of 20 European multinationals have voluntarily introduced arrangements for employee information and consultation at European-level within the EC and a further 15–20 within the Nordic area (EIRR 1993a, b). Of the companies listed in table 2.1, those known to have arrangements are asterisked. Within the EC, these 'prototype European works councils' (Gold and Hall 1992) are almost exclusively found among companies based in France, where the first arrangements were established in the mid-1980s, and in Germany. The number of companies concerned remains small: the significance of these arrangements lies both in their innovatory nature and in the fact that they anticipate in important respects the provisions of the European Commission's proposed directive on EWCs (see chapter 11). Such arrangements also demonstrate that some managements have seen positive advantages in meeting employee representatives at European level.

In a study of eleven of these companies, Gold and Hall (1992) identified a basic model among the French-based companies, which has clear parallels with the *comités de groupe* established under the 1982 Auroux legislation. They are joint bodies of management and employee representatives: on the employee side trade union and employee representation intersects, most commonly through the nomination of group employees by trade unions organized within the group. Most arrangements comprise relatively small numbers of participants – no more than 30 – meaning that by no means all subsidiaries within the group have direct representation. The companies meet the costs of the meetings, which are usually held annually, and function mainly to communicate information rather than for consultation (or negotiation). Their competence is confined to matters which are group-wide or which have cross-border ramifications. Variants on this basic model are evident, particularly among the German-based companies where the initiative has tended to come from group works councils (which under the German system comprise employees only). In some cases, arrangements remain informal and *ad hoc*. Most significant is the inclusion of a formal consultation procedure in the Volkswagen agreement.

These European-level information and consultation arrangements may potentially bring two forms of pressure to bear on national systems. Procedurally, the creation of European-level employee representative fora could be reflected in pressure for similar enterprise-wide developments at national level in Britain and Ireland, where such arrangements are virtually non-existent. Substantively, information obtained at these meetings, from employee representatives in other countries as much as from management, is likely to feed into national and local bargaining.

Organization-based industrial relations systems

The third challenge derives from diversification and the adoption of devolved or 'divisionalized' management structures. Such structures spread initially amongst large Anglo-American companies and by the early 1980s were well established amongst large German-based companies (Cable and Dirrheimer 1983). More recently the large holding groups in France, Italy and Spain have reorganized their internal management along divisional lines. This entails disaggregation into quasi-autonomous business divisions or units; delegation of responsibility for operating matters and devolution of financial accountability, in profit and loss terms, to the business divisions and units; yet at the same time, retention by corporate offices of strategic decision-making responsibility along with the capacity to audit and monitor management at division and business unit level. Typically, the large European company is increasingly made up of a number of 'strategic business units' – linked together in 'divisions', 'streams' and 'sectors' – whose managers have 'bottom-line' cost or profit responsibility for their activities. In many cases individual business units are encouraged to trade and compete with one another for capital investment as if they were independent businesses. *De facto* there is an 'internal market'.

Diversification and divisionalization can conflict in two ways with the systems of multi-employer bargaining which prevail in many European countries. First, concessions which make sense in one industrial sector may prove damaging to the company if extended to others in which it is involved. Second, the company may wish its subsidiaries to adopt a particular approach to employee management either because of some broader philosophy or because of the image it wishes to promote in the market. For these reasons diversified companies may question their continued participation in multi-employer bargaining.

The logic of devolving operational and financial responsibility under these management structures – that business-level managements should, as far as possible, be in a position to determine their own costs – is also a key consideration. The rationale for collective agreements at industry, sector or national level which determine major terms and conditions, and thereby an important element of costs, is called into question by the wider competitive imperatives which are leading companies to develop organization-specific employment systems (Dore 1989): such agreements take away managers' 'bottom-line' responsibilities. The result is a marked movement away from the role of the sector in establishing the framework within which industrial relations are conducted in large companies. In its place, corporate frameworks for policy formation, co-ordination and control are growing in importance. This is reflected in a widespread growth of collective bargaining at company and workplace levels, albeit often in the form of supplementary bargaining within a changing framework of multi-employer agreements (for further details see Sisson 1991; Ferner and Hyman 1992a).

This eclipse of industry and sectoral frameworks by those based on individual large companies has gone furthest in Britain but is also significant in other countries. In The Netherlands large companies have long stood outside multi-employer agreements: Visser (1992) reports that nearly all transnational negotiate their own agreements, with sectoral agreements being largely confined to small and medium-sized enterprises. Elsewhere, as in France, Italy and Spain (Ferner and Hyman 1992b; Goetschy and Rozenblatt 1992; Martínez 1992), although transnationals continue to participate in multi-employer bargaining, they have been prominent in the development of additional, decentralized bargaining at company level. In Sweden, another country where home-based transnationals dominate the industrial economy, the successful challenge to multi-industry bargaining in metalworking during the 1980s reflected the dominance of large transnationals such as Volvo; here too there is also a considerable amount of company bargaining (Kjellberg 1992: 107–9).

Until recently, although there has been a considerable amount of workplace bargaining with works councils, the trend towards decentralized bargaining had been least evident in Germany. Here regional multi-employer bargaining had tended to be the norm in most sectors; bargaining at this level, although co-ordinated by the national organizations on both sides, gave greater opportunities to deal with local issues. Unification, however, coupled with the impact of the recession in the early 1990s, has put considerable strain on the traditional system. IBM has recently opted out of multi-employer bargaining (EIRR 1993d) and the signs are that others may follow (Gow 1993). By opting out of multi-employer bargaining, it is argued, the larger companies will be better able to tailor the terms and conditions of employment to their particular circumstances. Even if they do not opt out, such companies can be expected to voice demands for greater flexibility in sector agreements and an increase in the role of workplace negotiations.

Looking to the future, a key question is what form the 'organization-based' systems will take. In particular, will they include collective bargaining with employee representatives? In the United Kingdom, initially, single-employer bargaining with shop stewards largely replaced multi-employer bargaining with full-time trade union officials. In recent years, however, there has been a movement away from union recognition: many newly established companies and those opening new sites prefer individual arrangements with employees to collective bargaining with trade unions (see, for example, Millward et al. 1992; Marginson Armstrong, Edwards and Purcell 1993). Whether similar developments will take place in other European countries remains to be seen. Much will depend, as the next sections argue, on the preferences of Euro-company managements, the legal framework, and, in particular, the provision that national systems of industrial relations make for statutory forms of employee representation in the workplace.

Moreover, it is important to remember that, however significant they may be for industrial relations developments, Euro-companies represent only a small fraction of the total number of companies. Small and medium-sized companies account for the overwhelming majority in every member state; they are especially important, in terms of the proportion of the labour force they employ, in Spain, Portugal, Ireland and Italy (Eurostat 1990; Sisson et al. 1992). Such companies, along with the subsidiaries of some of the large 'holding' companies, are unlikely to have the time or resources to develop their own employment systems. In the circumstances, there is little reason to expect the wholesale break-up of national 'systems' of multi-employer bargaining which prevail across much of the European Economic Area.

Structures, Styles and Strategies

The impact of the triple challenge posed by the emergence of Euro-companies on the balance between new European-level forms of regulation and centrally driven though locally enforced arrangements, will in part depend on the possibilities offered or closed off by different national systems of industrial relations. The outcome will also be contingent on the broader political developments in the European Community and EFTA considered in chapter 11. However, management policy approaches are likely to vary within and between the different European countries according to such factors as differences in corporate governance structures, management style, business strategies and internal organization.

Corporate governance structures

In exploring ways in which management approaches to industrial relations are likely to vary, it is useful to distinguish Euro-companies by both the institutional features of the countries where they are based and their own strategy, structure and style at a transnational level. A crucial institutional difference between countries lies in systems of corporate governance which, it will be argued, have important implications for approaches to employee management in Euro-companies.

Two distinct modes of corporate ownership and control can be identified within Europe: the Anglo-American 'outsider' system and the continental 'insider' system (Albert 1991; Franks and Mayer 1992). The continental 'insider' system encompasses two main variants: the 'Latin' and the 'German–Nordic'. A third variant of the 'insider' system, the 'Japanese', is gaining some influence within Europe as a result of recent international investment flows.

The 'Anglo-American' mode, found in British, Irish, North American and Australasian-based companies, is characterized by dispersed networks of shareholdings, a high degree of institutional share ownership, highly developed stock markets, an active market for corporate control and an emphasis on short-run financial returns backed up by intensive internal monitoring and performance evaluation. Financial control is exercised through a 'constellation of interests' rather than through relations with specific financial institutions. There is a tendency for investment strategies to be driven by purely financial criteria rather than considerations of longer-run industrial performance (Lane 1989; Scott 1991). In Britain, one reflection is the preponderance of conglomerates and the relative absence of manufacturers amongst large capital noted earlier.

The 'continental' mode, of which the French and German systems of corporate ownership and control represent the two main variants, is distinguished by interlinked networks of corporate, institutional or family shareholdings, a financial system based on long-term bank credit, a less developed stock market, less exposure to hostile takeover and an emphasis on longer-run performance. Internal controls tend to be operational rather than financial in character. Financial control is exercised through specific institutional relations (Lane 1989; Scott 1991). As a consequence, investment strategy is shaped by longer time horizons and commitment to the development of existing assets, reflected in the numerical strength of large German- and French-based manufacturers as compared with Britain (Gardner 1993).

The French and German systems differ in some respects: investment-holding companies play an important controlling and co-ordinating role in France, where bank influence is less pronounced than it is in Germany; and longer-term commitments to product and process innovation and associated skill development are more marked in Germany (see chapter 7). The extent of the stakeholder rights accorded to employees and their representatives also differs between the two countries (see below).

Systems of corporate governance in other continental European countries tend to resemble one of these two. In addition to France, the 'Latin' variant includes Belgium, Italy, and in a less developed form owing to the dominance of foreign and state-owned capital, Spain and Portugal. The 'German–Nordic' variant covers Austria and the Nordic countries as well as Germany.

The distinction between 'outsider' and 'insider' systems of corporate governance serves to highlight two salient differences which have industrial relations consequences. First is the contrast between exposure to hostile takeover and a concentration on short-run financial performance characteristic of the 'outsider' system, and protection from hostile takeover and concentration on longer-run performance associated with 'insider' systems. Arguably, these features of 'insider' systems tend to encourage owners to display greater commitment to their assets than is the case in outsider systems. Thus, under 'insider' systems employees are more likely to be regarded as enduring assets who form a potential source of competitive advantage, and to be associated with an employee development approach to labour management. In turn, employees, and other stakeholders, may also be encouraged to make longer-term commitments to the company. Because of the mediating role of different national systems of education and skill formation, this tendency will not be uniform across countries. It is likely to be most evident in systems which support investments in skills beyond current needs, as is the case in Germany (see chapter 7).

Under 'outsider' systems, by contrast, employees are more likely to be regarded as disposable liabilities and to be associated with a cost minimization approach to labour management. In Britain, Lane argues that this tendency is reinforced by an educational and skill formation system which places a low premium on sustained training. As such, employee management is more likely to be of strategic concern to companies based in 'insider' systems, and therefore to be the subject of centrally determined approaches and policies. Companies based in 'outsider' systems are more likely to see employee management as solely a matter for the operating units.

A second difference concerns the rights of stakeholders other than shareholders, including employees and their representatives. Under 'outsider' systems, such stakeholders enjoy few rights. The threat of takeover is the main discipline on the existing management. Indeed, a change in management direction can frequently only be secured by a change in ownership. Under 'insider' systems, incumbent managements have greater immunity from takeover. Internal supervision by other stakeholders, such as banks and employee representatives, is greater. This means that changes in management direction can more easily be secured without recourse to a change in ownership. The rights that employees or their representatives have as stakeholders can be considerable. Streeck (1987) argues that the consequences of such status rights for the organization of work as well as for industrial relations are far-reaching.

The nature and extent of such employee rights under 'insider' systems vary across countries, reflecting the specific ways in which the provisions of corporate legal systems combine with those of industrial relations systems. Status rights tend to be more extensive under the 'German–Nordic' than under the 'Latin' mode. They are most extensively recognized under Germany's system of corporate governance, where employees are able to exercise a degree of control over management decisions at two levels: at site and company levels where works councils have the right of veto over specified categories of management action, and, in large companies, through representation on the supervisory board. Examples of the effective exercise of these countervailing powers by employee representatives are provided by Windolf (1993). The formal situation differs in the Nordic countries. Here basic agreements between the employers' and trade union confederations require management to inform and consult with employees and their representatives at group level (Hall et al. 1992). In practice, status rights are considerable.

In France works councils enjoy less extensive rights of consultation, although the 1982 Auroux laws broadened the scope of consultative rights and, importantly, gave employees the right to establish works councils at company as well as site level. In Italy the 1970 Workers' Statute gave employees the right to form workplace representative structures. Although employees (or their representatives) have no formal role in corporate governance, in practice the provisions of the Statute have served to entrench employee rights by giving an informal veto over management decisions. Further, in all the other countries mentioned above, together with The Netherlands, employees have rights to be consulted, or at the least to be informed, about management decisions affecting their interests taken at higher levels of enterprises within the same country (for further details, see Hall et al. 1992).

By creating European-level structures for consulting and informing employee representatives about management decisions at a transnational level, companies based in 'insider systems' have extended internationally rights already recognized under domestic systems. In this sense, group works councils at national level can act as a springboard for the creation of European bodies. For companies with their roots in 'outsider' systems, however, such an innovation represents a radical departure from a form of corporate governance in which rights over decision-making are vested solely in shareholders. This in part explains the hostility of British-based transnationals to EC proposals which would require the creation of EWCs (see chapter 11).

Are such substantial differences in forms of corporate governance structure likely to persist as companies based in contrasting systems become increasingly European in the scale, scope and organization of their operations? Or will there be some measure of convergence? Pressures for reform are evident within both 'insider' and 'outsider' systems. In Germany and the Nordic countries concern focuses on the inability of current structures to promote effective industrial restructuring and rationalization that takeover allegedly secures in outsider systems, and on giving greater emphasis to shareholder rights; and in Britain there is pressure to strengthen internal controls on incumbent managements and to induce a more 'long-term' perspective, seen as virtues of insider systems. Whether tangible changes will emerge is, however, difficult to predict at this stage.

Certain forms of ownership may also be associated with distinctive approaches to industrial relations. In this respect, one important group is state-owned enterprises. Significantly, in France these enterprises were among the first to reach agreements at company level in the 1950s (Goetschy and Rozenblatt 1992). Also French state-owned companies have been prominent among the relatively small number of transnationals which have established European-level information and consultative structures, in part because of the particular political orientation of their top managements (Gold and Hall 1992). In Italy, the state-holding enterprises IRI and ENI have been a major source of innovatory practice in industrial relations (Ferner and Hyman 1992b). In Germany, Volkswagen's pioneering initiative in conceding consultation, as well as information, rights to employee representatives at European level is linked with the distinctive industrial relations structures and policies it developed as a state-owned company.

Management style and organization

Although structures of corporate governance shape management approaches in certain ways, they still permit choice. The ways in which choice is exercised will vary according to differences in management style and organization, including considerations of business strategy and internal structure, between companies.

Discussion of the influence of management style dates back to Perlmutter's (1969) classification of transnationals according to the cultural influences acting on their style of management. Initially Perlmutter distinguished between companies which are 'ethnocentric' and 'polycentric' in approach. In ethnocentric companies, overseas subsidiaries are wholly owned and managed as a cultural extension of the parent by managers from the 'home' country. Polycentric enterprises are characterized by local participation in ownership, and a management style which is locally determined and implemented by locally recruited managers. Whereas ethnocentric companies are likely to be centralized in their management of overseas operations, polycentric enterprises tend to be decentralized.

In terms of implications for industrial relations, ethnocentric transnationals can be expected to try to introduce employment practices from the source country in their overseas operations, whereas polycentric transnationals can be expected to adopt local practice. Thus the former are assumed to be innovators and the latter adaptors.

Evidence suggests that US-, and more recently Japanese-, owned companies tend towards an ethnocentric approach, whereas European-based transnationals have tended to be more polycentric (Capelli and McElrath 1992; Hamill 1984; Jain 1990; Lawler et al. 1992). An interesting question is whether Japanese-based companies exercise more central control over their European operations than do those based in North America.

Over time, Perlmutter (1969) expected transnationals to move from either an ethnocentric or a polycentric approach to a 'geocentric' style based on an international management structure which transcends national borders and differences in approach. Management style supposedly owes strict allegiance to neither 'home' nor 'host' countries. A similar structural development is envisaged by Porter (1986) as companies move from a 'multi-domestic' structure – where territory forms the prime axis of internal organization – to a 'global' structure – where the prime axis of internal organization comprises international businesses for particular products or services.

Globally, an increasing number of companies have been shifting emphasis away from territorial forms of internal organization, based on the national subsidiary, and towards international business organization (United Nations 1988). And a small, though increasing number of transnationals are transferring the headquarters, and research and development, functions of their different international businesses to overseas locations (Forsgren et al. 1992; Lorenz 1991). Yet how far such structural changes have been accompanied by the adoption of a truly geocentric, or global, management style is open to question. So too is the linear progression implied by Perlmutter's model. Hu (1992) argues that many 'global' companies remain essentially 'ethnocentric' in their management approach. Moreover, following our argument above, different systems of corporate governance, in combination with nationally specific systems of skill formation and industrial relations, are likely to impart an 'ethnocentric' dimension to the management systems of globally organized companies. Conversely, the persistence of regional and national differences between consumer markets within Europe may require a continuing 'polycentric' dimension to the management of globally structured companies (Edwards et al. 1993).

With the spread of global corporate structures, the influence of the host country is likely to diminish, while that of business requirements is likely to increase. Yet how far will the influence of the home country continue to be evident in shaping international management approaches to industrial relations? The creation of the SEM and the EEA, by further reducing differences between national markets, may stimulate European-level approaches to employee management among companies whose operations are globally structured. Where the primary emphasis remains on national subsidiaries, responsible for all businesses in an area, however, approaches to employee management are likely to remain nationally based. Either way, the possibility of European-level approaches to employee management suggests the emergence of a 'Eurocentrism' which is neither 'ethnocentric' nor 'geocentric'.

Strategy and structure

With moves towards global management structures, industrial relations policy is likely to be shaped much more by the nature of the particular businesses than by practices in specific 'home' or 'host' countries. As argued previously, the characteristics of some businesses are likely to enhance the importance of local industrial relations to corporate-level management, whereas those of other businesses mean that local practice is of little account. In the first case, the outcome is likely to be a distinctive, centrally determined approach. In the second, local operations, albeit centrally co-ordinated, can be expected to enjoy considerable autonomy.

The management rationale which underlies such differences flows from divisionalized structures. Within these there is a continuing tension between securing the benefits of decentralization, stemming from divisional and business unit autonomy, and those of centralization, stemming from the need to co-ordinate activities across different business units and divisions. The benefits of decentralization arise from the ability of business unit management to respond appropriately to particular circumstances, the opportunities for effective servicing of local markets and the incentive effects deriving from devolved financial accountability. The benefits of centralization arise from the ability to co-ordinate activities across different, though related, business sectors and from economies of scale in production. These tensions are resolved by companies in various ways, according to the nature of the business in which they are engaged.

Where there is a high degree of integration in production or service provision across countries, as in automobile manufacture or banks, transnationals will tend towards a centralized approach. This is also likely where companies carry out the same activity in several locations in different countries – as in food manufacturing or the retail sector – because of gains to be made in standardized operating procedures and/or common purchasing. A decentralized approach is likely where unrelated business activities are undertaken in different locations, as in a diversified conglomerate or industrial holding company. Evidence from The Netherlands, Italy and Britain indicates that centralization and decentralization in the management of industrial relations is closely associated with such differences in business strategy and management structure (Buitendam 1979; Hamill 1984; Perulli 1986; Marginson et al. 1988).

Different patterns of company expansion also affect industrial relations. Whereas in the 1970s companies favoured diversification across different products and services, in the 1980s and early 1990s they have focused on expanding into new markets for established lines of business (Ietto-Gillies 1992). Companies are more likely to pursue a common policy for employees across countries if such expansion is achieved by investment in new locations, rather than by acquisitions of, or joint ventures with, existing companies.

Further changes in the nature and form of divisionalized management structures are likely to enhance the attractiveness of a decentralized, though centrally co-ordinated, approach. Four particular developments are of note. First, profit responsibility has been devolved ever further to smaller business units serving ever more specific markets. Second, transnationals have externalized an increased proportion of their operational activities, through franchising and licensing arrangements and national and international subcontracting. Third, co-ordination through networks across different parts of the enterprise, rather than through hierarchy from the centre, has increased. Fourth, there has been a growing emphasis on commercial relationships between different parts of the enterprise, which have to tender for business from each other often in competition with external suppliers. All these developments are creating pressures to push responsibility for decisions on industrial relations matters down the organization.

Conclusion

The previous section described the three main challenges that Eurocompanies present to existing national systems of industrial relations. An important means by which the first challenge can be met is through information and consultation rights for employees and their representatives in respect of transnational management decisions or those which have clear cross-border implications. In the absence of any legislative requirement, such developments are more likely to occur in companies based in 'insider' systems and where centralizing pressures, the second challenge identified, are greatest. Such pressures, which may also be reflected in the adoption of a common policy across countries, will be stronger among companies which are primarily organized along international business lines rather than on the basis of national subsidiaries, and where either production or service provision is networked across locations in different countries or where similar activities are undertaken in different locations. Decentralizing pressures, the third challenge identified, will be strongest where companies remain organized around national subsidiaries and in diversified companies able to segment and stratify their activities across countries.

European Companies and National Industrial Relations Systems

Having demonstrated how Euro-companies may affect national industrial relations systems, we should now emphasize that the influence is not one-way: different systems of industrial relations place constraints on the approaches that companies can feasibly adopt. These constraints serve both to promote and to preclude particular approaches to industrial relations. Thus management's choice of approach to industrial relations takes place within 'different constellations' of industrial relations corresponding to different national systems, rather than within a single European universe (Marginson, Buitendam, Deutschmann and Perulli 1993). In some countries, such as Italy and Spain, Euro-companies will additionally confront important regional differences in skill formation and industrial relations systems (Perulli 1993). In turn, continuing differences between systems are likely to affect the ways in which transnational companies segment and stratify their activities across different European locations.

The structure of collective bargaining

A first difference between countries is the extent to which Euro-companies remain locked within multi-employer arrangements for collective bargaining over pay and major conditions. At one end of the spectrum, systems of centralized multi-industry bargaining remain more or less intact in Austria and Norway. In Germany, as indicated in a previous section, regional multi-employer bargaining also remains intact, although it is increasingly under pressure. In other countries, although multi-employer bargaining at sectoral level continues to set minimum rates and conditions, there is increasing scope for bargaining at company level. In The Netherlands, even though multi-employer bargaining persists, many large multinational companies have long opted out of these arrangements in favour of company agreements over pay (Visser 1992). In Britain, the movement from multi-employer arrangements has gone furthest: single-employer bargaining, most commonly at business or site level, is now the typical pattern.

Especially important in accounting for this variety is the extent to which multi-employer bargaining continues to serve employer objectives successfully. In many countries, for example, multi-employer agreements continue to neutralize the workplace as a focus of trade union organization and activity. By reducing competitive pay bargaining, multi-employer agreements also help to limit the overall levels of pay settlement to movements in productivity. In Britain, by contrast, multi-employer agreements are no longer capable of delivering these objectives, if they ever were (Sisson 1987; 1991).

The extent to which multi-employer agreements remain entrenched depends above all on the legal framework. Thus the incentive to participate in multi-employer bargaining is strongest in Germany, where agreements are legally binding; they impose a 'peace' obligation on trade unions; member companies cannot contract out; and, although rarely used, non-member companies can be obliged to follow the terms of the agreements because of the statutory provisions for extension. In France and Italy, where the right to engage in industrial action is much less restricted, the incentive to take part is not quite as strong. It is weakest in Britain, where multi-employer agreements, like other collective agreements, are binding in honour only and none of these conditions applies.

Support for the view that the 'collective' behaviour of management is largely to be explained in structural rather than cultural terms comes from the contrasting choices of US- and Japanese-owned companies coming to Europe. Most of these companies locating in the United Kingdom have stayed outside employers' organizations and multi-employer bargaining, whereas in other European countries such companies are very firmly in the system. Significantly, too, the same goes for the many British companies that have withdrawn from their employers' organizations in the United Kingdom to develop company-based systems. In each case, management's decision reflects the advantages and disadvantages of different structures of multi-employer bargaining rather than any principled commitment to independent or collective action (for further details of the 'cultural' and 'structural' explanations of management's collective bargaining behaviour, see Sisson 1987).

A final point is that multi-employer bargaining does not greatly limit the ability of companies to determine pay and conditions in accordance with their own business requirements. Very rarely, for example, do agreements provide for standard rates of pay, and they normally permit considerable flexibility in implementing most other terms and conditions. In short, multi-employer bargaining can give management the best of both worlds: this is why it is by no means certain that even Euro-companies will abandon it.

Workers' participation

A second difference lies in the extent to which legal frameworks make statutory provision for workers' participation and involvement. Most European countries have some kind of legal or centrally agreed provision for the establishment of works councils, whereas Britain and Ireland have none. There are marked cross-national contrasts in the powers of works councils. In Germany, for example, works councils are employee bodies and their powers include co-determination; in France they are joint management–employee bodies and the main emphasis is on information and consultation.

As noted earlier, several countries also have provisions for national-level enterprise- or group-wide councils for informing and consulting employees. These, it was argued, provide an important platform for the extension of similar arrangements to European level. In contrast, the absence of any similar statutory provision combined with the historical weakness of trade union organization at group level (Terry 1985) has meant that a national-level enterprise forum in Britain is very much the exception.

Established provisions for workers' participation and involvement can preclude some approaches to employee management whilst promoting others. Thus, legislative requirements have obliged Japanese-owned companies operating in Germany to establish works councils, although evidence indicates that managements have tried to circumvent their role. These companies have also been reluctant to introduce forms of direct employee participation widely used in Japan, such as quality circles, in case these should provide a platform for the extension of works council influence (Faust et al. 1993; Deutschmann 1992). By contrast, in Britain where there are no statutory provisions for employee representation, some Japanese-based companies have developed a distinctive form, the company council, which contrary to local custom is employee- rather than union-based. Quality circles are also much more widespread.

Second, there is evidence that policies to introduce group working and devolve a measure of decision-making on production matters to operative level have been facilitated in Germany and Sweden by the presence of organizationally secure systems of employee representation in the workplace. These have encouraged a longer-term, production-oriented perspective, and provided a strategic ally for top management in overcoming resistance from middle management and supervisors (Faust et al. 1993; *Financial Times* 1993).

Training systems

A third difference between countries is the relative importance of external and internal labour market institutions in shaping employment practice. Crucially important are differing vocational training systems. There are two broad types: the 'market' and 'educational' models (Campinos-Dubernet and Grando 1988). Under the 'market' model, characteristic of Italy and Britain, the company bears the main responsibility for training, there are few training institutions external to the company, and the volume of training tends to be driven by employers' short-term demand for labour. Hence there is a tendency towards skill shortages in periods of upturn, and in Britain at least, towards chronic underprovision of trained labour because of fears of poaching. Under the 'educational' model, characteristic of France and Germany, institutions external to the company play a major role in training, which is viewed in an educational perspective (although its status differs greatly between the two countries – see chapter 7), and the state of the labour market has much less effect on the volume of training.

Trained labour, at all levels, is more plentiful in France and Germany than in Britain (Prais 1990). Moreover, comparative evidence on the relationship between training provision and productivity points to clear connections between higher levels of skill, greater work-force adaptability and decision-making autonomy, and superior productivity in Germany compared with Britain (Prais 1990). This suggests that certain strategies are more feasible in some countries than others. Thus companies whose production requires a more highly skilled work-force able to work with a considerable degree of discretion are, *ceteris paribus*, likely to invest in locations where institutional arrangements promote extensive training and forms of workgroup autonomy. In contrast, companies engaged in routine production with low skill requirements may be more inclined to invest in locations with plentiful supplies of industrially disciplined though lower skilled labour.

Industrial relations systems and investment decisions

This brings us to a key issue underpinning the debate over the EC Social Charter: the extent to which different constellations of industrial relations institutions shape strategic business decisions of Euro-companies on matters such as capital investment programmes in new and existing processes, restructuring and rationalization. The debate is inconclusive, with evidence, for example, of particular countries being both the 'victims' and 'beneficiaries' of rationalization decisions by different corporations. None the less, some points are clear. First, in the case of many location decisions the industrial relations regime is of secondary importance to product market and infrastructure considerations. Companies often have to locate near their markets or customers regardless of industrial relations considerations, or they require ready access to good communications systems (*Financial Times* 1991). Second, evaluation of the comparative advantages of different industrial relations regimes is often more complex than it appears at first sight. Countries with higher labour costs – including Germany, France, Benelux and the Nordic countries – tend also to have higher productivity and skilled work forces, whereas the reverse tends to be true of countries – such as Greece and Portugal – with low labour costs (European Commission 1993). Within the EC, Britain and Spain appear to occupy an intermediate position. Locational decisions are likely to reflect the particular labour requirements of companies. Third, as already suggested in the case of works councils, the indications are that for US and Japanese companies especially it is perceptions of the freedom to manage, rather than simply social costs, which are of paramount importance. For example, management perceptions of the tightness of regulatory restrictions on hiring and firing differ sharply across EC member states (European Commission 1993).

Conclusion

How, and to what extent, Euro-companies modify their approaches to industrial relations appears to vary across countries. The extent of adaptation to local practice reflects the scope for variation permitted by different national systems. This is relatively low in those countries which legally impose a uniform set of institutional arrangements on companies, or which provide legal support for the generalization of the provisions of collective agreements, or which determine important aspects of terms and conditions or of employment practice by statute. Germany is an example of the first and second, France of all three.

Where all of these are absent, institutional permissiveness is greater. Britain and, to a lesser extent, Italy are examples. Thus when comparing, say, Britain with Germany, patterns of industrial relations and employment practice in the former are more contingent on management and trade union organization at sectoral and company levels than in the latter.

Other things being equal, Euro-companies will continue to segment and stratify their activities, in part according to the properties of national and regional systems in terms of skill formation, levels of productivity, levels of pay and non-pay benefits, representation rights and employment protection legislation. The adoption of global management structures and enhancement of information-processing capabilities, facilitating cross-country comparisons, are likely to increase companies' potential to engage in 'regime shopping' (Streeck 1991). The geographical scope of the resultant regime competition within Europe is also becoming wider: Hungary, the Czech Republic, Slovakia and Poland all offer an abundant supply of cheap – and at least in the first two countries – comparatively well-trained and disciplined labour. One result could be a tendency to undermine labour standards and conditions in institutionally less permissive systems of industrial relations. Alternatively, continued segmentation and stratification could reinforce rather than undermine existing differences between national and regional systems. Thus although unit labour costs across different countries and regions are likely to converge, given pressures arising from European economic and monetary integration, this could be on the basis of very different configurations of labour productivity and hourly labour costs.

Coming to Terms with European Integration

As well as the constraints of national systems, Euro-companies also face pressure for social policy measures to accompany moves towards economic integration. As Commons (1909) recognized nearly a century ago, the nature and extent of markets are major influences on industrial relations; like it or not, therefore, having been prime movers in the creation of the single European market, Euro-companies now have to face the inevitable industrial relations consequences. The pressures for such measures are coming from trade unions and the European Parliament as well as the European Commission. One is for EC-level measures, either in the form of directives or 'agreements' resulting from the process of social dialogue, covering the range of issues in the Social Charter. The other is for Euro-company level arrangements and, above all, for new institutions with rights to information, consultation and negotiation at European level on both a sectoral and enterprise basis. Both these developments are discussed in more detail in chapter 11. Moreover, the enlargement of EC membership to include most or all of the European Economic Area is likely to create additional pressures for new forms of European regulation of industrial relations, as is any further progress towards economic and monetary union within the EC.

These prospective developments raise questions about how Euro-companies will organize and extend their interest representation beyond current forms. Will UNICE, the European employers' confederation, be empowered to enter into European-level opinions and agreements with trade unions? Or will the preferred strategy be to augment the resources and authority of sectoral employers' organizations, with the aim of concluding sectorally specific arrangements? Alternatively, might Euro-companies eschew approaches through central or sectoral employers' federations at European level, in which national interests and those of small and medium-sized employers may well continue to loom large, in favour of their own distinct forms of interest organization? In which case, might a forum such as the European Round Table, which brings together the main European multinationals, seek to engage in the process of social dialogue? The answers will depend in part on the degree to which the EC succeeds in regulating industrial relations, and on progress towards economic and monetary union.

Of possible industrial relations developments, the one most likely to have an impact on Euro-companies in the short run is the proposed EWC directive. If implemented on a Community-wide basis, it would require almost a thousand companies to establish European-level arrangements for informing and consulting employees (Sisson et al. 1992). Implementation under the Maastricht Social Policy Protocol by the eleven member states, excluding the United Kingdom, would nevertheless affect up to 100 UK-owned transnationals because of the scale of their operations elsewhere in the EC. In this case, the total number of companies required to establish EWCs would be approximately 650 (Marginson, Hall and Sisson 1993).

Of all the member states in the EC, the impact of EWCs on industrial relations is likely to be especially profound in the United Kingdom. One reason is the United Kingdom's primary position within Europe as both the numerically largest home base for transnational companies and the most important host economy for transnationals based elsewhere. If, under the Social Policy Protocol, these companies are obliged to establish EWCs covering their operations elsewhere in the

EC, they will come under trade union pressure to include their UK employees as well (and may see managerial advantages in doing so). The second is that among the differences that exist in industrial relations from one country to another, those between the United Kingdom (and the Republic of Ireland) and the other EEA countries are especially marked. Most UK managers, even in companies based elsewhere in Europe, have little direct experience of statutory forms of employee participation, such as works councils. Where they exist in Britain, representative structures are almost always trade union based. Thus the introduction of a structure in which representatives are elected by all employees regardless of trade union membership, would represent a considerable innovation for established patterns of industrial relations in the United Kingdom.

Of other possible European industrial relations developments, the one that managements of transnational companies will oppose especially vigorously will be collective bargaining at European company level. This seems as true of those which have set up EWCs voluntarily (Gold and Hall 1992) as of those who refuse to take this step. A first reason is that such bargaining, either at group or divisional level, reduces the ability of employers to exploit the advantages of different labour market conditions. Second, it runs directly counter to the logic of decentralized management structures and devolved management responsibility discussed earlier. Although organizational logic might also point to the potential for transnational bargaining within international product or service divisions, for the reasons outlined earlier further decentralization of collective bargaining levels appears the most likely outcome. Third, in many European countries structures for collective bargaining over pay and major conditions remain formally separate from those for informing and consulting with employees within the enterprise. Companies will want to maintain this institutional separation; otherwise they increase the risk of giving trade unions a platform to become involved in the key strategic business issues of investment and disinvestment.

Unions also differ on the desirability of collective bargaining at Euro-company level. True, European industry federations of unions have been attempting to co-ordinate bargaining demands across countries. Also, the establishment of EWCs is a central objective of the European Trade Union Confederation, the European industry federations and individual unions. Even so, trade unions in many European countries remain as attached as most employers to existing systems of national multi-employer bargaining. National trade unions may well prove reluctant to yield the necessary authority and resources to European-level organizations to enable them to pursue transnational negotiations. For the foreseeable future, managements are unlikely to find themselves under strong pressure from unions to concede European-level collective bargaining.

Assuming that the managements of European companies will have to respond to legislative or 'social' initiatives from the Commission, however, it is possible to envisage the development of a 'triple' structure. First, in their anxiety to limit and, if possible, avoid altogether the impact of detailed legally binding directives, these managements may accept an increase in social dialogue at EC level. This may lead to framework 'agreements' or 'opinions' which provide for 'outline' procedures and some minimum conditions of employment (for example, hours and holidays). Second, they may also accept as part of this process that it will be necessary to introduce some form of EWC. Although such an institution may *de facto* become a vehicle for consultation, formal rights are likely to be restricted to information. Third, the preferred level of collective bargaining over working arrangements and payments structures, if not over pay levels, is likely to be the individual business unit within enterprises. The focus on individual units will be important in preventing European company bargaining as well as in contributing to the devolution of management responsibilities more generally. In some cases this business unit bargaining may entail a total withdrawal from the national system of multi-employer bargaining; in others it may mean a further shift of emphasis to the workplace within this framework. Much will depend on the nationality, strategy, structure and style of different companies and on the nature of national systems.

The opportunity that the introduction of EWCs provides for workers' representatives from different member states to meet and exchange information will be especially important for the development of a European system of industrial relations. Trade union representatives will have better information about pay and conditions elsewhere, which will enable them to introduce meaningful comparisons into bargaining and, in some cases, to extend concessions from one member state to another via forms of 'pattern' bargaining. Managements at group and divisional headquarters can also be expected to exercise greater co-ordination over the key decisions apparently taken in individual business units to avoid the setting of embarrassing precedents. In short, there could be a form of 'arms length' transnational bargaining: although managements and trade unions do not negotiate directly, the outcome is not dissimilar. The overall effect could be a growing convergence in the conditions of employment, if not necessarily pay levels, and the 'Europeanization' of industrial relations more generally.

Prospects

The emergence of a growing number of transnational companies able to integrate production, distribution and marketing across national borders raises wider questions about the organization of production; relations between different elements of capital; and processes of economic globalization.

The development of Euro-companies goes along with a revival in small and medium-sized enterprises (SMEs) within Europe. Whether these parallel developments represent a polarization of large and small capital is the subject of considerable debate. Does the revival of SMEs signify the flowering of an independent sector of capital, producing specialist, high quality products and services attuned to the needs of ever more discriminating consumers? Or does it reflect a process of organizational disaggregation, whereby an increasing range of formally independent suppliers, service providers, distributors and market outlets – including many subcontracted to undertake activities previously performed in-house – are brought within the strategic ambit of the transnational corporation? We tend to the latter view: management structures, information-processing capacities, performance control systems and available financial and communications infrastructures increasingly permit capital organized on a global scale to co-ordinate and control production and service provision on a devolved basis, both inside and outside the firm.

SMEs are likely to remain economically and numerically important, although within a European economy increasingly shaped by large conglomerations of capital. Their probable subordinate role in the development of the European (and global) economic system raises questions about relations between those southern European economies where SMEs are still the predominant form of national capital and the central and northern European states where large, transnational capital predominates. How far and how fast, for instance, will southern European economies find themselves locked into a division of labour in which they form the economic periphery to the transnational core?

A further complicating factor is the role of capital based in eastern Europe. At present the small-enterprise sector remains underdeveloped, although transnational companies have in recent years steadily increased their direct investment in medium and large-scale enterprises in the Czech Republic, Hungary, Slovakia and Poland, and have also made growing use of joint ventures and subcontracting arrangements with these enterprises. How far will industrial development in eastern Europe be shaped by indigenous forces? Or if, as seems probable, these economies become drawn into the ambit of large transnational capital which predominates in western Europe, will they extend, or displace, western Europe's economic periphery?

Relations between large and small capital also affect interest representation. Will Euro-companies develop distinct interests, which may lead them to question their involvement in national systems of industrial relations? Or will they seek to replicate in the industrial relations and political arenas the economic power they exercise over small and medium-sized capital? In which case, they seem likely to remain within multi-employer bargaining arrangements, while seeking scope for greater variation at enterprise level, and to exert political influence through the major employers' federations. Neither would necessarily preclude the development of distinct forms of interest representation, or moves towards organizationally specific employment and industrial relations policies, at European level.

A further set of questions relates to the distinctiveness of developments at European level, within a more general process of globalization. Many Euro-companies are world-wide in the scope of their operations. Some transnationals already organize their activities into global product or service divisions; for North American or Japanese-based companies, much will depend on the autonomy that world-wide headquarters grant regional operations. The distinctiveness of the 'Euro-company' may be less than evident in some cases. However, within a global economy which is becoming increasingly open to international economic forces, developments within Europe have a trajectory and momentum of their own. The creation of a common economic area, along with the gradual evolution of supranational economic and political institutions, are stimulating transnational companies to develop specific forms of organization and interest representation at European level. These merit distinct analytical treatment.

These wider developments may have substantial repercussions on industrial relations. In so far as small-scale capital becomes drawn into the strategic ambit of large, transnational companies, decisions affecting the incomes, working conditions and employment security of the work force in SMEs could increasingly be taken by corporate managements who are neither the direct employer nor within the scope of national jurisdiction. More generally, countries and regions within Europe could become locked into low pay, poor conditions and insecure employment equilibria which result from decisions taken by corporate offices based elsewhere in Europe, or further afield, over which they have little influence.

The ability to compare industrial relations performance across sites, or, for new investments, anticipated performance at potential sites, is enabling transnationals to exercise more general pressures on pay, benefits and working conditions across Europe. Current debates about 'Eurosclerosis' indicate the pressure that might be exerted to achieve more flexible working arrangements, less advantageous terms and conditions and less comprehensive employment protection in some of the most economically advanced countries of Europe. Moreover, these pressures increasingly operate at global level. The opening up of eastern Europe, and the development of highly educated work-forces and sophisticated infrastructures in the newly industrialized countries are multiplying the sources of pressure and thereby increasing the options open to transnationals. Their choices will in large measure shape the future of European industrial relations.

References

Albert, M. 1991: *Capitalisme contre Capitalisme*. Paris: Editions du Seuil.

Buiges, P., Ilkovitz, F. and Lebrun, J.-F. 1990: The impact of the internal market by industrial sector: the challenge for member states. *Social Europe*, Special Issue, Luxemburg: Office for Official Publications of the European Communities.

Buitendam, A. 1979: Personnel departments in industry: an empirical study of the structure and functioning of personnel departments in industrial organisations in The Netherlands. PhD thesis (unpublished), Groningen State University.

Cable, J. and Dirrheimer, M. 1983: Hierarchies and markets: an empirical test of the multidivisional hypothesis in West Germany. *International Journal of Industrial Organisation*, 1(1) 1–129.

Campinos-Dubernet, M. and Grando, J.-M. 1988: Formation professionelle ouvrière: trois modèles Européens. *Formation/Emploi*, 22, 5–29.

Capelli, P. and McElrath, R. 1992: The transfer of employment practices through multinationals. Paper to Third Bargaining Group Conference, University of California, Berkeley, March.

Commons, J. 1909: American shoemakers 1648–1895: a sketch of industrial evolution. *Quarterly Journal of Economics*, 24.

Deutschmann, C. 1992: Works councils and enterprise-level industrial relations in German transplants of Japanese firms. In S. Tokunga, N. Altmann and H. Demes (eds), *New Impacts on Industrial Relations: internationalisation and changing production strategies*, Munich: Iudicum.

Dore, R. 1989: Where we are now: musings of an evolutionist. *Work, Employment and Society*, 3(4) 425–46.

Dunning, J. 1993: *Multinational Enterprises and the Global Economy*: New York: Addison Wesley.

Economist 1993: Everybody's favourite monsters: a survey of multinationals. *The Economist*, 27 March.

Edwards, P.K., Ferner, A. and Sisson, K. 1993: People and the process of management. *Warwick Papers in Industrial Relations*, No. 43. Coventry: Industrial

Relations Research Unit.

European Commission 1993: *Employment in Europe: 1993*. Luxembourg: Office for Official Publications of the European Communities.

EIRR 1993a: Information and consultation in European multinationals – Part 1. *European Industrial Relations Review*, January, 13–19.

EIRR 1993b: Information and consultation in European multinationals – Part 2. *European Industrial Relations Review*, February, 14–20.

EIRR 1993c: The Hoover affair and social dumping. *European Industrial Relations Review*, March, 14–19.

EIRR 1993d: IBM goes it alone. *European Industrial Relations Review*, April, 16–18.

Eurostat 1990: *Enterprises in the European Community*. Luxembourg: Office for Official Publications of the European Communities.

Faust, M., Jauch, P., Brünnecke, K. and Deutschmann, C. 1993: *Dezentralisierung von Unternehmen: Bürokratie und Hierarchieabbau und die Rolle betrieblicher Arbeitspolitik*. Tübingen: Forschungsinstitut für Arbeit, Technik and Kultur.

Ferner, A. and Hyman, R. 1992a: Introduction. In Ferner and Hyman 1992c, xvi–xlix.

Ferner, A. and Hyman, R. 1992b: Italy: between political exchange and micro-corporatism. In Ferner and Hyman 1992c, 524–600.

Ferner, A. and Hyman, R. (eds) 1992c: *Industrial Relations in the New Europe*. Oxford: Blackwell Publishers.

Financial Times 1991: European investment locations. Supplement, 4 July.

Financial Times 1993: Resetting the clock. 10 February.

Forsgren, M., Holm, U. and Johanson, J. 1992: Internationalisation of the second degree: the emergence of European-based centres in Swedish firms. In S. Young and J. Hamill (eds), *Europe and the Multinationals*, Aldershot: Edward Elgar Publishing.

Franks, J. and Mayer, C. 1992: Corporate control: a synthesis of international evidence. Unpublished paper, London Business School and University of Warwick, November.

Gardner, S. 1993: Trends and trade-offs in the corporate structure–strategy of UK and German enterprises. Coventry: Industrial Relations Research Unit. (Mimeo.)

Goetschy, J. and Rozenblatt, P. 1992: France: the industrial relations system at a turning point? In Ferner and Hyman 1992c: 404–44.

Gold, M. and Hall, M. 1992: *European-Level Information and Consultation in Multinational Companies: an evaluation of practice*. Luxembourg: Office for Official Publications of the European Communities.

Gow, D. 1993: Employers deliver knock-out threat to German pay round. *The Guardian*, 16 October.

Hall, M., Marginson, P. and Sisson, K. 1992: The European Works Council: setting the research agenda. *Warwick Papers in Industrial Relations*, No. 41, Coventry: Industrial Relations Research Unit.

Hamill, J. 1984: Labour relations decision-making within multinational corporations. *Industrial Relations Journal*, 15(1) 30–4.

Hamill, J. 1992: Cross border mergers, acquisitions and alliances in Europe. In S. Young and J. Hamill (eds), *Europe and the Multinationals*, Aldershot: Edward Elgar Publishing.

Hu, Y. 1992: Global or stateless corporations are national firms with international operations. *California Management Review*, 34(2) 107–26.

Ietto-Gilles, G. 1992: *International Production: trends, theories, effects*. Cambridge: Polity Press.

Jain, H. 1990: HRM in selected Japanese firms, their foreign-owned subsidiaries and locally-owned counterparts. *International Labour Review*, 129(1) 73–90.

Kjellberg, A. 1992: Sweden: can the model survive? In Ferner and Human 1992c, 88–142.

Lane, C. 1989: *Management and Labour in Europe*. Aldershot: Edward Elgar Publishing.

Lawler, J., Atmiyanandana, V. and Zaidi, M. 1992: The role of home country culture in shaping HRM practices in subsidiaries of multinational firms. Paper to Third Bargaining Group Conference, University of California, Berkeley, March.

Lorenz, C. 1991: Sharing power around the world. *Financial Times*, 29 November.

Marginson, P., Edwards, P.K., Martin, R., Purcell, J. and Sisson, K. 1988: *Beyond the Workplace: managing industrial relations in the multi-establishment enterprise*. Oxford: Blackwell Publishers.

Marginson, P., Armstrong, P., Edwards, P.K. and Purcell, J. with Hubbard, N. 1993: The control of industrial relations in large companies. *Warwick Papers in Industrial Relations* No. 45, Coventry: Industrial Relations Research Unit.

Marginson, P., Buitendam, A., Deutschmann, C. and Perulli, P. 1993: The emergence of the Euro-company: towards a European industrial relations? *Industrial Relations Journal*, 24(3) 182–90.

Marginson, P., Hall, M. and Sisson, K. 1993: European-level employee information and consultative structures in multinational enterprises. *Issues in People Management*, 7. London: Institute of Personnel Management.

Martínez, M. 1992: Spain: constructing institutions and actors in a context of change. In Ferner and Hyman 1992c: 482–523.

Millward, N., Stevens, M., Smart, D. and Hawes, W. 1992: *Workplace Industrial Relations in Transition*. Aldershot: Dartmouth Publishers.

Mueller, F. and Purcell, J. 1992: The Europeanisation of manufacturing and the decentralisation of bargaining: multinational management strategies in the European automobile industry. *International Journal of Human Resource Management*, 3(1) 15–34.

Perlmutter, H. 1969: The tortuous evolution of the multinational corporation. *Columbia Journal of World Business*, January–February, 9–18.

Perulli, P. 1986: *Pirelli 1980–85: Le relazioni industriali*. Milan: FrancoAngeli.

Perulli, P. 1993: Towards a regionalisation of industrial relations. *International Journal of Urban and Regional Research*, 17(1) 98–113.

Porter, M. (ed.) 1986: *Competition in Global Industries*. Boston: Harvard University Press.

Prais, S. (ed.) 1990: *Productivity, Education and Training*. London: National Institute of Social and Economic Research.

Scott, J. 1991: Networks of corporate power: a comparative assessment. *Annual Review of Sociology*, 17, 181–203.

Servain-Schreiber, J.-J. 1967. *Le Défi américain*. Paris: Editions Denoël.

Sisson, K. 1987: *The Management of Collective Bargaining: an international comparison*. Oxford: Blackwell Publishers.

Sisson, K. 1991: Employers' organisations and industrial relations: the significance of the strategies of large companies. In D. Sadowski and O. Jacobi (eds), *Employers' Associations in Europe*, Baden-Baden: Nomos.

Sisson, K., Waddington, J. and Whitston, C. 1992: The structure of capital in the European Community: the size of companies and the implications for industrial relations. *Warwick Papers in Industrial Relations*, No. 38. Coventry: Industrial Relations Research Unit.

Streeck, W. 1987: The uncertainties of management and the management of uncertainty. *Work, Employment and Society*, 1(2) 281–308.

Streeck, W. 1991: More uncertainties: German unions facing 1992. *Industrial Relations*, 30(3) 317–49.

Terry, M. 1985: Combine committees: developments in the 1970s. *British Journal of Industrial Relations*, 23(3) 359–78.

United Nations 1988: *Transnational Corporations in World Development*. New York: United Nations.

United Nations 1993: *World Investment Report 1993: transnational companies and integrated international production*. New York: United Nations.

Visser, J. 1992: The Netherlands: the end of an era and the end of a system. In Ferner and Hyman 1992c: 323–57.

Windolf, P. 1993: Codetermination and the market for corporate control in the European Community. *Economy and Society*, 22(2) 137–58.

3

The State as Employer

Anthony Ferner

Introduction

The public sector in European countries, following decades of post-war expansion, has been swept up in general economic restructuring. It has been at the centre of things: as protagonist, as scapegoat, as political symbol of change. The role of the state in the provision of welfare – health, education and social security – has provoked a literature of the 'overloaded state', of 'fiscal crisis', in which an overextended public sphere was seen as 'crowding out' the wealth-generating private sector. Such longer-term trends were compounded by the effect of economic crisis, leading to worsening public sector deficits in the 1970s (CEC 1989: 139–43).

These developments encouraged a widespread political response in the 1980s. Government policy sought to 'roll back' the state. Over the decade, the rise in public expenditure as a proportion of gross domestic product (GDP) was stemmed if not reversed in most European countries (Oxley et al. 1990), although falling tax revenues and growing demands on social security budgets during the early 1990s recession masked the underlying trend.

From the end of the 1980s, new pressures for reform of the state have arisen from European integration, and more generally from the intensification of international competition. The efficiency of the state sector is seen as one key factor of competitiveness in the single European market, while the convergence conditions set out in the Maastricht Treaty set precise targets for the level of national debt and public expenditure deficits.

The rolling back of the state has taken two forms. First, governments have redefined the area of legitimate state action, and have withdrawn from certain activities by privatization, 'hiving off' and 'contracting out' of services. Second, they have tried to reform the provision of public services. This has brought about a radical shake-up in the way in which the public administration is managed. In particular it has entailed the imposition of private sector styles and structures of management: the 'market' has penetrated the very core of the state. These developments are summarized in the following section.

Restructuring has had a marked impact on many aspects of industrial relations and personnel management in the state. The growth of public employment has been slowed if not reversed, while structures of bargaining and participation, pay determination, work organization, career structures and so on have been the subject of reform projects, as described in the third section of the chapter.

The main analytical focus of the chapter, however, is on three more general issues arising from the restructuring of the state. First, what is the foreseeable trajectory of the state as employer? How permanent are current developments? How valid is the project of 'commercializing' the state and its industrial relations? The answer to these questions, considered in the fourth section, will depend on whether the various elements of the new public management 'fit together' as a coherent whole, or whether they suffer from their own internal contradictions: most fundamentally, can a culture of public service be reconciled with the mechanisms of the market?

Second, although reform has been widespread, reform projects have varied greatly in the degree, timing and speed of change, in the content, and in the style of implementation from country to country. What is the reason for these variations? The argument of the fifth section attempts to untangle various political and institutional threads of explanation and to propose different models of state industrial relations.

Third, a strand of debate has raised the possibility of the growing convergence of state and private sector industrial relations. This has generally been in response to the introduction of private sector models of collective bargaining and work-force representation in countries where the doctrine of state sovereignty traditionally held sway. An associated move has been the erosion of the special status often granted to public employees. Is there a limit to this process, a mode of operation that is irreducibly 'of the state', or will the public/private distinction become increasingly blurred? These points are taken up in the conclusion.

Reconstructing the State

The 1980s brought a profound change of emphasis in efforts to control the state. The classic concern with 'top–down' budgetary constraints on spending was increasingly supplemented by 'a more intense scrutiny of the internal functioning of public sector organizations' (OECD 1990: 9). In other words, what states do and how they do it is now as important a question as how much they spend. The change has been driven by the arrival of the so-called 'new public management' in the United States and Britain (e.g. Aucoin 1990; Hood 1991), but the influence of Anglo-Saxon concerns has spread throughout Europe, as demonstrated by the OECD surveys of new initiatives in public sector management (OECD 1992; 1993a).

The main thrust of new developments is on changing the way in which state services are delivered, which in turn has affected the internal organization and management of the state. First, decision-making authority and the corresponding financial responsibility have been devolved to individual units and agencies, although within more rigorous frameworks of accountability. The emphasis of managerial jobs has shifted from following bureaucratic procedures to producing easily definable 'outputs'. Results can then be measured against targets, allowing managers to be held accountable (OECD 1990: 11). In a number of countries such as Belgium, France, Spain, Italy, Sweden and Denmark – though not Britain – there has been a delegation of powers from the national state to the regions or local authorities, as well as within managerial units.

Second, a related development has been the separation of policy-making from executive functions. Since the late 1980s, for example, the Swedish government has been devolving managerial responsibilities to some 200 state agencies (Gustaffson 1987; OECD 1991: 85–91; Wise 1993), a process accelerated with the arrival of the centre-right government in September 1991. Perhaps the most prominent example has been the 'Next Steps' initiative in the British civil service, under which central government employees are being decanted from ministries into 'executive agencies' (Corby 1991). These are semi-autonomous organizations responsible for their own management, resources and industrial relations, albeit under the policy directives and framework of financial control laid down by ministers. They are thus a key example of managerial decentralization within the state. The British government now estimates that by 1995 some 450,000 civil service employees (75 per cent of the total) will be working in agencies. Elsewhere, such developments have affected state trading organizations rather than central government. Previously operating as government departments within the central state administration, rail, telecommunications and postal authorities in Italy, France, Germany and The Netherlands have acquired greater managerial autonomy and an organizational structure more akin to that of private enterprises.

Third, there have been efforts to introduce elements of market competition into the untraded public services sector. Again, Britain has led the way in its reforms of health and education. Schools can now 'opt out' of local authority control, gaining more control over their resources, including the management of industrial relations. Schools can increase their funds by competing successfully to attract students (Keep 1992). In the Health Service the role of *purchaser* has been separated from that of *provider* of services, and the allocation of health care resources is now decided more by contract between different units than by co-ordinated planning.

Fourth, Britain has gone furthest in introducing 'market testing'. This means that large areas of public service provision are examined to see whether they could be more cheaply or efficiently provided by private operators. Already, very large areas of local government and health service operations are subject to 'compulsory competitive tendering', and there is currently market testing of tens of thousands of central government jobs. Similar developments are on the agenda in Sweden under the government's administrative reform programme (OECD 1992: 86, 89).

Finally, the logical conclusion of these experiments with the 'marketization' of the state has of course been the total elimination of state involvement in the provision of services, as has occurred in the public trading sector in Britain with the privatization of most of the important public corporations (Vickers and Yarrow 1988; Colling and Ferner 1993). Elsewhere, privatization has been more pragmatic and subdued (Vickers and Wright 1988; Ferner 1991). During the 1980s, even countries with large nationalized sectors of industry – Italy, Austria and Spain, for example – did little beyond selling a few non-strategic companies and offering minority shareholdings in some of the remainder. In Greece and Portugal, loudly-heralded privatization plans have yet to amount to much; the October 1993 election victory of PASOK in the former is likely to delay existing plans further. Only in France has there been a programme to match that of Britain: first under Chirac's prime ministership in 1986–8 (Durupty 1988); and again following the right's electoral landslide in the spring of 1993. The Balladur government intends to sell all remaining nationalized companies operating in competitive sectors.

There are some signs of a renewed interest in privatization elsewhere, partly as a result of political upheavals – the victory of the right in Sweden, the crumbling of the post-war political system in Italy, and German unification. Among the most important developments are plans for the 'corporatization' and eventual privatization of German state railways, and for a large-scale sale of state assets in Italy; in preparation for the latter, the big holding companies IRI and ENI and electricity company ENEL have been converted into public companies. It remains to be seen how many of these projects will actually be implemented.

The overall picture, therefore, is one of general change, although its extent is very varied. On the one hand, the transformation of the public sector is a response to general pressures of public expenditure crisis and broader economic restructuring, of internationalization and European integration; on the other, as a later section explores in more detail, its variability suggests that the precise form is determined by country-specific factors.

The two great elements of transformation – the cut-back and redistribution of state expenditure and the reform of the internal functioning of the state – have had pervasive ramifications for industrial relations. The chains of influence are both direct and indirect. Constraints on expenditure have focused attention on personnel costs, which constituted around two-thirds of current government consumption in most European countries at the end of the 1980s. Changing management structures have placed public managers in a different framework of incentives and responsibilities, creating new pressures for change in aspects of industrial relations and human resource management – work organization, payment systems, bargaining levels, and so on. In addition, as Fudge (1990: 91) argues, private sector ideas of labour market flexibility and flexible personnel management 'are being diffused into the public sector and, in particular [impacting] on reforms of central state bureaucracies'. More directly, in many countries industrial relations in the public sector have been the subject of direct government action: through pay policy, staffing targets, reform of bargaining systems and the regulation of industrial conflict. The following section summarizes the main developments.

Reform of the State and Industrial Relations[1]

Public sector employment

The growth in public employment of the 1960s and 1970s has been slowed, although not generally reversed (see table 3.1). With the ex-

Table 3.1 Public sector employment in Europe, 1979–1990

	Annual average growth rate				Share in total employment				
	1970–5	*1975–9*	*1979–84*	*1984–90*	*1970*	*1975*	*1979*	*1985*	*1989*
Austria	4.1	3.0	1.9	2.7	13.2	16.3	17.6	19.1	21.1
Belgium[b]	3.0	4.1	0.9	0.7	13.6	15.6	18.3	19.9	19.9
Denmark[a]	6.5	4.6	2.5	0.7	17.2	23.6	26.9	30.2	30.1
Finland	5.0	4.3	3.2	2.2	12.1	14.8	17.2	18.9	20.6
France	2.0	1.7	1.8	1.0	17.6	19.0	19.9	22.1	22.8
Germany[a]	3.8	1.9	1.0	1.5	11.1	13.8	14.7	15.5	15.6
Greece[b]	2.6	3.3	2.2	2.5	7.4	8.2	9.1	9.4	10.1
Ireland	4.1	4.5	1.9	−0.8	12.0	14.4	16.1	18.3	17.9
Italy	3.8	2.6	1.4	1.3	12.3	14.6	15.8	16.6	17.4
Luxembourg	3.0	2.2	1.5	3.0	9.4	9.7	10.6	11.3	11.4
Netherlands	2.1	2.5	0.7	0.3	12.2	13.6	14.7	16.1	15.1
Norway[b]	5.0	5.3	3.7	2.8	17.9	21.7	24.3	28.1	29.3
Portugal	4.0	6.2	6.2	3.4	7.9	8.5	10.5	13.3	14.6
Spain[c]	7.6	5.0	2.9	4.0	5.5	7.8	10.0	12.8	13.7
Sweden[b]	5.3	4.6	2.2	0.0	20.9	25.7	29.9	32.9	31.8
Switzerland[b]	3.7	2.7	1.4	0.9	7.5	9.0	10.1	10.2	10.5
UK	3.1	0.8	−0.3	−0.2	18.1	20.9	21.2	21.8	19.6

[a] latest year available 1990; [b] latest year available 1988; [c] latest year available 1987.

Source: Oxley and Martin 1991: 168

ception of the United Kingdom and Ireland, the state sector continued to grow as a proportion of total employment in the 1980s in most European countries, although there were signs of a downturn in the latter part of the decade (Oxley et al. 1990: 49; Oxley and Martin 1991; Cusack et al. 1987). The overall figures conceal considerable variations between different areas of employment. Central government has declined somewhat relative to local government (OECD 1993a: 366), although health and education employment has continued to expand in a number of countries. Even in Britain, most of the shrinkage in civil service employment came from the fall in blue-collar staff, and the early 1990s have seen a renewed growth in white-collar numbers.

The major decline has been in state-owned enterprise where privatization and restructuring have combined to cause some dramatic falls in employment. Yet again, Britain provides the most dramatic example: two million employees of public enterprises in 1979, under three-quarters of a million in 1992. In countries such as Italy, Spain and Austria, state firms continued for a while to play their traditional role as 'social buffers' helping maintain employment, while in France, the early years of the Mitterrand presidency saw a massive nationalization programme, with state firms being used to buttress employment policy (Rand Smith 1990). Nevertheless, by the latter half of the 1980s, numbers were falling pretty well everywhere.

Pay determination

In a context of public expenditure restraint, governments have been preoccupied with the control of public sector pay as the largest component of current costs. The statistical evidence suggests that although the real earnings of public employees have often been rising slightly in the 1980s and early 1990s, public sector earnings as a whole have fallen relative to those of the private sector. The decline was particularly sharp in the latter part of the 1980s in the United Kingdom and in Germany, less so in France, Italy, The Netherlands and the Scandinavian countries (Oxley and Martin 1991).

Government concern with public sector pay is hardly new, of course. However, the 1980s and 1990s have brought additional pressures. First, growth of state sector employment meant that public pay had a correspondingly greater impact. This was manifested in the increasing wage leadership role of state employees, for example in bargaining rounds in Denmark and Sweden. Second, attention has been focused on public sector pay as a result of European integration, in particular the signing of the Maastricht Treaty and (until the exchange rate mechanism (ERM) crisis of mid-1993, at least) the convergence conditions for European monetary union. This has been true even for those governments – notably Italy and Greece – which have taken a more relaxed view of government deficits (compare IMF 1990). Recent developments in Italy suggest that whatever happens to the exchange rate mechanism, the drive for public expenditure restraint will proceed regardless (see below).

Governments have given priority to 'ability to pay' criteria over alternatives such as fair comparisons. Mechanisms linking public sector pay implicitly or explicitly to private sector groups or to inflation have been overridden or weakened. In The Netherlands, for example, the government imposed a pay cut on public employees in 1983, against the traditions of the 'trend mechanism' (Visser 1990: 227–8), while public sector pay in France was 'de-indexed' in 1982, being linked to inflation targets rather than actual price rises. Compensation clauses in Swedish public sector agreements were abolished in 1986 (Kjellberg 1992: 111). More recently, the British government's pay norm of 1.5 per cent for all public employees in 1993–4, to be followed by a virtual pay freeze in 1994–5, neutralizes the work of pay review bodies covering some 900,000 employees.

As in earlier decades, expenditure and pay constraints have been a major factor in some spectacular outbreaks of industrial conflict in the public sector (Ozaki 1987). In Germany, for example, the first major strike in the public sector for two decades took place in the spring of 1992.

A newer development in pay determination has been the use of pay as a tool of managerial flexibility, in line with the emerging emphasis on market-driven service provision. This is in part a reaction against the rigidities of traditional pay and grading structures, based on inflexible job categories and seniority-based pay and promotion. The very rigidity of structures encouraged a 'remuneration jungle' (Treu 1987b) of debased incentive schemes, as in the Italian public service where the proliferation of bonuses, special payments and job classifications has been the subject of wide-ranging proposals for reform (for example, Treu 1991). Similarly, in France, the rigidity of the famous *grille* has led to a plethora of bonuses to boost salary levels, sometimes amounting to 30–40 per cent of pay (Bach 1992).

Efforts are being made, therefore, to make existing systems more flexible, particularly in response to local labour market conditions (for example, Wise 1993; OECD 1990: 39, 75). The most important manifestation of this development is the introduction of performance-related pay for managers and more junior staff in many European countries during the 1980s (Maguire and Wood 1992). It has been carried furthest in Britain where individual merit pay for non-manual employees is now widely used in the civil service, health, and local government since 1987 (Colling and Ferner 1993; OECD 1992: 73–4).

The pursuit of labour flexibility

The use of performance-related pay is only one aspect of a more general trend towards greater flexibility in the way labour is deployed. In the largely white-collar areas of central and local government, flexibility has centred on changes in contracts, career paths, occupational mobility and grading structures (Treu and de Felice 1990). Increased mobility between different subgroups within the public sector is a key issue, for example, in the reform of the French public administration, where hundreds of specialist *corps* have created rigid barriers to job mobility (de Closets 1989). Increasingly, public managers are being recruited from the private sector.

Another form of flexibility, again taking the private sector as a model, is the rapid expansion of 'non-standard' forms of contracts, especially part-time and temporary employment (ILO 1988). The vast majority of non-standard employees are women, and they often have considerably lower job security and fewer employment benefits than full-time employees (pp. 130–5). The increase has been particularly marked in the United Kingdom, where it is encouraged by government policy (IRRR 1988a), and in France and Germany.

The special employment status of civil servants – as *Beamte, titulaires* or *ambtenaren* – in many countries has also been challenged by the search for flexibility. An example is the weakening of the 'alimentation' principle that determined remuneration for German civil servants according to length of service and grade status (Blenk 1987), although it remains strong. In France, the notably sympathetic tone of the de Closets Commission (1989) towards the *statut de la fonction publique* was qualified by the recognition of the need for greater mobility and flexibility.

The reform of structures of representation

Two sometimes conflicting processes have been operating in parallel in the reform of structures of collective bargaining in the public sector. First, with the devolution of power and the pursuit of greater flexibility, there have been pressures for the decentralization of bargaining and, in some cases, for the break-up of long-standing arrangements. Though decentralization has become a major strand of state industrial relations reform in The Netherlands (*EIRR* 1992a) Sweden (Gustaffson 1987) and elsewhere, Britain is again in the vanguard of developments. The traditional public sector principles of 'Whitleyism', whereby industrial relations for all groups of staff were conducted through elaborate multi-tiered machineries of negotiation and consultation, have been eroded. There is a gathering trend towards the fragmentation of national agreements and the development of local bargaining arrangements, in both public administration and the remaining state corporations such as the Post Office (see Colling and Ferner 1993). The rise of the internal market, 'opting out' by schools and hospitals, and the formation of executive agencies, are likely to strengthen further these developments. Moreover, important groups of employees have been removed from collective bargaining, either by the formation of pay review bodies (notably for health professionals and teachers), or by the use of 'personal', individually negotiated contracts for senior staff, as in British Rail.

The second general tendency runs, in some ways, counter to this. While Britain is moving away from a highly formalized system of joint regulation, other countries have been institutionalizing employment relationships within the public sector. This modernization is ambiguous. At one level, it is part of the general reform of the state and the search for greater efficiency by the sweeping away of outdated practices. At another level it entails the extension of pluralist institutions of industrial relations from the private sector to the state. In most continental European countries, the legal doctrine of state sovereignty had been accompanied by the unilateral determination of the terms and conditions of state servants. Even in Sweden, public servants achieved full bargaining rights and the right to strike only in the 1960s (Kjellberg 1992: 102). The 1980s and 1990s have seen a widespread erosion of the doctrine of state sovereignty, notably in France, Italy, The Netherlands and Spain.

In Spain, the construction of a new structure of industrial relations in the public sector (OIT 1985: 117–22) was part of the transition from dictatorship to democracy. Pluralist institutions were created from scratch in a compressed period of time. This was not solely or even primarily driven by concerns with state efficiency, but rather with the consolidation of a viable alliance of pro-democracy interests in conditions of considerable political instability.

Both Italy and France saw further major steps in a process, stretching back to the 1960s, of modernizing public sector industrial relations. In France, the 1983 law on the public service formally permitted collective bargaining (Bazex 1987: 95–7). In Italy, the 1980s saw a continuation of the trend from *de facto* to legally regulated collective bargaining in the public administration, particularly with the law 83/1983 (Treu 1987b). However, the failings of the 1983 law (Cecora 1990), and the climate of looming crisis at the end of the 1980s, have led to proposals for further radical reform. This has now been caught up in the more general restructuring of the Italian state and politics, as is discussed below. Finally, The Netherlands moved decisively away from unilateral determination of the terms and conditions of *ambtenaren* (civil servants) during the 1980s towards what Rood (1990) calls the 'equivalence of relations' between employers and unions. The public sector strike ban was lifted in 1981 and under the 1988 Protocol the centrally determined employment conditions of *ambtenaren* could no longer be altered by government without the prior approval of the unions (*EIRR* 1992a, 21–3).

Thus, as in Britain, modernization of state industrial relations in France, Italy and The Netherlands has been driven at least partly by a desire to clarify and rationalize structures of representation and bargaining, within a climate of state expenditure constraint. However, unlike Britain and like Spain, the reform of the institutional framework of public sector industrial relations has also been the result of a move from state unilateralism to joint determination, by both granting bargaining rights to groups of employees and extending the scope of bargaining to cover new issues and levels.

The Viability of the New State Model

How coherent is the new commercial model as a form of state organization? Two of its defining features are decentralization and individual performance incentives. Each is found in at least incipient form in most western European countries (see OECD 1993b). Their introduction has been motivated by the desire to reduce costs of services and increase the efficiency of providing them. Each, however, poses considerable problems for state employers, to the extent of interfering with other state goals.

The decentralization of management organization may undermine both the central control over strategic state policy and the fabric of implicit understandings and culture of public administration. For example, in Britain the breakdown of central government into semi-autonomous agencies, with considerable management autonomy over pay and conditions, may bring to an end the notion of the 'unified career bureaucracy' (Corby 1991) and, paradoxically, discourage mobility between different parts of the state.

Decentralization also poses the question of how devolved bargaining structures can be reconciled with the central control of pay and other major components of public expenditure. As Oxley et al. (1990: 19) point out, there is likely to be strong resistance to devolution from finance ministries anxious to retain central control over pay as part of budget-setting. Continued political intervention in the setting of pay norms is likely to undermine local bargainers by making it difficult for them to deliver the devolved, 'market-led' remuneration packages on which their human resource strategies are built (compare Colling and Ferner 1993).

For individual agencies, decentralized bargaining can impose higher payroll costs (Wise 1993: 82). Where public unions are strong and retain their ability to co-ordinate information and action across different parts of the public sector, devolved bargaining may enhance their capacity to make 'leap-frogging claims', levering up pay to a greater extent than would be possible under a more centralized system. Information costs for each individual agency increase, as do the costs of resourcing decentralized bargaining functions, including developing the necessary negotiating skills of local managers. Seifert (1990: 56), writing about developments in the British health and education sectors, foresees 'a massed web of local agreements which will prove a nightmare to negotiate and implement'.

Decentralization may also leave its mark on the pattern of public sector conflict. Increasingly it is likely that a new pattern of 'micro-conflict' (Treu 1987b) will replace the traditional set-piece battles of public sector industrial relations. This derives from two sources. First, acquiescence in pay moderation has eroded the authority of central unions, and favoured the growth of alternative, disseminated forms of representation in the shape of powerful occupational groups with sectional demands for higher earnings or the restoration of earnings differentials. The *cobas* in Italy and the *coordinations* in France have been the most prominent examples of a widespread phenomenon which also encompasses more formally organized, occupationally based 'autonomous' unions such as the Spanish train-drivers SEMAF and the Italian airline pilots, Appi. Freed from the moderating influence of central union organizations, *cobas* and the like have exploited their often considerable industrial muscle to press their demands (see chapter 10). Second, the decentralization of management authority and bargaining structures means that the site at which industrial pressure can most effectively be applied is shifting to lower levels, while the proliferation of lower-level interactions increases the chances of conflict. The tendency in several countries (Italy, Spain, Ireland and Portugal among them) to regulate strikes in essential services by legislation, codes of conduct and so on, is unlikely to be effective in coping with micro-conflict: the very forces of fragmentation have weakened unions' control of their members, and much of the decentralized conflict is likely to be 'unofficial', even semi-clandestine in nature.

In short, to borrow Treu and de Felice's (1990: 74) now uncomfortably resonant image, decentralization runs the risk of provoking the 'Balkanization of [public sector] structures and representation, which certainly would not favour social harmony and responsible attitudes'.

The importation of the performance ethic is likewise dissonant in many respects with the requirements of public administration. Individual performance-related remuneration has in general suffered from a number of well-known problems of performance measurement, appraisal and reward (for example, Kessler and Purcell 1992). In the public sector, however, additional problems arise. First, performance-related pay conflicts with employee perceptions of 'fairness' (compare de Closets 1989: 217): the culture of public administration is saturated with an emphasis on the rate for the post, which is after all one of the expressions of the historical struggle to create professional public bureaucracies free of political interference and patronage. Feelings of unfairness may also be heightened by aspects of labour market segmentation in the public sector, particularly in relation to gender. Wise (1993: 89) cites evidence from Sweden that the wage gap between the sexes widens with the implementation of individualized pay. Second, by its nature, much public sector work does not lend itself to easy measurement (OECD 1993b). It has proved easier to measure volume than quality despite the increasing political emphasis on the latter. One result is that employees' energies are likely to be diverted into easily measurable and hence positively rewarded behaviour even where this may be less than optimal for the objectives of the organization. Wise (1993: 84) cites the example of the Swedish Labour Inspectorate. Since safety inspectors were evaluated on the number of sites they visited, they tended to concentrate on compliant sites with good safety records and avoid the more time-consuming problematic ones. Third, with restraints on public expenditure, the motivating effect of merit pay systems has been undermined by limits on the resources available, leading to complaints of unfairness and arbitrary treatment (OECD 1993b).

Most fundamentally, however, performance-related pay symbolizes 'the importation of commercial values into what were previously considered as community services' (IRRR 1988b: 4). Inevitably, this has led to demands by unions that if parts of the public sector are being run like a business, 'then staff should receive the salaries and fringe benefits on offer in the private sector' (IRRR 1988a: 13). Thus the performance ethic is at odds with and may undermine the public service ethic, and in particular the value of intrinsic, non-monetary motives that have traditionally been important aspects of public sector behaviour (Wise 1993: 86).

For all these reasons, one may question whether the performance ethos can achieve its stated aims of furthering efficiency in the public sector. Rather, it seems to have certain *tacit* functions relating to the political climate in which it has been introduced. This function is a *symbolic* one, whereby state agencies adopt the techniques of the private sector in order to signal to their political masters that they are taking seriously the exhortations to enhanced efficiency and financial responsibility. Such symbolic communication has been especially important in countries such as Britain where the onslaught on traditional management in the public sector had a strong ideological component. It also applied to Sweden where, as Wise (1993) argues, the new public management represented a form of 'crisis management' in which the important thing was to be seen to be doing something; its efficacy was a second-order consideration. In short, decentralization and the performance ethic have, to borrow the terms of Trice and Beyer (1984:

656–7), both a 'technical' function concerned with efficiency, and an 'expressive' function concerned with the communication of 'messages' to a set of public audiences.

New management systems and techniques are laden with ambiguities, and they have shown a propensity to generate new tensions in service provision. As a result, they have failed to provide a clear-cut, 'one best way' technical solution to the problems of what the state does and how it does it. Instead, there is a considerable political 'space' for different national paths to the restructuring of the state. This national variation forms the subject of the following section.

National Variation in the Reform of the State

Despite the predictions of an increasing homogeneity of European societies and states, what is striking, as Crouch argues, is the 'persistent variety of western Europe' (1993: vii) which has its origins in long historical development. Thus the inherent tensions between a 'market logic' and public service provision intersect with more particular obstacles to the new state model, rooted in the nature of national models, especially industrial relations. The general influences of economic and political restructuring discussed above have had a broad though far from uniform effect on public sector industrial relations. The divergences in approach are as striking as the similarities. The Thatcherite programme in Britain represents one extreme of the spectrum: an ideologically propelled political project of hacking the state down to size, and with it the allegedly over-powerful public sector trade unions. Nowhere else has there been such enveloping animosity to what the post-war public sector stands for; or such a thorough dismantling of the old ways of doing things in industrial relations; or such comprehensive privatization of the state; or such far-reaching reform of the remaining administrative apparatus. In other European countries, modernization of the state has been pragmatic, gradualist, accomplished with labour rather than against it, often going hand-in-hand with the consolidation of pluralist industrial relations institutions within the state. This section aims to delineate a number of models of state response in the 1980s and 1990s; and thereby to propose some strands of explanation for the differences. If Britain is out on a limb, why should this be so?

The essence of the argument is that in most countries the restructuring of the state has been delayed by its role as employer at the centre of a web of socio-political alliances and institutions. This appears to have given rise to efforts to *negotiate* the restructuring of the state, to mitigate the impact on the underlying alliances, and hence on systemic stability. This encourages a more consensual and cautious approach to reform. In some instances, public employment has been so enmeshed in the fabric of the system that it has been difficult to restructure without dismantling the supporting accommodations. Below, some key examples – Sweden, Italy, Spain, France and Germany – are examined in more detail.

Key cases in the reform of the state

The Swedish model

The expansion of public employment in Sweden was a product of the success of the 'Swedish model'. The labour movement's strategy was one of achieving social solidarity through income redistribution. On the one hand, centralized, though autonomous, national bargaining between the peak organizations LO and SAF allowed the pursuit of wage equalization policies. On the other, a massive edifice of social welfare and collective provision was constructed under the aegis of successive Social Democratic governments. This fuelled the rise in public employment. Between 1960 and 1990, the public sector proportion of LO's active membership rose from 22 to 41 per cent.

Yet, as the accounts of analysts such as Fulcher (1991: chs 8, 10) and Kjellberg (1992) make clear, the rise of the public sector was to alter the dynamics of the model and deal some critical blows to its viability. The growing weight of public employment was recognized in the granting of full bargaining rights and the right to strike in 1966, since when most legal conflicts have affected the public sector. A teacher's strike that same year could be seen as marking the beginning of the Swedish model's decline (Fulcher 1991: 207). From the 1970s, the public sector challenged the traditional wage leadership of the export sector, and struggles over 'comparability' between public and private sector were a major driving-force of pay determination in the 1970s and 1980s. 'Leap-frogging' was institutionalized by the introduction of comparability clauses in 1975 (Fulcher 1991: 215). This dynamic led to a series of major conflicts in the public sector in the 1980s as SAF tried to return to the classic, export sector-led model of the 1960s. More generally, the strategy of solidarity was seriously eroded. The public sector itself was also increasingly fragmented, with antagonistic blocs of interests emerging around lower-paid non-manuals represented by the LO/TCO 'Gang of Four' – the mainly female Local Authority Workers were the largest LO union by the 1980s – and higher-paid employees in unions belonging to the confederation of professional associations SACO/SR, who pressed for higher differentials.

Concern about the growing tax burden of rising pay within an expanding state sector helped forge an implicit anti-public sector alliance of private sector unions, employers and the Social Democratic government (see Swenson 1992: 52–61). In 1986, for example, the leaders of key unions in the private sector condemned the mediation commission's concession of public sector comparability with the private sector (Fulcher 1991: 214). At the same time, the problems for the private exporting sector were being aggravated by growing international competition, restructuring and European integration (Myrdal 1991). One reflection of this development was the breakaway of the Metal Workers from centralized bargaining in 1983. The ability of LO to co-ordinate a strategy on behalf of labour as a whole was thus being undermined on two flanks as the confederation became increasingly polarized between the Metal Workers and the Local Authority Workers. With the integrity of LO endangered, the model itself could only continue to disintegrate.

The contribution of the expanding public sector to the crumbling of the Swedish model may help explain why Sweden has witnessed some of the strongest moves to rein back the sector by the reform of state structures since the mid-1980s. For example, there have been attempts to decentralize public sector bargaining within centralized co-ordination and tighter financial control (Fulcher 1991: 299–301). SAV, the state's bargaining agency, was strengthened and put under the control of the ministry of finance in 1985, and bargaining was devolved to different subsectors.

The Swedish case displays, therefore, the way in which the model generated some of the causes of its own decline in a deepening tension between core export interests and the expanding state sector. The stresses were bound to be intensified by the increasing international competitive pressures and economic integration in the European Community. Since the election of the centre-right government in 1991, there has been a broader-based attack on the foundations of the old Swedish model. The political accommodations that underlay it, particularly the role of public sector employees, are likely to be increasingly challenged.

The Italian model

The post-war Italian model, like the systems of eastern Europe, has gone from apparent immutability to full-scale disintegration in a matter of months. The two events are not of course unconnected, since the collapse of communism removed the need for the anti-communist bulwark represented by four decades of Christian democrat hegemony. This took the lid off some of the explosive pressures contained within the system of 'blocked democracy' at a time when external pressures for change – notably from European integration – were challenging the assumptions of the model.

Public employment has played a key role in the Italian system. Italian general government employment[2] grew by about 27 per cent between 1970 and 1980, and then by a further 360,000 or 19 per cent between 1980 and 1990 (*Annuario Statistico Italiano*). This contributed to a public sector deficit among the highest in Europe. Public sector expansion was an integral part of the accommodations that underlay the Italian model. An implicit bargain united the dynamic, industrialized north with the poor south. A massive transfer of resources was effected, very often by means of public employment in both central and local government and in state enterprises. In addition, the latter played a key role in post-war industrial development and their location decisions were often determined by broad political considerations of developing the Mezzogiorno. As is now being graphically revealed, the transfer paths were both formal and official, and informal and corrupt, resting on an intricate web of clientelist relations that linked private and state industry, central government, local power structures, and even organized crime.

The state sector was also crucial in what Hyman calls the 'tacit pillarization' of Italian society, accommodating the diverse components of the governing alliance of Christian democrats and socialists. Thus the major state-sector holding companies were the fiefdoms of particular political parties and, as is now becoming clear, were part of the systematic web of illegal financial operations that paralleled the formal flows of resources.

The industrial relations of the public sector have been influenced by its key role in the political mosaic of post-war Italy: unofficially as a source and site of patronage, more openly as a symbol of the conciliation of different interests – particularly organized labour – within the polity. A key instance has been the role of state enterprises such as IRI in developing employee and union participation (through the 1984 IRI 'Protocol' for example). The whole complex alliance of interests generated its own dynamic of public employment growth that ran counter to the pressures for public expenditure control and reform. Efforts to modernize public sector bargaining structures in the early 1980s (Ferner and Hyman 1992: 570–3) were a relative failure (Cecora 1990): 'the rigidity of the legal machinery of 1983, inspired in the need to control expenditure, has not withstood the centrifugal and sectoral pressures that it was supposed to control' (Treu 1991: 310). Reform failed to address such costly anomalies as the so-called 'baby pension' which allowed public employees to retire in their mid-thirties after twenty years of service – it is estimated that 87 per cent of employees retired early, often to take up new jobs (*EIRR* 1992b: 9–10).

An integral component of the current political crisis has therefore been the pressure for further reform of the state and its industrial relations. The rallying cry of the reformers (see also Cecora 1992) has been the *privatizzazione* of industrial relations in the public sector – that is, making them more like those of the private sector. Treu (1991: 315–16) argues that this will be no guarantee against continuing collusive behaviour between public employers and their employees, and needs to be combined with management decentralization and the exposure of public services to competitive pressures on the British model. Government initiatives in the wake of the ERM crisis of autumn 1992 have included a large privatization programme, the freezing of public sector recruitment and pay, and an attack on the pension advantages of public employees. The decree law 421/1992 introduced further radical reform and 'privatization' of bargaining structures and industrial relations, bringing the 3.6 million public employees under the same legal framework of employment as applies to private sector workers (*EIRR* 1993a: 19–21).

The prognosis for the Italian crisis, and hence for the role of the public sector, remains highly uncertain. If the beneficiaries of the old system are able to stage an effective counter-attack, the role of public employment as a principal locus of accommodations is likely to be preserved, albeit in the framework of more reform of a cosmetic nature. If, on the other hand, the disintegration of the system continues at its present dizzying pace, the dismemberment of the system of state alliances will allow scope for more radical options, including the Treu strategy of a Thatcher-style privatization of the state from within.

The Spanish model

The Italian model of public sector employment relations has its echoes elsewhere in southern Europe. In Spain, for example, the rise of public employment – up by 50 per cent as a proportion of total employment between 1976 and 1989 (see also table 3.1) – has reflected the political alliances on which the transition from dictatorship to democracy was based (see Martínez 1992). For example, a growth of government structures has accompanied the dispersal of political power to the 'autonomous communities', which may be seen as an attempt to maintain the unity of the Spanish state and to hold centrifugal forces in check. Public enterprise was used until the mid-1980s as a tool of political consensus to ease the social impact of economic crisis: its role was reflected in the maintenance of levels of state industry employment in the face of mounting losses. Part of the process of democratization has also been the spread of pluralist industrial relations to the public service. Early post-Franco collective bargaining in the public enterprises was seen as a 'model' leading the way for the private sector (Ferner 1988).

There are even more direct parallels with Italy in the way in which the ruling party – in this case the socialist PSOE – has constructed a web of patronage and clientelism around state employment, creating thousands of posts for its adherents. The public sector has also been the conduit for the illicit flows of resources that oil the political accommodations on which the system rests. It is as yet unclear whether the socialists' loss of an overall majority in the June 1993 elections has created the conditions for a challenge to the system. In general it is questionable whether the socialists' political strategy can survive its contradictions, since it has rested on committing Spain securely to European integration. But this in turn has set limits to the political role of the public sector. The pressures for economic convergence are now leading to cuts in public expenditure and employment, privatization, and rationalization. However, PSOE's electoral dependence on the votes of public employees – evident again in the June 1993 elections – is likely to inhibit the extent of reforms. Much will depend on the impact of coalition politics on the internal accommodations within PSOE itself. In the medium term, an eventual electoral victory of the right may bring about a more radical restructuring of the state, although it may also produce a more unstable version of the Italian model as the right in its turn attempts to colonize the state while its mandate lasts.

The French model

In France as elsewhere, the 1980s witnessed growing concern with the efficacy and cost of the state in the light of new challenges of international competitiveness and European integration. There has been regular, tight, direct intervention in pay bargaining, for example, which has provoked repeated conflict. Under the socialists, however, the 1980s debate on the role of public administration is remarkable for the contrast it offers with the British case.

The analysis and recommendations of the government-appointed de Closets Commission on *The Effectiveness of the State* (de Closets 1989) are familiar enough: lack of initiative, inflexibility, over-complex and rigid pay and grading structures requiring more flexible employment and better performance evaluation. The analysis points to some of the 'dysfunctional' consequences of the distinctive state tradition in France: for example, the proliferation of specialist, hermetic, rigid *corps* of functionaries impeding flexible responses to new challenges. However – in marked contrast to the Italian case – the Commission defends the *statut de la fonction publique* which offers guaranteed employment to public servants. It argues that 'reform will be achieved with the civil servants and not without them or against them' (p. 115). While advocating decentralization and clearer management objectives, it firmly rejects the 'mechanical transposition' of management techniques from the private sector (for which in any case the appropriate systems of management control do not exist – Bach 1992).

It remains to be seen whether the conciliatory tone towards employees and unions will survive the election of a centre-right government in 1993, or whether a radical critique of the role of the state *à la Thatcher* will be launched. Even in the latter event, however, the parameters of state reform will be markedly different from the British case. The tradition of French public administration has always stressed the sovereignty and autonomy of the state and its inaccessibility to the organized interest groups of civil society (Crouch 1993: chs 9, 10). The *dirigiste*, interventionist French state continues to play a leading role in economic modernization and restructuring. This has not been seriously challenged on the left or right of the political spectrum, even though, as successive nationalization and privatization programmes show, the degree of direct intervention of the state in the economy has been the subject of contention.

The German model

The German experience has been one of moderate economic deregulation in the labour market (Jacobi et al. 1992), and similarly measured restructuring of the state sector. Despite the ideological rhetoric of the conservative CDU/CSU/FDP coalition government, privatization in the 1980s was limited (with the special exception of the *neue Bundesländer*), and essentially symbolic in nature (Esser 1988). Even where technological and market pressures for deregulation were fierce, as in telecommunications, the pattern was one of 'soft deregulation' rather than privatization on the British model (Esser 1988: 69–70; Webber 1987). Within the public service sector there has been debate on the weakening of *Beamte* status, but there has not been the same 'privatization' of employment relations as in Italy or The Netherlands, despite the increasing blurring of the boundaries between the work of *Beamte* and other public sector employees, and the *de facto* harmonization of their terms and conditions. Nor has there been the same degree of decentralization and 'marketization' of public sector activities as in Sweden or Britain.

How is one to explain the difference in the restructuring of the state in Germany, compared, say, with Sweden or Britain? First, constitutional structures and political relationships are important. Thus radical change in the status of public sector organizations such as the telecommunications or railway authorities requires a two-thirds majority in parliament. Moreover, power is disseminated in the federal political system, so that the *Länder* are frequently able to intervene in political debates about state restructuring: for example, the state of Lower Saxony refused to participate in the privatization of VW, in which it held a 20 per cent stake (Esser 1988: 68).

Second, the links between the labour movement and the political system are much broader than in Sweden or Britain. Unlike Sweden, for example, the presence of a Conservative administration does not exclude the unions from political influence: Christian democrat trade unionists have guaranteed institutionalized representation in the unions' governing bodies and, conversely, several senior CDU politicians have a strong trade union background (Jacobi et al. 1992). This union element within the CDU has been vociferous in its opposition to labour market deregulation, and in general its presence places limits on the scope of government restructuring strategies, in stark contrast to the British case. As Webber (1987: 3) argues, in relation to the deregulation of telecommunications, the Christian democrats were constrained by the socially diverse nature of their political base, which meant that 'the pursuit of a neo-liberal telecommunications policy amounts to a high-risk political adventure'.

State employees themselves also have direct access to the political system. Some 40 per cent of Bundestag deputies are *Beamte*, and their strong presence 'which is also reflected in the composition of the various parliamentary committees, is one of the reasons why the interests of civil servants are not likely to be neglected' (*EIRR* 1993b: 26). The process of interest representation that compensates for the absence of collective bargaining rights for *Beamte* also allows them to exert structured influence at the political level. In addition to formal representation, they have achieved 'informal influence at practically all stages of the legislative process' that determines their remuneration (*EIRR* 1993b; Jacobi et al. 1992: 256–62).

Third, the German public sector is much smaller than that of Sweden or Britain. Public employment (excluding public enterprises) amounted to around 16 per cent of total employment in 1990, compared with 32 per cent in Sweden and 20 per cent in the United Kingdom. Moreover, the rate of growth of public sector pay was considerably lower than in Sweden. In the late 1970s, public sector pay in Germany was already declining significantly relative to the private sector (Oxley and Martin 1991: 166–7). Labour costs in the public sector did not, therefore, have the same political resonance as they did in Sweden, where they contributed to one of the highest rates of personal income tax in the world (Swenson 1992: 72–3).

As a consequence, the structural conditions for a broad anti-public sector alliance were not present to the same degree as in Sweden. Despite the reliance of Germany, as Sweden, on the dynamism and competitiveness of its manufacturing export sector, there was not the same concern about the impact of public sector pay costs on competitiveness in the export sector. The key private sector union, IG Metall, refused to join an anti-state alliance. Indeed, it saw the public sector unions as allies in maintaining its capacity within the peak union federation, the DGB, to pursue militant policies at the head of the German labour movement (on the 35-hour week, for example) (Swenson 1992: 62–72).

The restructuring of the state sector in Germany is complicated by a factor unique to the country: reunification. On the one hand, considerable energy and resources have been devoted to the complex and time-consuming process of establishing the West German system of public sector industrial relations in the east. On the other, the impact of reunification may be indirectly undermining the relative moderation of state restructuring. In April–May 1992 the first major strike in the public sector for almost two decades caused widespread disruption of rail and air transport, the postal system and refuse collection. The strike reflected widespread feelings among public sector workers that they were being asked to pay through wage moderation for the economic consequences of reunification. By their timing in the negotiating round, the public sector negotiations and the ensuing strike also became the focus of the concerns of German workers more generally to limit the erosion of their real incomes as a result of the burden of reunification.

The crisis of state finances and the faltering of the German economy as a result of German unification may encourage a more radical restructuring of the state. Straws in the wind include planned cuts in unemployment and social benefits – which the DGB has dubbed the most devastating assault on the welfare state since the early 1930s (*Financial Times* 2 July 1993) – and plans for the privatization of the rail and telecommunications networks. None the less, there are strong indications that the process will be a highly controlled one, based on negotiated compromise between the interested parties. For example, the privatization of *Deutsche Telekom* has been agreed by the Social

Democrats, but on condition that the state retain a 51 per cent stake and that there continue to be cross-subsidization between domestic and business services. The bargaining power of the SPD in the privatization debate derives from the constitutional constraint of the required two-thirds majority referred to above, which means that the reform can be effected only with SPD support.

Explaining national variation

Thus the strategies for the reform of public employment and industrial relations have been conditioned by the different ways in which the public sector is enmeshed in networks of political accommodations in different countries (compare Goldthorpe 1984). In countries such as France recent pressures for reform are unlikely to challenge the basic historical tradition of the strong interventionist state. In Italy and in a different way in Sweden, thoroughgoing state reform reflects and hastens the disintegration of a system in which public employment has played a key and distinctive role. This very role helps explain why such reform has been 'blocked' for so long. In Spain, alliances based on the role of the state as employer have provided crucial underpinning for the passage from dictatorship to democracy, although it remains to be seen if they will be transmuted into an enduring 'system'.

One question is why, despite incipient developments elsewhere, Britain remains the only country to adopt the radical market solution to the problem of the state. At one level, the answer must address the long-standing historical traditions of the modern British state rooted in *laisser-faire* liberalism (Crouch 1993), reflecting the relative strength and confidence of civil society. 'Rolling back the state' makes more sense in such a culture than in the strong interventionist culture of France, or in the Italian culture of political patronage and the 'archipelago' state (Donolo 1980) in which a plurality of civil and political interest groups are inextricably intermingled.

Yet one must still ask why, on a shorter historical time scale, the assumptions of the post-war welfarist consensus have been so brusquely overturned in Britain. One factor must be the mechanics of the British political system which has allowed the 'elective dictatorship' of a minority party for a decade and a half, giving it the space and time to implement a strategy that breaks sharply with the past. This may be contrasted with the logic of coalition politics in Germany and, notoriously, in Italy, which dampens any tendencies to radical restructuring. Another argument is that 'strategies count' (Lash and Urry 1987: 282): Thatcherism was able to marginalize the unions because, in contrast to Germany or Sweden, organized labour had failed to play an active role in shaping new forms of work organization or worker participation (pp. 282–4; compare Terry in chapter 9 of this volume). While this analysis applies more to private manufacturing than to the public sector, which had a long tradition of management–union co-operation in change (Hyman and Elger 1981; Ferner 1988), Lash and Urry are right to draw attention to the sectionalism that sharpened divisions between public and private sectors. These divisions were symbolized by the 1979 'Winter of Discontent' of public service conflict which played a major role in the demonology of Thatcherism.

Conclusion: the Convergence of Public and Private Sector Industrial Relations?

Some observers have argued that the adoption of private sector models of industrial relations within the state is leading to a *convergence* between the two sectors (for example, Treu 1987b). There are grounds for thinking that convergence is likely to be limited as long as the state operates according to a different 'logic' from the private sector: that is, it supplies goods and services by democratically accountable agencies, according to priorities defined in the political sphere rather than the market (Ferner 1988; Keep 1992; Stewart and Ranson 1988). Criteria of provision frequently revolve round notions of 'need', 'public interest' or 'universality' of service (compare Fudge 1990). However, the privatization of the state 'from within' by the adoption of private sector management models may lend increasing support to proponents of the convergence thesis by eroding the characteristic dynamic of state industrial relations, and by blurring once clear boundaries between the state and the private sector.

Yet the arguments of previous sections suggest that the convergence between the public and private domains has its limits in the contradictions that arise within the new model of public management. The closer managerial behaviour approximates to the private sector model, through decentralization and 'commercialism', the harder it is to use public agencies coherently to implement policies defined by the political process. Constant tension is likely to arise between the 'political logic' of governments who define what services should be provided, and the 'agency logic' of the devolved management units charged with providing them. Two outcomes are possible. One is that governments will reassert greater central control over devolved management units, and define more closely the nature of the services to be produced. The other, increasingly evident in the post-Thatcher Conservative government in Britain, is that the state withdraws from service *definition* (as well as service provision); in other words, the market, rather than politics, increasingly determines what is produced. However, the high price in terms of the depletion of traditionally understood public services – already painfully obvious in current British controversies on transport or energy policy and on the introduction of market disciplines in health and education – can be expected to provoke a backlash, leading once more to greater political involvement in the definition of public services.

The polarization of political positions about the role of the public sector in Britain is likely to imperil serious debate about the conditions of efficient provision of public services. The excesses of Thatcherism have discredited many of the tools of the new public management which are tainted with the free market ideology that inspired them. They will inevitably be counterposed to the resurgent ethic of public service. Yet it is clear that the structural demands upon public expenditure – from the challenges of competitiveness and training, through the health and welfare of an ageing population to the management of the environment – will be growing faster than state resources. The increased efficiency in the organization and performance of work and the remuneration of public employees will be an urgent question. But the traditional sources of co-operative change in the British public sector will have been seriously eroded if not permanently lost by the aggressive strain of commercialism that has been pursued. Elsewhere in Europe, a more gradualist approach will have conserved the basis for consensual work-force involvement in ongoing reform.

Acknowledgements

I am very grateful to Paul Edwards, Richard Hyman, Berndt Keller, Anders Kjellberg and David Winchester for comments on drafts of this chapter.

Notes

1   A more detailed account of industrial relations developments in the public sector can be found in Ferner 1991: 2–10.
2   This includes some autonomous enterprises such as the postal service; however, to ensure comparability over the period, it excludes the railways, which assumed corporate status from 1987.

References

Aucoin, P. 1990: Administrative reform in public management: paradigms, principles, paradoxes and pendulums. *Governance*, 3(2) April, 115–37.
Bach, S. 1992: Restructuring public services employment practices: a comparison

of British & French health care reform. Dissertation, MA in Management Learning, University of Lancaster.

Bazex, M. 1987: Labour relations in the public service in France. In Treu 1987a, 83–109.

Blenk, W. 1987: Labour relations in the public service in the Federal Republic of Germany. In Treu 1987a, 49–81.

Cecora, G. 1990: Pubblico impiego: motivazioni e opportunità per la riforma. *Industria e Sindacato*, 43, December, 3–8.

Cecora, G. 1992: La situazione nel pubblico impiego: problematiche e proposte di riforma. *Industria e Sindacato*, 34, 8–18.

Colling, T. and Ferner, A. 1993: Changing forms of participation: the impact of privatisation and 'commercialisation'. Paper commissioned for ISVET, Istituto per gli studi sullo sviluppo economico e il progresso tecnico, Rome, June.

Commission of the European Community (CEC) 1989: Public finances and fiscal policy in the community. In *Facing the Challenges of the Early 1990s, European Economy*, 42, November, 137–59.

Corby, S. 1991: Civil service decentralisation: reality or rhetoric? *Personnel Management*, February, 39–42.

Crouch, C. 1993: *Industrial Relations and European State Traditions*. Oxford: Clarendon Press.

Cusack, T., Notermans, T. and Rein, M. 1987: Political–economic aspects of public employment. Globus Research Group Publication Series 87–2. Berlin: Wissenschaftszentrum Berlin für Sozialforschung.

de Closets, F. (Commission Efficacité de l'Etat du Xe Plan) 1989: *Le pari de la responsabilité*. Paris: Payot.

Donolo, C. 1980: Social change and transformation of the state in Italy. In Scase, R. (ed.), *The State in Western Europe*, London: Croom Helm, 164–96.

Durupty, M. 1988: *Les Privatisations en France*. Paris: La Documentation Française.

EIRR (*European Industrial Relations Review*) 1992a: Netherlands: new industrial relations in the public sector. *EIRR 221*, June, 21–3.

EIRR 1992b: Italy: Massive reform plan. *EIRR 223*, August, 9–10.

EIRR 1993a: Italy: public sector employment reformed. *EIRR 231*, April.

EIRR 1993b: Germany. Industrial relations in the public sector. *EIRR 233*, June, 25–8.

Esser, J. 1988: Symbolic privatisation: the politics of privatisation in West Germany. *West European Politics*, 2(4) 61–73.

Ferner, A. 1988: *Governments, Managers and Industrial Relations. Public enterprises and their political environment*. Oxford: Blackwell Publishers.

Ferner, A. 1991: Changing public sector industrial relations in Europe. Warwick Papers in Industrial Relations, 37. Coventry: Industrial Relations Research Unit.

Ferner, A. and Hyman, R. (eds) 1992a: *Industrial Relations in the New Europe*. Oxford: Blackwell Publishers.

Ferner, A. and Hyman, R. 1992b: Between political exchange and micro-corporatism. In Ferner and Hyman 1992a, 524–600.

Fudge, C. 1990: Flexibility reconsidered: selected issues. In OECD, *Flexibile Personnel Management in the Public Service*, Paris: OECD, 91–9.

Fulcher, J. 1991: *Labour Movements, Employers and the State. Conflict and co-operation in Britain and Sweden*. Oxford: OUP.

Goldthorpe, J. (ed.) 1984: *Order and Conflict in Contemporary Capitalism*. Oxford: Clarendon Press.

Gustaffson, L. 1987: Renewal of the public sector in Sweden. *Public Administration*, 65, Summer, 179–91.

Hood, C. 1991: A public management for all seasons? *Public Administration*, 69, Summer, 3–19.

Hyman, R. and Elger, T. 1981: Job controls, the employers' offensive and alternative strategies. *Capital and Class*, 15, 115–49.

ILO (International Labour Office) 1988: Joint Committee on the Public Service, 4th Session, Report I, *General Report*. Geneva: ILO.

IMF (International Monetary Fund) 1990: Italia: consultazioni 1990. *Industria e Sindacato*, 43, December, 9–11.

IRRR (*Industrial Relations Review and Report*) 1988a: Public sector working practices and pay – shake-up? *IRRR 408*, 19 January, 10–13.

IRRR 1988b: Restructuring in the public sector: variations and themes. *IRRR 419*, 5 July, 2–7.

Jacobi, O., Keller, B. and Müller-Jentsch, W. 1992: Germany: codetermining the future. In Ferner and Hyman 1992a, 218–69.

Keep, E. 1992: Schools in the marketplace – some problems with private sector models. *British Journal of Work and Education*, 5(2) 43–56.

Kessler, I. and Purcell, J. 1992: Performance related pay: objectives and application. *Human Resource Management Journal*, 2(3) 16–33.

Kjellberg, A. 1992: Sweden: can the model survive? In Ferner and Hyman 1992a, 88–142.

Lash, S. and Urry, J. 1987: *The End of Organized Capitalism*. Oxford: Polity Press.

Maguire, M. and Wood, R. 1992: Private pay for public work? *OECD Observer*, 175, April–May, 29–31.

Martínez, M. 1992: Spain. Constructing institutions and actors in a context of change. In Ferner and Hyman 1992a, 482–523.

Myrdal, H.-G. 1991: The hard way from a centralised to a decentralised industrial relations system – the case of Sweden and SAF. In Sadowski, D. and Jacobi, O. (eds), *Employers Associations in Europe: policy and organisation*, Baden-Baden: Nomos, 191–210.

OECD (Organization for Economic Co-operation and Development) 1990: *Public Management Developments. Survey – 1990*. Paris: OECD.

OECD 1991: *OECD Economic Surveys 1990/1991. Sweden*. Paris: OECD.

OECD 1992: *Public Management Developments. Update 1992*. Paris: OECD.

OECD 1993a: *Public Management: OECD Country Profiles*. Paris: OECD.

OECD 1993b: *Private Pay for Public Work. Performance-related pay for public sector managers*. Paris: OECD.

OIT (Oficina Internacional del Trabajo) 1985: *Situación sindical y relaciones laborales en España*. Geneva: OIT.

Oxley, H., Maher, M., Martin, J., Nicoletti, G. 1990: The public sector: issues for the 1990s. Working Paper no. 90, OECD Department of Economics and Statistics. Paris: OECD.

Oxley, H. and Martin, J. 1991: Controlling government spending and deficits: trends in the 1980s and prospects for the 1990s. *OECD Economic Studies*, 17, Autumn, 145–89.

Ozaki, M. 1987: Labour relations in the public service. 2. Labour disputes and their settlement. *International Labour Review*, 126(4) July–August, 405–22.

Rand Smith, W. 1990: Nationalizations for what? Capitalist power and public enterprise in Mitterrand's France. *Politics & Society*, 18(1) 75–99.

Rood, M. 1990: European integration and Dutch public service labour relations. In W. Dercksen (ed.), *The Future of Industrial Relations in Europe*, Netherlands Scientific Council for Government Policy, 77–81.

Seifert, R. 1990: Prognosis for local bargaining in health and education. *Personnel Management*, June, 54–7.

Stewart, J. and Ranson, S. 1988: Management in the public domain. *Public Money and Management*, Spring/Summer, 13–19.

Swenson, P. 1992: Union politics, the welfare state, and intraclass conflict in Sweden and Germany. In M. Golden and J. Pontusson (eds), *Bargaining for Change. Union politics in North America and Europe*, Ithaca/London: Cornell University Press, 45–76.

Treu, T. (ed.) 1987a: *Public Service Labour Relations*. Geneva: ILO.

Treu, T. 1987b: Labour relations in the public service in Italy. In Treu 1987a, 111–43.

Treu, T. 1991: Il pubblico impiego: riusciremo a farlo entrare in Europa? *Il Mulino*, 40(2) March–April, 307–21.

Treu, T. and de Felice, A. 1990: The future of labour relations in the public service. In W. Dercksen (ed.), *The Future of Industrial Relations in Europe*, Netherlands Scientific Council for Government Policy, 65–75.

Trice, H. and Beyer, J. 1984: Studying organizational cultures through rites and ceremonials. *Academy of Management Review*, 9(4) 653–69.

Vickers, J. and Wright, V. 1988: The politics of industrial privatisation in western Europe: an overview. *West European Politics*, 11(4) 1–30.

Vickers, J. and Yarrow, G. 1988: *Privatization. An economic analysis*. Cambridge, Mass. and London: MIT Press.

Visser, J. 1990: Continuity and change in Dutch industrial relations. In G. Baglioni and C. Crouch (eds), *European Industrial Relations. The challenge of flexibility*. London: Sage Publications, 199–242.

Webber, D. 1987: The Assault on the fortress on the Rhine. The politics of telecommunications deregulation in the Federal Republic of Germany. Paper for the Conference of the Council of European Studies, Washington DC, 30 October – 1 November.

Wise, L.R. 1993: Whither solidarity? Transitions in Swedish public-sector pay policy. *British Journal of Industrial Relations*, 31(1) March, 75–95.

4

European Trade Unions: the Transition Years

Jelle Visser

The Challenge

In a recent review, Regini (1992) identifies three problems of trade union organization which have dominated the agenda of union policy and research in the past thirty years. In the 1960s the problem of *collective mobilization* was a major preoccupation. Union growth stagnated because unions based primarily on skilled manual workers seemed unable either to represent the interests of a growing labour force in mass production or to organize the rapidly increasing world of white-collar employees. The 'resurgence of class conflict' (Crouch and Pizzorno 1978) in the late 1960s lifted these doubts and initiated a new phase of union growth and influence. The new problem was how the increased power, confidence and militancy of unions could be reconciled with economic growth and political stability.

Concertation and *neo-corporatism* became thus the new foci of attention. The main trend in European industrial relations in the period of economic turbulence unleashed by monetary destabilization and the oil crisis of the early 1970s was a growing politicization of functional interests and economic management. Interests and demands, particularly when represented by trade union peak federations, were increasingly mediated in the political arena (Schmitter and Lehmbruch 1979; Berger 1981). Processes of political exchange seemed to replace, in part, outcomes dictated by the logic of the market. This development reflected, and perhaps further promoted, the strength of organized labour, legitimizing its presence in new policy areas. It encouraged the centralization of decision-making in and between organizations in the search for aggregate solutions to problems of cost inflation, wage restraint and unemployment. Within this common trend, national differences in the objectives, processes and results of concertation tended to widen (Scharpf 1987), as did the degree of control over industrial relations in firms and workplaces (Goldthorpe 1984; Visser 1987).

The main topics of the 1980s were *decentralization, flexibility* and *human resources management* (Kochan and McKersie 1986; Baglioni and Crouch 1990). The features that had accompanied concertation in the preceding decade, including centralization, macroeconomic management and union involvement, came under attack in a new environment dominated by intensified global competition, industrial restructuring, flexible production systems, and the search for micro-adjustment at the level of firms (Piore and Sabel 1985). The rediscovery of the firm and flexibility in determining economic performance in international markets convinced managers that they had to look for differentiated and customized, rather than uniform, responses to variable product markets, technology and labour markets. In consequence there was a shift in the centre of gravity from the national level to that of the firm, and from the political arena back to the industrial. The political fall-out from the failure of concerted incomes policies and the soaring rate of unemployment helped tilt the balance of power in favour of capital. Governments became less supportive, and unionization tended to fall throughout the western capitalist world (Visser 1991). Employers have increasingly attempted to encourage direct employee participation through expression groups, quality circles, team discussion and job consultation methods, while the distinction between consultation and collective bargaining has often become harder to draw (Windmuller 1987). Despite some decentralization in most trade union movements in western Europe following the up-surge in shop-floor militancy of the 1970s, many seemed ill-prepared for the new management policies of the 1980s.

In the final decade of the twentieth century, trade unions simultaneously face the problems of collective mobilization, concertation and flexibility (Regini 1992). Collective mobilization has become a problem for many union movements after a decade of decline in membership levels and militancy (Shalev 1992). Both trends are especially pronounced in the market sector of the economy, though they vary widely between countries. In some cases, in particular France and Spain, collective worker organization is extremely low – even lower than the United States and Japan. Though the decline has slowed in recent years, it is not clear where it will stop, especially if high unemployment, labour flexibility and downward pressures on standards continue or even increase. Unionization levels in Germany have been more stable; but the system of collective bargaining, the achievements of unions, and the rights of workers are currently under attack in ways unknown since the foundation of the Federal Republic. Swedish union membership, while still between 80 and 90 per cent of all wage and salary-earners, has declined in recent years for the first time since the mid-1920s. With unemployment approaching 10 per cent in 1993, the Swedish 'full employment' of the 1970s and 1980s seems to have been buried unceremoniously, just as, a decade ago, 'Keynesianism in one country' collapsed when French socialists had to yield to the pressure of world capital markets.

Union Decline

The 1980s stand out as a unique period of union decline in post-war Europe. One has to go back to the 1920s and 1930s to find a comparable decline and stagnation of trade union organization. This decline began in the later years of the 1970s, generalized in the 1980s, and was more pronounced in the private sector of the economy (see table 4.1).

Employment expansion in the public sector, however, assisted union growth in three of the five countries which seemed to evade the general trend of decline in the 1980s: Sweden, Finland and Norway. Expansion of public sector jobs, many part-time, also helped to keep unemployment levels down. Union participation in the administration of unemployment insurance goes some way to explain why Belgian and Danish unions, despite high unemployment, could also defy the downward trend.[1] These are the only countries in which unions still

Table 4.1   Union density rates (averages per period) – total (1) and market sector (2)

	A	B	CH	D	DK	IRL	F	GB	I	NL	N	SF	S
(1)													
60–67	58	44	35	34	60	47	20	40	29	38	53	37	66
68–73	55	47	30	33	61	52	22	44	37	37	51	54	69
74–79	52	56	32	37	71	55	21	50	49	37	53	67	76
80–85	53	57	31	36	77	51	15	48	46+	31	56	70	82
86–91	47	56	25	34	75	44	10	41	38+	25	57	71	84
(2)													
1980	49	–	24	33	–	–	16	45	43	26	47	64	80
1990	41	–	21	31	72	–	8	37	32	19	44	65	81

– = not available; + = probably higher by some percentage points.

Source: Visser 1992a

recruit more than half of all employees in employment. Even in these countries, the upward trend in union density which had begun in the late 1960s was reversed. Membership levels fell in Belgium between 1982 and 1988; in Denmark between 1986 and 1989; and for the first time since the mid-1920s in Sweden in 1990, though in 1991 the growth of white-collar unions made up for the losses of blue-collar unions.

Britain, France, Ireland, The Netherlands, as well as Spain and Portugal, witnessed severe union decline. In Ireland and The Netherlands the blood-letting stopped in the late 1980s. In recent years Dutch unions have gained members, but given the extraordinary increase of (part-time) jobs after 1984 – according to OECD statistics, the largest in Europe – these gains do not represent increased density, which stagnated at 25 per cent, down from 37 before 1979. In Italy our data refer only to the three official confederations: increased membership in independent unions, critical of the moderation of the confederations, makes up for an unknown proportion of the losses.

Finally, the three German-speaking countries have in common more or less stable union membership levels: years of small losses after 1982 were followed by years of small gains. As in Britain or France, economic recovery after 1984 was not reflected in growing union strength. Austria, Germany until reunification, and Switzerland share the experience of slow demographic growth and stagnant, if not declining, civilian employment, with older cohorts of workers and emigrants leaving the labour market and a rather low rate of entry. Hence the decline in union density was rather moderate: four percentage points in Germany between 1980 and 1990, six in Austria and Switzerland. In 1990 the unification of Germany swelled the ranks of the German unions, especially those in the *Deutscher Gewerkschaftsbund* (DGB). Union density in the five ex-DDR *Länder* is estimated at 50 per cent, well above the West German rate shown in table 4.1. Changes in union administration and the current labour shake-out in the east German economy make it likely that the density will fall towards the west German level of around 35 per cent.

Explanatory Framework

How may we explain the pattern of decline in unionization? Why did it occur in the 1980s, and why did it affect some countries (Britain and France, for example) more than others (Scandinavia)? Many explanations have been proposed in the literature: sectoral employment change away from high density industries and firms, economic factors increasing the pressure on unions and workers, changes in values and public opinion regarding trade unions and collective organization, hostile legislation and increased opposition of employers towards unions, and inadequate union-organizing policies (for an overview of the evidence with respect to each of these, see Visser 1993; also chapter 5 of this volume).

The discussion may be helped by the distinction in figure 4.1 between conceptions of unions as *organizing agencies* and as *passive recipients* of changes in their environment. In the latter category are structuralist explanations of union decline which leave little room for unions as active organizers of their membership markets, let alone as strategic actors capable of changing the dynamics of these markets. Structuralist explanations include some versions of the 'business cycle theory' of union growth (Visser 1987) and those emphasizing demographic change, shifts in the composition of employment, and social-cultural change which, supposedly, has eroded working-class communities and lifestyles. In contrast are theories which emphasize the failure of trade union leaders to respond adequately to the current crisis of representation (for Britain, see Mason and Bain 1993). Some have argued that union leaders might not be sufficiently committed to growth as a priority. Recruitment opportunities might be lost because of rivalry and lack of co- operation between unions, inefficient organization, insufficient mobilization of resources, inadequate services, or policies which alienate potentially helpful employers. The problem is that these explanations are presented in an *ad hoc* and *ex post facto* manner. There is often no way of telling what would have occurred had unions done nothing or had they done something quite different. In short, we need a theory of union behaviour with respect to worker organization.

In figure 4.1 the distinction between an environmental or interventionist approach is cross-cut with a second dimension contrasting theories based on individual worker choice or union organization and those emphasizing the social and institutional embeddedness of these actors in the world of co-workers and employers. In rational choice theory the decision of workers to join a union is presented as a calculation in which benefits and costs are weighed and utility is maxi-

	environment	intervention
actor	WORKER	UNION
network	CO-WORKERS	EMPLOYERS

Figure 4.1   Unionization

mized. This approach is dominated by the 'free-rider' problem: individual workers have no incentive to join the union because they will enjoy the benefits whether or not they co-operate in achieving them (Olson 1965). The problem for social scientists is to explain why so many cost-conscious workers do nevertheless join.

Resource mobilization theory offers an explanation. In Klandermans' (1984) version of the theory, workers participate when they are convinced that the goals matter to them, that their own participation makes a difference, that others will join, and that together they stand a chance of success. This approach deviates from Olson's logic in that the belief that others will participate does not reduce but strengthens the willingness to join. The belief that a 'critical mass' will be reached is closely related to interest homogeneity within groups and their integration in social networks through which others are reached and participation can be monitored (Marwell and Oliver 1993).

We may also apply a version of rational choice theory to trade union recruitment and organizing efforts. For instance, assuming constant rather than diminishing costs for the recruitment of each additional member and considering that these costs have to be borne by members who have already joined, one can explain why union density tends to be lower in large countries (Wallerstein 1989). Similarly, rising marginal costs for organizing workers in small firms, or workers with an expected short duration in the labour force, may explain the absence of organizing efforts (Dunlop 1949; Rojer and Visser 1993). But institutional rules and the interdependence with employers are equally important. Do unions have to gain recognition from employers company by company, as under the National Labor Relations Act rules in United States? Alternatively, does recognition at national level help unions in organizing workers in smaller firms, or does it lower the target rate of unionization because membership is no longer critical to recognition? Clegg's (1976) comparative theory of union growth based on the interdependence between union and employer organization through collective bargaining has much to offer.

An adequate explanation of union growth and decline will address each of the four elements in figure 4.1 and show how they relate in a particular conjuncture. It is assumed that the model is limited in space and time, applying to a particular region and historical era. In the remainder of this chapter I shall move anti-clockwise through figure 4.1, starting in the upper left field with a discussion of external pressure, then discuss social and organizational interdependence, and finish with some observations about how unions might act.

Unemployment

Unemployment is the primary environmental constraint on unions. Since the late 1960s the level has stabilized at a higher rate after each recession. There was a sharp rise in all but three main European countries after the first oil crisis, and another after 1980 (see table 4.2). Even in Sweden and Switzerland, where unemployment remained below 3 per cent in the 1980s, the situation has since deteriorated; while once unimaginable double-digit unemployment rates have been experienced in most western European countries.

Unemployment is often incorporated in business cycle models of union growth, although the empirical findings are not very convincing. Unemployment turns out to be an unstable and rather weak predictor of union decline (Bain and Elsheikh 1976; Fiorito and Greer 1982; Hirsch and Addison 1986). In the microeconomic foundation of business cycle theory, unemployment is supposed to affect the costs and benefits which workers consider in their decision to join a union or to retain membership. However, it may equally be argued that unemployment affects the decision of unions to organize workers, employers to resist unions, and co-workers to act in solidarity.

Rising unemployment may increase the expected benefit of union membership where workers believe that the union is effective in defending their jobs. Large and highly visible job losses should erode this belief. Moreover, when unemployment is endemic, the opportunity for selection between workers increases and employers may choose to discriminate against union members; such discrimination was common practice among Italian employers, for example, until the Workers' Statute made it a criminal offence (Guigni et al. 1976). In this case, the costs of membership rise steeply. Finally, under conditions of

Table 4.2 Unemployment rates (average % per period)

	A	B	CH	D	DK	IRL	F	UK	I	NL	N	SF	S
60–67	2.0	2.1	0.0	0.8	1.6	4.9	1.3	2.0	4.9	0.7	1.0	1.5	1.6
68–73	1.4	2.5	0.0	1.0	1.0	5.7	2.6	3.3	5.7	1.5	1.7	2.6	2.2
74–79	1.6	6.3	0.3	3.2	5.5	7.6	4.5	5.0	6.6	4.9	1.8	4.4	1.9
80–85	3.0	11.2	0.6	5.8	9.3	12.5	8.3	10.5	8.6	10.1	2.6	5.1	2.9
86–91	3.4	9.0	0.7	5.6	8.9	15.5	9.8	8.8	10.5	8.6	3.8	4.9	2.0
92	3.7	7.8	2.5	7.7	11.2	16.1	10.2	9.9	10.5	6.8	5.9	13.0	4.8

Source: OECD *Labour Force Statistics*, various years (standardized definitions, except in Austria, Denmark, and Ireland before 1983; figures for Germany before 1992 refer to West Germany)

rising unemployment, union income is likely to decline and union officials will be preoccupied with fighting plant closures and job losses, having neither the means nor the time to campaign for new members. In sum, we should expect an inverse relationship between unemployment and union growth, in particular when unemployment remains high, when employment discrimination is legally possible, and when unemployment is concentrated among workers in areas and jobs where union membership is customary.

Union members who leave their jobs discontinue membership for two main reasons. First, because there are no selective benefits accruing from membership. Although union campaigns for more jobs may help, unions are rarely in a position to select union members for these new jobs. Similarly, although unemployed workers benefit from union campaigns for higher unemployment benefits, a rise in benefit is a public good for all concerned. The selective benefits of union membership are all targeted at the workplace (for example, grievance handling, a voice in decision-making), from which the unemployed worker is excluded. The second reason for leaving the union is the disintegration of the network of co-workers to which individuals belonged when they were in employment. It is well established that long-term unemployed workers tend to become isolated and find it difficult to continue relationships with their old workmates. Trade union membership is maintained through networks of social relationships among co-workers; hence, one would expect (long-term) unemployed workers to discontinue membership, especially when they cannot reasonably hope to return to their old jobs. Historically, union attempts to organize networks of unemployed workers on the basis of their identity as unemployed have always failed (Pollard 1969; Garraty 1978).

There is an important qualification to all this. If unions do influence rehiring, unemployed workers are likely to stay in the union. Rising unemployment will also attract to the union workers who have a job yet are uncertain about their future. Thus workers in the *cassa integrazione* usually retain membership in the Italian unions. In countries such as Belgium, Denmark, Finland and Sweden, where unions have maintained a role in the administration of the unemployment insurance system, unemployment appears to have a positive effect on union growth (Rothstein 1989).

Marginal Workers

The aggregate unemployment rate is a poor measure of downward pressure on union membership and bargaining power; its distribution and structure matter a great deal. I have shown elsewhere that until the early 1980s the rise in unemployment in Europe hardly affected union growth (Visser 1986). Despite the decline in manufacturing jobs and the rise in unemployment, mainly of manual workers, during the 1970s, union membership did not fall proportionately. Indeed, until 1979 union density in manufacturing rose in all European countries for which data are available, with the exception of France,[2] where union decline began well before the end of the decade (Visser 1991: 110, table 4.4). In Germany, Switzerland and The Netherlands, with the contraction of manufacturing employment absolute union membership stagnated or fell slightly, though density increased. In Sweden, Denmark, Finland, Belgium, Italy and Great Britain the number of union members in manufacturing rose, thanks to a continuing high level of collective organization among male manual workers and the recruitment of female and white-collar employees. In Britain, more than one million manufacturing jobs were lost between 1968 and 1979; yet union membership rose by about the same number over the period, and density increased from 50 to 70 per cent; indeed, this phenomenon of employment contraction and membership expansion was reproduced in 13 of the 16 subdivisions within manufacturing (Bain and Price 1983: 11, 14–15, table 1.5).

Why did unemployment make no inroads into union membership? From surveys and union membership files we know that in Britain, Germany, or The Netherlands unemployed workers do not generally retain their membership, unless unemployment is a typical seasonal experience of short duration and workers expect to stay in the same trade (Barker et al. 1984; Lewis 1989; on The Netherlands, Veltman 1986). However, workers who became unemployed in the 1970s may not have been union members to begin with; and unions may have been able to compensate for losses by recruiting other workers who kept their jobs or entered employment for the first time. The first labour-intensive industries hit by the recession, and subject to 'runaway' investments in low wage countries, were clothing, leather and textiles. These had low union densities compared with most other branches of manufacturing. Moreover, the first groups of workers forced to leave in these and other industries worked in smaller subcontracting firms, and tended to have fewer job rights and lower skills; the 1973–4 crisis and its aftermath also hit women and immigrants to a much greater extent (OECD 1983).

Studies of unemployment in the 1970s show that the unemployed came in large numbers from small firms and from among the lesser skilled. While long-term unemployment was concentrated among older people with low skills and in depressed regions, the experience of frequent spells of unemployment was typical for (re-)entrants into the labour market. Except for older males in larger firms, these groups did not figure prominently in trade unions. Stern, analysing the 1978 data on unemployment in Britain, found that it was unlikely that men becoming unemployed had been holders of career jobs, in spite of an aggregate unemployment rate of 5.5 per cent of the civilian labour force. He concluded from this that the pressure from unemployment on unions and union wages was still very small (1982: 376). In the 1970s the inverse relation between unemployment and government popularity weakened for the first time in Britain, which has been interpreted as an erosion of communalist values (Husbands 1985). The uneven experience of unemployment may well have been the main explanatory factor.

The bias of unemployment risks against marginal workers will be increased when seniority rules apply and local representatives (shop stewards, works council representatives, union district officers) are in a position to influence firing decisions (or the recall list, as in Italy). This bias was mobilized by the drift to workplace control in the 1970s and the extra protection provided for long-serving employees by law or collective agreements in the aftermath of the 1973–4 crisis (Visser 1987). Hohn (1983) concluded from case studies in German industry that selection in favour of union membership affected not only firing but also hiring decisions: workers with career histories and social characteristics typically associated with union membership are more readily accepted by the existing work-force. Works council representatives had little difficulty in justifying a preference for well-trained, German, male workers with stable career patterns, because this was the constituency which had elected them and the backbone of union strength. Streeck concluded on the basis of similar case studies that 'the qualities of workers which have traditionally been viewed as conducive to union membership also enhance job security: high level of qualification, long period of company service, male, married, indigenous, etc.' (Streeck 1981: 90, my translation). The increased capacity of unions to protect themselves and their members against the threat of unemployment is, in the German case, related to the 1972 reform of the *Betriebsverfassungsgesetz*, which strengthened the position of union members in the works council and enhanced its rights in matters of personnel policy. Together with the continued presence of union officials on supervisory boards, this engaged unions and councils in a policy of stabilizing the employment of the core labour force in large firms against unpredictable and wasteful fluctuations in product demand (Streeck 1992).

From 1980, with the onslaught of recession and the restructuring of entire industries such as shipbuilding, cars, printing and mining, in which unions had traditionally been strong, selection through union networks became less effective since entire firms and establishments were forced to shut down. Union jobs disappeared and unemployment began to have an impact on union membership. Large and nationalized firms collapsed when governments stopped providing subsidies. The crisis of heavy industry and large firms, in which unions were overrepresented, contributed to the large drop in union membership in manufacturing between 1980 and 1984 in Great Britain (Waddington 1992) and The Netherlands (Visser 1987). Similar though less severe contractions took place in Ireland, Italy, Austria, Switzerland and Germany. Given its distribution, the rise in unemployment was directly reflected in declining unionization.

In a cross-national comparison of union density and unemployment rates of ten European countries, I could establish no relationship between the change in unionization between the late 1960s and the late 1970s and the rise in unemployment over that period. However, allowing for the special cases of Belgium, Denmark, Finland and Sweden, where for institutional reasons unemployment is expected to boost union membership, I found a strong negative correlation between the rise in average unemployment between 1977–9 and 1983–5 and the mean annual membership growth between 1980 and 1985 ($r = .-71$) (Visser 1987). Across 18 OECD countries the change in the average unemployment rate between the second half of the 1970s and the 1980s explained 44 per cent of union membership decline after 1980 (Visser 1991: 105–6).

Inflation

Inflation is the second environmental factor whose impact on unions differs clearly between the 1968–83 period and later years. According to OECD data, inflation rose together with unemployment in many countries from an average of 3.7 per cent in the 1960s to 8.3 per cent in the 1970s and even 9.1 per cent between 1980 and 1983, though it fell to 4.5 per cent in the later 1980s. In econometric studies of union growth, inflation, along with unemployment, is a recurring variable.

Consumer price inflation is expected to increase the need for union organization.

> In as much as workers perceive an increase in the rate of change of retail prices as a threat to their standard of living . . . they are more likely to become and remain union members in an attempt to maintain this

standard. In addition, . . . employers may be more prepared to concede worker demands partly because increases in labour costs can be passed on more easily to customers. (Bain and Elsheikh 1976: 62–3)

Flanagan et al. (1983) add another reason, especially relevant in the high inflation environment of the 1970s: white-collar employees unionize because they want to protect their pay relative to manual workers who have often obtained automatic cost-of-living adjustments.

However, the role of inflation in union growth is ambiguous. Although some earlier studies in the United Kingdom, notably Bain and Elsheikh's (1976), found a strong impact, Carruth and Disney (1988) showed that their model could not explain the sharp downturn in unionization during the 1980s. The overall power of their model was improved by incorporating a dummy variable for the years of Labour government. Similar regression models have been developed for the United States, Australia, Canada, Italy, Ireland, Germany, Sweden and The Netherlands (Ashenfelter and Pencavel 1969; Sharpe 1971; Swidensky 1974; Bain and Elsheikh 1976; Romagnoli 1980; Visser 1987; Roche and Larragy 1990). While these studies all estimate some impact from cyclical factors such as inflation, wages and unemployment, no model is consistently successful (see also Neumann et al. 1989). This gives support to the view that institutional factors – setting countries and periods apart from one another – should be made the focus of explanation.

Decentralization of Production and Sectoral Change

One of the most robust variables in econometric studies of union growth is the (lagged) density rate. Union density is taken to indicate 'saturation' (Rezler 1961: 4) resulting from the demographic characteristics of the remaining non-unionized workers, for example workers in services and in small firms, women employees, part-timers. In this case the role of the union as organizer is invoked most explicitly by Sharpe (1971), who argues that the marginal costs of organizing increase when unions try to organize progressively smaller firms.

Establishment size appears to have a large effect on union density. According to one survey in West Germany it varied from 4 per cent in units with 1–9 employees to 58 per cent in those with over 2,000 employees (Bertl et al. 1988). In Norway 1980 density varied between 18 per cent in establishments with fewer than 5 workers to 67 per cent in those with 200 or more. In The Netherlands the employment share of the small firm sector, under 35 employees, has risen to almost 40 per cent, compared with less than 25 per cent of all union members (van den Putte et al. 1991). In Britain a strong association, albeit not linear, between workplace size and unionization is well established (Elsheikh and Bain 1980; Millward and Stevens 1986: 53–62). In a recent panel study of 3,000 trade union members and ex-members in The Netherlands, carried out in 1991 and again in 1993, we found that a markedly larger proportion of members had left the union in firms with fewer than 35 employees, and in workplaces where few others were perceived to be member of the union (Klandermans et al. forthcoming). Under these conditions the possibility that a supportive network of co-workers will be maintained is remote. From the point of view of the worker, the effectiveness of the union is doubted, hence its expected benefit in the workplace will be low and the social cost of isolation high.

Hence sectoral employment shifts from unionized to non-unionized sectors are significant for unionization. Several estimates have been made of the contribution of such shifts to the recent decline in unionization. In a shift-share analysis, on the basis of 10 sectors (defined at the 1-digit level of the International Standard Industrial Classification (ISIC)) and with 1970, 1975 or 1980 as base year, a structural drag on unionization was found in most countries. However, its magnitude was small, and it was unable to explain more than 50 per cent of the actual decline in any country (Visser 1991: 114). But this does not take into account shifts within sectors from large to small firms. Booth (1989), using a more detailed classification for Britain, found that 5.3 percentage points of the 12.5 point decline in union density between 1979 and 1987 could be attributed to sectoral shifts in employment, while Waddington (1992) attributed around two-thirds of the decline between 1979 and 1987 to such shifts. The latter also notes that most of the drag took place between 1980 and 1983, because 'compositional effects are associated with unemployment and the differential effects of the "shake out"' (Waddington 1991: 304). On the basis of the British Workplace Industrial Relations Survey (WIRS) data, he is able to argue that the adverse effect of declining establishment size is compounded by the weakness of union organization in establishments where employment is expanding: average density in establishments in which employment fell by one-fifth or more between 1980 and 1984 was 60 per cent, whereas in establishments whose work-force expanded by one-fifth or more it averaged 21 per cent.

There are two facts which are not easy to accommodate in structural explanations, however. First, in the 1970s union membership and density in industry rose in many countries despite employment contraction. To make contraction of employment responsible for union decline a decade later seems inconsistent, unless of course it can be shown that contrary movements of other structural determinants of union membership characterize the two periods. Decentralization is more pronounced in the 1980s and tends to reverse a process of concentration and vertical integration of earlier decades. Second, the decline of membership in countries such as Britain or The Netherlands during the early 1980s affected nearly all unions, irrespective of the expansion or contraction of the sectors in which they operated. This suggests a general change, which is determined not by the employment structure of firms and sectors, but by shifts in economic, cultural or political conditions.

Social Control

Workers' expectations concerning the union are critically related to their reason for joining in the first place. These expectations affect their attachment to the union and their satisfaction with what the union is or does. We know very little about changes over time in such variables. In the *Affluent Worker* study, Goldthorpe et al. (1968: 96–7) drew a distinction between those who had 'internalized' British union traditions and those for whom support for the union was merely 'a matter of calculation'. For the first group the

> union has often represented more . . . than simply a means of economic betterment; it has also been seen as a form of collective action in which solidarity was an end as well as a means and as a socio-political movement aiming at radical changes in industrial institutions and in the structure of society generally. (p. 107)

The authors argue that this variation may be more a matter of social integration than of individual values. Klandermans (1986: 190) concurs that 'participation is inextricably bound up with the group culture, and the individual decision to participate is influenced by the group to which the individual belongs'.

Goldthorpe et al. (1968: 167–8) found that of trade union members in the three Luton plants they studied, those who had joined 'with little volition on their own part', but because of social pressure or closed shop agreements, 'clearly outnumbered the minority – 20 per cent overall – who stated that they had become union members as a matter of principle or duty'. About half of all union members stated that they 'were attracted by what would often be the individual, or at any rate highly sectional advantages of belonging to a labour organization'.

Van de Vall (1970: 125–9), in his study of union members in The Netherlands in the mid-1950s, found that individual reasons, in particular what he called 'conflict insurance' (that is, the provision of legal and material assistance in the case of individual grievances) provided the most important motive for workers to join. One-third of the members had joined primarily as a result of pressure from others, particularly because of personal infiuence in the family or at work. 'Sociocentric' arguments, relating to the collective achievements of unions from which others should also benefit, appeared to be the overriding motive for only about one-fifth of members. Fortunately, we can compare these attitudes over time. In 1991, roughly equal proportions – 40 per cent – of union members in The Netherlands mentioned collective and individual reasons as the principal motive for joining a trade union. Idealistic motives and social pressure, which taken together had provided the principal stated reason for one-third of those in Van de Vall's study, were the principal grounds for under 10 per cent and 3–4 per cent respectively in the later study.

The kind of community pressure found in the 1950s has largely disappeared. It would indeed be surprising to find the mechanisms of social control described by Gadourek in his study of Sassenheim, a rural-industrial area in the 'modern' western part of Holland: non-members were 'either directly or indirectly (e.g. by letters put anonymously into their coats during the working hours) reminded that they actually profit from work done by the unions without paying their dues in return' (Gadourek 1956: 131). There is no reason to believe that this description of the behaviour in the Catholic part of the community did not also apply to the smaller Protestant and socialist pillars (*zuilen*). Indeed, as argued by Kruyt and others, pillarization strengthened social control in the community. Unions in The Netherlands have not been successful in substituting social control mechanisms once available in the community or through the family with social control in the workplace. (However, even today, the probability of joining a union doubles when one parent is, or has been, a union member (Klandermans et al. 1992).) The absence of union representation in the firm has been a major disadvantage in this regard and it is probably one of the most important reasons for the divergence in unionization trends between Belgium and The Netherlands since the 1950s (Mok 1985).

Finally, social control and preferences also affect the attachment to the union after joining. Union members who discontinued their membership between 1991 and 1993 more often mentioned individual motives for joining in the first place. Social pressure, on the other hand, was to a greater extent recognized as a motive for joining among workers who had retained membership.

Social Attitudes

Unfortunately, there exists little comparative evidence of changes in social values and public opinion with regard to collective worker organization. Opinion poll data may help show whether the perceived need for unions has decreased as a result of statutory employee rights (works councils, health and safety rights, etc.) and the focus in recent years on the individual employee in the context of human resources management. Lipset (1984) has argued, with respect to American unions, that the decline of their standing in public opinion has precipitated their decline. Although the majority of American people still 'approve' of unions and see them as a necessary counterweight to management, opposition to unions rose steeply in the 1970s. The net popularity score of labour unions reported in opinion polls – the percentage of respondents approving of unions minus those disapproving – declined from 57 per cent in 1953, when union density peaked, to a low of 20 per cent in the early 1980s (Lipset 1986: 201, table 5). Despite the severe retrenchment of American unions, still almost half of those questioned believed that unions were too powerful. Data for Australia (Peetz 1990), Canada (Lipset 1990) and Britain (Edwards and Bain 1988) also point to a decline in the rating of trade unions in the 1970s, although in Canada and Britain this was not reflected in membership decline. The net popularity of British unions recovered in the 1980s from 15 per cent in 1979 to 47 per cent in 1988. This may be interpreted as reflecting union weakness (Edwards and Bain 1988) and sympathy for the underdog. These ratings may be seen as indicators of the performance and legitimacy of unions, and therefore inform the strategic choices of employers and governments. Thus the Conservative government elected in 1979 could afford to take on the trade union movement in Britain, despite the apparent strength suggested by the comparatively high union density at the time.

Since the first poll in 1960, the percentage of West Germans who reply that 'unions are necessary' has remained constant at 60–70 per cent; between 4 and 11 per cent reply that unions are not necessary (Niedenhoff and Pege 1987: 33). Similarly, in our biannual surveys, from 1989 till 1993, we find that three-quarters of the Dutch population agree with the statement that unions are necessary, and between 45 and 55 per cent agree with specific industrial action on issues varying from general wage increases, nurses' pay, and working-time reduction.[3] These figures indicate, at least in the German and Dutch cases, that unions have a high degree of public recognition and legitimacy. Perhaps this reflects an image of unions as capable of promoting general interests that go beyond the special interests of their members. These outcomes do, however, raise the question of free-riding. About two-thirds of all workers approve of union objectives and rate their performance on the whole as satisfactory, but less than one-third join (Kriesi 1993). Are unions capable of mobilizing this potential for collective action?

Employer Choice

Before returning to that question, one more anti-clockwise step within figure 4.1 must be taken. Probably the dominant pressure for change in industrial relations since the early 1980s has come from increased product competition, in combination with the opening of world markets. The regulatory framework of European social policy and industrial relations is under increasing pressure from lower-cost domestic and foreign competitors. As important is the change in market structures caused by greater uncertainty and more specialized consumer tastes, and by the flexible technologies that make it possible to meet these efficiently (Piore and Sabel 1985). As is argued by Kochan et al. (1984) with reference to the United States, these changes have provoked a strategic reconsideration of management–union relations. In their explanation of management choices concerning union representation, the authors take for granted employers' preference for operating without a union, since it is 'deeply ingrained in American ideology'. The priority given to acting on this preference 'is conditioned by the feasibility or the costs of doing so. The feasibility, in turn, depends basically on how highly unionized the firm is'(Kochan et al. 1986: 491).

In the 'strategic choice' approach, the power dependency relations between firm and union are decisive, with contrasting ideologically informed preferences taken as given. Only the prior strength of trade unions, their capacity to offer resistance, will restrain management and at least 'buy time'. In Kochan's theory, management appears curiously unconstrained by choices of other firms. It is in my view necessary to arrive at a fuller understanding of employer behaviour by considering the different institutional conditions under which they must realize their goals. In this connection, I propose a return to Clegg's (1976) theory of employer behaviour and union representation.

Clegg claims that international variations in union density can be explained with the help of three critical aspects of the industrial relations system: the extent of collective bargaining, the depth of bargaining and union security. Extent of collective bargaining is defined as coverage, that is, the number or proportion of wage and salary earners whose terms of employment are subject to collective bargaining. Coverage is closely related to the level at which unions are recognized. It co-varies with centralization, which can be defined as the level at which bargaining is usually conducted. Bargaining depth is understood as the degree to which union organization extends down to the shop-floor, rather similar to what Kjellberg (1983) calls decentralization and Crouch (1993) articulation of interest representation. If union officials and stewards have frequent contact with those whom they represent and continually renegotiate with management solutions to problems as they arise in the workplace, then bargaining is said to have depth. Finally, Clegg uses the term 'union security' in the broad sense of union recognition. It includes the benefits conferred by employers on the union as an organization, helping it to become a predictable and reliable bargaining agent. Union security in the narrow sense – the existence of a post-entry closed shop, check-off, or employer funding of training for union representatives – reflects the employers' acceptance of the union as the legitimate representative of the work-force.

Union recognition is closely related to centralization. If unions and employers negotiate a collective agreement at sector level, they have a mutual interest in protecting the contract against non-organized outsiders. If coverage is very high, as in Sweden, or extension of the contract to employers outside the signatory employers' federation is customary, as in Germany, or statutory, as in Belgium or The Netherlands, the incentive of employers to run a non-union firm is diminished. Instead, employers have an incentive to join the branch-level employers' association because they experience the consequences of its policies anyway. This may apply especially to the larger companies, which stand a chance of exerting influence; small firms may occasionally take a free ride.

Under a centralized multi-employer bargaining structure, union recognition is likely to be decided centrally for all member firms, though observance may vary. In fact, employers in Sweden, Germany and The Netherlands have used their combined strength to force unions to accept a measure of centralized control over shop-floor behaviour, and to acknowledge the employer's 'right to manage'. Consequently, bargaining depth has been restricted. For unions there may be a trade-off, the outcome of which is also influenced by the prior existence of craft-based unionism at plant level.

Fiercer competition in the product market may increase employers' resistance to union demands, and they may be tempted to leave multi-employer agreements and 'go it alone'. In this case they would bear the full costs of union opposition; indeed, employers' associations often use the union to force non-compliant employers into line, and the union is only too happy to oblige. Only if employers know that other firms will follow without delay are they likely to take this road. The alternative is to work through the association, for instance by exerting pressure to negotiate a cheaper and leaner collective agreement, and by demanding greater freedom to determine employment relations at the level of the firm. Such a strategy may jeopardize the 'neutralization' of the workplace.

In the United States this kind of collective insurance among firms is absent and each firm is on its own. Blanchflower and Freeman (1990) show that the differential in wages between union and non-union firms is much larger than in Sweden, Austria or Germany, where the union mark-up is very small; the United Kingdom occupies a position between these extremes (according to early 1980s data). Like Kochan et al. (1984), the authors argue that the rising union mark-up has increased the incentive for employers to oppose the union. Unionized employers are at a disadvantage compared with non-union employers, especially if the higher union wage is not fully compensated by higher productivity. The restriction on employer autonomy may be sufficient reason for an American employer to opt for an union-free environment, even if this choice is inefficient from a purely economic point of view. In companies where they are recognized and have negotiated a contract, American 'job control' unions have an almost unparalleled bargaining depth. They police meticulously and in an adversarial fashion day-to-day employment relations in the firm.

The Cascade of Decline

In Britain, the 1990 Workplace Industrial Relations Survey (Millward et al. 1992), offers a picture of the consequences of the decline of multi-firm bargaining. In the 1980s there was a 'substantial reduction' in multi-employer bargaining over rates of pay. Only 13 per cent of manual and 6 per cent of non-manual employees reported multi-employer bargaining in 1990, against 26 and 16 per cent in 1984 (p. 229), resulting in the collapse of employers' organizations. A large part of the decline in bargaining coverage is explained by the disappearance of recognized unions, and union representatives or shop stewards, in a growing number of (smaller) establishments. Aggregate union density in the United Kingdom dropped to 37 per cent; in establishments of 25 employees and more, density declined from 58 per cent in 1984 to 48 per cent six years later (p. 58). The researchers note that in addition to the effect of the disappearance of the closed shop, 'the most striking feature . . . is the increase in the proportion of establishments with no members at all'. It should be added that reduced collective bargaining did not encourage employers to introduce alternative forms of representation such as joint consultation; such mechanisms, traditionally a minority phenomenon in Britain, have most often operated in large unionized firms, and their incidence also declined in the 1980s.

The Trade-off between Coverage and Depth

Data on bargaining coverage are scarce; however, the OECD has recently provided some standardized statistics. Data for eight countries are presented in table 4.3 and probably reflect the full range of cross-national differences. The two extremes are Sweden on the one hand, and the United States and Japan on the other. In Sweden both union density and bargaining coverage are very high as a proportion of the work-force; in the United States and Japan, both are very low. In Japan bargaining coverage is even smaller than union density, reflecting the

Table 4.3 Bargaining coverage and union representation in 1990

country	extension	union density	bargaining coverage	ratio
Sweden	no	81	83	1.02
Germany	yes	31	81	2.61
Netherlands	yes	19	71	3.74
France	yes	8	91	11.38
Spain	yes	9	68	7.56
Great Britain	no	37	47	1.27
United States	no	15	18	1.20
Japan	no	23	23	1.00

Note: density rates refer to market sector

Source: Visser 1992a; coverage data from OECD 1993

fact that some unions in the government sector are not legally entitled to negotiate collective agreements. In Germany, the Netherlands, France and Spain, the coverage of collective agreements exceeds union density by a wide margin.[4] The principal reasons are the high degree of employer organization, the continued importance of centralized (multi-employer) bargaining for entire sectors and regions, and the voluntary or statutory extension of collective agreements to workers employed in non-member firms. Only in Sweden is union coverage co-terminous with bargaining coverage: although the legal facility of extension was offered to the unions by the social democratic government in 1934, it was rejected because it would, in the unions' view, diminish the incentive for workers to become members (Kjellberg 1990).

The problem of 'free-riding' is exacerbated by extension, but does not begin there. It also exists for workers under company agreements, unless contracts are restricted to union members only. Where bargaining depth is significant, and the union has a visible role in supervising the agreement at the workplace, the benefits of membership are increased and the costs to non-members are also raised. Bargaining coverage is an important factor in determining whether there will be a union in the workplace for workers to join. Bargaining depth infiuences the actual decision of the worker to join when a union is present (Visser 1992b).

In Clegg's theory, depth and coverage are independent dimensions; however, I would contend that extensive coverage, which can be obtained voluntarily only under multi-employer bargaining conditions, presupposes a somewhat reduced bargaining depth. In other words, the Swedish case is exceptional and cannot be stable in the long run; or, to paraphrase Elvander (1990), employer interest in collective solutions is incompatible with decentralization under conditions of high union density and low unemployment.

Conclusion: What should Unions do?

What lessons should trade unions draw from all this? In his survey of the Thatcher years, Towers (1989: 180) identifies five possible strategies for British unions: 'work for a Labour government and supportive legislation; merge with other unions; recruit new members in the fastest-growing industries and among previously neglected groups; improve services to members; and revise trade union purposes'. All of this would probably help. Although Labour, if it regains power, might reverse some of the most vicious measures of the Conservatives, it will not bring back the legal or political environment of the 1970s. Mergers concentrate union resources and may help to structure activities in more efficient ways; however, most mergers have been defensive and opportunistic, making union structure in Britain more complex than ever. Elsewhere in Europe, attempts to concentrate resources in the union movement have been slow. Generally, peak organizations have declined in importance and funding. Unions have no alternative but to organize in new areas – probably introducing new methods of tapping potential sympathy for collective action. The decline in union membership, and popularity, among young people in various countries is probably the most alarming aspect of union decline. It seems highly unlikely that the current generation will ever reach the level of collective mobilization of its predecessors. Providing better services and introducing a more 'business-like' approach is not a panacea, although it would certainly help dispel an image of inward-looking conservatism. In some unions, paradoxically, the status of customer may provide more rights than that of member. A change of purpose refers, in the British case, to attempts to define a less adversarial type of unionism. Both the American business union and the Japanese company union have fared badly since the mid-1970s, so it seems curious that they inspire confidence in Europe. A merger of the principles of craft and industrial unionism may have more to offer, combining inter-firm and inter-group solidarity with greater attentiveness to individual career interests.

The big question for the future of trade unions in Europe is, in my view, whether the German model will survive. This model combines extensive bargaining coverage (over 70 per cent of all employees); continued multi-employer bargaining, with collective agreements that are still fairly detailed though increasingly leaving issues to be determined at lower levels; strong employer associations with a proven capacity for policy co-ordination; a small number of concentrated industrial unions, directed from the centre and able to chose when and how to use their capacity to strike; and wide-ranging and detailed procedures of employee consultation in firms organized through a second channel of representation which is, in part, independent from both union and employer. This configuration survived the breakdown of national concertation (*konzertierte Aktion*) in the 1970s and the pressures of decentralization and flexibility in the 1980s. Müller-Jentsch et al. (1992: 101) observe that

> in contrast to the situation in the United Kingdom and the United States, decentralized collective bargaining does not take the form of single-employer agreements, but rather implies the gradual transfer of traditional bargaining functions to management and works councils.

They add that this process has tended to blur the thin line between bargaining and consultation. Within German unions this leads to tensions. Nevertheless, given their past track record in dealing with strong works councils, German unions may be better prepared than most to handle these pressures. They must simultaneously accommodate the pressure of world markets, be extremely attentive to the macroeconomic implications of their behaviour, and respond to works councils by taking account of developments in individual firms and local markets. Indications are that the stormy unification with the five eastern *Länder* has strained the system to its limits. It is too early to tell whether the recent announcement by *Gesamtmetall*, Germany's powerful engineering and steel employers' association, that it will terminate current collective agreements in the western *Länder*, is a tactical manoeuvre or the beginning of the end of the post-war system. It can certainly be interpreted as a harbinger of extreme tensions in a hitherto successful system of industrial relations.

In 1987 I predicted that

> to the extent that labour markets, under the present standards of employment, insurance and wage compensation, fail to absorb a sufficient large number of people looking for jobs, the pressure towards more flexible and generally lower standards of protection concerning hiring and firing, minimum and maximum hours, overtime regulations, minimum wages and social insurance provisions, will continue. (Visser 1987: 233)

Unions' power and legitimacy will continue to erode unless they find a way of promoting a feasible and creative policy of full employment. This cannot but include the acceptance of greater variation and flexibility in how people work and are rewarded, and it has to show a greater capacity than hitherto for concerting diverse interests. In other words, the problem of collective mobilization will not be solved in isolation. The 'new frontier' is whether it will be possible to reconstruct a policy of social solidarity on a European scale, open to other regions of the world, though without entailing a levelling down in social conditions. Like the editor of the French newspaper *Le Monde* (2 October 1993), I believe that the stakes are high:

> To the extent that unemployment continues to rise and the chances of a resumption of economic growth become more remote, a single strategy tends to impose itself on European governments: the destruction of the system of collective protection patiently built up over the last forty-five years and which still distinguishes the way of life in the Old Continent. [My translation]

There is still a task for trade unions, though they may have to unlearn many of their past habits. New constituencies have to be reached, probably in novel ways. Concertation of interests can no longer be confined to the narrow boundaries of the national state but must have an international dimension. A policy of small concessions may not be the best approach to a reinvention of social solidarity under conditions of fiexible production, global competition and increasingly differentiated life chances within the working classes of contemporary Europe.

Notes

1 Although data on union membership are incomplete, the cases of the two very small countries, Iceland and Luxembourg, should probably also be placed in this category of stable unionism (Visser 1991: 101, 125–6).
2 In Austria, manufacturing employment continued to expand (Visser 1991, p. 110, table 4.4).
3 UvA-FNV project, *FNV-barometer* no. 2–11, University of Amsterdam, Faculty of Politics and Social-Cultural Sciences.
4 In Germany and The Netherlands sectoral agreements are fairly rich in both substantive and normative terms, allowing adjustments at the level of firms only under certain specified conditions. In France and Spain they are often 'agreements on aims rather than on procedures or content' (Reynaud 1988) and contain minimum provisions on pay. Legal statutes on union recognition and representation in both countries may be more important than collective bargaining.

References

Ashenfelter, O. and Pencavel, J.H. 1969: American trade union growth 1900–1960. *Quarterly Journal of Economics*, 83, 434–8.
Baglioni, G. and Crouch, C.J. (eds) 1990: *European Industrial Relations*. London: Sage Publications.
Bain, G.S. (ed.) 1983: *Industrial Relations in Britain*. Oxford: Blackwell.
Bain, G.S. and Elsheikh, F. (1976) *Union Growth and the Business Cycle*. Oxford: Blackwell Publishers.
Bain, G.S. and Price, R. 1983: Union growth: dimensions, determinants, and destiny. In Bain (ed.), 3–34.
Barker, A., Lewis, P. and McCann, M. 1984: Trade unions and the organization of the unemployed. *British Journal of Industrial Relations*, 22(3) 391–404.
Berger, S. (ed.) 1981: *Organizing Interests in Western Europe. Pluralism, corporatism and the transformation of politics*. Cambridge: Cambridge University Press.
Bertl, W., Rudak, R. and Schneider, R. 1988: *Arbeitnehmerbewusstsein im Zeichen des technischen und sozialen Wandels*. Düsseldorf: DGB/Hans Böckler Stiftung.
Blanchflower, D. and Freeman, R. 1990: Going different ways: unionism in the U.S. and other advanced OECD countries. London: London School of Economics, Centre for Economic Performance, Discussion paper no. 5.

Booth, A. 1989: What Do Unions Do Now? Discussion paper in economics, no. 8903, Brunel University.

Caruth, A. and Disney, R. 1988: Where have two million trade union members gone? *Economica*, 55, 1–20.

Clegg, H.A. 1976: *Trade Unionism Under Collective Bargaining: a theory based on comparisons of six countries*. Oxford: Blackwell Publishers.

Commons, J.R. *et al.* 1918: *History of Labour in the United States*. New York: Macmillan, 3 volumes.

Crouch, C.J. 1993: *Industrial Relations and European State Traditions*. Oxford: Clarendon Press.

Crouch, C.J. and Pizzorno, A. (eds) 1978: *The Resurgence of Class Conflict in Western Europe Since 1978*. London: Macmillan.

Dunlop, J.T. 1949: The development of labor organization: a theoretical framework. In R.A. Lester and J. Shister (eds), *Insights into Labor Issues*, New York: Macmillan, 163–93.

Edwards, P. and Bain, G.S. 1988: Why are trade unions becoming more popular? Unions and public opinion in Britain. *British Journal of Industrial Relations*, 26(3) 311–26.

Elsheikh, F. and Bain, G.S. 1980: Unionization in Britain: an inter-establishment analysis based on survey data. *British Journal of Industrial Relations*, 18(2) 376–85.

Elvander, N. 1990: Income policies in the Nordic countries. *International Labour Review*, 129(1) 1–21.

Fiorito, J. and Greer, C.R. 1982: Determinants of U.S. Unionism. Past research and future needs. *Industrial Relations*, 20, 1–32.

Flanagan, R.J., Soskice, D.W. and Ulman, L. 1983: *Unionism, Economic Stabilization and Incomes Policies: European experience*. Washington DC: The Brookings Institution.

Gadourek, I. 1956: *A Dutch Community*. Leyden: Stenfert Kroese.

Garraty, J.A. 1978: *Unemployment in History*. New York: Harper and Row.

Goldthorpe, J.H. (ed.) 1984: *Order and Conflict in Contemporary Capitalism*. Oxford, London: Clarendon Press.

Goldthorpe, J.H., Lockwood, D., Bechofer, F. and Platt, J. 1968: *The Affluent Worker: Industrial Attitudes and Behaviour*. Cambridge: Cambridge University Press.

Guigni, G., *et al.* 1976: *Gli anni della conflittualità permanente. Rapporto sulle relazioni industriali in Italia*. Milan: Angeli.

Hirsch, B.T. and Addison, J.T. 1986: *The Economic Analysis of Unions: New approaches and evidence*. London: Allen & Unwin.

Hohn, W. 1983: Interne Arbeitsmärkte und Betriebliche Mitbestimmung – Tendenzen 'Sozialen Schließung' im 'dualen' System der Mitbestimmung. Berlin: Wissenschaftszentrum, IIM/IMP paper 83-2.

Husbands, C. 1985: Government popularity and the unemployment issue, 1966–1983. *Sociology*, 1(1) 1–18.

Kjellberg, A. 1983: *Facklig organisering i tolv länder*. Lund: Archiv.

Kjellberg, A. 1990: The Swedish trade union system: centralization and decentralization. Paper to 12th World Congress of Sociology, ISA, Madrid, 9–13 July (mimeo).

Klandermans, P.G. 1984: Mobilization and participation in trade union action: a value expectancy approach. *Journal of Occupational Psychology*, 57, 107–20.

Klandermans, P.G. 1986: Psychology and trade union participation: joining, acting, quitting. *Journal of Occupational Psychology*, 59, 189–204.

Klandermans, P.G., Sharda, N., van den Putte, B., van Rij, C., Saris, W., van den

Veen, G., Visser, J. 1992: Participatie in vakbonden. Een opiniepeiling onder CNV- en FNV-leden. (Participation in Trade Unions. A Survey among CNV and FNV members), Amsterdam: University of Amsterdam/Nimmo-PSCW.

Klandermans, P.G., Sharda, N., van den Putte, B., van Rij, C., Saris, W., van der Veen, G., Visser, J. 1992: Participatie in Vakbonden II: veranderingen in de jaren negentig. (Participation in Unions II: changes in the 1990s), Amsterdam: University of Amsterdam/Nimmo-PSCW.

Klandermans, P.G., Sharda, N., van den Putte, B., van Rij, C., Saris, W., van den Veen, G., Visser, J. forthcoming: Veranderingen in vakbondsparticipatie (Changes in Trade Union Participation). Amsterdam: University of Amsterdam/Nimmo-PSCW.

Kochan, T., Cappelli, P. and McKersie, R. 1984: Strategic choice and industrial relations Theory. *Industrial Relations*, 23(1) 16–39.

Kochan, T., Katz, H., and McKersie, R. 1986: *The Transformation of American Industrial Relations*. New York: Basic Books.

Kochan, T., McKersie, R., and Chalykoff, J. 1986: The effects of corporate strategy and workplace innovations on union representation. *Industrial and Labor Relations Review*, 39(4) 487–501.

Kriesi, H. 1993: *Political Mobilization and Social Change. The Dutch Case in comparative perspective*. Aldershot: Avebury/European Centre Vienna.

Lewis, P. 1989: The unemployed and trade union membership. *Industrial Relations Journal*, 20, 271–9.

Lipset, S.M. 1986: Labor unions in the public mind. In S.M. Lipset (ed.), *Unions in Transition. Entering the second century*, San Francisco: ICS Press, 287–321.

Lipset, S.M. 1990: *Continental Divide. The Values and Institutions of the United States and Canada*. London and New York: Routledge.

Marwell, G. and Oliver, P. 1993: *The Critical Mass in Collective Action. A micro-social theory*. Cambridge: Cambridge University Press.

Mason, B. and Bain, P. 1993: The determinants of trade union membership in Britain: A survey of the literature. *Industrial and Labor Relations Review*, 46(2) 332–51.

Millward, N. and Stevens, M. 1992: *British Workplace Industrial Relations 1990*. Aldershot: Gower Publishing.

Mok, A. 1985: Arbeidsverhoudingen in Nederland en België (Industrial Relations in the Netherlands and Belgium). *Tijdschrift voor Arbeidsvraagstukken*, 1(1) 1–17.

Müller-Jentsch, W., Rehermann, K. and Sperling, H.J. 1992: Socio-technical rationalisation and negotiated work organisation: recent trends in Germany. In Rojot and Tergeist (eds), 93–111.

Neumann, G., Pedersen, P.J. and Westergard-Nielsen, N. 1989: Long-run international trends in aggregate unionization. Revised paper Public Choice Society meeting, Linz (mimeo).

Niedenhoff, H.-U. and Pege, W. 1987: Gewerkschaftshandbuch 1987, Cologne: Institut für deutschen Wirtschaft.

Olson, M. 1965: *The Logic of Collective Action. Public goods and the theory of groups*. Cambridge, Mass.: Harvard University Press.

Organisation for Economic Co-operation and Development (OECD) 1993: The level and coverage of collective bargaining: a cross-national study of patterns and trends. Note by the Secretariat. Paris, September 1993.

Pedersen, P.J. 1982: Union growth in Denmark, 1911–1939. *Scandinavian Journal of Economics*, 583–92.

Pedersen, P.J. 1989: Langsigtede internationale tendenser i den faglige organisering og den politiske venstrefløj. *Oekonomie e Politik*, 62(2) 91–9.

Peetz, D. 1990: Declining union density. *Journal of Industrial Relations*, 32(2) 197–223.

Piore, M.J. and Sabel, C.F. 1985: *The Second Industrial Divide*. New York: Basic Books.

Pizzorno, A. 1978: Political exchange and collective identity in industrial conflict. In Crouch and Pizzorno (eds), 277–98.

Pollard, S. 1969: Trade union reactions to the economic crisis. *Journal of Contemporary History*, 4(4) 101–16.

Price, R. and Bain, G.S. 1983: Union growth in Britain: retrospect and prospect. *British Journal of Industrial Relations*, 21(1) 46–68.

Ramsay, H., Pollert, A. and Rainbird, H. 1992: A decade of transformation? Labour market flexibility and work organization in the United Kingdom. In Rojot and Tergeist (eds), 169–95.

Regini, M. (ed.) 1992: *The Future of Labour Movements*. London: Sage Publications.

Reynaud, J.-D. 1988: La négociation de la qualification. *European Journal of Sociology*, 29, 78–101.

Rezler, J. 1961: *Union Growth Reconsidered. A critical analysis of recent growth theories*. New York.

Roche, W.K. and Larragy, J. 1986: The trend of unionization in the Republic. In *Industrial Relations in Ireland. Contemporary issues and developments*, Dublin: University College Dublin, Department of Commerce.

Roche, W.K. and Larragy, J. 1990: Cyclical and institutional determinants of annual trade union growth and decline in Ireland: Evidence from the DUES Data Series. *European Sociological Review*, 6, 49–72.

Rojer, M. and Visser, J. 1993: De ene sector is de andere niet. Keuzegedrag, netwerkvorming en werknemersorganisatie (Cross-sectoral differences in worker choice, networks and union organization). *Tijdschrift voor Arbeidsvraagstukken*, 9(2) 182–98.

Rojot, J. and Tergeist, P. (eds) 1992: *New Directions in Work Organization. The industrial relations response*. Paris: OECD.

Romagnoli, Guido (ed.) 1980: *La sindicalizzazione tra ideologia e pratica. Il caso italiano* (2 vols). Rome: Edizione Lavoro.

Rothstein, B. 1991: Labour market institutions and working class strength. In S. Steinmo, K. Thelen and F. Longstreth (eds), *The New Institutionalism. State, society and economy*, Cambridge: Cambridge University Press.

Scharpf, F.W. 1987: *Sozialdemokratische Krisenpolitik in Europa*. Frankfurt: Campus (1990: *Crisis and Choice in European Social Democracy*. Ithaca: Cornell U.P.).

Schmitter, P.C. and Lehmbruch, G. (eds) 1979: *Trends towards Corporatist Intermediation*. Beverly Hills and London: Sage Publications.

Shalev, M. 1992: The resurgence of labour quiescence. In Regini (ed.), 102–32.

Sharpe, I. 1971: The growth of Australian trade unions: 1907–1969. *Journal of Industrial Relations*, 13.

Stern, J. 1982: Job duration of men becoming unemployed. *British Journal of Industrial Relations*, 20(3) 373–6.

Streeck, W. 1981: *Gewerkschaftliche Organisationsprobleme in der sozialstaatlichen Demokratie*. Königstein/Ts: Athenäum.

Streeck, W. 1992: *Social Institutions and Economic Performance. Studies of industrial relations in advanced capitalist economies*. London: Sage Publications.

Swidensky, R. 1974: Trade union growth in Canada: 1911–1970. *Relations Industrielles*, 29, 435–51.

Towers, B. 1989: Running the gauntlet: British trade unions under Thatcher, 1979–1988. *Industrial and Labor Relations Review*, 42, 163–89.

van der Vall, M. 1970: *Labor Organizations. A macro- and micro-sociological analysis on a comparative basis*. Cambridge: Cambridge University Press.

van den Putte, B., Visser, J. and van Rij, C. 1991: De Vakbond in het Bedrijf (The Union in the Workplace). Amsterdam: University of Amsterdam, Nimmo-PSCW.

Veltman, J. 1986: Uitkeringsgerechtigd en toch georganiseerd (Union membership retention among benefit recipients). Amsterdam: University of Amsterdam, Department of Sociology, unpublished MA thesis.

Visser, J. 1986: Die Mitgliederentwicklung der westeuropäischen Gewerkschaften. Trends und Konjunkturen 1920–1983. *Journal für Sozialforschung* (Vienna) 26(1) 3–34.

Visser, J. 1987: In search of inclusive unionism. Thesis, University of Amsterdam. Also published as special issue of *Bulletin of Comparative Labour Relations*, 18.

Visser, J. 1991: Trends in union membership. OECD *Employment Outlook*, 97–134.

Visser, J. 1992a: Trade union membership data-base. University of Amsterdam, Department of Sociology/Sociology of Organizations Research Unit.

Visser, J. 1992b: Why countries differ. Explaining cross-national variation in union organization. Mimeo, International Industrial Relations Research Association, 158–76.

Visser, J. 1993: Syndicalisme et desyndicalisation. *Mouvement Social*. (Special issue edited by Robert Boyer and Jacques Freysinnet), 17–40.

Waddington, J. 1992: Trade union membership in Britain, 1980–1987: unemployment and restructuring. *British Journal of Industrial Relations*, 30(2) 287–335.

Wallerstein, M. 1989: Union organization in advanced industrial democracies. *American Political Science Review*, 83(2) 481–52.

Windmuller, J.P. 1987: *Collective Bargaining in Industrialised Market Economies: a reappraisal*. Geneva: ILO.

5

Changing Trade Union Identities and Strategies

Richard Hyman

The purpose of this chapter is to explore both common trends and national particularities in trade union responses to hard times. My concern is as much to raise questions as to propose answers, but also to develop some conceptual and analytical ideas of relevance to the understanding of contemporary European trade unionism.

I ended a recent survey of the state of European trade unions by suggesting that classic models of class unionism had been eclipsed, and that the dominant form in the 1990s might be characterized as 'business unionism with a social conscience' (Hyman 1991: 637). In the present chapter I adopt a different focus, but the underlying concern is the same. Trade unions throughout western Europe have for more than a decade been faced by unprecedented challenges to established patterns of internal and external relations. The nature and severity of these challenges have varied between countries, and the pattern of responses has differed likewise. The general consequence, however, has been to put in doubt inherited conceptions of the character and purpose of unions as collective organizations or social movements, and to encourage or provoke the search for new definitions of trade union identity.

In the following discussion I analyse in some detail the key changes in the environment of trade union action since the 1970s, and the challenges they pose; then I suggest a conceptual framework for analysing trade union dynamics; and finally I consider alternative models of evolving union identity.

Changing Contexts of Trade Union Action: Challenges and Opportunities

It is a familiar argument that in the space of two decades the environment of industrial relations in much of Europe has been transformed. Analysts often emphasize, first, the restructuring of capital (closely associated with an increased role for transnational enterprises) and the occupational and sectoral recomposition of employment; second, the pressures of intensified global competition under unfavourable economic circumstances; third, the undermining of traditional political points of reference; fourth, what many regard as the altered priorities and orientations among unions' actual and potential memberships.

Restructuring of capital and employment

Changes in the structure of capital and employment in recent years constitute, to some extent, the continuation of long-term trends; however, the cumulative effect of incremental adjustment may at a certain stage amount to a qualitative transformation. On the one hand, large companies covering many establishments – often in different countries and in a number of sectors – have become increasingly influential actors in industrial relations, particularly under the impetus of the single European market (see chapter 2). On the other hand, the SME sector has increased in numerical prominence, encouraged by deliberate government policy in most of Europe as well as by the growth of the service sector and increased subcontracting by manufacturing firms and public employers. Almost universally, patterns of industrial relations, including the degree of union membership and recognition, differ radically between the large- and small-firm sectors. Changes in company structure are thus associated with a polarization in industrial relations regimes.[1]

These trends overlap with the sectoral and occupational restructuring of employment. All European economies have displayed parallel long-term historical shifts, though the pace and extent of transformation differ considerably between countries. Agricultural employment – in much of Europe, the largest sector of the economy well into the twentieth century – has been shrinking in relative and, latterly, also in absolute terms for many decades. In some countries, the major growth sector for much of the present century (often drawing on a large influx of rural labour) was manufacturing, and associated industries such as mining and transport. But recent decades have seen a process of 'de-industrialization' (far more marked, say, in Britain than in Germany), with the major expansion occurring in service employment. In most of Europe, services have become the largest single sector of employment: following either a 'northern' model whereby the early consolidation of extensive provision of state welfare had substantial labour market effects; or a 'southern' model in which the long persistence of a large agricultural sector precluded the growth of large-scale industrial employment, and recent urbanization has been associated with expanding private services. In the latter case, there has thus been a direct transition from a 'pre-industrial' to a 'post-industrial' economy. Two other developments have been associated with these trends: the shift from agriculture to manufacturing normally entailed a substantial increase in dependent employment and a corresponding decline in family labour and self-employment, but in some areas of services this move has been reversed. More clear-cut has been a growth in female employment – commonly the majority of the work-force in the service sector – though in some countries (notably Britain) employed to a large extent on a part-time basis. Partly as a result of these sectoral trends, there has been a long-run decline in the proportion of the labour force in manual occupations: in most countries they are now outnumbered by white-collar employees (among whom, again, the proportion of female employees is universally higher than in manual occupations).

None of these trends is conceptually or empirically unambiguous; occupational or sectoral classification of employment involves notorious complexities (Hyman 1978). The manual/white-collar distinction is largely a matter of somewhat arbitrary convention, even though in many European countries this convention rests on strong institutional and even legal supports. The boundary between manufacturing and services is likewise problematic, not least because, even in manufacturing firms and establishments, often only a minority of employees participate directly in physical production. The tendency in recent years for companies to divisionalize their organization and to contract out many of their activities has in itself contributed significantly to a purely nominal expansion of the service sector. Moreover, the essential heterogeneity of services must be emphasized: we are speaking not of one sector but of a variety, which present very different patterns of opportunities or obstacles for trade unions. Thus in the public sector, levels of unionization are in most countries relatively high, often reflecting positive attitudes among public authorities towards union recognition and collective bargaining. (For this reason, the growth in public services in the 1960s and 1970s not only cushioned the employment effects of 'de-industrialization' in most European countries but also offset the potential adverse effects on unionization; conversely, subsequent policies to contain or reduce public employment by budgetary restrictions and privatization have contributed to both high aggregate unemployment and declining unionization.) Private services are themselves diverse; in particular, there is a sharp distinction to be made between those areas such as retail distribution, hotels and catering which depend primarily on a low-paid and vulnerable – and overwhelmingly female – work-force with few formal qualifications, and other more specialized services with a high proportion of professional or quasi-professional employment. It is, however, true that both types of service work can present serious, though qualitatively different, obstacles to unionization.

Most commentators have stressed the negative implications of such changes for trade unions, and have indeed presented structural shifts as a key explanation of decline and disorientation. The 'compositional argument' for declining union density is familiar, if sometimes contested (Kelly 1990) or qualified (see chapter 4), and will not be examined further here. More complex is the impact of corporate and employment restructuring on the character of trade unions and their internal dynamics.

Among both academic analysts and trade union strategists there is a broad consensus that structural change has weakened the internal coherence of trade unionism and unleashed a variety of centrifugal pressures (Crouch 1986; Müller-Jentsch 1988). Five tensions in particular have been regularly emphasized. The first is the destabilization of the traditional balance of power within central confederations, often associated with a loss of confederal authority. This has been a familiar theme in discussions of Scandinavian trade unionism: in Sweden, for example, the metalworkers ceded numerical predominance within LO to the local authority workers' union in the late 1970s, and major differences between the two over collective bargaining strategy have contributed to the disintegration of co-ordinated macroeconomic wage policy (Kjellberg 1992; Pontusson 1992; Swenson 1992; for Denmark, see Scheuer 1991 and 1992). Second, in those countries where white-collar employees have traditionally been unionized separately from manual workers, the numerical dominance of the manual confederation is being eroded. Again, Sweden provides a stark example: the proportion of union members affiliated to LO had fallen to 60 per cent by the late 1980s. Third, structural change has blurred jurisdictional boundaries, creating inter-union competition for members even in countries with traditionally stable demarcations (unprecedented conflicts between industrial unions within the German DGB; rivalry between manual and white-collar unions in Swedish engineering over the recruitment of new technically qualified categories of production workers). Fourth, centralized authority within individual unions has in many countries been weakened by an increased internal differentiation of interests, and by tendencies towards the decentralization of collective bargaining (themselves encouraged by the efforts of large companies to regulate employment relations in the light of their own distinctive priorities). Finally, the harsher environment in product and labour markets has created new interest divisions: between the employed and the unemployed, workers in exposed and sheltered sectors, those with 'typical' and 'atypical' employment contracts, those with new specialized skills and those with redundant qualifications or none (Offe 1985: chapter 3; Pérez-Díaz 1987). The ability to reconcile such differentiated interests presents radical challenges for trade unions: inspiring Crouch's question (1990: 359): 'unions may have a long-term future, but do union *movements*?'

These developments are in practice complex and often contradictory: it is misleading to present them in too stark and mechanical a manner. As I have argued elsewhere (Hyman 1992), the thesis of interest disaggregation is often exaggerated and oversimplified. The task of unions has always been to harmonize and reconcile a multiplicity of particularistic interests: the generation of solidarity has always been a project at best incompletely realized. Often, indeed, strategic unity within trade union movements has been achieved only by imposing the priorities of one segment of the work-force upon all other groups. In most countries, national trade unionism was primarily the product of collective organization of male full-time employees in such 'core' sectors of industrialization as metal-working, mining, docks and railways. The agenda of the emergent institutions of collective bargaining was shaped by the specific employment circumstances of such workers; its appropriateness for the working class more generally was rarely questioned. Moreover, the methods of job control pursued within traditional trade union practice commonly involved the defence of inherited restrictions on occupational entry or the construction of new demarcations between internal and external labour markets (Rubery 1978): typically the only immediately available defences for unionized workers whose employment status and bargaining leverage were precarious. However, trade union action which consolidated the position of a relatively protected and advantaged category of 'insiders' by the same token reproduced the vulnerability and disadvantage of a (possibly larger) category of 'outsiders'. Since the latter were unlikely to be unionized – or if unionized, to possess influence within union policy-making – the traditional bias within the politics of trade unionism was normally unchallenged.

It is therefore possible to interpret many of the recent tensions and conflicts within trade union movements as marking the end of trade unionism in the unquestioned image of the male manual manufacturing worker. Rather than a crisis of trade unionism, what has occurred is a crisis of a specific, narrowly based *type* of trade unionism. Groups within the work-force whose distinctive experiences and interests were in the past largely excluded from the agenda of national trade unionism have become increasingly willing and able to assert their own collective priorities.

Certainly one possible outcome of an altered balance of power may be 'a kind of internal paralysis of union behaviour and decision-making' (Golden 1992: 322). But the situation may be interpreted, more positively, as rendering more transparent those differences of interest which were previously suppressed. The need to devise and negotiate new bases of solidarity presents trade unions with a major challenge, which some may be constitutionally incapable of addressing effectively. But a central issue for comparative analysis of trade unionism in the 1990s is the different patterns of response, both within and between countries. Undoubtedly there are lessons to be drawn in explaining contrasting outcomes in union success in aggregating variegated interests.

Economic stringency

Historically it has been common to discuss trade union identities in terms of two overlapping antinomies: one, a tension between collective bargaining over terms and conditions of employment ('pure-and-simple unionism') as against broader social and political concerns; the other, between defensive and reactive responses to employer and government initiatives, and efforts to impose unions' own industrial relations agenda.

Generalizing heroically, one may argue that in post-war Europe these dichotomies were typically resolved in a novel fashion. Even trade union movements which traditionally had embraced broad political ambitions, whether communist or social democratic, became increasingly preoccupied with a collective bargaining agenda; at least in so far as employers were prepared to recognize and negotiate with *them*. To this extent, inherited political identities became increasingly rhetorical. Yet at the same time, the autonomy of 'industrial relations' in its traditional sense was increasingly undermined; the terrain of collective bargaining itself becoming decisively shaped by politically driven macroeconomic policy and legislative regulation of employment relations. 'Business unionism', in the American sense of the term, was evidently not a serious option. The outcome, almost universally in western Europe, was trade union fixation upon a new set of priorities which might best be labelled 'political economism': a dual concern with negotiations with employers and with influencing the broader framework of such negotiations.

Concurrently, the economic environment of trade union action was more favourable than in any previous historical epoch. For several decades the context was one of sustained GNP growth and relatively tight labour markets. A margin existed for regular improvements in workers' standard of living and in other terms of the employment contract. For a generation of union members and their representatives, increased real wages and other gains became the expected outcome of each bargaining round. From the late 1960s, moreover – often as a result of rank-and-file pressure upon more conservative leaderships – union demands, and achievements, in collective bargaining embraced qualitatively new issues: working conditions, organization of production, division of labour, career development. To an important extent, trade unions appeared to be reshaping the collective bargaining agenda rather than merely responding to employers' priorities. Political economism thus appeared to be the basis for an essentially *progressive* mode of interest representation.

Since the advent of the global economic crisis in the 1970s – stagnation or even decline of GNP, rapid increases in unemployment, and intensified international competitiveness – the terrain of collective representation has been transformed. The margin for real improvements has diminished or disappeared; indeed, as employers attempt desperately to restructure and economize, industrial relations has become the arena for different varieties of concession bargaining. Almost as a grotesque parody of the qualitative 'new demands' of radical trade unionists in the 1960s and 1970s, the rhetoric of humanization and employee involvement has been transmuted within the new managerialism as a means of integrating (core) workers within the constraints of corporate competitiveness in hard times.

Economic stringency puts in question the whole consolidated postwar mode of union representation. Unions which until recently based their membership appeal so centrally on their capacity to negotiate regular improvements in the returns to labour now find themselves mediating the freezing or even reduction of wages; those which made job protection their central function find themselves regulating the terms and rapidity of 'downsizing'. The contradictions of political economism in hard times are transparent: governments and employers can be expected to sustain willingly the unions' role as interlocutors in the processes of political exchange, and more generally to support the national regimes of industrial relations established as part of the various post-war settlements, *only* to the extent that unions underwrite policies of retrenchment and restraint. Nevertheless, this in turn is likely to provoke rank-and-file disenchantment, reflected either in a haemorrhaging of membership, or in *Cobas*-style insurgency by strategically located groups – or both.

This is the most transparent, and most frequently debated, dilemma of current trade union identity and strategy; various responses are considered in more detail below. What may be noted at this stage is the extent to which the unravelling of post-war political economism presents a polarization of options, one of which entails a narrower and particularistic conception of economism, the other a broader and more generalizing political agenda. Even if many elements among the 'new demands' of earlier decades are fatally contradicted by the constraints of intensified competition, can unions successfully address areas of experience and aspiration within the working class which have traditionally been external to the agenda of collective bargaining? And can they simultaneously respond to the need for 'conscious politicization of the diverse domains of traditional and non-traditional bargaining policy' (Altvater and Mahnkopf 1993: 263; my translation)? These are the overriding questions demanding strategic imagination within European trade unions today.

The erosion of partisan attachments

Historically, the dominant trade unions in continental Europe derived many of their defining characteristics from their relationship with a political party (social democratic, communist, or in some cases Christian democratic). (Britain provides the main counter-example of a country where 'modern' trade unionism became consolidated before the formation of a working-class party.) Such ideological identities imposed some restraints on unions' characteristic tendency to give overriding priority to advancing the immediate sectional interests of those in membership. Social democratic and communist unions identified – albeit in very different ways – with a broader working-class constituency; confessional unions drew on alternative forms of populist discourse. Whether from the perspective of class struggle or social partnership, these various ideological identities offered an obvious rationale for the development of political economism.

Ideologically, the traditional points of reference are in confusion. The collapse of communism in eastern Europe precipitated the dramatic climax of a longer-term trend: the gradual relaxation of politically driven strategy in most Mediterranean countries with powerful communist parties; only the French Confédération Générale du Travail persists as a relic of the bygone age of Stalinist trade unionism (though the decision of PCF secretary Marchais in 1993 to leave the scene may perhaps result in change even here). Secularization had previously eroded much of the ideological basis of confessional trade unionism, with Catholic confederations in France and (more ambivalently) Italy switching to a socialist identity, and in The Netherlands actually merging with the socialist unions. As for social democratic trade union ideology, its coherence as a political project rested partly on the rationale of anti-communism, partly on the credibility of a 'democratic class struggle' (Korpi 1983) succeeding by a combination of macroeconomic management, active labour market policy and a redistributive welfare state. The first support has evaporated; the second has disintegrated, as economic crisis has destroyed the basis of 'Keynesianism in one country' (Pontusson 1992). If the social democratic connection today requires that unions endorse one or other variant of 'socialist monetarism', this is no longer a popular or a progressive option.

The loss of old political identities entails obvious dangers. One is strategic disorientation, as former guiding principles are lost. Associated is the risk of syndicalist opportunism, a rejection of any political dimension to trade union practice, and in particular of those class or populist visions which transcended narrow sectional concerns. In the process, the claim of unions to represent a 'sword of justice' rather than merely a vested interest (Flanders 1970: 15) would disappear.

Yet here too there is a more positive potential. Arguably, many of the ideological identities derived from the struggles and commitments of former generations of trade unionists had become little more than empty icons and legitimations for organizational conservatism. At the very least – in such countries as Italy, Spain and Portugal – the prospect now exists for organizational reconstruction to repair the damaging divisions of past decades. Much more generally, the loosening of old ideological bonds does create more scope for advocacy of new perspectives: the redefinition of the relationship between collective bargaining and broader socio-political action, in ways which transcend post-war models of political economism.

A further point deserves emphasis. In their different ways, all the old trade union ideologies were internationalist in inspiration. Increasingly, however, political economism entailed a preoccupation with national production and the nation-state. As was argued in the Introduction to this volume, the eclipse of Keynesianism in one country is a trauma which purely national trade union strategies cannot survive. The crisis of national trade unionisms cannot be resolved except through new forms of trade union transnationalism. Whether effective cross-national co-operation (let alone genuine common strategy) is attainable can of course be questioned. But at least the bias of national vested interests has altered at the same time as ideological obstacles have disappeared; the idea of the trade union internationalism is no longer self-evidently utopian.

The decline of collectivism?

The eclipse of old trade union ideologies reflects, in the view of some analysts (for example, Zoll 1982), a more general erosion of societal collectivism. Across Europe, for most post-war decades, mainstream politics of both right and left accepted many of the assumptions of the 'social state' as regulator of economic relations and provider of social benefits and protection. However, economic crisis has coincided with (and helped encourage) a transformation of the political agenda, with a new emphasis on market liberalism and individualism. A related cultural shift is the increased centrality of consumption rather than production in shaping personal identities and interests.

Some writers directly associate a weakening of collectivism with the restructuring of employment. Early trade unionism was typically rooted in the 'occupational communities' of skilled workers or the relatively undifferentiated work situation of labour in the expanding sectors of mass production. For white-collar workers with individualized career expectations there is a far more complex and problematic relationship between individual and collective interests (Lockwood 1958); the same is true of workers with new, technologically specific skills in scarce supply (Kern and Schumann 1986; Gulowsen 1988). If they unionize at all, they often do so to ensure 'fair' conditions for the pursuit of their personal career interests. The more general displacement of traditional forms of trade union collectivism is an explicit objective of some employer strategies which aim to personalize the employment relationship. Equally problematic for unions are management attempts to redefine the company as the point of reference for workers' collective interests and loyalties: attempts assisted by the material reality of intensified inter-firm competition.

'Farewell to solidarity' would be too simplistic a conclusion to draw (Hyman 1992). The 'embourgeoisement' of the working class – a theme of sociological debate in Britain several decades ago – had provoked complaints by Marx and Engels in the 1860s. The stereotype of traditional proletarian solidarity is revealed by any detailed study of labour history to be little more than a myth: aligning individual, sectional and broader collective interests has always involved a difficult effort in the structuring and mobilization of identity and consciousness. In this sense, the 'instrumental collectivism' attributed by British sociologists in the 1960s to a new, 'privatized' working class (Goldthorpe et al. 1968) has always formed one of the foundations of union organization. We may recall that the pioneering theoretical analysis of British unionism (Webb and Webb 1897) referred to the 'method of mutual insurance' as the earliest principle of working-class collectivism.

Nevertheless, there seems little doubt that real though complex changes in culture and consciousness have occurred, which present serious problems for traditional trade union practice. These affect, first, the readiness of employees to become and remain trade union members; second, their expectations from trade unionism (and hence to some extent, where alternatives exist, their choice of union); third, the relationship between trade union attachment and other interests and identities both within and outside employment. The last, in turn, influences both loyalty and participation: members' 'willingness to act' (Offe and Wiesenthal 1985) in terms of both involvement in the internal life of the union and readiness to follow its advice or instructions (particularly in the face of contrary appeals from other sources).

Hence the decline in union membership which has occurred in most European countries, while certainly influenced by structural changes in employment, may at the same time be seen as a reflection of attitudinal shifts (see chapter 4). Although the sharp reduction in industrial disputes which was an even more notable feature of the 1980s in many national systems was certainly shaped by the harsh economic climate, it may also be interpreted, in part, as a sign of diminished mobilizing potential. (In addition, the growing proportion of trade unionists working in the public services face the dilemma – or in extreme cases, crisis of conscience – that any industrial action has its immediate impact on the consumer rather than the employer, and may have the consequence of alienating popular sympathy.) The increasing numbers of female employees bring new concerns to industrial relations but face particular obstacles in achieving effective representation in trade union policy formation, a source of a variety of potential conflicts and tensions (Bakker 1988). Trade unions in many countries report serious difficulties in persuading younger workers, even if they take up membership, to participate in union activities and accept representative positions: there is a disjuncture, it is suggested, between the traditional trade union agenda and the aspirations and interests of a new generation of workers (Görner 1993).

Here too, challenges to established trade union practice may also constitute opportunities. To continue to attract members, trade unions are obliged to reformulate their rationale: to the extent that traditional objectives have lost their relevance or credibility in new circumstances, workers' interests must be reassessed and redefined. As traditional – and typically hierarchical and bureaucratic – modes of internal organization become ineffectual, systems of communication and decision-making must be reshaped to suit the realities of social relations in the 1990s (not, as so often, the 1890s). As conventional methods of struggle appear to have diminished in effectiveness, or to hit the wrong target, so trade unions are in many cases led to re-evaluate the nature and purpose of collective action, and reappraise the dynamics of social and economic power.

Reformulating the Issues: How (far) can Trade Unions Influence their own Future?

How far, in practice, have European unions succeeded in turning challenges into opportunities? A comprehensive and systematic answer is scarcely possible: the detailed evidence is not obtainable cross-nationally in a form available to a single author. A firmly grounded assessment would require a massive task of comparative research.

The problem is, however, not only a matter of information but also of conceptualization. To guide inquiry and understanding, appropriate tools of analysis must be developed. The principal concern of the remainder of this chapter is therefore to suggest ways of organizing and interrogating the complex experience of trade unions in different countries.

Experience is complex, among other reasons, because the dynamics of trade unionism entail a series of constraints and determinants, in some cases mutually reinforcing, in others contradictory. Trade union identity may be viewed as both the point of origin and the end-result of these interconnecting processes, which I term interests, democracy, agenda and power. Their interrelationship is presented schematically below; I go on to discuss each in turn.

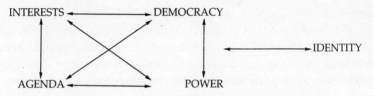

Figure 5.1 A model of trade union dynamics

Interests

Whatever other characteristics they may possess, trade unions are universally organizations for the representation of interests. It is important to note that this is true in a double sense: unions (and union movements) act on behalf of specific constituencies, with criteria of inclusion which of necessity are at the same time principles of exclusion; and they focus on distinctive aspects of their constituents' individual and collective experiences.

The question of constituencies comprises in part the issue of trade union structure: whether unions recruit from an occupationally or sectorally narrowly demarcated group of employees, or whether they are more 'encompassing' (Olson 1982: 47–8) in their coverage. Yet other important issues are also involved. First, in what respects and in what circumstances do unions act as private interest organizations, concerned exclusively with their actual members, as against identifying with a broader constituency? The distinction between a 'private' and a 'public' orientation refers partly to the relationship between union members and non-members within the same employment unit (who may all be seen as candidates for union representation, or as radically separate – and perhaps opposed – groups); partly to the degree to which separate unions are able and willing to harmonize their strategies of interest representation; and partly to the extent to which the interests of such sections of the community as pensioners and the unemployed (who in most countries have not traditionally been recruitment targets of trade unions) influence their policy-making.

Second, how far do unions frame and pursue the interests of their own memberships in ways which exclude and oppose those of other constituencies (whether unionized or non-unionized); and how do unions – particularly those with heterogeneous memberships – reconcile internal differences of interest? The future of trade unionism, Freyssinet (1993: 9; my translation) has suggested, rests on 'its capacity to construct a global project around which can be built alliances to render partially contradictory interests sufficiently convergent'. There are obvious differences in national experience: for example, IG Metall has succeeded in aligning its policies with those of public sector unions in Germany, avoiding the damaging conflicts which weakened the cohesion of their Swedish counterparts (Swenson 1992). At another level, Leisink (1993) has shown how differing occupational and gender interests among unionists in the printing industry have been more effectively aligned in The Netherlands than in Britain. In both these examples, differences in organizational structure were important though not all-important in shaping the outcomes; the evidence is that strategy does make a difference.

Most unions, whatever their egalitarian pretensions, have typically been biased in the composition of their officials and activists towards relatively high-status, male, native-born, full-time employees. Intentionally or otherwise, the programmes developed in collective bargaining, and even more crucially those issues assigned real priority, reflect the dominant concerns of these hegemonic groups. The question increasingly recognized in recent years is how far union interest representation can genuinely include constituencies formerly marginalized as a result of such factors as gender, ethnicity and employment status.

Representation of interests also concerns the more elusive question of human needs and aspirations which are held relevant for trade union action. Here, the key issue is the extent to which workers – and their representatives – regard employment as a largely self-contained sphere of social existence generating a clearly bounded set of industrial relations problems, or as an aspect of their lives so interconnected with other experiences and social relations that unions must necessarily range widely in their activities. Here, the question of interests links directly to that of the trade union agenda, to be discussed below.

Historically, there seems to have been a definite reciprocity between the two dimensions of interest representation. In general, unions based upon narrow membership constituencies have limited their concerns to specific job-related questions; more encompassing organizations have often addressed a wider range of issues. To the extent that unions are having to grapple with the tensions resulting from increased differentiation among their constituents, how far is this encouraging a more extensive view of the qualitative range of interests to be represented? Such a tendency is perhaps illustrated by the German metalworkers' programme *Tarifreform 2000* (IG Metall 1991). Its emphasis on the expansion of training opportunities and the harmonization of pay scales, as well as issues of working conditions and collective control of production, can be interpreted as a deliberate effort to address concerns shared by women and men, higher- and lower-skilled, manual and white-collar, and in ways which permit a reconciliation of potentially conflicting interests.

'Interests can only be met to the extent that they are partly re-defined' (Offe and Wiesenthal 1985: 184). It is a sociological truism that the elusive notion of interests has both objective and subjective dimensions, and that the relationship between the two is never fixed. Through their own internal processes of communication, discussion and debate – the 'mobilization of bias' – unions can help shape workers' own definitions of their individual and collective interests. Cumulatively, the outcomes compose the patterns of commonality and conflict among the interests of different groups and hence contribute to the dynamics of sectionalism and solidarity within labour movements. How far unions in fact attempt to redefine interests, and possess the organizational capacities to do so successfully, certainly varies considerably both between and within countries.

Democracy

Organizational capacity relates problematically to union democracy: the forms of membership participation and relationships among and within leaderships, activists, and the membership more generally. To speak of trade unions as social actors is in one sense a reification. Organizations do not act: specific individuals and groups act in their name and with their resources (and may be constitutionally authorized to do so). Yet reification is not (or not only) a logical error: it reflects social reality. Social organizations embody traditions, routines and norms which constrain the actions of members and officials. Trade unions, as 'historical deposits and repositories of history' (Turner 1962: 14), possess an organizational facticity which is often resistant to creativity and innovation.

Trade unions are, however, organizationally distinctive in possessing a democratic rationale: their claims to representativeness of their constituency rest on the existence and actual functioning of internal structures of accountability to membership interests. (As in any other organization, reality may differ from rhetoric.) Since the Webbs, it has been common to distinguish between two models of union democracy: participative and representative. This distinction is often linked to what may be termed the 'efficiency *versus* democracy' thesis: the argument that unions' capacity to act effectively on behalf of their members is inhibited if membership participation in policy-making is direct and organic, and facilitated if democratic procedures are purely formal and indirect. As I have argued elsewhere (for example, Hyman 1975: chapter 3), such arguments are tendentious. Without membership participation it impossible to establish that the interests which trade unions represent (however 'efficiently') are indeed those with which members identify; and without active involvement, the capacity to mobilize collective resources – power – in support of these interests is constrained. As Regalia has put it (1988: 361), 'unions are orgnizations in which the (democratic) requirement of responsibility and receptiveness to rank-and-file preferences is also a condition for survival itself'. It may be persuasively argued that the bureaucratic-hierarchical model of union organization which follows logically from the efficiency-*versus*-democracy argument has itself contributed greatly to the subjective alienation or disenchantment within trade union constituencies which underlies many of the unions' contemporary problems.

A different critique of union democracy is that of Streeck (1988: 316), who suggests that 'democracy and solidarity may have become incompatible'. In his view, increasing differentiation of interests within trade union constituencies means that intra- and inter-union conflict can be contained only where centralized authority rather than rank-and-file democracy prevails. This thesis could be related to Turner's distinction between 'exclusive democracies' and 'popular bossdoms' as models of British union development: according to his analysis (which has strong resonances with that of the Webbs), activist democracy was viable only in small unions with an occupationally homogeneous membership; larger, more heterogeneous unions could be held together only with strong central discipline, often given legitimacy by membership loyalty to a charismatic leader. It is important to stress that centralizing and authoritarian tendencies can also be externally driven; for example, the pressures to gain external legitimation have contributed to the retreat of the Spanish Comisiones Obreras from the spontaneist traditions of *asambleísmo* (Martínez Lucio 1992: 92).

This analysis, though consistent with much historical evidence, can also be questioned. Pragmatically, it is doubtful whether solidarity can be imposed: to be effective it must be debated and negotiated. If recent European experience is indeed of a fragmented and often mutually frustrating pursuit of particularistic interests, this reflects in part the degree to which 'solidarity' within national trade union movements was formerly mechanically enforced rather than organically generated. Conceptually, the analysis is also deficient unless the relationship between democracy and leadership is clarified. Historically, the syndicalist view that leadership and activist democracy were incompatible was often reciprocated by bureaucratic leaders – as an argument for restricting democracy. However, the issue is less straightforward: there are different types and meanings of leadership, just as there are different types and meanings of democracy. For contemporary European trade unionism a vital question is whether, and how, the two may be reconciled. Resolving these dilemmas is the more difficult, it may be added, precisely because of the compositional changes in employment and union membership which have already been discussed. In general, traditions of decentralized, participative union democracy have been strongest among skilled, male, manual workers in whose image trade unionism itself has traditionally been formed. Workers without similar labour market advantages, occupational culture and patriarchal assertiveness lack the same basis for upward control within their unions. Yet do 'new' types of trade unionists bring alternative resources to the task of constructing new forms of union democracy?

It is indeed clear that large national organizations cannot function on the basis of decentralized spontaneity alone. Unions are

> not simple mouthpieces of their members. Their bargaining power rests not only on their organizational strength but also on their ability to interpret, aggregate and select the demands of their actual and potential members and translate them into strategic choices. (Dufour and Hege 1992: 407; my translation)

Hence there is a need for co-ordination and strategic planning, and the current challenges faced by unions make this need the more urgent. What is less clear is whether bureaucratic forms of centralization and leadership are a necessary, or an adequate, response to this need. Formal meetings, hierarchical structures of decision-making, constitutionally prescribed positions of official authority – not only Weber's defining characteristics of bureaucratic organization, but also the structures of his 'iron cage' precluding autonomy and creativity – have traditionally provided the main model of trade union organization. Within some European unions, recent years have seen a search for alternative organizational forms – facilitated by advances in the technology of telecommunications and microelectronics – which might reconcile the possibilities of leadership and democracy, and by enhancing union adaptability in a rapidly changing environment also contribute to greater effectiveness. Experimentation with networks, working groups or discussion circles has become increasingly common: partly to meet the needs of more member-friendly organization, but also to rebuild a relationship between leaders, activists and ordinary members in ways which make strategic initiative effective because democratically developed.

Agenda

The agenda of trade unions may be defined as the expression in action of the interests which they seek to represent, and also the outcome of their internal processes of democracy and leadership. It encompasses not only the demands pursued in collective bargaining with employers, but also the subjects covered by public campaigns, political lobbying and negotiations with governments.

Identifying the formal agenda is relatively straightforward: it is documented in conference resolutions, programmatic declarations, bargaining submissions, publicity briefings and internal communication media. However, union leaders and representatives are usually adept at constructing an agenda sufficiently comprehensive to reflect the specific interests of the broadest possible cross-section of their constituents. Nevertheless, any negotiation – whether in collective bargaining or 'political exchange' (Pizzorno 1978) – requires processes of give-and-take, in which each party concedes elements of its formal agenda in exchange for success in others. Which items are abandoned, and which pursued with more persistence, not only depends in part on the dynamics of the bargaining relationship, but also reflects a structure of priorities which is more often implicit than explicit. (Indeed, to admit the existence of priorities is virtually to concede that certain demands are largely tokenistic.) Yet to the extent that the *real* agenda of any union is defined by such priorities, its nature has to be inferred from actual practice and cannot simply be identified with formal declarations.

It is common in the analysis of collective bargaining to distinguish between quantitative and qualitative demands. The first type covers the terms of the market exchange between workers and employers: wages and other financial compensations for employment, and hours of work. Traditionally these issues have been central to the collective bargaining agenda, precisely because, it is usually argued, quantitative demands do not challenge managerial authority, their cost to the employer can be readily calculated, and they permit many gradations of compromise settlement. Where collective agreements apply across a whole industry, quantitative negotiation may traditionally have even been welcomed by employers as a means of taking labour costs out of competition; while trade unions – at least those with established bargaining relationships with employers – have tended to give priority to those issues on which concessions are most likely to be offered.

Qualitative demands, by contrast, are those which concern the actual conditions of work, the determination of effort levels and the control of production. To the extent that these put in question the employer's 'right to manage' they have often been strongly resisted: for example, providing the rationale for several lock-outs in the history of British engineering industrial relations, and forming the content of the German employers' notorious *Tabukatalog*. Traditionally, the expectation of powerful opposition has often inhibited unions from pursuing such demands, at least as part of their 'real' agenda.

It is a familiar theme of comparative industrial relations that the late 1960s and 1970s saw a radicalization of the trade union agenda, in part a consequence of increased rank-and-file militancy and assertiveness (and linked by some theorists to the rise of the lower-skilled 'mass worker' as a key actor), and that pressure for concessions on qualitative demands resulted in major official disputes in many countries. The point has been made, however (for example, Kirchlechner 1978: 175–6), that many qualitative demands and grievances were diluted and reduced 'to an economic core' within official union policy-making in order to facilitate compromise in negotiations with employers. To the extent that this occurred, potentially disruptive discontents became institutionalized.

How have such dynamics been affected by a decade or more of economic crisis? Several propositions may be suggested. First, increased transnational competitiveness and a shift in the balance of regulation between multi-employer and single-employer levels mean that quantitative demands are less of a 'soft' option for trade unions than in former times. Second, many qualitative demands have obvious cost implications. For example, the Swedish demand for 'good work' (Kjellberg 1992) may have been presented as consistent with quality-conscious firms' interest in developing non-Taylorist forms of work organization; however, experience in the 1990s suggests that employers, under the pressure of cost competition, are returning to more traditional systems of production – as shown, for example, by Volvo's closure of its showpiece 'humanized' plants at Kalmar and Uddevalla (Cressey 1993; Sandberg 1993). The notion of a consensual strategy to increase the quality of working life now seems manifestly utopian. Accordingly, trade union policy-makers are caught between the twin constraints of shaping an agenda which will attract, by reflecting the interests of, the changing constituencies which they seek to represent;

yet which at the same time will be realistically attainable either by negotiations with cost-conscious employers or through political channels which are themselves conditioned by sensitivity to issues of national competitiveness.

One response is to focus on the 'qualitative' dimensions of contemporary managerial discourse. 'Humanizing human resource management' is a slogan which has gained some resonance among British unions in the 1990s.[2] Increasing union concern, across Europe, with the issue of initial and further vocational education and training indicates an attempt to frame an agenda which can be legitimated in productivist terms while appealing to members' own interests. Another direction of agenda reconstruction is an emphasis on procedural demands – from new institutions of workplace consultation to European works councils – which have no necessary and direct cost implications for companies (though indeed challenging traditional 'employer prerogatives'). A key question has to be the extent to which different types of union agenda in the 1990s are conceived as susceptible to 'positive-sum' (and hence consensual) resolution. In part the answer is shaped by different national (and union) traditions: social partnership as against more adversarial relationships. However, central also are perceptions and dynamics of power.

Power

Power is almost certainly the most contentious and elusive concept in social analysis. It is not my intention here to review the general debate, which is, however, relevant in indicating that trade union power has at least three dimensions: first, the ability to achieve unions' objectives in the face of resistance; second, winning an institutional or legal framework within which their agenda is better able to be realized; third, the capacity to influence attitudes and perceptions – of employers, governments, the 'general public' and their own members – so as to create a favourable ideological climate. It should be added that the fashioning of trade union power entails an uphill struggle. Labour is at a disadvantage at the levels of both social action (large employers have far greater resources than workers and far closer links to political elites and opinion leaders) and social structure (in a competitive market economy, there is an underlying socio-economic dynamic privileging employers' pursuit of profitable production). Despite familiar stereotypes of trade unions as 'overmighty subjects', the reality is that even the most cohesive and strategically sophisticated of workers' collective organizations can only partly offset the structured imbalance of power which confronts them.

Power does not exist in isolation from concrete issues: it varies according to the questions in contention, precisely because the ability of all parties to industrial relations to mobilize material and ideological resources is in part issue-specific. Hence the question of power links to that of the union agenda. Moreover, unions, as organizations of the relatively powerless, cannot derive significant power from a simple quantitative addition of their members' individual resources; power requires a qualitative transformation, based on a collective 'willingness to act' (Offe and Wiesenthal 1985), which in turn depends on appropriate internal processes of information, consultation, discussion and decision-making. Such internal dynamics (what in Germany is known as *Willensbildung*) connect power to the dimension of union democracy and union leadership. Further, 'willingness to act' is necessarily dependent on the centrality with which issues affect the interests which unions seek to represent, and their success in persuading their constituencies that action (and even sacrifice) is indeed essential to defend and advance these interests. Hence power and interests are intertwined.

Within most national labour movements it has been traditionally assumed that trade union power derives primarily from the capacity to strike, which thus represents 'a trade union's capacity to realize its demands' (Müller-Jentsch 1985: 22). Most academic contributions within labour economics and game theory have similarly identified the relative power of unions and employers with their (actual or anticipated) relative preparedness to resist the demands of their counterparts in collective bargaining. If this is indeed the essential foundation of union power, a pessimistic reading of recent trends is unavoidable. In almost the whole of western Europe, strike activity has diminished – often substantially – since the 1970s (see chapter 10); in France, where the decline has been among the sharpest, Goetschy and Rozenblatt (1992: 416) have written of a 'crisis of militancy'. According to most conventional analyses, adverse economic circumstances reduce the preparedness of unions and their members to strike. (Even though some of those strikes which do occur may be unusually bitter and protracted, these are typically defensive and most often unsuccessful.) In a number of countries, governments have increased the legislative obstacles to effective strikes. And as has already been indicated, sectoral and occupational changes in employment and union membership as well as underlying cultural shifts are commonly interpreted as restraining strikes: because workers feel vulnerable to employers' counter-sanctions; or lack the strategic capacity to cause rapid disruption of production which many traditional workers possessed; or feel inhibited by professional norms or loyalties to clients; or have lost the will or confidence necessary for effective collective action.

Some unions have indeed attempted to overcome these difficulties. In Germany, imaginative methods of mobilizing members – *neue Beweglichkeit* – through brief demonstration stoppages and selective strikes have achieved some success. In Britain, the legal obligation to hold pre-strike ballots has stimulated more effective methods of internal union communication and campaigning, and thus paradoxically is seen as a source of greater collective strength. In Italy – as in the years around the 'hot autumn' of 1968 – unofficial militants have shown considerable ingenuity in devising forms of action which cause disruption at mimimal cost to the workers concerned.

It is, however, necessary to emphasize that many of the efforts to rebuild unions' strike capacity have qualitative connotations: what is typically intended is not the strike as trial of strength, as familiar in economists' models as in labour iconography, but rather the strike as symbolic demonstration. If this is a power resource, its significance is often socio-political rather than narrowly economic. The importance of this point is that the traditional conception of the strike as an endurance test between union and employer addresses only the first dimension of union power identified above: the direct impact on the outcomes of collective bargaining. If union power at this level has diminished, the possibility of compensating influence at other levels becomes the more important.

Here the concept of political exchange is relevant. In introducing this notion, Pizzorno (1978: 278–80) raised the question: how, when an employer decides to close an 'uneconomic' factory, can a union sometimes prevent this? For the workers in the factory to strike can have no impact, at least in simple economic terms, since the employer no longer wants their labour. Pizzorno's answer rests on the distinction between three different types of bargaining. The individual contract between worker and employer consists of an exchange between pay and work performance. Collective bargaining between unions and employers (or their associations) exchanges standardized improvements in the terms of employment for predictability and regularity in workplace social relations. In political exchange, the government makes concessions to trade unions (in the example above, endeavouring to keep the factory open) in return for union support for social order and legitimacy. In this sense, the political equivalent of the strike is the mobilization of protest, dissent and even disorder (perhaps indeed including strike militancy).

This analysis differs in important respects from 'neo-corporatist' interpretations of union–government relations, familiar for several decades in northern Europe. Within corporatist theories, unions are seen as achieving political influence as a reward for restraint in collective bargaining: governments gain industrial peace, price stability and a favourable climate for investment; unions in return obtain a favourable social and macroeconomic regime. The 'political economy of distribution' (Hibbs 1978) is thus shifted from the industrial to the political arena. Yet in this analysis, unions' ability to win economic gains through the 'political market-place' rests ultimately on their industrial strength; political marginalization thus follows logically from reduced strike capacity.[3] It is for this reason that Müller-Jentsch (1988: 179–80) has spoken of a 'crisis of political exchange' accompanying economic crisis.

The implications of economic stringency for what may be termed the 'Italian model' of political exchange are, however, different. In this perspective, unions relate to governments less as vehicles of economic restraint than as representatives of social interests. Under an unstable political system in which the popular legitimacy of government is uncertain – precisely the situation in the Italian 'blocked democracy' since the second world war – trade union endorsement of government action offers a valuable *political* resource. (Similar concerns have applied in other southern European countries re-establishing democratic institutions after dictatorship, though here, political exchange has often been complicated by inter-union ideological conflicts more severe than in Italy.) Today, governments across Europe struggle to manage new social tensions when their own freedom of action at national level seems increasingly constrained, and when the social consensus supporting traditional political institutions faces new challenges. It could be argued that in such a context, the value of trade unions as participants in political exchange is enhanced rather than diminished, and hence that other European countries are likely to learn Italian.

However, what governments can offer in such circumstances is tightly constrained – as the Spanish government, for example, made very clear, even while declaring its support for the principle of concertation, in the aftermath of the 1993 general election. Thus the key issue for unions is the costs and benefits of political exchange in such a situation. The costs are the potential alienating effects on their constituencies if unions support unpopular policies (which helps explain why German unions were not directly party to the 'solidarity pact' designed to share the costs of unification). The benefits depend on unions' strategic skill and cohesion, their ability to formulate a credible agenda to pursue within political exchange,[4] and their past and current success in developing the second and third dimensions of power identified previously.

This implies an extension – or rediscovery – of unions' role as campaigning organizations: effective participation in political exchange must be supported by the mobilization of bias at societal level. Unions and union movements which have achieved greater success in this respect are those which have helped generate broad definitions of membership interests, formulated and propagated an extensive agenda, and cultivated alliances with social movements whose concerns overlap with theirs. For example: unions which link the defence of public transport to a more general consumer and environmental agenda are able to mobilize greater influence than those which focus solely on their members' employment interests. The search for allies outside their own immediate membership is necessarily linked to an overt commitment to a wide definition of interest representation. If trade unions' (relative) success in pursuing political economism in the first post-war decades rested on a conception of economic power which is now deprived of many of its material foundations, the complex challenge of cultivating new forms of social and political power must be met if they are to sustain a relevance and effectiveness.

Identity

Trade union identity relates dialectically to the interconnecting dynamics of interests, democracy, agenda and power. Historically, as suggested previously, three main identities either struggled for supremacy or else coexisted. The first viewed unions as interest organizations with exclusively labour market functions; the second treated them as vehicles for raising workers' status more generally and hence advancing social justice; the third regarded them as 'schools of war' in a struggle between labour and capital. The dominant identities embraced by particular unions, confederations and national movements – themselves reflecting the specific national context in which workers' organizations historically emerged (Crouch 1993) – have necessarily helped shape the interests with which they identify, the conceptions of democracy informing members, activists and leaders, the agenda they pursue, and the type of power resources which they cultivate and apply. Identities may be viewed as inherited traditions which shape current choices, which in normal circumstances in turn reinforce and confirm identities.

Yet in a period of crisis, trade unions – like any other organization – may be driven to choices (redefinition of interests, new systems of internal relations, broadening or narrowing of agenda, altered power tactics) at least partly at odds with traditional identities. As this occurs, the question 'what are we here for?' (the words of a former general secretary of the British Trades Union Congress) has to be addressed. To the extent that old beliefs, slogans and commitments – the ideological supports of union self-conceptions – are undermined, an explicit and plausible redefinition of trade union purpose is essential if 'the capacity itself of labour movements to pursue the social and political construction of solidarity' (Regini 1992: 13) is to be salvaged. The future of trade unions 'will depend above all on . . . whether we find a new way of conceiving and practising trade unionism' (Accornero 1992: 42; my translation).

There have been few examples of European trade unions explicitly and systematically reviewing their identities, though there have been some. In Italy, for instance, the formerly communist-linked CGIL confederation devoted its 1991 congress to a self-critical assessment of its past and a programmatic reorientation to a post-communist present. To sustain a role in the future, it concluded, the union must build solidarity by campaigning actively for a programme of rights which integrates workers' interests as employees and as citizens (CGIL 1991). In Germany, the DGB has launched a wide-ranging discussion of future strategy (*Zukunftdebatte*) in which fundamental questions of trade union identity are posed. How extensively such initiatives affect members and activists, and how far they are more than ceremonial in terms of their impact on actual practice and hence real union identity, is not altogether clear. Nevertheless, it is evident at least that there is growing awareness that old identities are increasingly inadequate.

Strategy or structure? One assessment of the German discussion of future scenarios notes 'the paradox of an open debate within the "iron cage"' (von Randow 1993). Are unions seeking strategic choices when no room for choice remains? In the face of powerful external forces, how far can European unions survive as subjects rather than merely objects of history? The answer depends to an important extent on how far union strategists can distinguish the necessary from the contingent in current socio-economic transformations, identifying space for realistic yet imaginative intervention. Any plausible alternative identity must satisfy these essential though difficult criteria.

Towards the Millennium: Alternative Trade Union Identities

Analysing American trade unions almost half a century ago, Mills (1948) described their leaders as 'managers of discontent'. To ensure members' continued identification with union organization, it was necessary to maintain their consciousness of employment grievances and unsatisfied aspirations; yet to achieve a stable relationship with employers, dissatisfaction had to be contained and regulated. As many subsequent authors indicated, this process of 'antagonistic co-operation' could become a precarious enterprise. In Germany, Müller-Jentsch (1985) has likewise sketched the tensions provoked when unions, as 'intermediary organizations', face the risks of excessive militancy (antagonizing employers) or excessive co-operation (alienating the membership). Where union identity is shaped by the business union model, these contradictory pressures are almost inevitably intensified in times of economic stringency: the margin for mediation disappears. Famously, Sam Gompers, the most forceful protagonist of the American business union model, described his organization's objectives in the single word: 'more'. A similar 'common-sense' response is hardly available in an era of concession bargaining.

Political economism provided scope for a broader identity than Gompers' 'pure-and-simple unionism': although collective bargaining might constitute the core of day-to-day union priorities, intervention in the political arena – however pragmatically informed – could be presented as an expression of more radical ideological traditions. Nevertheless, the contradictions stemming from the 'dual character' of trade unionism (Zoll 1976) remained: unions acted as mediators between workers and governments as well as employers, and bargaining at macroeconomic level generated inter- as well as intra-union tensions. As suggested earlier, the progressive character of political economism depended on favourable economic conditions; in hard times, it no longer offers the basis for a coherent trade union identity.

What alternatives are available? Four emergent identities may be suggested, and are presented in table 5.1.

The first model, premised on an irreversible displacement of collectivism by individualism, sees the future of unions as providers of services to workers as individuals. Though presented by some advocates (Bassett and Cave 1993) as a distinctively new trade union identity, this has indeed an ancient heritage: the earliest unions devel-

Table 5.1 Trade union identities

Focus of Action	Key Function	Ideal Type
Individual worker	Services	Friendly society
Management	Productivity coalition	Company union
Government	Political exchange	Social partner
Mass support	Campaigning	Social movement

oped out of societies providing 'friendly benefits' to their members. It should be noted, however, that there is a variable relationship between individual services and collective identity. The Webbs referred to the nineteenth-century role of such benefits as the 'method of mutual insurance' precisely because the system offered collective material support to individuals with common work-related interests. Or again: the traditional emphasis of many unions on supporting and representing individual workers in disputes with their employer addresses the vulnerability which is part of employees' shared experience in the employment relationship. Unions which offer a wider range of services may do so as a means of responding to a broader conception of workers' interests (although – as the *Neue Heimat* débâcle in Germany demonstrated – they will not necessarily prove more successful in fiercely competitive markets than dedicated building societies, banks or travel agencies). However, an organization whose sole or dominant identity is to provide commercial services to discrete customers is not easily recognizable as a trade union.

The second model adapts to the altered balance of power between unions and employers, and the structural pressures on firms to survive despite intensified competition. Here, the co-operative dimension of intermediary unionism is reinforced: the union becomes part of a 'productivity coalition' (Windolf 1989) with management, collaborating in policies to enhance company performance. Again, this is not necessarily a novel orientation: trade unions can scarcely neglect the commercial viability of their members' employers.[5] In Germany, 'company egoism' has long been recognized as a countervailing force to union efforts to build cross-employer solidarity; while in Italy, 'microcorporatism' or 'microconcertation' (Regini 1991) was a notable development of the 1980s. However, in adverse economic circumstances, company-level productivity coalitions can easily imply a competitive underbidding of either job protection or conditions of employment, with unionism organizationally intensifying the fault lines of intra- and international conflicts of employee interests. Fragmentation into company unionism along Japanese lines represents the ultimate logic of this model.

The model of trade unionism as interlocutor of government has already been discussed. This role has a firm basis in those countries where state benefits for unemployment, sickness and retirement are explicitly regarded as elements in the 'social wage', in the determination of which trade unions possess a legitimate representative status. It has clear antecedents in the tradition of political economism, and in both the 'northern' and the 'southern' European variants of political exchange. The dilemmas of social partnership parallel at macro level the micro-dilemmas of productivity coalitions: do unions sustain or even enhance their external representative status (recognition by employers and governments) only at the cost of internal representativity, by legitimizing painful policies without securing compensating benefits for their constituencies? As suggested earlier, to escape this dilemma it is essential for unions to pursue a distinctive agenda, oriented to the specific interests they claim to represent, and with the resources necessary for independent leverage within political exchange. In other words, political exchange is not viable as a self-contained activity of trade union leaders. They can represent a constituency only if organically bound to it by the dynamics of union democracy; and they can realistically pursue alternative strategies only by winning popular support. This is particularly true, it should be added, if trade unions attempt to develop mechanisms of political exchange at supranational level: the feeble results of 'social dialogue' within the EC reflect the failure to mobilize informed backing among unions' own constituents.

This leads to the final model: trade unions as populist campaigning organizations. Economic interest organization and social movement have been two of the ideal types often identified as polar opposites in the analysis of trade union character. What is significant is the degree to which, after many decades in which political economism seemed to displace strong ideological identities in most European trade union movements, the campaigning model previously associated with class or populist politics is being rehabilitated. The traditional tensions between interest organization and social movement cannot be ignored, however; not least because on many of the key socio-political issues (such as curbs on environmentally damaging industries, or taxation to sustain public services) there are conflicting interests among trade unionists themselves. Yet those unions – the majority –

whose membership base is unstable and whose traditional power resources are unreliable seem impelled to embrace at least some elements of the social movement model.

In practical terms, no trade union can fully assume any of these four identities; and if it could, it would no longer remain a trade union as that institution has traditionally been understood, at least in western Europe. Nevertheless, the contradictions of political economism in hard times generate a search for new identities, and European unions will increasingly give priority to one or other of the four outlined. The choices will reflect specific union traditions and also national contexts: as the millennium approaches, there are few reasons to expect the emergence of a standardized Euro-union.

Notes

1   This development in Britain has been documented by Millward et al. 1992.
2   The term was first used, I think, by (Lord) Bill McCarthy in a paper to the Trades Union Congress in 1991.
3   Part of the left critique of neo-corporatist theory was that union commitment to bargaining restraint tended to demobilize and alienate the membership, undermining the 'willingness to act' and thus reducing the need for governments to make concessions to labour in the political market-place.
4   Over a decade ago, Ross (1981) offered a comparative assessment of national union movement efforts to introduce 'Keynes-plus' programmes within political decision-making; his analysis remains relevant today.
5   Unless – as was at least theoretically the case in the 'golden age' of the Swedish industrial relations model – macro-level labour market policies ensured alternative employment opportunities for workers whose companies could not meet collectively agreed standards.

References

Accornero, A. 1992: *La Parabola del sindacato: ascesa e declino di una cultura*. Bologna: il Mulino.
Altvater, E. and Mahnkopf, B. 1993: *Gewerkschaften vor der europäischen Herausforderung: Tarifpolitik nach Mauer und Maastricht*. Münster: Westfälisches Dampfboot.
Bakker, I. 1988: Women's employment in comparative perspective. In J. Jenson, E. Hagen and C. Reddy (eds), *Feminization of the Labour Force: paradoxes and promises*, Cambridge: Polity Press, 17–44.
Bassett, P. and Cave, A. 1993: *All for One: the future of the unions*. London: Fabian Society.
CGIL 1991: *Strategia dei diritti: etica della solidarietà*. Rome: Ediesse.
Cressey, P. 1993: Kalmar and Uddevalla: the demise of Volvo as a European icon. *New Technology, Work and Employment*, 8, 88–90.

Crouch, C. 1986: The future prospects for trade unions in western Europe. *Political Quarterly*, 57, 5–17.

Crouch, C. 1990: Afterword. In G. Baglioni and C. Crouch (eds), *European Industrial Relations*, London: Sage Publications, 356–62.

Crouch, C. 1993: *Industrial Relations and European State Traditions*. Oxford: Clarendon Press.

Crouch, C. and Pizzorno, A. 1978: *The Resurgence of Class Conflict in Western Europe since 1968*, Vol. 2: *Comparative Analyses*. London: Macmillan.

Dufour, C. and Hege, A. 1992: Conclusion. In IRES, *Syndicalismes: dynamique des relations professionnelles*, Paris: Dunod, 399–427.

Ferner, A. and Hyman, R. (eds) 1992: *Industrial Relations in the New Europe*. Oxford: Blackwell Publishers.

Flanders, A. 1970: *Management and Unions: the theory and reform of industrial relations*. London: Faber.

Freyssinet, J. 1993: Syndicalismes en Europe. *Le Mouvement Social*, 162, 3–16.

Goetschy, J. and Rozenblatt, P. 1992: France: the industrial relations system at a turning point? In A. Ferner and R. Hyman (eds), 404–44.

Golden, M. 1992: Conclusion: current trends in trade union politics. In M. Golden and J. Pontusson (eds), 307–33.

Golden, M. and Pontusson, J. (eds) 1992: *Bargaining for Change: union politics in North America and Europe*. Ithaca: Cornell University Press.

Goldthorpe, J.H., Lockwood, D., Bechhofer, F. and Platt, J. 1968: *The Affluent Worker: industrial attitudes and behaviour*. Cambridge: Cambridge University Press.

Görner, R. 1993: DGB und Gewerkschaften müssen sich der Beteiligung Jugendlicher öffnen. *Die Mitbestimmung*, 4, 40–2.

Gulowsen, J. 1988: Skills, options and unions. In R. Hyman and W. Streeck (eds), *New Technology and Industrial Relations*, Oxford: Blackwell Publishers, 160–73.

Hibbs, D. 1978: The political economy of long-run trends in strike activity. *British Journal of Political Science*, 8, 153–77.

Hyman, R. 1975: *Industrial Relations: a Marxist introduction*. London: Macmillan.

Hyman, R. 1978: Occupational structure, collective organization and industrial militancy. In C. Crouch and A. Pizzorno (eds), 35–70.

Hyman, R. 1991: European unions: towards 2000. *Work, Employment and Society*, 5(4) 621–39.

Hyman, R. 1992: Trade unions and the disaggregation of the working class. In M. Regini (ed.), *The Future of Labour Movements*, London: Sage Publications, 150–68.

IG Metall 1991: *Tarifreform 2000: ein Gestaltungsrahmen für die Industriearbeit der Zukunft*. Frankfurt: IG Metall.

Kelly, J. 1990: British trade unionism 1979–89: change, continuity and contradictions. *Work, Employment and Society*, 4, Special Issue, 29–66.

Kern, H. and Schumann, M. 1986: *Das Ende der Arbeitsteilung?* Munich: Beck.

Kirchlechner, B. 1978: New demands or demands of new groups? Three case studies. In C. Crouch and A. Pizzorno (eds), 161–76.

Kjellberg, A. 1992: Sweden: Can the model survive? In A. Ferner and R. Hyman (eds), 88–142.

Korpi, W. 1983: *The Democratic Class Struggle*. London: Routledge.

Leisink, P. 1993: *Is Innovation a Management Prerogative? Changing employment relationships, innovative unions*. Coventry: Industrial Relations Research Unit.

Lockwood, D. 1958: *The Blackcoated Worker: a study in class consciousness*. London: Allen and Unwin.

Martínez Lucio, M. 1992: Spain: constructing institutions and actors in a context of change. In A. Ferner and R. Hyman (eds), 482–523.

Mills, C.W. 1948: *The New Men of Power: America's labor leaders*. New York: Harcourt, Brace.

Millward, N., Stevens, M., Smart, D. and Hawes, W.R. 1992: *Workplace Industrial Relations in Transition*. Aldershot: Dartmouth Publishing.

Müller-Jentsch, W. 1985: Trade unions as intermediary organizations. *Economic and Industrial Democracy*, 6, 3–33.

Müller-Jentsch, W. 1988: Industrial relations theory and trade union strategy. *International Journal of Comparative Labour Law and Industrial Relations*, 4(3) 177–90.

Offe, C. 1985: *Disorganized Capitalism*, Cambridge: Polity Press.

Offe, C. and Wiesenthal, H. 1985: Two logics of collective action. In C. Offe, 170–220.

Olson, M. 1982: *The Rise and Decline of Nations: economic growth, stagflation and social rigidities*. New Haven: Yale University Press.

Pérez-Díaz, V. 1987: Unions' uncertainties and workers' ambivalence. *International Journal of Political Economy*, 108–38.

Pizzorno, A. 1978: Political exchange and collective identity in industrial conflict. In C. Crouch and A. Pizzorno (eds), 277–98.

Pontusson, J. 1992: Introduction: organizational and political-economic perspectives on union politics. In M. Golden and J. Pontusson (eds), 1–41.

Regalia, I. 1988: Democracy and unions: towards a critical appraisal. *Economic and Industrial Democracy* 9(3) 345–71.

Regini, M. 1991: *Confini mobili: la construzione dell'economia fra politica e società*. Bologna: il Mulino.

Regini, M. 1992: Introduction: the past and future studies of labour movements. In M. Regini (ed.), *The Future of Labour Movements*, London: Sage Publications, 1–16.

Ross, G. 1981: What is progressive about unions? *Theory and Society*, 10(5) 609–43.

Rubery, J. 1978: Structured labour markets, worker organization and low pay. *Cambridge Journal of Economics*, 2(1) 17–36.

Sandberg, Å. 1993: Volvo human-centred work organization – the end of the road. *New Technology, Work and Employment*, 8, 83–7.

Scheuer, S. 1991: *Leaders and Laggards: who goes first in bargaining rounds?* Coventry: Industrial Relations Research Unit.

Scheuer, S. 1992: Denmark: return to decentralization. In A. Ferner and R. Hyman (eds), 168–97.

Streeck, W. 1988: Editorial Introduction. *Economic and Industrial Democracy*, 9(3) 307–17.

Swenson, P. 1992: Union politics, the welfare state, and intraclass conflict in Sweden and Germany. In M. Golden and J. Pontusson (eds), 45–76.

Turner, H.A. 1962: *Trade Union Growth, Structure and Policy*. London: Allen and Unwin.

von Randow, M. 1993: Gewerkschaftliche Zukunftsdiskussion im DGB – aber wie? *Gewerkschaftliche Monatshefte*, 6/93, 375–85.

Webb, S. and Webb, B. 1897: *Industrial Democracy*, London: Longman.

Windolf, P. 1989: Productivity coalitions and the future of European corporatism.

Industrial Relations, 28(1) 1–20.
Zoll, R. 1976: *Der Doppelcharakter der Gewerkschaften: zur Aktualität der Marxschen Gewerkschaftstheorie*. Frankfurt: Suhrkamp.
Zoll, R. 1982: Krise und Solidarität. *Gewerkschaftliche Monatshefte*, 4/82, 222–6.

6

Does Feminization Mean a Flexible Labour Force?

Jill Rubery and Colette Fagan

Introduction

Labour market developments in Europe over the past decade have displayed two common features: a continuous feminization of the labour force, and moves to deregulate the labour market and supposedly increase its flexibility. These two developments are often seen as interconnected, with women providing the flexible labour force to be deployed in low-paid casual or part-time work. Despite a narrowing of the gender gap in participation rates, persistent differentiation in the character and use of female and male occupations has encouraged the view that female labour may play a particular role in the 'flexibilization' of the labour market.

However, recent research into women's employment and labour market organization has revealed that similar trends and patterns between countries mask significant differences in both the intensity and the form of moves towards flexibility. Given variations in the initial extent of labour market regulation, a major push towards deregulation in one country might still leave it with a higher level of labour standards and more effective regulation than were present in another country before deregulation began (Brunhes 1988; Rubery 1988). Not only is there little evidence of convergence in the degree of regulation, there is also widespread evidence of continued differentiation in labour markets and patterns of work organization. Various authors have suggested that some countries may be pursuing labour market strategies aimed at positive flexibility, developing a more skilled labour force and a more responsive industrial system, while others may be attempting, more negatively, to intensify the pace of work, shift risk to employees and minimize costs (Lane 1991).

The implications of such forms of work as self- or part-time employment may differ according to their prevalence and function in national industrial systems (Rubery 1988; Rodgers and Rodgers 1989). For example, part-time work may be used to reduce total labour hours and even to reduce average wage levels, or alternatively to retain skilled workers in their jobs over the period of childbearing. Similarly, self-employment may be a means to a flexibly specialized system of industrial production and organization as is found particularly in the 'third Italy', or alternatively a reaction to unemployment or a development from the growth of services and the contracting out of peripheral activities.

Equally complex problems arise when we look in more detail at the increasing feminization of labour markets. Again there are strong and certainly more than superficial similarities in the position of women across countries. Women still have lower participation rates than men and are more likely to be employed as part-time or temporary workers (Meulders and Plasman 1989; Meulders et al. 1993; Rodgers and Rodgers 1989). Occupational segregation is still a major feature of all European labour markets and is increasing for some groups of women (Rubery and Fagan 1993). Finally, women consistently earn less than men across Europe even in the same occupations or industries (Blau and Kahn 1992; Equal Opportunities Commission 1992; Rubery 1992a).

However, set against these common characteristics, and against the tendency for gender segregation and differentiation to be constantly renewed and recreated even when previous patterns of differentiation break down, must be put the evidence of surprising variations in the experience of women between countries.

Characteristics that are often taken as central to women's disadvantage in employment in one European country are found not to hold in others. For example, women in Britain are extensively employed in part-time work, and the birth of a child frequently leads to withdrawal from the labour market. Yet this is not true elsewhere, so that the issue of what happens to 'women returners' is less important outside Britain (Dex and Walters 1989).

Different systems of pay determination and regulation, and differential access to social security payments, change the relative risk of women receiving very low wages or suffering discrimination in the pay structure because of lack of seniority, lack of qualifications or biased assessments of merit. Different systems of pay determination influence not only the overall gender pay gap, but also which particular groups of women are likely to be low paid (CERC 1992; Rubery 1992a). Moreover, different systems of training and patterns of work organization can change the quality of work in female-dominated areas, affecting job content, skill and productivity, although not necessarily relative pay levels (O'Reilly 1992; Gregory 1991; Prais et al. 1989; Jarvis and Prais 1989; Steedman 1987; Steedman and Wagner 1989).

Despite this evidence of diversity we still have to confront the continued differentiation in women's and men's employment position in all countries. This cannot be explained solely by the organization of sexual relations; the specific form of gender differentiation within the workplace can only be understood with reference to the interaction between the different elements of the economic and social system.

The Relationship between Feminization and Flexibility: an Institutional Framework for Analysis

Figure 6.1 summarizes four sets of economic and social institutions relevant to the analysis of labour market flexibility. The interrelationship between the different domains is conceptualized as a dynamic process, complete with tensions and contradictions, and not as a harmonious and static structure (Rubery 1992b: 249). No one set of institutions determines the operation of another.

The system of social reproduction includes both familial and state systems of childrearing and support for the unemployed and inactive. Included here are formal state regulations which define social entitlements and responsibilities in relation to both the welfare state and the domestic sphere of support for 'dependent' family members (Wilson 1977; Lewis 1983; Glendinning and Millar 1987). Social attitudes to labour market participation, particularly for women, young and older people also come within this sphere. It is perhaps in this domain that the structuring of gender relations is most apparent, with the sexual division of labour in the home and the welfare state creating a pool of female secondary workers to provide a flexible labour supply. However, both historical and national comparative analysis demonstrates that the organization of social reproduction is neither independent of, nor determined by, wider economic and political pressures; rather the system is relatively autonomous (Humphries and Rubery 1984).

Therefore, to understand any links between feminization and flexibility, the structuring of labour supply must be analysed in conjunction with the other sets of institutions identified in figure 6.1. Gender relations permeate each category because of the different em-

LABOUR MARKET REGULATION
Legal regulation
(i) employment rights
(ii) fiscal system
(iii) regulation of collective bargaining

Voluntary regulation
(i) regulation at industry, occupation
or market level
(ii) regulation at company or
establishment level

SOCIAL REPRODUCTION

Familial and state systems of support
for:
(i) childrearing
(ii) unemployed and inactive

Social attitudes to participation

Domestic division of labour

INDUSTRIAL SYSTEM
Industrial composition and
organization
(i) sectoral composition
(ii) size distribution of firms and
ownership
(iii) systems of vertical/horizontal
integration

Organization practices
(i) employer policies and competitive
strategies
(ii) institutional systems of work and
employment organization

LABOUR MARKET SYSTEM

Labour market flows
(i) between non-employment,
unemployment and employment
(ii) between training and employment
(iii) job moves within firms or
between firms
(iv) between non-standard or atypical
work and non-employment/
unemployment and permanent/full-
time employment

Source: adapted from Rubery 1989b: figure 8.1

Figure 6.1 Framework for the analysis of labour market flexibility

ployment positions of women and men. The labour market system covers movements between non-employment and employment, between training and employment, and between job positions within the labour market. It also affects whether atypical or non-standard employment represents an escape route from unemployment or non-employment, or a trap into permanently insecure employment. Labour market flows are critical to understanding, for example, the impact of discontinuous employment on women's career opportunities, and their participation in flexible employment forms. These flows differ between countries, with those countries having systems based on internal labour markets exacting greater penalties for discontinuity than those based on occupational labour markets (Eyraud et al. 1990; Marsden 1986).

The industrial system provides the demand-side picture to the pattern of flexible employment. It includes both the aggregate industrial structure and the specific organizational practices within the firms that make up the industrial system. These practices arise out of the actions of the actors within the system – out of the competitive strategies adopted by employers in relation to product markets and the labour process, and the patterns of pay, working-time and work organization that are negotiated for and defended by trade unions.

Finally, the system of labour market regulation provides the legal and administrative regulations and voluntary collective bargaining institutions which shape the employment system. These set the constraints and opportunities for employers, unions and individuals within the labour market. At the same time, these regulatory institutions are altered through activity and change elsewhere in the system. The interaction of the four categories of institutions affects the extent and type of labour market flexibility which evolves. And as gender differentiation in employment arises out of the organization of the economic and social system, it is highly probable that when the economic and social system is in a state of flux and transformation, gender will be an important element in the transformation. Not only will men and women be affected differently by the transformation, since they occupy different and segregated positions in the labour market; they will also play different roles in labour market change and reorganization. At the same time, the different societal systems of social and economic institutions mean that this gender impact varies between countries.

Hence to identify and understand these relationships, we need to consider both the differences in roles played by men and women and the national differences in the role of gendered employment relations in labour market transformations and restructuring (Rubery 1988; 1989a). While a detailed focus on the components of national economic and social systems is not the purpose of this chapter, the analysis reflects the framework outlined here.

The member states of the European Community are used for the empirical analysis, for both theoretical and practical reasons. The theoretical interest lies in the regulatory umbrella of the EC and the resulting pressures, however weak, towards convergence in national systems of regulation and organization. The practical advantage is that the annual EC labour force survey is available for cross-national comparative analysis. This source is compiled from information collected in national surveys which are designed on the basis of certain agreed principles and definitions in order to make them comparable (Eurostat 1988; Dale and Glover 1989; Hakim 1991).

All empirical studies have to address questions of conceptual validity and measurement reliability: what a concept such as 'part-time work' means, how it should be measured and the accuracy of the adopted measurement are issues which are continually present.

A further complication arises in cross-national analysis, precisely because the research examines the impact of different national contexts. This means that data collection and interpretation have to be sensitive to the diverse national institutional systems and historical backgrounds (Dale and Glover 1989).

To organize this analysis the various and often interrelated ways in which women's position in the labour market differs from that of men can be grouped under four headings. First, women's participation patterns tend to differ from men's more continuous activity patterns. This means that women may provide a flexible labour reserve, either to be expelled in order to reduce measured unemployment levels or to be mobilized to fill new or precarious areas of employment.

Second, the industrial and occupational segregation of women and men during restructuring will result in differential rates of job loss and gain for each sex. Segregation is also related to the differentiation of employment conditions between men and women and the lower valuation of tasks defined as 'women's labour'. Changes in the pattern of occupational segregation may therefore be expected to relate to internal transformations of occupational and industrial sectors, with increased feminization associated with moves towards more deskilled, lower-paid or lower status employment.

A related feature is the differential participation of men and women in various atypical employment forms. These are often regarded as synonymous with the flexibilization of the employment system. However, while men are less likely than women to work part-time, they are more likely to be in self-employed subcontracting.

Finally, flexibility is often associated with policies to reduce the cost of labour. Women tend to possess fewer labour market resources than men, and therefore depend more on institutional protections, whether by collective agreements or legislation, which provide a floor to wage levels. Labour market transformations designed to weaken such protection and increase the opportunities for wage inequalities are again likely to disadvantage specifically the female labour force (Rubery 1992a). This is considered further in a later section.

All four aspects of gender differences in employment relations are related to recent developments in the organization of labour markets. However, wide variations can still exist between European countries in the ways in which labour markets have been transformed as well as in the role of gender within this process. We thus need to look in turn at participation, segregation, atypical working and pay to identify and account for these variations.

Women as a Flexible Labour Supply?

Do women act as a 'reserve army', entering the labour market when employment expands and retreating when the economy takes a downturn? In the preceding section we argued that the organization of social reproduction is relatively autonomous, and that the labour supply is not determined by labour market demands (Humphries and Rubery 1984). Hence we should expect to observe some lack of 'fit' between the increase in the female labour supply and trends in employment and unemployment in recent decades. At the same time women's employment patterns remain more discontinuous than men's, partly because of the social organization of reproduction, which contributes to the segmentation of employment along gender lines and hence to women's disproportionate participation in non-standard or 'flexible' employment.

Women as a reserve labour pool?

Women's activity rates have consistently increased over the last 20–30 years. Between 1960 and 1990 the recorded labour force in the European Community increased by just under 29 million, of which over 20 million were women (CEC 1992: 61). For most countries, the strong surge in women's participation rates began in the 1970s; in the United Kingdom, it took place in the 1960s, while in Spain and Greece the major surge was in the 1980s (CEC 1992: 58–9).

This historical variation is to some extent reflected in the different female activity rates reached by 1990 (see table 6.1). Although the highest rates tend to be found in the northern countries, and the lowest in the southern, it is noticeable that Portugal ranks high. National variations in education and retirement have an impact on activity patterns; for example a higher proportion of both sexes remain in education until the mid-twenties in Belgium than elsewhere (Eurostat 1992: table 2). Yet variations persist when the age group is narrowed to 25–49 years to control for different education and retirement patterns.[1]

The feminization of the labour market has been accompanied by wider changes in social attitudes and behaviour in other spheres of life – reflected in and galvanized by the sex equality legislation of the 1970s stemming from article 119 of the Treaty of Rome – which suggest that this transformation is 'irreversible, lasting, widespread . . . a basic trend that is redrawing the contours of the labour market' (Maurani 1992: 1).

Table 6.1 Female activity and part-time rates by country, age and motherhood, 1990

| | Activity rates | | Part-time employment[a] 14 years + | Activity rates of mothers age 20–59 by age of youngest child[b] | | |
	14 years +	20–59 years		2 years or less	3–6 years	7–14 years
Denmark	61	84	38	84	90	90
UK	52	72	43	47	62	76
Portugal	47	64	9	69	71	66
France	46	68	24	62	69	73
Germany	45	65	34	42	53	62
Netherlands	43	57	59	40	45	54
Belgium	36	55	26	64	69	62
Italy	35	50	10	50	51	47
Greece	35	49	8	47	49	50
Ireland	35	48	18	37	32	32
Luxembourg	34	49	17	37	39	40
Spain	32	46	12	40	44	37
Eur12	42	61	28	50	57	59

Notes:
[a] Part-time work is self-defined by the respondents stating whether they consider themselves to be employed part-time.
[b] The survey design records only one adult or married/cohabiting couple as the 'household head' per address. This means that the calculation of activity rates for mothers excludes some mothers, such as those living in a household with their parents.
Source: EC Labour Force Survey – Eurostat (1992: table 1) and unpublished analysis

First, the share of formal educational qualifications held by women is increasing, and women now make up around half of all higher education students in most countries (CEC 1992: 133). Educational attainment tends to create a greater attachment to the labour market, both for the greater potential earnings and different career aspirations which result (PA Cambridge Economic Consultants 1991: 63–4). Hence we can expect to see a 'generation effect' as the greater education attainment of younger cohorts of women feeds into the raises overall average activity rates in the coming years.

Second, increased female activity and education rates have co-incided with changes in patterns of family formation and systems of reproduction. Compared with previous generations, women tend to be older when they have their first child and to have fewer children, and rates of divorce and lone parenthood are rising (PA

Cambridge Economic Consultants 1991). The greater instability of marriage combined with greater educational and employment experience has probably increased women's desire for financial autonomy.

Finally, much of the increase in women's activity rates has coincided with slower employment growth and rising unemployment. There is little evidence, therefore, of a strong 'discouragement' effect leading women to quit the labour force and become an inactive labour reserve. Instead, women are remaining in the labour market, with recorded female unemployment rates which are higher than those for men in every country except the United Kingdom (Eurostat 1992: table 1).

However, formal unemployment rates underestimate the real level of available female labour supply, for the demarcation between the status of 'economically inactive' and 'unemployed' is slippery.[2] Institutional systems of entitlement to unemployment benefit as well as dominant social attitudes concerning who counts as unemployed affect the category of non-employment in which people are placed. In particular, women's unemployment is often disguised as inactivity, namely 'looking after the home'.

However, this is not equivalent to a 'flexible buffer' of female labour which is readily expelled from the market in times of recession. Furthermore, we need to look at other groups of labour which may be transformed into a reserve labour pool, particularly since male activity rates have remained constant or fallen while those for women have increased. At one end of the age spectrum, young people remain in education longer than in previous generations. At the other end, retirement ages have fallen, particularly for men, because of earlier public pension entitlement and early retirement schemes designed partly in response to rising unemployment (Meulders et al. 1993: 3; CEC 1992: 74). This changing gender and age profile of national labour forces may generate pools of young and older workers whose activity rates are sensitive to economic cycles (Rubery 1989b), particularly in countries where fiscal policy is squeezing the real value of pensions or financial support for students. New pools of workers are also available as a result of the restructuring of eastern European countries, either as migrant labour or through the relocation of certain production processes.

Women as a discontinuous labour supply?

Despite the continued increase in female activity rates in every country, women still tend to have more discontinuous employment patterns than men, associated with the family formation years. Male employment rates across the European Community tend to increase up to the mid-twenties as men make the transition from education to the labour force, and then to level off before falling again from the mid-fifties. However, this gender difference coexists with marked national variations in female age-related activity patterns (Dale and Glover 1989; Meulders et al. 1993), which can be summarized in a broad typology according to the extent and type of discontinuity: a left-handed peak, an M-shaped curve and a plateau (see figure 6.2). Interpretation is complicated, for these activity curves are derived from cross-sectional data and so are changing as a result of the 'generation effect': the more continuous labour market behaviour of younger generations of women moving up through the age groups. Hence in most countries with either a 'peak' or 'M-shaped' curve the age-related discontinuities are less pronounced than in previous years (Maurani 1992; Meulders et al. 1993; Dale and Glover 1989).

Women's activity rates increase in countries with a left-handed peak as they make the transition from the education system into the labour force (figure 6.2a). In these countries activity rates are highest for women in their twenties and thirties, followed by a decline. This reflects a tendency for women in older age groups to quit the labour force when they marry or start a family and to re-enter the labour market intermittently. These countries currently have the lowest female activity rates in the European Community, with the exception of Portugal which is third in the ranking (see table 6.1).

The variation in the steepness of the decline in the peaks reflects the weaker impact of motherhood upon women's activity rates in some of these countries. Indeed, the economic activity rates for women with children increased substantially between 1985 and 1991 (EC Childcare Network 1990; 1993). In all of the 'peak' countries except Greece and Luxemburg, activity rates are higher for mothers whose youngest child is aged 6 or under than for mothers with older children, who are themselves older on average. Furthermore, in Belgium and Portugal these rates exceed the average activity rates for all women in the 20–59 year age group. This suggests a possible movement towards a plateau rather than an 'M-shaped' curve in at least some countries – reflecting a strong generation effect exerted by the labour market behaviour of younger age groups (table 6.1).

In contrast, the influence of motherhood is different in Germany,[3] The Netherlands and the United Kingdom (figure 6.2b). Here it is the age of children which is important, for the main pressure reducing economic activity is the presence of young children. The second peak corresponds to women's return to employment once their children are older. These countries have the steepest rise in activity rates as the

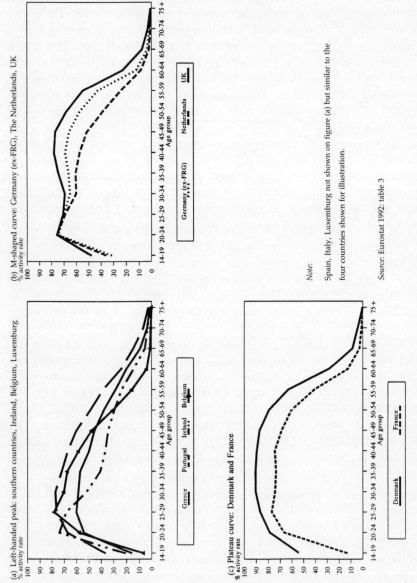

(a) Left-handed peak: southern countries, Ireland, Belgium, Luxemburg

Greece   Portugal   Ireland   Belgium

(b) M-shaped curve: Germany (ex-FRG), The Netherlands, UK

Germany (ex-FRG)   Netherlands   UK

(c) Plateau curve: Denmark and France

Denmark   France

Note:

Spain, Italy, Luxemburg not shown on figure (a) but similar to the four countries shown for illustration.

Source: Eurostat 1992: table 3

Figure 6.2   Patterns of women's activity rates by age group, 1990

youngest child reaches school-age and women return to employment (table 6.1).

A plateau, as is found in Denmark and France (figure 6.2c), indicates that neither marriage nor motherhood has a significant impact. Instead, high overall activity rates reflect continuous participation in the labour market, mirroring the predominant activity pattern for men throughout the European Community. Denmark has the most pronounced plateau-shaped curve, with a female participation rate similar to that for men. The rate is 80 to 90 per cent even for mothers with children aged under 2 years (table 6.1). The impact of children on women's activity in Denmark is now limited to the type of activity (whether full- or part-time) rather than whether or not they participate.

Both the incidence of part-time employment and the extent of childcare facilities are important influences on national variations in activity rates. Although mothers are disproportionately employed part-time compared with childless women (who are younger on average); nevertheless, most employed mothers (61 per cent) in the European Community in 1991 had full-time jobs (EC Childcare Network 1993: 12).

The highest availability of childcare provision is found in the plateau countries (Denmark, France), yet a similar level is found in Belgium where the activity rates are lower (EC Childcare Network 1990: table 3). Denmark has one of the highest part-time rates, but France does not, indicating that part-time jobs are not a necessary requirement for high female activity rates. Furthermore, part-time work is not common in the southern countries, and there are no signs of it increasing, yet this has not prevented the rapid rise in activity rates for younger cohorts or the high activity rates in Portugal.

Table 6.1 shows that part-time employment is high in the 'M-shaped' countries, associated with employment discontinuity and the 'woman returner' pattern. This is in contrast to the high and continuous activity in Denmark which also has a high part-time rate. The United Kingdom and The Netherlands (along with Ireland) have the lowest level of public childcare provision in the European Community. Although the level is higher in Germany, children have to go home for two hours at lunch-time and primary school attendance is mostly for mornings only (EC Childcare Network 1990: table 3).

The marked national variation in the extent and form of the discontinuity in women's participation rates reveals the influence of factors other than motherhood or the organization of childcare. Other social and economic policies, for example the taxation system (Spencer 1986; Dex and Walters 1989), as well as dominant social attitudes and

conventions concerning domestic roles and responsibilities also influence the structure of the female (and male) labour supply. In particular, the wider interrelationship with labour market institutions which
structure the demand and organization of employment, such as the
incidence of part-time work, is important when seeking to understand
the extent of the relationship between feminization and flexibility. It is
to these demand-side institutions that we now turn.

Economic Restructuring: Desegregation and Resegregation?

Women and men are segregated in the labour market. The gender
boundaries to the types of jobs the sexes usually do mean that in effect
women and men are in different labour forces, and are not readily
substitutable. Economic restructuring therefore has a different impact
upon women and men, and simple hypotheses that women act as a
buffer or cushion for male employment must be rejected. Nevertheless, the specific characteristics of women's role in the labour market
may be important in reshaping and refashioning the employment
system. This arises in part from the high share of women among the
new entrants to the labour force.

In the 1980s, employment expanded in every member state, the
growth of the service sector offsetting continued job losses in agriculture and industry. By 1990 the service sector accounted for over 60 per
cent of total employment in the European Community, compared with
just over 40 per cent at the end of the 1960s. The rate of employment
growth was greater for women than men in every country (*Bulletin on
Women and Employment in the EC* 1993) with female employment
growth disproportionately concentrated in the service sector (Rubery
and Fagan 1993: figure 1.3).

Women have not benefited equally in all countries from economic
restructuring. For example, in southern European countries the persistent decline in agricultural employment has had a particularly negative impact upon women (Rubery and Fagan 1993: table 3; CEC 1992:
36–40). The rapid shift from a generally rural-based economy and the
parallel reorganization of work has led to waged employment instead
of unpaid work on the family farm for some women, and unemployment or underemployment for others (CEC 1992: 58). By 1990, agriculture still occupied over 10 per cent of those in employment in Greece
(24 per cent), Portugal (18 per cent), Ireland (15 per cent) and Spain (12
per cent). Women remain disproportionately concentrated in agriculture compared with men in both Greece and Portugal, making them

particularly vulnerable in these countries to further agricultural contraction over the 1990s.

Between a third and a half of men's employment is in the industrial sector, depending upon the structure of the specific national economies (CEC 1992: 36–40). This sector is male-dominated, with the share of jobs held by men ranging from over 80 per cent in the Benelux countries to just under 70 per cent in Portugal (see table 6.2). Stagnating or falling employment levels have primarily affected men, whereas women have maintained or slightly increased their share of employment in most industries. This reflects the pattern of occupational segregation: women's concentration in clerical and other non-manual jobs has protected them during a phase of industrial restructuring that has hit male-dominated manual jobs particularly hard (Rubery 1988; Meulders et al. 1993: chapter 2).

However, within the industrial sector the position of some groups of women may be more insecure, because of both discriminatory redundancy policies, and their concentration in more precarious jobs and some of the more vulnerable and labour-intensive industries such as textiles and clothing (Meulders and Plasman 1991). Occupational segregation does not therefore always protect women; it can also construct women as a flexible reserve, even within a sex-segregated employment system (Rubery 1988).

The service sector provides the main source of employment and employment growth for women. In nine countries, over 70 per cent of women's employment is in services. Even in Greece, Portugal and Italy the figure exceeds 50 per cent. More than 40 per cent of men's employment is also in this sector, although the level fails to reach 60 per cent in any country (CEC 1992: 36–40). The majority of the service sector work-force is female in Denmark, Germany, France and the United Kingdom, all countries which have high female activity rates. But the mobilization of female labour is not an essential requirement for the development of a service economy, for the male-dominated service sector is an important part of the economies in the Benelux countries.

However, the growth of the service sector and the expansion of female employment are closely linked. This is confirmed by the analysis presented in table 6.2. The increase in total female employment between 1983 and 1990 was highest in the United Kingdom, followed by Spain (see column 1). The next two columns estimate the portion of employment growth which was due to the restructuring of employment between agriculture, industry and services and the portion which was due to the change in the gender shares of the sector work-forces.

Table 6.2 The structural and gender share components of female employment growth and sex segregation in employment in agriculture, industry and services

	Female employment growth 1983–90 as % of female employment in 1983[a]	Structural and gender share breakdown of female employment growth[a]			Women's % share of employment in 1990 in:			
		Structural	Gender share	(Interaction)	Agriculture	Industry	Services	All employment
Denmark	13	12	*	(1)	23	27	56	46
UK	22	18	3	(1)	23	23	54	43
Portugal	10	6	3	(1)	50	31	47	42
France	7	5	2	(0)	34	25	52	43
Germany	17	13	3	(1)	44	25	51	40
Netherlands	13	8	5	(0)	27	16	47	38
Belgium	16	8	7	(1)	26	19	46	38
Italy	10	5	5	(0)	35	25	39	34
Greece	14	4	9	(1)	45	24	37	35
Ireland	10	5	5	(0)	10	22	45	33
Luxembourg	13	11	2	(0)	33	11	46	34
Spain	18	12	6	(0)	27	17	42	32

[a] = 1987–90 data for The Netherlands, Portugal and Spain. * = less than 0.5%.

Source: Calculations based on Eurostat Labour Force Survey Results, table 26 in published volumes for 1983, 1987 and 1990

The gender share effect was equal or similar to the structural effect in Belgium, Ireland, and Italy, so we can estimate that half of total female employment growth in these countries was due to women increasing their share of employment within sectors over and above the effect of economic restructuring. The strongest gender share effect occurred in Greece, accounting for nearly 65 per cent of total female employment growth.

In the previous section these four countries were seen to have 'peaked activity curves' (along with Spain, Portugal and Luxembourg). We have already argued that the female labour supply in these countries is being rapidly transformed by the attitudes and behaviour of younger generations of women and that 'plateau' rather than 'M-shaped' activity curves might develop in the future. The gender share effects estimated here support this interpretation, for they suggest that this changing character of the labour force is feeding through into a changing gender profile in the work-force.

By contrast, in the other eight countries the strongest effects were structural, indicating that most of the increase in female employment was associated with growth in the service sector. For these countries, continued employment expansion for women may depend on continued structural change that favours female-dominated occupations and industries. However, while the expansion of service sector employment and the increase in female activity have been closely linked during the last decade, certain service industries such as banking and finance are now shedding considerable numbers of jobs after having recruited large numbers of women in the 1970s and early 1980s. This new vulnerability to service sector restructuring adds to that which women employed in agriculture and in some traditional manufacturing industries face in the recession of the 1990s.

Although restructuring has provided more employment opportunities for women, it has not dismantled segregation. Across Europe, employment growth at the top of the occupational hierarchy, in conjunction with women's rising qualification levels, has produced some desegregation in professional areas. But this has mainly occurred in public sector employment, and the public/private divide may become an increasingly significant gender boundary in the future (Crompton and Sanderson 1990; Rubery and Fagan 1993). Women have also increased their share of the expanding clerical grades and other traditionally female jobs, while making few inroads into the male-dominated manual jobs where job prospects are bleaker.

Within this general pattern, the role women have played in the reshaping of employment systems has varied. First, there is no immediate prospect of convergence between countries because of national variations in both the sex shares and growth rates of different occupations. Second, the extent to which women are drawn into occupations as cheap sources of labour also varies. Women's entry into higher-level jobs in the public sector has been accompanied by falling pay levels in some countries, although elsewhere feminization has accompanied stable or even improved pay and conditions. And conditions in the male labour market have created reserve pools to fill vacancies in male-dominated manual work (Rubery and Fagan 1993). This suggests that the role of women in providing a source of cheap and alternative labour is still shaped by historically determined boundaries between male and female jobs, by conditions in the male labour market and by systems of wage regulation (Reskin and Roos 1990). Furthermore this restructuring is producing both desegregation and resegregation of different parts of the employment system, leading to a 'polarization' of experiences as boundaries are created between different groups of women (Humphries and Rubery 1992).

Flexible Employment Forms: Gender and Country Specificities

An important feature of economic restructuring has been the growth of atypical employment, the three main forms of which are self-employment, part-time employment and employment on temporary contracts. This development is often taken as synonymous with a move to more flexible employment systems. And it is women's disproportionate participation in this type of employment that has led to an association being identified between flexibilization and feminization.

Atypical employment forms are often seen as an opportunity for employers to evade fixed overhead employment costs. However, the incidence of each category of atypical work varies by both country and gender, suggesting that the pattern is not mainly explained by employers' strategies to reduce fixed overhead costs. Instead the form and function of these types of employment differ between countries (Rodgers and Rodgers 1989).

If we look at self-employment we find that many of the differences in incidence between member states are explained by the size and organization of the agricultural sector, followed by other differences in industrial organization, including the dominance of family firms in service sectors. The use of subcontracting to minimize overheads and to shift risk provides only a small part of the explanation. Moreover, it is only in the United Kingdom that there has been a major expansion of self-employment over the past decade.

In all types of self-employment men tend to play a more dominant role than women. It is in specific forms of self-employment such as homeworking (for which no good data exist) and family working that women predominate. In 1990 nearly three-quarters of all family workers in the European Community were women and half of all family workers were found in agriculture. However, this is a form of atypical employment that has been declining along with agricultural employment. Only in Spain and Greece does this group remain an important part of total female employment (although there may be much under-reporting here).

It is in temporary and part-time work that we find more evidence of both growth over the decade and the disproportionate participation of women. There are problems in defining and measuring temporary work in a way that is relevant to different national regulatory regimes. The Labour Force Survey relies on self-definition of temporary work: people are asked whether their job has a fixed finishing date or task to complete. In countries where regulations provide greater protection for non-temporary staff, employers may make more effort to create specific categories of temporary jobs. No strong incentive exists in countries such as the United Kingdom where there is little job protection attached to so-called permanent jobs (Rodgers and Rodgers 1989). A further problem is that the survey takes place in the spring, when there is likely to be a low incidence of temporary seasonal workers. All those problems notwithstanding, we find that around 12 per cent of women and 8 per cent of men are on temporary contracts.

Men seem to provide a labour supply for temporary jobs at young ages, at their point of entry into the labour market. Young women are just as likely as young men to be on temporary contracts, but women continue to provide a temporary or flexible labour supply in their later years. This may imply that women returners in particular are likely to be found in temporary jobs.

However, the function and incidence of temporary work vary by country as well as by gender. Portugal and Greece have comparatively high rates of temporary contracts, but the highest incidence is in Spain (30 per cent), where it has become the normal type of contract for new jobs. In other countries temporary work may be confined more to specific sectors and particular types of jobs: for example, in Greece male temporary employment is less in the service sector than in agriculture and construction.

While in all countries except Greece the share of women on temporary contracts exceeds that of men, in some cases the differences are small. Furthermore, in five countries (Spain, Portugal, Greece, Germany and Denmark) a higher absolute number of men are on these contracts. There is a particular problem in Spain where the growth of temporary jobs for women has accelerated at a rate twice that for men in the 1980s. Moreover, for women there is often an interaction between temporary contracts and part-time work. In all countries other than Denmark and Germany part-timers are more likely to have temporary contracts than full-timers (*Bulletin on Women and Employment in the EC* 1993). This interaction may result in the creation of a segment of particularly marginalized employment, primarily filled by women.

Apart from family work, gender segregation is highest among part-time employees, two-thirds of whom are women. Growth of part-time jobs is often regarded as the main means by which the European labour market has become increasingly feminized. The expansion has been concentrated in the service sector, where over 80 per cent of all part-timers in the European Community were employed in 1990. Overall, 28 per cent of employed women in the Community worked part-time (4 per cent of men).

Considerable differences in the rate of part-time job growth occurred over the 1980s. Countries with low shares of part-time work continued to favour full-time jobs, and the absence of part-time job growth in Spain, Italy, Greece and Portugal coexisted with high female employment growth. By the end of the decade the expansion of part-time work in the northern countries had slowed down in most cases and marked differences in the national levels of part-time work continued to persist.

The highest female part-time rates are found in the United Kingdom and The Netherlands (table 6.1), and together these two countries account for 42 per cent of all female part-timers in the European Community. Almost half of the EC's male part-timers also live in these countries, but the form of men's part-time work is different. It occurs at different stages in their work histories, when they are young or old, and is often concentrated in different types of jobs (CEC 1992: 144). For example, half of the male part-timers in The Netherlands are under 25 and three-quarters of these are students or trainees. In contrast half of the women working part-time in The Netherlands were doing so because of family commitments (Meulders et al. 1993: 85).

National as well as gender differences in the types of jobs done by part-timers reflect the specificities of the market. Women working part-time are more segregated than women full-timers in each country, but comparison reveals variations in the extent to which part-timers are ghettoized into low-paid and precarious work, even between countries with comparable rates of part-time employment. For example, part-time employment is more extensive in some professional occupations in Denmark, Germany and The Netherlands compared with the United Kingdom (Rubery and Fagan 1993). Average hours worked by part-timers also vary between countries, with short part-time working (10 hours or less) more common in The Netherlands and the United Kingdom than anywhere else (Eurostat 1992: table 51).

Comparative case studies provide further understanding of how part-time employment differs between countries. For example, part-time employment may be used as a way of retaining skilled women within their current occupations, such as in the French banking sector, whereas in the United Kingdom women part-timers in this sector are used for less integrated and lower-level tasks, such as lunch-time cover (O'Reilly 1992). Likewise, variations in labour supply characteristics and the regulation of working-time lead to national differences in the number of part-time hours even for similar occupations such as sales work (for example, Gregory 1991).

Preferences for part-time work are influenced although not determined by labour demand. There is some match between the proportion of unemployed women looking for part-time work and the availability of part-time jobs, yet, for example, in Ireland the proportion of unemployed women who wanted part-time work exceeded the national part-time rate in 1990 while the opposite was true in Denmark (CEC 1992: 33–4). Similarly, more than a quarter of women employed part-time in Britain would like a job with longer hours (Marsh 1991) and between a quarter and a third of women part-timers in The Netherlands, Belgium, Spain and Italy want full-time work (Meulders et al. 1993: 86). And within countries, the extent of choice and constraint entailed in working part-time varies between sectors and higher and lower-level jobs (for example, Gregory 1991).

There is thus no mechanical relationship between the growth of atypical employment and the increasing participation of women in the economy. Likewise there can be no simple equation between feminization and employment flexibility. Women are overrepresented in particular atypical employment forms, but these differ markedly in incidence across the European Community. No single factor – for example, employment legislation – can explain these differences; all the institutions summarized in figure 6.1 must be considered in order to provide a full interpretation.

One important set of institutions is those which regulate systems of pay. Is the incentive for employers to create atypical jobs related to the savings gained from lower overheads or are there also more direct wage benefits to be gained? The pay and conditions of such employment may again be affected not only by gender, but also by the specific systems of pay determination and regulations prevailing in the member states.

Pay Flexibility and the Gender Pay Gap

Women are often regarded not only as flexible and disposable but also as a cheap labour force. To what extent has the feminization of the European labour force been the result of strategies or policies to reduce labour costs, including direct labour costs?

Research into pay structures within Europe is rather sparse and no definitive answers to this question can be given. However, from the limited data and research available certain key points can be made. First, women continue to be paid less than men throughout Europe, and there has been only slow progress in the 1980s towards closing that gap, despite women's movement into higher-level occupations and the implementation of EC Equal Treatment and Equal Pay directives in national legislative systems. Second, the majority of the low-paid in Europe are women, even though they account for less than half of the labour force. Third, women are disproportionately employed in sectors with weak systems of pay regulation, such as private services or small firms. Fourth, the gender pay gap is likely to be even larger than that revealed by surveys of pay because the survey coverage often excludes atypical and marginal employment in which women are disproportionately concentrated and which are precisely the types of employment likely to be excluded from minimum wage protection or collective agreements.

Finally, the pay position of women does, nevertheless, vary markedly between member states, and thus the extent to which feminization is synonymous with low pay depends on the specific institutions of wage determination within member states. For example, recent research has compared systems of pay regulation and the extent of low pay as a percentage of national median rates between the member states (CERC 1992; Bazen and Benhayoun 1992). The proportion of low-paid workers, that is those paid below two-thirds of the median wage, was found to vary between member states and to relate to the form of wage-setting in operation.

The incidence of low pay tended to be smaller in countries with an effective minimum wage system. In some countries, this may be the result of collective bargaining. However, union organization tends to be weak in those industries where women's employment is highest, and among atypical workers. Even where women and part-time or temporary workers are unionized, their influence on trade union bargaining priorities is often weak. Unless procedures exist to generalize minimum pay rates across industries and occupations (as in Germany, Italy, and possibly Denmark), collective bargaining along cannot prevent a deterioration in women's relative pay (particularly given current trends to decentralization in collective bargaining).

An alternative or supplementary protection is a statutory national minimum wage. This reduces the proportion of low-paid workers in France, Portugal, Luxembourg and perhaps also Greece (countries where in many cases the coverage of collective agreements is inadequate), and in The Netherlands and Belgium, where minimum wage legislation is combined with widely used extension mechanisms. The greatest incidence of low pay was found in those countries without either effective voluntary regulation of minimum pay or a national minimum wage (United Kingdom and Ireland). Spain also fell into this category; although it has a national minimum wage, this is set at such a low level (54 per cent of the median) that it fails to prevent low pay.

Although this overall national incidence of low pay was an important factor in predicting the rate of low pay among women, other factors also intervene. For example, in Portugal low pay was found to be more a problem for the less educated of both sexes than specific to women, and in The Netherlands the risk of low pay is particularly concentrated among young people.

These figures underestimate the incidence of low pay for both men and women because of the exclusion of the informal economy and atypical workers. Where these workers are self-employed, earnings data are difficult to collect and arguably not comparable with directly employed workers. However, part-time workers are also excluded and this leads to a major underestimate of the incidence of low pay among women. For example, the United Kingdom comes out as having the highest incidence of low pay among full-time workers, although only by a small margin. If part-timers were included, the relative position of the United Kingdom would be seen to be far worse. In the United Kingdom approximately 46 per cent of those paid below two-thirds of the adult full-time median wage are female part-timers, a group that earns only around 75 per cent of female full-time hourly earnings (Rubery 1993). In other countries, for example Germany and The Netherlands, the gap between part-timers' and full-timers' pay is much less marked (Rubery 1992a; Plantenga and Van Velzen 1993).

The average level of pay for women is also affected by the system of pay determination. Research suggests that the more centralized the system of pay determination, the narrower the differences in pay between industries and occupations and the smaller the overall gender gap (Whitehouse 1992; Blau and Kahn 1992). A narrow wage dispersion favours women as they tend to be concentrated at the bottom of the hierarchy and small differentials between industries prevent pay falling too far in the female-dominated sectors. Where decentralization and deregulation have occurred in payment systems, the evidence suggests that vulnerable groups of workers, such as women, have lost out. At the same time, some women have fared better than others under these changes, for example non-manual compared with manual women in the United Kingdom (Rubery 1992a).

The extent to which national systems have been deregulated is uneven. Moreover, not all women are employed in sectors with deregulated pay structures. In most European countries the public sector remains an important employment sector for women and is still highly regulated. However, the impact of flexibility in pay may not be fully evident until recent moves towards privatization, decentralization and individualization of pay through systems such as performance-related pay become more established. Nevertheless, marked differences in systems of pay determination across countries will continue to have a differential impact on the gender pay gap, and the extent to which women provide a source of cheap labour.

Conclusions

Four conclusions emerge from this survey of how the increased feminization of the European labour market has interacted with the reshaping of the employment system.

First, there is a clear gender dimension to all aspects of European labour markets. We found strong evidence of persistent and newly evolving patterns of segregation by industry, occupation and employment form. There is equally clear evidence of the continued economic inequality that accompanies this segregation: a higher incidence of low pay among women than men and continuing gender pay gaps at the aggregate and the industrial or occupational level.

Second, the integration of women into the economy is closely associated with new types of jobs and forms of employment: women have provided the main source of new labour for the growth of services and part-time work. However, the integration of women is not simply related to the increased flexibilization of the labour market.

Women are increasingly resisting the role of providing a flexible source of labour by developing more continuous employment patterns. Moreover, much female employment growth is explained by structural changes, and not by a switch of employers to new and more flexible forms of labour. Atypical employment shows no sign of becoming a predominant feature in female job growth by the end of the 1990s, while the importance of part-time work in expanding female participation varies markedly by country. Finally, the extent to which women provide a cheap, flexible labour force also depends upon wage determination institutions. In many European countries minimum wage protection even expanded in the 1980s and moves towards decentralized and flexible pay, although evident in other countries, have nowhere been taken to such extremes as in the United Kingdom.

The third conclusion is that the societal system shapes the form of integration of women into the economy. The influence of societal systems goes beyond differences in explicit regulations, or provision of resources specifically aimed to help women integrate into the labour market, such as childcare assistance. This influence extends not only to the quantitative measures of women's activity, such as shares of part-time work, but also to the qualitative assessment of the significance of these employment forms. In some instances part-time work is a means of employing low-paid and low-skilled labour to meet numerical flexibility requirements, but in others it is a way of retaining skilled labour. Sufficient examples of differences in national systems have been provided to cast doubt upon the thesis of convergence in the organization of European labour markets or in the form and level of gender inequalities. This suggests that one-dimensional studies, such as those which look at the incidence of occupational segregation across countries, provide limited information since the consequences of this segregation are likely to vary between countries. The consequences of inequalities are also likely to vary. For example, although in some countries there may be internal career paths associated with female-dominated jobs, such openings may be non-existent or blocked in others, and the level of pay in female-dominated occupations may vary greatly between countries. Moreover, even within mixed or integrated occupations, the implications for economic inequality are unknown unless information is provided on male and female pay differentials (Hakim 1993).

The final conclusion is that policy matters. The system of pay determination, the conditions associated with atypical working, the provision of childcare and access to education, all can and do have significant impacts on the extent and form of gender inequality. It may be true that in all countries gender inequality remains, but the failure to remove all discrimination is no reason not to support and press for policies that ameliorate its effects.

Notes

1   Portugal is the only member state where youths under the age of 15 can be legally employed full-time. In most countries education continues to at least 16, although the prevalence of further education and training beyond the official school–leaving age varies between member states and has changed a great deal over time (CEC 1992: 74; see also published tables in EC Labour Force Survey Results).

2   In the Labour Force Survey all persons of working age were defined as 'employed' if they performed at least one hour of work for a wage, salary or profit (in cash or in kind) in the reference week. People who were absent from their usual employment were included as employed. The 'unemployed' were defined as those people not employed, available to start employment within two weeks and actively seeking work, i.e. taking specific steps to look for work. People who were neither employed nor unemployed were defined as inactive (Eurostat 1988: 10–11).

3   Data for Germany relate to the former West Germany unless specified.

References

Bazen, S. and Benhayoun, G. 1992: Low pay and wage regulation in the European Community. *British Journal of Industrial Relations*, 30(4) 623–38.

Blau, F.D. and Kahn, L.M. 1992: The gender earnings gap: learning from international comparisons. *American Economic Review Papers and Proceedings*, May, 533–8.

Bulletin on Women and Employment in the EC. 1993: 2. EC Network on the Situation of Women in the Labour Market. Manchester: Manchester School of Management, UMIST.

Brunhes, B. 1988: *Labour Market Flexibility in Europe: a comparative analysis of four countries*. Working paper for the OECD Working Party on Industrial Relations.

CERC (Centre d'Etudes des Revenus et Coûts) 1992: *Low Pay in the European Economic Community*. V/20024/91-EN. Brussels: Commission of the European Communities (DG V).

Commission of the European Communities (CEC) 1992: *Employment in Europe 1992*. COM(92) 354. Luxemburg: Office for Official Publications of the European Communities.

Crompton, R. and Sanderson, K. 1990: *Gendered Jobs and Social Change*. London: Unwin Hyman.

Dale, A. and Glover, J. 1989: Women at work in Europe: the potential and pitfalls of using published statistics. *Employment Gazette*, 299–308, June.

Dex, S. and Walters, P. 1989: Women's occupational status in Britain, France and the USA: explaining the difference. *Industrial Relations Journal*, 20(3) 203–12, Autumn.

Equal Opportunities Commission 1992: *Women and Men in Britain*. London: HMSO.

EC Childcare Network 1990: *Childcare in the European Communities 1985–90* (*Women of Europe*, Supplement, no. 31). Brussels: Commission of the European Communities Women's Information Service (DG X).

EC Childcare Network 1993: *Mothers, Fathers and Employment 1985–1991.* V/5787/ 93-EN. Brussels: Commission of the European Communities (DG V).

Eurostat 1988: *Labour Force Survey: methods and definitions.* Luxembourg: Official Publications of the European Communities.

Eurostat 1992: *Labour Force Survey Results 1990.* Luxembourg: Official Publications of the European Communities.

Eyraud, F., Marsden, D. and Silvestre, J.-J. 1990: Occupational and internal labour markets in Britain and France. *International Labour Review*, 501–17.

Glendinning, C. and Millar, J. (eds) 1987: *Women and Poverty in Britain.* Brighton: Harvester Wheatsheaf.

Gregory, A. 1991: Patterns of working hours in large-scale grocery retailing in Britain and France. *Work, Employment and Society*, 5(4) 497–514, December.

Hakim, C. 1991: Cross-national comparative research on the European Community: the EC Labour Force Surveys. *Work, Employment and Society*, 5(1) 101–17, March.

Hakim, C. 1993: Segregated and integrated occupations: a new framework for analysing social change. *European Sociological Review*, 9(3) 289–314.

Humphries, J. and Rubery, J. 1984: The reconstitution of the supply side of the labour market: the relative antonomy of social reproduction. *Cambridge Journal of Economics*, 8(4) 331–46, December.

Humphries, J. and Rubery, J. 1992: The legacy for women's employment: integration, differentiation and polarization. In J. Michie (ed.), *The Economic Legacy 1979–1992*, London: Academic Press, 236–54.

Jarvis, V. and Prais, S.J. 1989: Two nations of shopkeepers: training for retailing in France and Britain. *National Institute Economic Review*, 58–74, May.

Lane, C. 1991: Industrial reorganization in Europe: patterns of convergence and divergence in Germany, France and Britain. *Work, Employment and Society*, 5(4) 515–40, December.

Lewis, J. (ed.) 1983: *Women's Welfare, Women's Rights.* London: Croom Helm.

Marsden, D. 1986: *The End of Economic Man.* Brighton: Harvester Wheatsheaf.

Marsh, C. 1991: *Hours of Work of Women and Men in Britain.* Equal Opportunities Commission Research Series. London: HMSO.

Maurani, M. 1992: The position of women on the labour market: trends and developments in the twelve member states of the European Community 1983–90. Summary report. (*Women of Europe*, Supplement, no. 36). Brussels: Commission of the European Communities Women's Information Service (DG X).

Meulders, D. and Plasman, R. 1989: *Women in Atypical Employment.* EC Women in Employment Network. V/1426/89, Brussels: Commission of the European Communities (DG V).

Meulders, D. and Plasman, R. 1991: *The Impact of the Single Market on Women's Employment in the Textile and Clothing Industry* (*Social Europe*, Supplement 2/91). Brussels: Commission of the European Communities (DG V).

Meulders, D., Plasman, R. and Vander Stricht, V. 1993: *Position of Women on the Labour Market in the European Community.* Aldershot: Dartmouth Publishing House.

O'Reilly, J. 1992: Where do you draw the line? Functional flexibility, training and skill in Britain and France. *Work, Employment and Society*, 6(3) 369–96, September.

PA Cambridge Economic Consultants 1991: *Study on the Relationship Between Female Activity and Fertility.* Volume 1: *Synthesis Report: Issues and policy in the relationship between female activity and fertility.* V/639/91-EN. Brussels: Commission of the European Communities (DG V).

Plantenga, J. and Van Velzen, S. 1993: *Wage Determination and Sex Segregation in Employment: the case of The Netherlands.* Report for the European Commission Network on the Situation of Women in the Labour Market.

Prais, S.J., Jarvis, V. and Wagner, K. 1989: Productivity and vocational skills in services in Britain and Germany: hotels. *National Institute Economic Review,* 52–74, November.

Reskin, B. and Roos, P. 1990: *Job Queues, Gender Queues: explaining women's inroads into male occupations.* Philadelphia: Temple University Press.

Rodgers, G. and Rodgers, J. (eds) 1989: *Precarious Jobs in Labour Market Regulation: the growth of atypical employment in Western Europe,* Geneva: ILO.

Rubery, J. (ed.) 1988: *Women and Recession.* London: Routledge and Kegan Paul.

Rubery, J. 1989a: Precarious forms of work in the United Kingdom. In G. Rodgers and J. Rodgers (eds), *Precarious Jobs in Labour Market Regulation: the growth of atypical employment in Western Europe,* Geneva: ILO, 49–74.

Rubery, J. 1989b: Labour market flexibility in Britain. In F. Green (ed.), *The Restructuring of the UK Economy.* Brighton: Harvester Wheatsheaf, 155–76.

Rubery, J. 1992a: Pay, gender and the social dimension to Europe. *British Journal of Industrial Relations,* 30(4) 605–22.

Rubery, J. 1992b: Productive systems, international integration and the single European market. In A. Castro, P. Mehaut and J. Rubery (eds), *International Integration and Labour Market Organization,* London: Academic Press, 244–56.

Rubery, J. 1993: *Wage Determination and Sex Segregation in Employment: report for the UK.* Report for the European Commission Network on the Situation of Women in the Labour Market.

Rubery, J. and Fagan, C. 1993: Occupational segregation of women and men in the European community. (*Social Europe,* Supplement, 3/93). Luxembourg: Office for Official Publications of the European Communities.

Spencer, N.S. 1986: Taxation of husband and wife: lessons from Europe. *Fiscal Studies,* 7(3) 83–90, August.

Steedman, H. 1987: Vocational training in France and Britain: office work. *National Institute Economic Review,* 58–70, May.

Steedman, H. and Wagner, K. 1989: Productivity, machinery and skills: clothing manufacture in Britain and Germany. *National Institute Economic Review,* 40–57, May.

Whitehouse, G. 1992: Legislation and labour market gender inequality: an analysis of OECD countries. *Work, Employment and Society,* 6(1) 65–86.

Wilson, E. 1977: *Women and the Welfare State.* London: Tavistock Publications.

7

Industrial Order and the Transformation of Industrial Relations: Britain, Germany and France Compared

Christel Lane

Severe recession, changes in world markets and in production technology have confronted managements and labour with new challenges, provoking transformations in industrial relations in all advanced societies. Despite some common trends, however, national systems of industrial relations have adapted to these external influences in their own distinctive ways. Common global pressures have not brought about convergence but only adaptations of pre-existing patterns of industrial relations structures and styles. Enduring national distinctiveness reflects the fact that industrial relations systems are a part of a wider social configuration, termed Industrial Order, which shapes their development.

The first section of this chapter discusses the concept of Industrial Order and its utility for understanding both continuity and change in national industrial relations systems. The second part outlines the essential features of Industrial Order in Britain, Germany[1] and France and indicates how the various components of that order interact with the conduct of industrial relations. It does so in broad, general terms, neglecting many of the variations within each country.[2] The third section demonstrates the utility of the concept of Industrial Order by focusing on one major aspect of recent change in the industrial arena: transformations in production, such as changes in work organization and associated labour relations, as well as in the related areas of training and technological change.

The Concept of Industrial Order

Social scientists analysing industrial change in the 1980s have been compelled to recognize that capitalist economic organization, despite a strong underlying homogenizing dynamic, has many distinctive national variants. But if most sociologists accept that each society is a distinct historical formation, few have used this insight as a systematic guide to their investigations. Even fewer have explored the implications of the interpenetration of social institutional structures with economic organization. The notion of Industrial Order implies such systemic interpenetration.[3] It focuses on the interdependence between industrial organization – the structure and behaviour of firms and their relations with other firms – and the social institutional environment in which they are embedded. Although such an environment is usually national in character because of the homogenizing impact of state regulatory activity, the absence of a strong political centre or a strong emphasis on voluntarism in industrial affairs can lead to the creation of more than one Industrial Order within national boundaries.

Industrial Orders assume their distinctive character during critical phases of industrialization. That process was itself shaped by preindustrial social structure and particularly by the way the transition from the guild to the industrial system was accomplished. However, Industrial Order developed gradually over time in response to external stimuli and as the result of internal struggles between key economic actors. Given that an Industrial Order always evolves from complex interaction between its various constituent elements, development is usually continuous, and radical discontinuous transformations are the rare outcome of war and revolution.

The constituent elements of Industrial Orders are those institutional complexes which shape the conditions under which the factors of production are made available, as well as the ways in which they are deployed and co-ordinated in processes of production and exchange both within and between firms. The following institutional complexes are thus included: the state, both as a direct economic rule-maker and as an institution which prominently shapes the rules of other important institutions; the financial system; the system of education and training, particularly the training of industrial managers and employees; the system of industrial relations; and, lastly, various intermediate associations, such as trade associations, Chambers, etc. which influence the ways in which firms acquire, maintain and co-ordinate resources. Thus the basic components of Industrial Order are the same in all advanced capitalist societies, although their specific institutional forms differ, and different elements will assume importance for different areas of decision-making. There are also societal variations in the degree of mutual coherence and consequent tightness of fit between the component elements of the Industrial Order: a consequence of the degree to which the state historically has regulated industry.

Institutions are complexes of both formally fixed rules and regulations and informally generated conventions, customs and cultural understandings. Their influence over industrial organization stems from the fact that they constrain or channel the actions of critical organizational actors – in this case management and representatives of labour – in crucial ways. They influence what kind of goals are taken up, how they are pursued and how resultant policies are implemented. Although organizational actors generally prefer familiar recipes for action, they occasionally endeavour either to circumvent or to change institutional rules. However, such change is very difficult to effect as individual rules form part of a whole web of mutually sustaining rules. Institutional inertia is thus far more pronounced than innovation. This explains the exceptional degree of continuity even of Industrial Orders which have been long associated with undistinguished economic performance.

This emphasis on continuity in Industrial Order should not, however, obscure the occurrence of constant incremental change. Although any single change may be slight, the cumulative effect over time may be considerable, even if usually recognized only with the benefit of hindsight. Change within an Industrial Order can be initiated both by external agents, such as the occupying forces in Germany after the second world war, or by critical internal actors in response to outside challenges or in attempts to influence the business environment. Organizational actors are particularly likely to initiate change if external events have brought about a change in the pre-existing balance of power. Actors are thus not completely determined by institutional structures but engage in strategic manoeuvring within set parameters (Thelen 1991). The capacity for implementing such change is, in turn, structured by institutional rules within subsystems of Industrial Orders. Such institutional structures thus shape actors' capacities for action in that they provide differential space and resources for proactive intervention. Outside challenges are, of course, much more frequently directed at economically uncompetitive Industrial Orders, particularly during crucial stages of industrial development and at times of intense international competition. At such times, outside challenges lead to a flurry of blueprints for change, without necessarily achieving a basic change of direction. This may induce a sense of permanent institutional crisis, but it will not necessarily lead to a breakdown of Industrial Order.

Industrial Order: Britain, Germany and France Compared

Britain

The salient features of British Industrial Order are its long persistence without radical institutional and ideological change, such as resulted from defeat in war in other countries. Lack of rationalization over time has led to highly fragmented institutional structures.

A high degree of continuity in state structures and ideology was accompanied by minimal political involvement in industrial organization. This resulted in the diffusion of a voluntarist attitude throughout the Industrial Order and explains the comparatively weak links between its elements. Governments modified their traditional arm's-length relationship with industry only belatedly and in haphazard fashion, and responses to the problems of industry were amateurish. The centralized nature of the state and the rather feeble development of corporatist structures has also weakened policy implementation. When a more interventionist industrial policy was developed from the 1960s, deficiencies in structures and personnel and lack of control over the financial system precluded lasting transformation. Intermediary associations of both capital and labour were strong enough to exercise their veto power but too weakly co-ordinated to intervene more proactively.

The financial system, shaped predominantly by Britain's imperial past and its role as the world's banking centre, has maintained the same arm's-length relationship with industry as the state. It has imposed constraints on industrial managements of high, short-term returns on capital, and the relative ease of take-over provides the necessary discipline to heed these constraints. It has forced managements into a strong preoccupation with financial affairs and has led to the pre-eminence of accountants among higher management. As a consequence, concern with manufacturing performance remains underdeveloped.

These pressures for short-term returns on capital have profoundly affected investment behaviour. British manufacturing has been notorious for insufficient investment, particularly in technologically advanced products and processes.

Underinvestment in capital equipment has resulted in underinvestment in human resources. The British system of vocational education and training (VET) was shaped during the early stages of industrialization, and unease about the low level and quality of technical and vocational training was voiced almost without interruption from the 1860s. The apprenticeship system survived the transition from the guild to the industrial stage, although it was operated in a very informal way, without government regulation and control and with only slight interest from the owner-managers of predominantly small firms in developing high standards. Turner (1962) has argued that this meant a transfer of control of the apprenticeship system to journeymen societies – the forerunners of craft unions. But other labour historians (More 1980: 146f.; Elbaum 1991: 198f.) claim that, although the unions attempted to assert such control and frequently achieved local success, they were too weak during the nineteenth and early twentieth centuries to achieve any strong measure of restrictive influence over apprenticeship training. Employers generally were free to train as little or as much as they chose. Their reasons for training were determined by immediate business needs and often by the ability to use apprentices as low-paid labour. The state had no role in industrial training, and the deficient development of general education for the mass of non-academic young people also deprived industrial trainers of a suitable basis for a good VET system.

Union influence over VET became, however, more strongly developed after the war. Craft unions managed to exert direct control over the intake of apprentices, as well as influencing employers indirectly to reduce the intake. The latter was the result of pay bargaining practices which had reduced differentials between apprentices and craftsmen and rendered the recruitment of apprentices too costly (Senker 1992: 28, 103). The sectionalism of craft unions prevented the development of a more inclusive system with broader access from all sections of the working class. Union control over training also led to sharp labour market divisions between skilled craftspeople and mere operatives (Marsden 1992) and has thus served to perpetuate a damaging division between craft unions and unions for 'general' and mainly semi- and unskilled workers.

The establishment of Industrial Training Boards in 1964, with tripartite representation, brought some rationalization and modernization of training. The statutory grant-levy system taxed employers who did not train and rewarded those who did. But Conservative governments soon cut short such forceful reform efforts.

The 1970s and, more so, the 1980s did indeed see a series of state-initiated reforms of training: the establishment of central bodies, such as the Manpower Services Commission and later the Training Agency, to develop training and lay down standards; the introduction of the Youth Training Scheme (YTS) and Employment Training (ET) as alternatives to the apprenticeship system; and, finally, the introduction of employer-dominated Training and Enterprise Councils. From the

1980s, however, government policy has been a mixture of, on the one hand, extensive regulatory and financial involvement and, on the other, an insistence that training has to become primarily a matter for employers, with strenuous attempts to marginalize unions in the area of training. Despite constant institutional and policy innovation, the level and prestige of skill training have remained low and highly skilled workers a small elite in most industries.

Thus, to sum up, the blame for a backward system of VET cannot be laid solely at the door of craft unions. It is in large measure attributable to a lack of leadership from management, characterized by short-termism, little interest in productive concerns and an inclination to compete on low price rather than on skill-based quality. Moreover, employers, lacking a capacity for solidarity, have tended towards skill-poaching rather than sustained training effort. Both the structure and the voluntarist ethos of the state have prevented state agencies from filling the vacuum left by the representative bodies of capital, and the absence of organizations supportive of high standards of training mediating between the state and individual firms has impeded policy implementation.

This disdain for technical skill in production and for product quality has also been evident in the approach to management training. Although this is now more professionalized, an emphasis on credentials is of quite recent origin. 'Practical men' and status lenders still have a strong weight among managers today, and among those with professional management skills, generalists predominate while engineering skills remain weakly represented.

The historical legacy has been particularly pronounced in the shaping of the system of industrial relations. The slow pace of industrialization favoured the gradual transformation of journeymen societies into craft unions and the persistence of remnants of craft organization among the workers. The absence of a sustained challenge from either the state or the predominantly small and weakly organized employers permitted unions to build up a system of representation and bargaining which gave workers strong influence over the terms and conditions of their work. Although employers frequently challenged union influence over the recruitment and employment of labour, such challenges consisted mainly of local skirmishes rather than all-out confrontation. Until recent decades, enduring prosperity, disunity and lack of state support made employers disinclined to challenge customary union rights in a sustained manner. Control over workers was mainly exerted through the piece-work system (Edwards et al. 1992: 4–5).

The system of industrial relations evolved at the workplace, and the state did not attempt to regulate it through legal rules. Rules of bargaining and employment and the definition of rights and obligations of either side of industry developed through daily practice at the workplace, and, by long usage, acquired authority as 'custom and practice'. Through long historical evolution there developed a system characterized by minimal involvement and 'arm's-length' relations on both sides, as well as by an adversarial approach, leading easily to industrial action rather than lengthy negotiation. Opportunistic behaviour was also encouraged by the lack of regularity in bargaining processes and the ensuing absence of a long-term perspective.

The organizational forms of labour representation – their weak centralization and professionalization (the ratio of full-time officials to members is comparatively low), the development of competitive multi-union structures – are all results of the peculiarities of British industrial development. The following are notable: the gradual advance of industrialism and the early dominance of craft unions; the small size of firms and the highly decentralized nature of production until the 1930s and longer; and the voluntarist stance of the state and the two sides of industry.

Closeness to the workplace and union structures and style, as well as management priorities, have interacted to structure concerns and capacities for action. Ambitious long-term strategies for the whole union movement, looking beyond immediate grievances and concerns, have rarely been contemplated and hardly ever implemented. Any nationally co-ordinated action by the TUC has usually been defensive rather than proactive. The steadily growing decentralization in bargaining has led to much greater pluralism than in the other two societies, not only in bargaining arrangements but also in reward systems, career patterns and in work and employment practices. The competitiveness of companies and industries was not the unions' concern.

The absence of monopolistic, professionalized and solidaristic labour organization in turn obviated the need for such organizations among employers. Indeed, in terms of membership, employer organizations have generally been weaker than unions. Such fragmented, competitive, loose and weakly professionalized organization has pertained on both industrial relations issues and broader business issues. Capital, too, has acted mainly defensively rather than in proactive and innovative ways in response to issues of industrial relations, narrowly defined, and wider business policies.

Germany

In Germany a mixture of traditional features and more recent (post-1945) institutional innovations has been welded into a tightly integrated whole. The salient features are a high degree of legal regulation and considerable self-organization of the industrial community. The web of legal rules leaves room for largely consensual negotiated adjustment, giving the Industrial Order its communitarian character (Lodge 1987; Allen 1987). But recent events, following reunification, have severely tried consensualism, and it remains to be seen whether it can prevail in the face of the resulting extensive economic, political and cultural turmoil now being experienced.

Although the ideology and organization of the German state show some sharp breaks between the pre- and post-war period, there have also been remarkable continuities. There is insufficient space to explore these, and the focus will be mainly on the post-war period. Both economic ideology and state structure have limited the power of the central state and have curtailed direct state intervention in the economy. The federal political structure divides economic resources and competences between the central and the regional governments (*Länder*). A horizontal division exists in macroeconomic management, the federal government sharing power with the independent *Bundesbank*, which has been able to play a decisive role in curtailing inflationary wage demands. The long tradition of industrial self-administration by the large banks and the trade associations and Chambers further limits state action in this field. During the post-war period, unions, too, have become part of this wider policy-making community, although largely in a consultative capacity. This quasi-political industrial community provides highly effective compensation for lack of state intervention, making German economic liberalism much less damaging to industrial development than the British version – though also inhibiting the growth of fully corporatist arrangements. Nevertheless the central state has been important in shaping industrial development by establishing the legal framework which has provided general norms and effective regulatory mechanisms, as well as establishing a social infrastructure highly supportive of industry.

The German financial system is bank-centred and credit-based and has a weakly developed stock market. Close ties between the large banks and firms, dating from the 1870s, are based on a plurality of factors: interlocking share ownership and supervisory board membership;[4] additional voting rights of banks acting as proxies for smaller stockholders; and the provision of long-term credit and consultancy services by the banks. The links between industrial firms and banks have also given the latter an important role in the restructuring of firms and whole sectors, forming so-called crisis cartels together with representatives of capital and labour.

These features of the German financial system have shaped management orientations towards investment in both plant and people. Enterprises have the opportunity to take a long-term perspective, encouraging technological innovation. Innovation in products and processes is paralleled by investment in appropriate skill training beyond current needs, which is not, as in Britain, viewed primarily as a cost.

The system of VET has been decisively shaped by the long preservation of the craft (*Handwerk*) sector, although restrictive craft practices have not been part of the German pattern. The uniform national regulation of VET and its widespread acceptance as essential to the German production model have ensured its broad diffusion through all sectors and sizes of firms. A much higher proportion of the labour force than in Britain or even France is formally trained at all levels.

VET has been administered in a tripartite manner throughout the post-war period. The representatives of labour play an important role, in both determining the content of VET and monitoring its implementation at enterprise level. The national homogeneity of training content, the range of the skills taught and the certification of skill by outside bodies – the Chambers – make for a high degree of functional flexibility and assure skilled workers of a strong position in both external and internal labour markets. The chance of progression in the system of VET, from skilled worker via technician and foreman right up to professional engineer, has further important effects: it provides common understandings and orientations and reduces divisions between hierarchical levels. This, in turn, contributes to the creation of a craft community and obviates the 'minimum involvement' relationship between management and labour, traditional in Britain.

German management education has been professionalized for a much longer period than in Britain (Locke 1984), although ascent from the ranks has always remained a possibility. Management is perceived in a more specialist way, and management education has reflected this perception. Technical expertise has been more highly prized than in Britain and has had a more practical bent than in France. It has resulted in a pronounced production orientation among German managements and has served to strengthen the craft community.

The system of industrial relations is a mixture of established German traditions—for example, centralization of bargaining authority, the works councils—and of structures devised after 1945, notably the principle of unitary rather than ideologically oriented unions. The predominantly authoritarian and paternalist labour relations of the pre-war period and the consequent high level of conflict has been transformed into co-operative relations in the democratic and in-clusionary political climate of the post-war period. The system of industrial relations is legally regulated in a nationally homogeneous way and entails a very orderly distinction between the competencies, rights and obligations of unions and works councils. Both legal defi-nition and actual operation of works councils and unions are said to have strengthened the consensual tenor of management–labour re-lations. Unions and employers are bound by law to engage in regular bargaining which engenders long-term perspectives and more co-operative attitudes among the social partners (Boyer 1992: 54). Juridification makes for a cumbersome system, slowing down de-cision-making, although, it is argued (Keller 1990; Thelen 1991), not an inflexible one.

The high degree of centralization, solidarity and professionalization of the system ensures that commitments made by national or regional leaders are usually honoured at lower level. Lastly, the extension of sectoral wage agreements to all firms in the sector, whether unionized or not, creates greater homogeneity of wage levels between firms of different sizes and prevents the development of downward pay flexibility and price competition, as well as weeding out inefficient firms more readily – hence the fairly uniform German emphasis on competition through superior quality and service rather than low price. These organizational features have encouraged union goals and capacities for action which are long-term and encompassing.

The various organizations of capital – employers' associations, trade associations and Chambers – display not only similar pro-fessionalization, solidarity and capacity for action but also higher levels of membership and greater material and power resources. The trade associations are oriented mainly to the larger firms, whose emergence early on in Germany's industrialization favoured such extensive self-organization. The Chambers, a modernized remnant of the guild system, are oriented more towards the needs of the small and medium-sized craft enterprises. The strength and solidarity of employers' associations make them formidable adversaries for the unions and partly account for the few, though usually lengthy, strikes.

This picture of unity and solidarity among both unions and em-ployers and of orderly conflict resolution has, however, become less convincing since unification of the western and eastern parts of Germany in 1990. The dual structures and practices of industrial rela-tions, formally transferred from the western to the eastern *Bundesländer*, are being undermined by informal divisions which strike at the very core of the system (Büchtemann and Schupp 1992; Hoss and Wirth 1992). The official union goal of attaining speedy wage parity between workers in the west and east has not only caused conflicts between unions and employers but also between western and eastern workers. Economically precarious eastern employers can pressurize politically inexperienced works councils into accepting wage settlements below those agreed in bargaining rounds at industry level. Moreover, locally owned and managed firms have different interests from those controlled by powerful western companies. Such divisions are a serious threat not only to the system of industrial relations but also to the whole Industrial Order of which it forms a vital part.

France

Industrial Order in France also consists of a mixture of traditional and modern elements but less tightly integrated than in Germany. The state is very much the focal element of Industrial Order and enforces a statist communitarianism in industrial organization, which, however, has had only limited success, stunting independent initiative from intermediary bodies.

The guiding economic ideology of *dirigisme* has deep historical roots. Economic governance has been highly centralized, with no corporatist policy-making; the organizations of labour have been particularly marginalized (Hall 1984). Power has rested particularly on a high degree of formal and informal control over the banking sector and hence over investment finance (Zysman 1983), as well as control over the Bank of France. Extensive nationalization of firms at various times during the post-war period has both reflected and enhanced state power in industry. Given the frequent turnover in governments in the earlier post-war decades, the permanent administrative staff became a very influential economic and industrial technocracy. Social cohesion and functional interchange among the governmental and industrial elites has served to smooth policy-making.

Concentration of power, together with the backwardness of industry at the end of the second world war, allowed the state to shape the development of both capital and labour. Industry expanded rapidly, as did the industrial labour force; the traditional skilled *artisanat* was soon outnumbered by low-skilled rural migrants. Wage inflation was prevented by price controls which forced employers to restrict pay increases (Hall 1984). Only after the protests of 1968 did the state begin to make significant economic and organizational concessions to organized labour (Stoffaës 1989: 108) and develop some tripartite bodies for decision-making on social issues (Goetschy and Rozenblatt 1992: 405).

The French financial system, like the German, is credit-based and large firms obtain their outside finance mainly as long-term bank loans, on terms influenced by the state. Although the influence of banks in industry is not as pronounced as in Germany, the consequences for managerial investment behaviour are comparable, generating a commitment to a longer-term perspective. This in turn encourages proactive human resource management (HRM); but this effect is countered by a much less developed productivist ethos among managements, dominated by recruits from socially and educationally elitist *grandes écoles*.

A comprehensive system of initial VET is a creation only of the post-war period when international competition began to expose the inadequacy of the French skill base. The ensuing school-based and state-organized system has progressively increased the proportion of the work-force trained to either 'skilled worker' or 'technician' level, bringing France closer to its German rival and steadily surpassing Britain (Steedman 1990). Although vocational education is certified, it does not provide young workers with a guarantee of a skilled position (Méhaut 1992; Marsden 1992).

In-company further training, which complements school-based initial training, has been encouraged by a state-enforced training levy and is now more extensive than in Germany (Méhaut 1992). This system ties French workers to internal labour markets, which in turn influences trade union recruitment and bargaining activities. It also serves to blur the boundary between skilled and semi-skilled and thus favours the principle of egalitarian general unions.

In contrast to the situation in Britain, the regulation of VET has never come under union influence (though today the unions are consulted more frequently than hitherto), nor has it been accomplished in the tripartite manner of Germany. As with many other aspects of industrial organization, the state has assumed a directing role in initial and advanced VET, while employer regulation of further training occurs in a state-determined regulatory framework.

Although French unions have deep historical roots, a system of industrial relations, with institutionalized representation and bargaining practices, has developed only recently and gradually. At national level, the state was traditionally hostile to collective organizations, which in turn were prone to political radicalism and ideological fragmentation. In addition, the long dominance of the French economy by generally anti-union owner-managed SMEs gravely undermined the influence of unions both in the enterprise and at the national political level. Until the mid-1970s there was little effective bargaining at enterprise level since both employers and unions were implacably opposed to it (Linhart et al. 1989: 102–3).

Legal regulation of industrial relations has not provided French unions and works committees with the strong legal participation rights of their German counterparts, nor do they have the strong customary rights of British unions over workplace matters. Weakness has been exacerbated by inter-union conflict.

Nineteenth-century French unionism was strongly influenced by anarcho-syndicalism; later, the largest union – the CGT – was closely allied to the communist party. This strong political engagement has resulted in ambiguity as to whether economic or political goals should predominate (Goetschy and Rozenblatt 1992: 404). Antagonism has frequently spilled over into the political arena, as in 1968: at times forcing the state to make substantial concessions to organized labour, resulting in a piecemeal strengthening of the industrial relations system and considerable employment rights.

Given the centrality of ideology for union recruitment and mobilization, French unions have subscribed to egalitarian principles of membership and have pursued solidaristic goals. Bargaining has normally occurred above the level of the firm, and has primarily concerned pay issues. Unions have been incapable of pursuing long-term goals, which would require a high level of organization and co-operation between federations; instead, objectives obtainable by spontaneous mobilization or state action have been favoured.

The weak organization and low capacity for action on the part of labour have been partly mirrored in the organization of employers. Employer organizations enjoy relatively high levels of membership (Goetschy and Rozenblatt 1992: 421), but have been internally divided; conflicts of interest between large and small capital have been more pronounced in France than in the other two countries. This heterogeneity of interests has prevented strategic action to alter the industrial relations system (Goetschy and Rozenblatt 1992: 422). Intermediary organizations of capital have had relatively little influence on national industrial policy formation.

The Impact of Industrial Order During the Last Decade

Recent economic, political and technological changes have transformed industrial relations, forcing unions onto the defensive as well as challenging them to operate more strategically. The following discussion concentrates on one area of challenge: the emergence of a new production paradigm and the ensuing efforts to restructure work organization and labour relations.

Many writers, such as Piore and Sabel (1984), Kern and Schumann (1984) and Boyer (1988), identify structural changes in production organization which signal the emergence of a new paradigm; however, they disagree over the extent and nature of the break. In this chapter, the term 'new production paradigm' is used to denote three features. First, the need to increase the variety and quality of products (Sorge and Streeck 1988) requires higher levels of both workers' skills and technological capacity and hence calls for greater investment in training and advanced forms of technology. Second, this in turn necessitates improved communication between functional departments, new forms of work organization and a more involved, co-operative and self-regulating work-force, entailing new management approaches to labour relations and deployment. Third, these changes result in new approaches to bargaining and raise new bargaining issues.

The following discussion attempts to establish, first, how the different national Industrial Orders have influenced unions to respond to these demands; and second, whether union responses have reinforced established institutional structures, perhaps aggravating institutional failure, or on the contrary have encouraged institutional innovation.

Britain

How have the two sides of British industry responded to the challenge? Improvements in skill training have been only partial, because of the persistence of short-termism. There have been few major policy responses from the union movement to increase the levels and scope of training. As a result, the initiative has shifted very decisively to the state and, to a lesser extent, employers, depriving unions of a previously important sphere of influence.

Moves to multi-skilling have been very slow and cumbersome, with as yet only modest results (Cross 1988; Rainbird 1990). This illustrates particularly well the institutional constraints on action in the British union movement. Local representatives have been enjoined to await national agreements before negotiating on this issue; however, no national agreements have been reached because acceptance of multi-skilling also means risking loss of sphere of influence, membership and identity (Rainbird 1990). These negative consequences could have been avoided by concerted action, but multi-unionism makes this very difficult to achieve.

This failure has, in turn, prevented innovative union policies on work organization and new technology. Although unions have recognized technological change and new forms of work organization as crucial fields of action, little concerted action has resulted (Rainbird 1990). Consequently, moves towards diversified quality production and associated forms of work organization, such as autonomous work groups, have proceeded in a hesitant and haphazard manner (Lane 1992b). The exercise of veto power has been generally more notable than proactive initiative. But such responses must be placed in the larger context of sharply deteriorating employment security, work intensification and a decisive shift in the balance of power towards a management not renowned for its innovative capacity, nor for making full use of shop-floor expertise.

In recent decades, British managements have placed considerable emphasis on worker involvement and HRM more generally (Storey and Sisson 1990; Millward et al. 1992), though with limited evidence of strategic co-ordination and only piecemeal implementation (Marginson et al. 1988). Despite the strongly implied and sometimes openly declared (CBI 1988) intention of HRM to bypass and marginalize the unions, the latter have taken no initiative to influence the implementation of HRM measures in their favour (Edwards 1987; Marginson et al. 1988; Ramsey 1991; Grahl and Teague 1991). Thus although labour relations have become superficially less adversarial, the new balance is unstable and has brought few gains for workers.

Lastly, there has been little change in either the form or substance of bargaining, except for a move towards even more decentralized bargaining at enterprise level in response to demands for greater flexibility in local decision-making (Brown and Wadhwani 1990: 64; Millward et al. 1992). There has been no notable shift away from bargaining for pay increases towards more qualitative issues, such as training, new technology or working-time (ibid.).

This brief overview has shown that British union responses to the emergence of a new production paradigm have been either poorly developed or mainly defensive. This has been partly due to the influence of an Industrial Order inimical to technological innovation and skill enhancement and to the co-operative resolution of problems; partly to the conventions of the industrial relations system itself, which limit capacity for proactive change and discourage institutional innovation; and partly to conjunctural factors, such as the depth of the crisis in the manufacturing sector and the hostility of the Thatcher governments, leaving unions little room for manoeuvre. The resultant immobility and loss of legitimacy on the part of the unions is bound to deepen institutional crisis in the longer run.

At the same time there has been a decisive change in the balance of power between the main industrial relations actors. For the first time in industrial history the state has abandoned its neutral stance on industrial relations and has actively intervened in favour of capital. Employers have utilized their new strength to achieve modest though significant changes in both labour relations and collective bargaining practices (Millward et al. 1992). But they have acted largely individually and have failed to develop a strategic approach to industrial relations (Edwards et al. 1992: 60).

Germany

The German industrial relations system has proved more stable despite a changed economic and political climate. There has been no significant realignment in the relationship between the three main actors, merely marginal change. Although employers have gained in influence, unions have remained a force to be reckoned with, and employers have refrained from pushing their new advantage very strongly. Because of the enduring co-operative bias of industrial relations, the state has been able, by and large, to continue its neutral stance and to respect the autonomy of the two sides of industry. Unions, in contrast to their British counterparts, have much more actively sought to minimize lasting damage to their established position and to shape industrial relations structures and issues to their own advantage. In evaluating their situation, however, it is important to remember that the industrial relations system interacts with other elements of Industrial Order in a way which provides much more positive and stabilizing reinforcement than has been the case in Britain.

Organized capital and labour have long agreed that a continuous improvement in initial vocational training is necessary to maintain international competitiveness. Unions have always made a positive input into policy formation, and works councils have had a vital monitoring function in the implementation of training standards. In 1987, however, a major new initiative was launched by the largest union, IG Metall, to protect labour against technological unemployment, and secure for workers the benefits of technological change (Mahnkopf 1992). A key concern was to extend union influence from initial VET into company-specific further training, in which unions and the certifying institutions had no role. Although the unions won concessions on this issue, so far implementation of this radical agreement has met with only partial success (ibid: 71f.). It has nevertheless provided a topical mobilizing issue and has changed the policy agenda in this very crucial area.

Labour flexibility has been a prominent issue. But while British employers have focused mainly on overcoming occupational demarcations, their German counterparts have concentrated on the rigidity of the internal labour market, which results from strong employment protection rights. Unions have had to agree to more flexible organization of working-time in exchange for major reductions in the working-week.

Unions have always insisted that employers should respond to competitive pressures with increased functional flexibility, not with numerical flexibility (job-cutting) or (downward) pay flexibility. In manufacturing industry they have been largely successful, partly because of the comprehensive industry coverage of wage agreements and partly because managements themselves are committed to quality rather than cost competition.

German unions have a long and quite impressive record of intervention in technological development, trying to influence both design and implementation (Cressey and di Martino 1991; Müller-Jentsch et al. 1992: 102f.). During the 1980s they moved to a more offensive strategy, pursuing explicit agreements over new technology (Linhart et al. 1989: 144). This remains a very contentious area where employer resistance is strong and union capacity for action limited by insufficient expertise (Altmann and Düll 1990). Nevertheless, unions have gained some notable successes in both national industry agreements and the extension of works council influence. Although works councils have only weak rights of information, not co-determination, over new technology, they have often used their stronger rights in other areas to trade against concessions on these more contentious qualitative issues (Linhart et al. 1989: 129). A recent investigation into works councils found that issues relating to new technology are very high on their agenda (Müller-Jentsch 1992: 20).

Union concerns with training and new technology are crucial for gaining influence over work reorganization resulting from systemic automation. The unions have long been active proponents of work group models that broaden skills and enrich jobs (Thelen 1991: 205). The principle of industrial unionism and the solidarity between skilled and semi-skilled this entails have encouraged more egalitarian work reorganization models than in Britain, favouring high and homogeneous levels of skill and job rotation within work groups. Works councils have been the main instrument of influence over work reorganization because of their information and consultation rights.

However, union efforts have been crucial in their continuous mobilization and education campaigns and their practical assistance to individual works councils (Linhart et al. 1989: 145). Their prominent role in the recent debate on 'lean production' is one example (Hans Böckler-Stiftung 1992). Managements, too, particularly in the car industry, now actively promote group work (Jacobi et al. 1992: 246). Consequently, greater and more consistent progress has been made than in Britain on the road away from Fordist methods of work organization (Lane 1992b).

The issue of greater employee involvement has been less salient than in Britain and less tied to the more general concerns of HRM. This may be because German management has long been able to rely on the co-operation of labour, which possesses legal rights of co-determination. Consequently the German debate has focused primarily on new forms of participation and involvement in the organization of production, sparked off by Japanese concepts such as quality circles and 'lean production'. After some initial hostility, the unions eventually decided to utilize this debate to gain new opportunities for works council participation. Hence German employers have been unable to exploit these developments to bypass and marginalize unions or works councils.

All these developments have brought changes in the content and level of bargaining. A distinct move away from quantitative goals towards more qualitative ones, such as working-time, employment security, training and participation in technological change, has been reflected in a growing number of framework agreements (Jacobi et al. 1992: 251). At the same time, unions have begun to search for new forms of pay determination in the wake of systemic automation, greater transparency of effort and more group work (Hildebrandt and Seltz 1985: 493; Altmann and Düll 1990: 119f.) The impact on unions has been double-edged. They have acquired new mobilizing issues, helping them to maintain an activist stance at a time when bargaining for more than routine pay increases has a low chance of success; however, qualitative issues and new problems in pay determination require a much more differentiated approach, which is not easily met by centralized industry-based bargaining. This may accelerate the move towards decentralization of bargaining and will require considerable organizational ingenuity for unions to keep the initiative and not become subordinate to works councils. Despite the interpenetration of unions and works councils, decentralization of bargaining towards works councils carries considerable dangers of undermining the current fundamentals of the German system which have helped it to function so well up to now.

To sum up, this difficult transition period in industrial development has been marked by active union efforts to retain the initiative. This stance has been promoted partly by more radical and more consistent change in production organization than in Britain, reflecting an Industrial Order which favours consensual solutions and is generally more responsive to the demands of the new production paradigm (Lane 1992b). Yet it is also a consequence of the institutional system of industrial relations itself. Its orderly structure and low level of internal conflict, centralization and high degree of professionalization permit strategic initiative and self-regulation by the two sides of industry, enabling the state to remain on the sidelines. Nevertheless, there are also signs that central features of the system of industrial relations may lead to increasing difficulties in the longer run (Jacobi et al. 1992; Linhart et al. 1989: 150).

France

In France, adaptation of the production system has reflected union weakness and the lack of autonomy of the two sides of industry. The French model, according to Boyer (1992), still displays insufficient use of skill resources on the shop floor. Although firms now invest strongly in training, this is still mainly for technical and managerial staff. The main training efforts have been undertaken by the state and by employers, and unions have not pressed strongly for training solutions which involve operatives on a more equal basis in further training and skill and pay upgrading. They have even blocked works committees which have some influence in the area of training (Amadieu 1992: 69).

Management has been anxious to reduce obstacles to functional flexibility which derive from the complex job classification system and pay grades (Eyraud et al. 1988). Efforts to increase flexibility through multi-skilling and group work have often been resisted by unions suspicious of management motives (Amadieu 1992: 62), although there have been some recent national agreements between the three sides of industry (Goetschy and Rozenblatt 1992: 435). More flexible working-time arrangements, often requested by employees, have led to an increasing individualization of the labour force (Goetschy and Rozenblatt 1992: 424). Despite union weakness, employers have not tried to increase numerical flexibility (Segrestin 1990: 122–3).

Automation of production processes made great strides in France during the 1980s, and the emerging new model is strongly technology-led. Technology policy, like all qualitative issues, has been a taboo subject for unions in the past as it was feared that negotiations would legitimize employer initiatives while gaining unions only small concessions. Until the late 1970s, unions were in any case hostile to enterprise bargaining, which effective regulation of technology would have required. From the early 1980s, however, the Conféderation Française Démocratique du Travail has pursued such agreements as a campaigning issue which might appeal to its growing white-collar members (Linhart et al. 1989: 107) though with little success (Eyraud et al. 1988: 75).

Process automation has encouraged work reorganization, typically using recruits from technical colleges, rather than the upgrading of existing workers. The new technology, according to Coriat (1992: 10) and Boyer (1992: 8f.), is being used to reduce reliance on manual workers and to control them more stringently than in the past, although there are partial exceptions to this rule, such as the car industry (Amadieu 1992).

Issues of work organization gained topicality from the introduction of expression groups under the 1982 Auroux laws. One of the prime purposes of such groups was to discuss changes in the workplace. This would not include unions directly; nevertheless, they could focus on such issues in their mobilizing campaigns. Although some union head offices have welcomed this opportunity, the rank and file have largely failed to take advantage of it. Local militants have either remained attached to old ideological orientations and have blocked management initiatives in such areas as group work, or they have had insufficient resources to exploit the expression groups for their own purposes (Linhart et al. 1989: 118f.).

As a consequence, management has retained the initiative. Implementation of a new production model has largely taken the old elitist direction and, although improving flexibility and response times, has retained the Fordist principle of a pronounced division of labour between conception and execution (Eyraud et al. 1988; Boyer 1992: 10; Coriat 1992: 10).

In France, too, the new production paradigm has brought initiatives to encourage more employee involvement and even co-operation. Given the traditionally antagonistic tenor of labour relations, this constitutes a major departure for both management and unions. Of the three main confederations, only the CFDT has accepted such a change whereas both the CGT and Force Ouvrière show 'suspicion of anything that smacks of joint management methods' (Amadieu 1992: 70). The main impetus has come from the Auroux laws, making enterprise bargaining compulsory and introducing the expression groups. Although both these developments were initially opposed by employers, they are now accepted and even welcomed for the new opportunities they afford in the area of labour relations (Hoang-Ngoc and

Lallement 1992: 2). Managements have since backed them up with other measures, such as profit-sharing and quality circles – both showing a strong growth during the 1980s (Goetschy and Rozenblatt 1992: 433).

Unions, as a result of ideological intransigence and weak organization, have on the whole failed to turn these new developments to their advantage. They have even been further weakened by the more direct relation between employers and employed, created by expression groups (Amadieu 1992: 70; Goetschy and Rozenblatt 1992: 423). Whereas Amadieu (1992) and Wilson (1991: 453–4) note some improvement in labour relations, Boyer (1992: 510) sees distrust as still the norm. This is likely to continue, despite a decrease in class conflict rhetoric, improved communication and greater realism on the parts of both union officials and workers, as the weakening of unionsleaves employees without guarantees that agreements will be implemented.

While the industrial relations agenda has changed and legislation has effected a partial shift of bargaining to the workplace, decentralization has not been drastic (Hoang-Ngoc and Lallement 1992: 4), and the late 1980s also brought a reversal of the trend (Bridgford and Sterling 1991: 266). Industry-level and economy-wide negotiations have remained important, general national norms are still being set and the role of the state in collective bargaining remains significant. A movement to more individualized pay has been reversed since the late 1980s, and standard length of service awards are still widespread (Amadieu 1992: 83).

To sum up, the move towards a new production policy has brought widespread changes in work organization and associated training practices. New bargaining issues have come to the fore, confronting unions with the need to adjust their policies and practices. Most French unions, particularly the CGT, have resisted such initiatives; where response has been more positive, as with the CFDT, the low level of organizational resources (few full-time officials) and underdeveloped capacity for sustained action have prevented them from exploiting these changes to arrest or reverse their decline. Despite sustained efforts by the state to strengthen the role of unions in the system, old patterns prevail, and state regulation remains a central characteristic of the system of industrial relations.

Conclusions

Since the late 1970s there has been a major industrial transition in the advanced countries, involving more or less radical adjustments in patterns of industrial organization in response to greatly intensified industrial competition, world recession and radical technological change. This chapter has investigated the impact of such transformation on one complex of industrial relations practices and has interpreted changes as being both constrained and facilitated by the social-institutional structures within which industrial relations are conducted. Each national system of industrial relations is inextricably linked to other institutional complexes, forming an Industrial Order which has influenced the manner and scope of industrial adjustment. The latter has, in turn affected the Industrial Order.

Britain's severe loss of industrial competitiveness has prompted Conservative governments since 1979 to pursue radical institutional and ideological change, including change in the state itself. Policies were based on the assumption that economic decline reflected rigidities in the labour market, and that both the system of industrial relations and that of VET needed to be restructured. It was not recognized that these institutional complexes are inextricably linked to other elements of the Industrial Order, and no attempt was made to restructure the organization of capital. Changes in the state itself during this period have been less concerned with a redesign of core structures than with increasing the centralization of state power and eliminating or weakening corporatist intermediate organizations which previously participated in industrial policy-making.

In view of this one-sided and increasingly autocratic approach to policy-making and implementation, it is not surprising that the resulting change has been only partial and inconsistent and that new institutional structures appear unstable. In the absence of a coherent strategy for renewal devised by the state, the organizations of capital or labour have provided no compensating strategic directives (Edwards et al. 1992: 61). Their capacities for strategic action have always been weak and have been further curtailed during the 1980s.

What then has been the nature of change in the system of industrial relations and how far, if at all, have these been complemented and supported by transformations in other parts of the Industrial Order? During the 1980s, union density and the coverage of collective bargaining structures declined, and there were many major changes in both structures and procedures (Millward et al. 1992). The creeping erosion of demarcation practices will eventually eliminate the principle of craft organization and will lead to a marked reduction in union fragmentation, particularly if it is accompanied by mergers between unions of the skilled and the semi-skilled. This process has been reinforced by a decisive shift in the system of VET from union-controlled apprenticeship schemes to employer-controlled institutions, as well as by more informal processes of dual-skilling. Unions have proved unable either to withstand change or to direct it to their own advantage.

Fundamental, albeit partial, reform of the system of industrial relations and less radical alteration of the training system have not been accompanied by changes of the financial system and by consequent transformation of management approaches to the creation and utilization of skill and to labour relations more generally. Short-termism has remained paramount, and new constraints on labour have not been balanced by new opportunities and participation rights. The government has been vehemently hostile to such rights – a striking contrast to Germany and France. This lack of integration between the various elements of British Industrial Order means that changes have been patchy, incoherent and unstable. Thus state action has been mainly concerned with curbing the power of the unions; it has done nothing to foster a more responsive and responsible union movement, or to encourage a more co-operative style of industrial relations.

In Germany, there has been no change to the Industrial Order beyond adjustment at the margin. This can be explained partly by the fact that the industrial crisis has been much less developed and concern with institutional restructuring less pronounced. However, institutional inertia also reflects the fact that the elements of Industrial Order are more tightly interlocked than in the other two societies, the degree of juridification is much greater, and the dispersion of state power in both vertical and horizontal terms is more pronounced.

Consequently change in the system of industrial relations during the 1980s has been more modest and has been the outcome of negotiated adjustment between organized capital and the unions, with the state staying very much on the sidelines. The principles of centralized bargaining and the unions' homogenizing regulatory functions have been weakened (Keller 1990: 386), and the relationship between unions and works councils has altered. During the 1980s, these changes were not drastic enough to undermine the dual system, nor to jeopardize centralized bargaining (Müller-Jentsch 1992: 34). But it remains to be seen whether these slight fissures in the industrial relations system of the old Federal Republic might turn into more serious ruptures in the all-German system evolving in the 1990s.

In contrast to the situation in Britain and France, unions have participated actively in the adjustment process and have lost much less ground to the employers. Employers still view unions as a factor of stability and predictability, and there are even signs that they now value the system of enterprise (though not board-level) co-determination more than in the past (Müller-Jentsch 1992: 22). The system of industrial relations remains well integrated into the Industrial Order, reinforcing and receiving reinforcement from other institutional complexes.

German reunification has provoked some uncertainty about whether this basically consensual Industrial Order will prevail in the future. Any forecast must, however, put gloomy analyses of the current industrial scene into a more holistic theoretical and longer-term historical perspective. If the analysis of Industrial Order developed in this chapter is persuasive, the long-term prognosis must be more optimistic. First, the system of industrial relations is accepted and valued by both sides of industry; though employers may pursue marginal adjustments, it is not to the advantage of capital to jeopardize it. Second, the industrial system is tightly integrated with, and supported by, other elements of the Industrial Order, and is, indeed, an indispensable part of the new Germany. Third, although we are experiencing the merging of two different Industrial Orders, there have been several institutional and cultural features shared by both. In the integration of the two, the markedly greater size, population, industrial might and political legitimacy of the old Federal Republic should ensure that its Industrial Order will prevail in the territory of the former GDR.

In France some significant changes have taken place in the system of industrial relations. Collective bargaining at the enterprise level now appears well accepted, even if it has not ousted national and industry-level bargaining. This institutionalization, together with the greater dialogue between employers and employed, has reduced the level of antagonism in relations between capital and labour. According to Michon (1992: 8), major social conflicts are no longer linked to labour disputes, as was the case in the past. But the lack of incorporation of the CGT into this new pattern and signs of increased militancy in the FO make the new compromise brittle. These changes have come about solely as a consequence of state intervention. Neither unions nor management have taken an active part in bringing them about but have initially even opposed change, and the state has had to compensate for the organizational weakness of unions. Despite the best intentions of state functionaries, their intervention has done nothing to strengthen unions; instead it has contributed to their further decline.

Another major change in French Industrial Order has been in the system of VET. Emphasis on raising the quality of human resources has been well integrated with a concerted move towards automation. However, the system of VET has not as yet had a strong impact on work organization and, through this, on labour market and industrial relations structures. The state has changed its ideological approach to the governance of the economy towards a more liberal stance, particularly from the mid-1980s onwards. But the inability of the state to withdraw from collective bargaining shows that the aim of eliminating *dirigisme* is difficult to translate into practice. The centrality of the state in French Industrial Order has contradictory effects: not only fostering consistency in industrial policy-making and integration between elements of Industrial Order, but also inhibiting the active involvement of intermediary organizations of both capital and labour, resulting in a patchy implementation of policy and resistance to change.

In conclusion, the exceptionally serious external challenges experienced by advanced economies from the middle 1970s onwards have begun to overcome long-established institutional inertia and to reshape elements of Industrial Order. This has been much more pronounced in Britain and France – where there has been a marked shift in the balance of power away from labour – than in Germany. In both France and Britain the main initiative for change has come from the state, whereas in Germany the two sides of industry have remained involved in industrial policy-making and have been moderately successful in shaping changes to their own advantage. In all three societies continuity in Industrial Order has been more notable than radical transformation, particularly in the style in which crucial institutional actors have grappled with changes in institutional arrangements (Crouch 1993).

Notes

1 Although this chapter makes some reference to developments in the reunited Germany, the discussion is mainly concerned with the original Federal Republic.
2 A more nuanced account is given in Lane 1991 and 1992a.
3 The concept was introduced, though not systematically elaborated, by Herrigel (1989). It is preferred to a similar concept, Business System, coined by Whitley (1992) and used by myself in an earlier publication (Lane 1992a). The term 'system' has become too closely associated with a functionalist orientation which assumes stable integration and thus underemphasizes historical development and social change. Although a systems approach does not neglect social actors, it leaves insufficient scope for action transforming system parameters. Such an emphasis on social actors and their ability to transform institutions is given prominence in the writing of 'new institutionalists', such as Hall (1984 and 1986) and Thelen (1991) who have inspired the approach taken in this chapter. These writers have, however, been concerned with discrete institutions rather than with the whole complex of institutions interacting in Industrial Orders.
4 German firms have a two-tier structure. The supervisory board, comprising shareholder and employee representatives, has a role in strategic decision-making and appoints (and can dismiss) the management board which exercises day-to-day control.

References

Allen, C.S. 1987: Germany, Competing Communitarianisms. In G. Lodge and E. Vogel (eds), *Ideology and National Competitiveness: an analysis of nine countries*, Boston: Harvard Business School Press, 79–97.

Altmann, N. and Düll, K. 1990: Rationalization and participation: implementation of new technologies and problems of the works councils in the FRG, *Economic and Industrial Democracy*, 2(3) 1–27.

Amadieu, J.-F. 1992: Labour–management co-operation and work organization change: deficits in the French industrial relations system. In OECD, *New Directions in Work Organisation*, OECD: Paris, 60–91.

Beisheim, M., von Eckardstein, D. and Müller, M. 1991: Partizipative Organisationsformen und industrielle Beziehungen. In W. Müller-Jentsch (ed.), *Konfliktpartnerschaft*, Munich: Rainer Hampp Verlag, 123–38.

Boyer, R. 1988: *The Search for Labour Market Flexibility*. Oxford: Clarendon Press.

Boyer, R. 1992: How to promote cooperation within conflicting societies? Paper presented at the Conference on Convergence and Divergence in Economic Growth and Technical Change, MERIT, University of Limburg, Maastricht.

Bridgford, J. 1990: French trade unions: crisis of the 1980s. *Industrial Relations Journal*, 21(2) 126–35.

Bridgford, J. and Sterling, J. 1991: Britain in a social Europe: industrial relations and 1992. *Industrial Relations Journal*, 22(4) 1991, 263–72.

Brown, W. and Wadhwani, S. 1990: The economic effects of industrial relations legislation since 1979. *National Institute Economic Review*, February, 57–70.

Büchtemann, C. and Schupp, J. 1992: Repercussions of reunification: patterns and trends in the socio-economic transformation of East Germany. *Industrial Relations Journal*, 23(2) 90–106.

Castro, A., Méhaut, Ph. and Rubery, J. 1992: *International Integration and Labour Market Organisation*. London: Academic Press.

Confederation of British Industry 1988: *People – the Cutting Edge*. London: CBI.

Coriat, B. 1992: Incentives, bargaining and trust. Alternative scenarios for the future of work. Paper presented at the Conference on Convergence and Divergence in Economic Growth and Technical Change, MERIT, University of Limburg, Maastricht.

Cressey, P. and di Martino, V. 1991: *Agreement and Innovation. The international dimension of technological change*. Hemel Hempstead: Prentice Hall.

Cross, M. 1988: Changes in working practices in UK manufacturing 1981–88. *Industrial Relations Review and Report*, 415, May, 2–10.

Crouch, C. 1993: *Industrial Relations and European State Traditions*. Oxford: Clarendon Press.

Daniel, W. 1987: *Workplace Industrial Relations and Technical Change*. London: Frances Pinter.

Düll, K. and Lutz, B. (eds) 1989: *Technikentwicklung und Arbeitsteilung im internationalen Vergleich*. Frankfurt: Campus.

Edwards, P. 1987. *Managing the Factory*. Oxford: Basil Blackwell.

Edwards, P., Hall, M., Hyman, R., Marginson, P., Sisson, K., Waddington, J. and Winchester, D. 1992: Great Britain: still muddling through. In A. Ferner and R. Hyman (eds) 1992, 1–68.

Elbaum, B. 1991: The persistence of apprenticeship in Britain and its decline in the United States. In H. Gospel, *Industrial Training and Technological Innovation. A comparative and historical study*. London/New York: Routledge.

Eyraud, F., d'Iribarne, A. and Maurice, M. 1988: Des entreprises face aux technologies flexibles: une analyse de la dynamique du changement. *Sociologie du Travail*, 1(30) 55–77.

Ferner, A. and Hyman, R. (eds) 1992: *Industrial Relations in the New Europe*. Oxford: Blackwell Publishers.

Fox, A. 1985: *History and Heritage. The social origins of the British industrial relations system*. London: George Allen and Unwin.

Goetschy, J. and Rozenblatt, P. 1992: France: the industrial relations system at a turning point? In Ferner and Hyman (eds) 1992, 404–44.

Grahl, J. and Teague, P. 1991: A new deal for Europe. In A. Amin and M. Dietrich (eds), *Towards a New Europe. Structural change in the European economy*, Aldershot: Edward Elgar Publishing, 166–78.

Hall, P. 1984: Patterns of economic policy: an organizational approach. In S. Bornstein, D. Held and J. Krieger (eds), *The State in Capitalist Europe*, London: Unwin Hyman, 21–53.

Hall, P. 1986. *Governing the Economy*. Oxford: Oxford University Press.

HBS, IGM, IAT, FhG 1992: *Lean Production/schlanke Produktion. Neues Produktionskonzept humanerer Arbeit?* Düsseldorf: HBS.

Herrigel, G.B. 1989: Industrial order and the politics of industrial change: mechanical engineering. In P.J. Katzenstein (ed.), *Industry and Politics in West Germany*, Ithaca and London: Cornell University Press.

Hildebrandt, E. and Seltz, R. 1985: Trade union technology policy between the protection of status and work structuring. *Economic and Industrial Democracy*, 6, 481–99.

Hildebrandt, E. and Seltz, R. 1989: *Wandel betrieblicher Sozialverfassung durch systemische Kontrolle? Die Einführung computergestützter Produktionsplanungs- and Steuerungssysteme im bundesdeutschen Maschinenbau*. Berlin: Rainer Bohn Verlag.

Hoang-Ngoc, L. and Lallement, M. 1992: The decentralization of industrial relations in France: trends towards microcorporatism?. Paper presented at the International Working Party on Labour Market Segmentation, Cambridge, July.

Hoss, D. and Wirth, B. 1992: Relations of trust in East German industry? Paper presented at the Conference on Convergence and Divergence in Economic Growth and Technical Change, MERIT, University of Limburg, Maastricht, December.

Hyman, R. and Streeck, W. (eds) 1988: *New Technology and Industrial Relations*. Oxford: Basil Blackwell.

Jacobi, O., Keller, B. and Müller-Jentsch, W. 1992: Germany: codetermining the future. In Ferner and Hyman (eds) 1992, 218–69.

Keller, B. 1990: The future of labour relations in the Federal Republic of Germany, *Labour and Society*, 15(4) 379–99.

Kern, H. and Schumann, M. 1984: *Das Ende der Arbeitsteilung? Rationalisierung in der industriellen Produktion*. Munich: C.H. Beck.

Landes, P. 1969: *The Unbound Prometheus. Technological change and industrial development*. Cambridge: Cambridge University Press.

Lane, C. 1989: *Management and Labour in Europe. The industrial enterprise in Germany, Britain and France*. Aldershot: Edward Elgar Publishing.

Lane, C. 1990: Vocational training, employment relations and new production concepts in Germany: some lessons for Britain. *Industrial Relations Journal*, 21(4) 247–59.

Lane, C. 1991: Industrial reorganization in Europe: patterns of convergence and divergence in Germany, France and Britain. *Work, Employment and Society*, 5(4) 515–39.

Lane, C. 1992a: European business systems: Britain and Germany compared. In R. Whitley (ed.), *Firms and Markets in Europe: the role of social institutions in structuring market economies*, London: Sage Publications, 64–97.

Lane, C. 1992b: Between control and commitment: the changing pattern of production and labour relations in Britain and Germany. Paper presented at the Conference on Convergence and Divergence in Economic Growth and Technical Change, MERIT, University of Limburg, Maastricht.

Linhart, D., Düll, K. and Bechtle, G. 1989: Neue Technologien und industrielle Beziehungen im Betrieb – Erfahrungen aus der Bundesrepublik Deutschland und Frankreich. In K. Düll and B. Lutz (eds), *Technikentwicklung und Arbeitsteilung im internationalen Vergleich*, Frankfurt and New York: Campus, 93–160.

Locke, R. 1984: *The End of the Practical Man: entrepreneurship and higher education in Germany, France and Great Britain 1886–1940*. Greenwich: JAI Press.

Lodge, G. 1987: Introduction. Ideology and country analysis. In G. Lodge and E. Vogel 1987, 1–28.

Lodge, G. and Vogel, E. (eds) 1987: *Ideology and National Competitiveness: an analysis of nine countries*. Boston: Harvard Business School Press.

Mahnkopf, B. 1992: The 'skill-oriented' strategies of German trade unions: their impact on efficiency and equality objectives. *British Journal of Industrial Relations*, 30(1) 61–81.

Marchington, M. and Parker, P. 1990: *Changing Patterns of Employee Relations*. Hemel Hempstead: Harvester Wheatsheaf.

Marginson, P. and Sisson, K. 1988: The management of employees. In P. Marginson, P.K. Edwards, R. Martin, J. Purcell, K. Sisson, *Beyond the Workplace*, Oxford: Basil Blackwell, 80–122.

Marsden, D. 1992: Trade union action and labour market structure. In A. Castro, Ph. Méhaut and J. Rubery (eds) 1992, 150–74.

Méhaut, Ph. 1992: Further education, vocational training and the labour market: the French and German systems compared. In A. Castro, Ph. Mehaut and J. Rubery (eds) 1992, 162–74.

Michon, F. 1992: The dynamics of the French industrial relations. Towards an 'archeo-corporatism'? Paper presented at the Conference of the IWPLMS, Integrating Economies: Disintegrating Societies, Newnham College, Cambridge.

Millward, N., Stevens, D., Smart, D. and Hawes, W. 1992: *Workplace Industrial Relations in Transition: The DE/ESRC/PSI/ACAS Surveys*. Aldershot: Dartmouth Publishing.

More, C. 1980: *Skill and the English Working Class, 1870–1914*. London: Croom Helm.

Müller-Jentsch, W. 1992: Works councils in Germany. Draft Paper. University of Bochum/Germany.

Müller-Jentsch, W., Rehermann, K. and Sperling, H.-J. 1992: Socio-technical rationalization and negotiated work organisation: recent trends in Germany. In OECD (ed.), *New Directions in Work Organization; the industrial relations response*, Paris: OECD, 93–112.

Piore, M. and Sabel, C. 1984: *The Second Industrial Divide*. New York: Basic Books.

Rainbird, H. 1990: *Training Matters: union perspectives on industrial restructuring and training.* Oxford: Basil Blackwell.

Ramsey, H. 1991: Reinventing the wheel? A review of the development and performance of employee involvement. *Human Resource Management Journal,* 1(4) 1–22.

Segrestin, D. 1990: Recent changes in France. In G. Baglioni and C. Crouch (eds), *European Industrial Relations,* London: Sage Publications, 93–126.

Senker, P. 1992: *Industrial Training in a Cold Climate.* Aldershot: Avebury.

Sorge, A. and Streeck, W. 1988: Industrial relations and technical change. The case for an extended perspective. In R. Hyman and W. Streeck (eds), *New Technology and Industrial Relations,* Oxford: Basil Blackwell, 19–47.

Steedman, H. 1990: Improvements in workforce qualifications: Britain and France 1979–88. *National Institute Economic Review,* August, 50–61.

Stoffaës, C. 1989: Industrial policy and the state: from industry to enterprise. In P. Godt (ed.), *Policy-Making in France. From de Gaulle to Mitterand,* London: Pinter Publishers, 105–26.

Storey, J. and Sisson, K. 1990: Limits to transformation: human resource management in the British context. *Industrial Relations Journal,* 21(1) 60–5.

Thelen, K.A. 1991: *Union of Parts. Labour politics in postwar Germany.* Ithaca and London: Cornell University Press.

Turner, H.A. 1962: *Trade Union Growth, Structure and Policy.* London: Allen & Unwin.

Whitley, R. 1992: Societies, firms and markets: the social structuring of business systems. In R. Whitley (ed.), *European Business Systems,* London: Sage Publications, 15–45.

Wilson, F.L. 1991: Democracy in the workplace: the French experience. *Politics and Society,* 19(4) 439–62.

Zysman, J. 1983: *Governments, Markets and Growth: financial systems and the politics of industrial change.* Ithaca, NY: Cornell University Press.

8

Beyond Corporatism: the Impact of Company Strategy

Colin Crouch

Most schools of industrial relations theory were caught off guard by the rise of corporate and managerial strategies as the most dynamic forces affecting industrial relations since the early 1980s. Now, however, we face glib generalizations about the importance of the company and management initiatives which suggest that virtually nothing else, including inter-country differences, need be discussed. This chapter will redress the balance by demonstrating the continuing importance of cross-national variation. Company strategies operate differently according to national context, and institutional (and therefore supra-company) structures continue to differentiate countries and sectors within countries.

Theoretical and Historical Background

My approach in this chapter is to present a long-term historical perspective, examining the development of industrial relations in the period of growth and consolidation of mass production and its more recent decline. I begin by sketching a formal deductive model, such as is familiar in economic analysis, of employers' strategies and their relationship with trade unions. Next I present some 'stylized facts' to illustrate the typical evolution of collective bargaining at multi-employer level. I go on to discuss the evidence from different western European countries of challenges to existing bargaining systems. Finally, I consider how far this experience matches the predictions of the model, and how differences might be explained.

This deductive model entails drastic simplification. It distinguishes only two levels of action in industrial relations: low (company) and high (industrial or national). It also assumes that the importance of each level for industrial relations can be measured by the number of interactions between employers and their organizations on the one hand, and workers and their organizations on the other. Further, it assumes that while the total volume of interactions may change over the long term, in the short term an increase in interactions at one level can occur only with an equivalent reduction at the other.

In addition, the model makes assumptions about the preferences of workers and employers. It is difficult for workers to establish and sustain collective organization, and the costs and obstacles are increased at higher levels. Low-level action is also preferable in that it is easier for workers to control the policies and actions of their representatives. However, this preference is counteracted by the fact that higher-level action reduces vulnerability to competitive pressures affecting individual firms, and also permits strategic intervention, particularly in the political arena.

In practice, workers themselves cannot choose between levels of industrial relations action: they lack the strategic capacity for such a choice. Only when there are established organizations which can act at higher levels does choice become possible. Even then, unions rarely take the initiative to alter the structure of industrial relations; rather they respond to initiatives of employers or governments.

It is assumed that employers normally prefer to retain unilateral autonomy at company level; that if forced to deal with workers' organizations, they wish to keep such interaction to a minimum; that they favour higher-level collective bargaining, if this helps sustain their 'managerial prerogatives' within the workplace; and that otherwise they may have no strong preference between the two levels of action.

Employers are better placed than workers to take strategic decisions (Offe and Wiesenthal 1980; Crouch 1982). Participating in a collective organization entails few if any risks, and (in all but the smallest firms) can be delegated to professional staff. However, individual firms – at least large firms – do have a real choice, in that they can be influential industrial relations actors even outside a collective organization. Further, many firms organize collectively for reasons other than industrial relations (for example, in trade associations) and thus acquire an organizational capacity which can easily be carried over into industrial relations (Crouch 1993).

To summarize: where there is little industrial relations activity, neither side may be in a position to exert strategic choice on the level of action. When action is intense, both parties may be able to do so. At intermediate levels, employers are more likely than workers to possess strategic choice.

This means that in the early stages of industrial relations development, only low-level action is possible. As workers develop organizational capacity they may pursue higher-level action in order to counteract their weakness at company level. Over time, employers may concede the demand for higher-level regulation, although insisting in return that company-level action should be reduced. Eventually, if workers continue to develop their organizational strength, they may press – successfully – for increased influence at the lower level also.

This will result (figure 8.1) in a U-curve of low-level industrial relations activity. The trajectory at the higher level is the opposite. Initially, as organizations on each side develop their capacity, interaction will increase. Eventually, however, as pressure of the lower level builds up, employers in particular face a choice. If higher-level regulation no longer insulates them from company-level pressure, they may well prefer to switch back to low-level regulation; but they also have the option of pursuing stronger high-level regulation to combat problems at the workplace. The dynamics of changing levels of action are complex. They may involve a mass of spontaneous low-level actions, or more strategic decisions by high-level actors. Much will depend both on the relationships and mutual preferences of actors at each level, and on the degree of articulation between the different levels on each side.

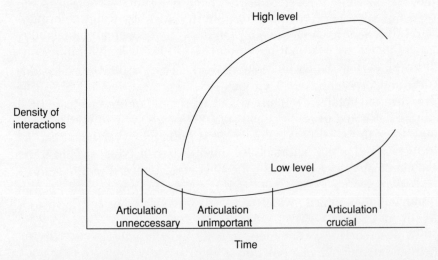

Figure 8.1 Density of interactions over time at two levels of bargaining

To repeat, this model is drastically oversimplified. The assumption that workers' power just accumulates over time leaves out the possibility of successful employers' counter-offensives. Further, the capacities of both employers' and workers' organizations for strategic action cannot be derived from logical assumptions of rational interest, but depend on inherited (or borrowed) institutional legacies, which are usually specific in time and place. Individual countries' and sectors' positions will be affected by the timing of their industrialization. Such a theoretical scheme also leaves out such upheavals as world wars, fascist regimes and other examples of employers using political strength to crush workers' ability to form organizations. However, something of the historical trajectory outlined can be seen to rest behind the specificities of individual national cases, serving as an underlying theoretical rationale behind more complex immediate events.

Figure 8.1 stands as a reasonable representation of the stylized facts of western European labour history. There has typically been a period of early industrialization around craft production, the organization of labour being almost entirely restricted to skilled craft workers who have developed a capacity for local or low-level action though nothing more. This period, normally ending in the last decades of the nineteenth century, has usually been followed by the spread of organization to less-skilled workers who do not have the craftsmen's capacity for local organization and must at least try to build their strength on the protection of large-scale organization and action at the high level. They have needed large organizations to provide sheer organizational strength to compensate for labour-market weakness; to reduce competition in the labour market by trying to bring a range of employers to bargain in common; and to exercise some political influence to persuade government to establish minimum conditions that they do not have the strength to secure through collective bargaining.

Higher-level bargaining was not always forced on employers. Where unions developed strength at company level, employers might find themselves vulnerable to piecemeal pressure tactics and therefore combine to create a united front. Industry-level regulation had the attraction of taking wages out of competition, and could also help to neutralize the workplace from trade union activity (Sisson 1987: 13), protecting managerial authority within production.

The growth of higher-level regulation encouraged worker organization on industrial union lines, and also stimulated demands for higher-level, sometimes national, political action. This included not just bargaining arrangements or the legal establishment of workers' rights, but also macroeconomic policy favouring employment. This development takes a long time, but typically reached a point of rapid expansion some time between 1935 and 1950.

In some respects the whole prolonged period constitutes a 'Fordist' episode, though ironically in the United States, the country where Fordism originated, the supra-company level of bargaining did not develop far. In European countries these work processes often combined with a development of labour movement politics differing from the United States. Perhaps more important, these countries lacked the US system of anti-trust law that has inhibited the growth of business associations and employers' associations. A kind of European Fordism therefore developed with distinctive branch-level and national political structures.

Relative success in the achievement of a framework of branch- or national-level collective bargaining, or Keynesian macroeconomic demand management, often gave workers of all kinds enough security at enterprise level to make new low-level demands, putting pressure on the capacity of the high-level system. In many countries such a period dates predominantly from the achievement of full employment some time in the late 1950s or early 1960s, culminating in the explosion of shop-floor militancy in the late 1960s and 1970s.

Typologies of Inherited Systems

There are two primary sources of variation in the way in which the abstract forces described so far operate. First, the balance of power between capital and labour determines which side is able to be more effective in shaping the system at any one time. For simplicity I shall treat it in terms of the relative strength of labour in the exchange. Second is the question of the varying access of capital and labour to organizational resources going beyond those which develop more or less 'automatically' from the bargaining relationship. Although this access is likely to vary between capital and labour, I shall initially treat this as a joint question. Asymmetries will be dealt with as they affect individual cases.

Combining degree of union strength and extent of co-ordinating capacity gives the major potential alternative outcomes shown in figure 8.2. It is assumed, first, that the higher the relative strength of labour, the greater the problems of managing high-level systems of industrial relations; second, that manageability at a given level of labour strength will rise, the greater the co-ordinating capacity of the two sides. Where co-ordinating capacity is weak, the only form of

	High	I. Unstable collective bargaining	IV. Tense neo-corporatism
Strength of organized labour		II. Stable collective bargaining	V. Stable neo-corporatism
	Low	III. Ineffective labour organization	VI. Stable neo-corporatism through social promotion

Low   High

Extent of co-ordinating capacity of capital and labour

Figure 8.2 Different forms of high-level industrial relations systems

regular interaction that is possible is collective bargaining; at low levels of labour strength this can be a stable model (II), although as labour's strength grows, its bargaining power will cause macroeconomic problems which the system lacks the capacity to accommodate, rendering the system unstable (I). At the extreme of labour weakness, workers may not be able to insist on any joint regulation at all (III).

When the social partners possess capacity for strategy and articulation, they are likely to develop neo-corporatist structures (IV and V). These make it possible to contain workers' strength at higher levels of labour's organizational power than under weakly co-ordinated systems, though there will still be tension as this rises in level (IV). The only other point that requires to be demonstrated is the possibility of co-ordinative ability by weak labour movements (VI). According to most theories, including that outlined so far above, labour acquires a co-ordinating capacity only as it develops organized power. The exception occurs in societies where, for some exogenous reason, the state (or possibly employers) needs to give organized labour a place of recognition that its industrial strength does not strictly 'deserve', what Katzenstein (1984), thinking primarily of Switzerland, terms a form of 'social promotion'.

Implications of the New Company-Level Industrial Relations

We are now in a position to review what has been happening in different kinds of systems over the past 15 to 20 years. The initial thrust behind the recovery of low-level action from the late 1960s onwards was not the development of post-Taylorist, flexible-specialization production regimes, but the resurgence of shop-floor confidence. A new generation of workers took full employment and a framework of trade union legitimacy for granted, although they were experiencing grievances as the easy growth of the initial post-war decades was coming to an end (Soskice 1978). The initial response of employers was to try to reduce the role of this new low level and to continue to place their confidence in the high, external level, either defending or trying to strengthen its neo-corporatist qualities. Where employers' organizational capacity at this level was weak, governments took the initiative.

However, workers' resurgence was quickly followed by the growth of 'new production concepts', the spread of Japanese managerial philosophy, the development of human resource management (HRM), and similar processes. Some though not all of these developments were clearly responses to shop-floor assertiveness. Further, individual companies needed to restructure in order to deal with such major challenges as changed conditions of production following the two oil shocks and other sources of commodity-price inflation, the impact of microprocessor technology on production and administration, and the emergence of the new industrializing economies in the Far East. Such restructuring could not be accommodated within the structure of branch-level agreements. Moreover, managements began seeking to regain the initiative in personnel relations, and therefore to 'redomesticate' elements of personnel policy that they had, under Taylorist conditions, been content to pass up to extra-firm negotiation.

While unions' capacity for strategy is challenged by an autonomous resurgence of their own lower levels, firms are able to respond strategically, because employers have greater control over the levels at which interaction will take place. They have therefore seized the initiative over reshaping industrial relations. Their strategies have varied considerably, often as a matter of corporate choice, as is anticipated in the theory where employers are given discretion in choice of strategy at this point. Some managements just want to regain power over the deployment of the work-force. Others want to develop company cultures and involvement models that require liberation from both external sources of determination of pay and conditions and of extra-firm patterns of participation and discussion of work matters. This is accompanied by a move at company level away from industrial relations and towards human resource management. Both approaches usually entail reducing interactions with unions. Both also often imply cutting back on high-level action by passing a growing number of questions to company-level determination.

However, employers' determination to make major changes will vary with their experience of existing high-level institutions, and with the incentives and opportunities presented to them by their particular context defined in terms of figure 8.2. The greater the strength of organized labour, the more likely will employers use the new company prominence to decentralize industrial relations. This means they should be expected to challenge existing arrangements of forms I, IV, V, possibly also II, and replace them with company-level bargaining; and to take full advantage of union weakness to develop non-union personnel strategies in III and VI. However, where employers themselves have a strong capacity for co-ordination (IV–VI), they will be less inclined to sacrifice the scope this affords for strategic capacity at higher levels than the firm.

If this reasoning is correct, preferences for the company level will be strongest where the existing structure has taken forms I–III, though there will be differences among these: form I gives the clearest incentive to break supra-company arrangements; III gives the easiest opportunities, but also less *need* for change, because workers and their representatives will already be particularly co-operative; II raises questions of letting sleeping dogs lie.

Questions of sleeping dogs are also raised, under different circumstances, in V and VI, while IV opens the possibility of considerable struggle between powerful co-ordinated unions and employers who, though similarly co-ordinated, consider that their opportunities to 'beat' the unions may be stronger if they themselves sacrificed the supra-company level.

Diversities of European Experience

If common pressures have been mediated through different past experiences, it should be possible to analyse differences by reference to the above models of prior structures. In so doing it is necessary for simplicity of presentation to assume that individual countries constitute examples of one or a limited number of these models. It must be acknowledged that a full account would have to recognize far greater diversity within nations, particularly according to different sectors of the economy, and with certain large corporations in particular being able to establish their own systems.

Collective bargaining systems

I and II: Unstable and stable collective bargaining

No western European countries emerged from the 1970s with pure (as opposed to semi-corporatist) *national* collective bargaining systems in a state of stability. Individual sectors and companies, however, followed the pattern in a number of countries, particularly perhaps in parts of the services sector, where there is usually detachment from national political issues and a non-militant, primarily white-collar work-force. There has been no real conflict of levels because of the weakness or non-existence of sector bargaining, so that employers have had little difficulty in reinforcing company-level action. Crises have sometimes resulted for unions, however, as British banking illustrates (Purcell 1993). Employers have used their improved power position to renegotiate agreements reached during the 1970s, especially over working hours.

Unstable collective bargaining was more widespread. Employers themselves have a very low level of co-ordination in this pattern and are therefore most likely to use new company-level policies aggressively to break from all high-level action and reduce union influence in general. Pattern I had become particularly common in several British, Irish and Italian sectors. Workers and unions had developed considerable strength at shop-floor level; in Britain and Ireland this had been a long-run tendency, while in Italy it had developed rather rapidly since the 1960s.

Employers' organizations had been weak, particularly in the United Kingdom, and business associations for non-labour purposes had not been particularly important. Central bodies (CBI and Confindustria) lacked co-ordinating power. All three countries had experienced important neo-corporatist experiments in the 1970s – partly as employers responded in the way anticipated in the theory of reinforcing the centre in the light of the low-level challenge, though mainly because governments had become desperate at the inflationary crisis (which was exceptionally severe in all three) and repeatedly sought means for bringing unions and employers' associations together to try to reach agreements (Crouch 1977, 1993; Hardiman 1988; Regini 1982).

All three countries possessed a structure of branch-level employer organizations and collective bargaining. This was weakest in Italy, where, despite strong statutory support, it was hampered by the long history of exclusion of the communist unions and by extreme regional disparities. The same disparities did, however, mean that regional branch-level bargaining, especially in the north, had an importance it had long ago lost in the United Kingdom, and more closely resembled the German pattern.

From the early 1980s all three countries witnessed a failure of the weakly based neo-corporatist experiments, a collapse of earlier bargaining structures and militant attacks by employers on union actions and achievements as managements sought to regain the initiative. This ostensibly confirms the thesis of a new thrust for company-level managerial control. However, only in the United Kingdom does the evidence support the thesis of a collapse of industrial relations institutions, in public as well as private sectors; the Italian situation was considerably more complex and differentiated, while Ireland continued with attempts at stabilizing higher-level co-ordination. Throughout the 1980s in the United Kingdom, though with gathering speed towards the end of the decade, bargaining above company level, especially over wages, declined in the private sector almost to the point of disappearance (Crouch 1990a; Edwards et al. 1992; Millward et al. 1992; Purcell 1993). One consequence has been the collapse of employers' associations in many branches. Once they have lost their role in industrial relations, their other membership services can often be replaced with accountancy-based consultancy firms (which are particularly prominent in the British economy). British business has therefore begun to lose any capacity for formulating common ideas on labour issues on the basis of practical, task-oriented associations. At national level the CBI has been replaced by the Institute of Directors as the main spokesman for business interests, reflecting the latter's closer affinities to Thatcherite ideology.

Within larger companies decentralization went even further, as managers in individual establishments were increasingly given discretion over matters of pay and conditions (Purcell 1987). This discretion is usually exercised within a tight framework of budgets and policy guidelines, but employees and unions are unable to progress beyond the local manager to debate these. Interestingly this within-firm decentralization went furthest within manufacturing; in many services sectors, such as banking and retail trade, individual establishments are too small for local pay-fixing to be feasible. The public sector remained rather more centralized, though much of it has been privatized. Within what remained government has pursued a dual strategy of maintaining rigid central controls over aggregate pay rises while seeking to imitate the private sector by breaking up national bargaining machinery for other matters. Conservative governments since 1979 have also pursued a sustained policy of assisting the reassertion of managerial power, with a succession of legislative changes to weaken unions and diminish employee rights. Further, most tripartite bodies within which unions exerted some national influence have been abolished; it is significant, for example, that the tripartite Manpower Services Commission has been replaced with local Training and Enterprise Councils, the members of which are leading *individual* business persons, and which lack any national-level organization capable of co-ordination.

Although the evidence is mixed, it seems that most managements have simply reasserted unilateral control rather than pursuing sophisticated human resource management. However, in individual companies there are examples of both human resource management and continuing co-operation with unions within a changed power relationship (Millward et al. 1992). Although union membership has declined, and in new areas of employment it is particularly weak, there is only limited evidence of direct exclusionary policies by firms.

Overall, the British pattern has moved from type I to II where unions exist; elsewhere III is becoming the predominant form. In some respects – for example, the abandonment of an incorporationist approach towards unions by government and employers, and of attempts at national co-ordination in pay determination – the period has been one of considerable change of direction. The changes have, however, been atavistic in reinforcing some fundamental characteristics of British industrial relations; a matter of making a virtue of necessity. What had been seen as a weakness of co-ordination has become a determination to avoid all co-ordination. And the long-perceived discontinuity between high and low levels is being tackled by the abolition of the former.

In Ireland, where there was a stronger legacy than in the United Kingdom or Italy of successful co-ordination of pay bargaining, appropriate to the small size of the country, government returned to a search for tripartite national agreement after a break of only five years of neo-liberal experiment as wage inflation continued to cause problems (von Prondzynski 1992).

The Italian situation is more varied, and overall does not conform to the expectations of the theory for a case of unstable collective bargaining. In particular there has been considerable variance and change in employers' strategies. The 1980 Fiat dispute and subsequent approaches to bargaining by Federmeccanica and others indicated a considerable desire among employers to follow the British road: to weaken unions and push for company-level industrial relations. However, similarly not only to Ireland but also to Germany, The Netherlands, Belgium and Denmark, aggressiveness by employers and right-of-centre governments in the early 1980s was not sustained (Ferner and Hyman 1992b; Negrelli and Santi 1990). Neither co-operative approaches at company-level nor sectoral nor even national bargaining and co-ordination attempts disappeared from the agenda.

At intervals Italian governments have renewed the call for central negotiations over wage restraint and the renegotiation of the *scala mobile*. More generally they have continued to seek the national integration of the main unions, ending the earlier decades of oppositional exclusion of the communist union, in particular. Employers, including Fiat, also returned to a policy of seeking union co-operation over modernization and restructuring.

One motive for employers here has been the continuation of shop-floor militancy by groups of workers organized outside the framework of the main unions. This has been particularly important in the public service, where groups representing the more highly paid groups (most prominently railway engine-drivers and schoolteachers) have formed *Cobas*, outside and hostile to the unions and rejecting the latters' shift to a more co-operative role (Bordogna 1992). A thorough-going move to company- or establishment-level bargaining would mean rejecting the established unions for these groups. Employers have obviously been reluctant to do this.

This situation, together with the fact that Italian business is still constructing industrial relations institutions, has meant that national, sectoral and regional levels of action have continued to play important roles at various times. The country's regional heterogeneity, combined with the recent rise in the importance of regional government, have led to a particularly important growth in branch-level bargaining within regions (Regalia 1988). At the same time the general motives for adopting stronger company-level profiles have also been operative. The overall outcome has been a rich complexity of behaviour, with no obvious single trend.

Unlike the United Kingdom, the Italian economy is dominated by small firms. In many of these, unions have no role at all, although one achievement of Italian unions during the 1970s and 1980s was to establish a foothold in this sector, especially in the flourishing industrial centres of central Italy (Trigilia 1986). This was sometimes achieved through local political party links that bound firms, unions, local governments and other local institutions in a network supportive of economic development. These relationships have continued to thrive. Sometimes they affect workers with insecure terms of employment more usually associated with non-unionized firms. However, unions continue to find that they can obtain some advantages for their members in these situations, and they have often co-operated in regulating work procedures. A further important factor here which also explains the diversity and complexity of the Italian case is that because of a poor record of trustworthiness in official institutions, informal, face-to-face arrangements are often more significant in Italy than organizational ones. Unions have become part of these processes.

In addition to the heterogeneity discussed here, we need a political variable to explain further the greater diversity of the Italian experience compared with Britain, and the more diluted nature of the drive for company-level action. There has been no frontal political attack on unionism similar to that in the United Kingdom. Until the major change of March 1994, all major political parties have had their union links, so it is difficult for any party to launch such an attack. (A similar point applies to Ireland where, during the 1980s, governments were formed either by coalitions including the Labour Party or by Fianna Fail, a party not unlike Democrazia Cristiana in its all-embracing character.)

Further, and again unlike the United Kingdom, Italy is a country in which there have been considerable anxieties about national integration: continuing urban terrorism from extremes on right and left; extraordinary regional diversity; until the 1970s the alienation from the rest of society of a powerful communist party and its union associates; in more recent years aggressive regional separatist movements. Even without their union links, Italian parties would have been cautious about alienating and isolating organized labour from national life. Major employers and employers' associations have shared this view, at least because of the continuing role of shop-floor militancy. This has combined with the obvious desire of the unions, especially the former communists, to try to play a constructive economic role. In ways directly contrary to what one would have expected on the basis of their past histories, the United Kingdom and Italy have diverged from their temporary convergence during the 1970s, with Italy seeking an articulated and incorporationist structure of industrial relations and the United Kingdom pursuing extreme disaggregation and union exclusion.

III: Ineffective labour organization

Outside Scandinavia most employment in private services lacks any organization of labour at all, and in much of France, Portugal and Spain this situation characterizes far larger sectors of the economy. In these cases employers are left virtually free to pursue whatever strategy they like. The resolution of tension between levels should hardly be an issue for management, who should be expected by the theory simply to pursue company-level bargaining. Nevertheless, in some instances weak unions may have played an important role, and subsequent developments have been of considerable interest.

French history furnishes many examples of this. Union organization has long been weak, and employers in most firms have considered themselves able to ignore them (Reynaud 1975; Goetschy and Rozenblatt 1992). On the face of it, therefore, there was no period of growing high-level action. However, this is too simple. The past legacy of French labour is of occasional capacity to generate highly disruptive, if short-lived, conflict. On several occasions, most notably 1936 and 1968, this has been sufficiently important for French labour to wield political influence, potentially challenging the social order. Following these instances, and also during the period of national reconciliation after 1944, legislation has been passed erecting industrial relations and bargaining institutions at a number of levels, from national to company.

These legal mechanisms have produced fields of industrial relations activity which have been found useful by both unions and employers. The former have taken advantage of the opportunity to attain prominence despite their underlying weakness, even though they traditionally rejected the concept of negotiation and agreement. Employers made use of extra-company bargaining in order to keep unions out of the plant.

During the 1980s French union membership levels, like those in most other countries, declined. In France, however, that reduced them to a very low level indeed; according to some estimates membership in private-sector manufacturing is as low as 5 per cent. Many French employers have taken the opportunity to reassert complete managerial control and remove firms from any connection with extra-company institutions. Legal reforms by the Socialist government in the early 1980s designed to advance worker representation ironically furthered this trend (Goetschy and Rozenblatt 1992; Segrestin 1990). The *lois Auroux* imposed an obligation on employers to consult and bargain with their work-forces on a range of issues. Because the obligation was imposed on companies, the level at which unions have been weakest, it gave firms a justification for avoiding the supra-company levels that had been the unions' toehold within the system.

However, in this context it has been remarkable that there has actually been a *growth* of collective bargaining at branch level since the early 1980s (Crouch 1993: chapter 7; Goetschy and Rozenblatt 1992). Employers too have had ineffectual organizations, and this has been widely perceived in France as a weakness in comparison with

Germany (Maurice et al. 1982). There have therefore been attempts to increase their role and significance, in particular by the Socialist governments of the 1980s. The employer organizations, alongside government, have found it opportune to make overtures to the unions at such a period, and they have been keen to negotiate various framework agreements at sectoral and national level on the introduction of new technology, training, and a range of other non-pay issues. All the unions other than the CGT have been happy to take advantage of these opportunities.

It is, however, a matter of debate whether these changes have had much practical importance. The avoidance of union channels in the development of such new company-level strategies as quality circles has been noted, though in this respect France is similar to many other countries (Goetschy and Rozenblatt 1992). Most uncertainty concerns whether there has been real change *within* the existing French model of company-level managerial determination. Some accounts point to the change in the structure of French capital, away from the small family firm to the modern large enterprise, and to the spread of HRM techniques. Others suggest that there has been little change in the hierarchical character of the typical French firm, large or small.

Fears that organized labour, if not incorporated in some way, might become a threat to social order, once so important in France, probably have far less importance today for French policy-makers, which helps explain why recent French developments have been far less intense than those in Italy. In Spain, Portugal and Greece, where a transition to democracy did not occur until the 1970s, the issue is very live (Martínez Lucio 1992; Estivill and de la Hoz 1990; Barreto 1992; Pinto 1990; Kritsantonis 1992). Despite the extreme industrial weakness of unions, they have been capable of considerable militancy, and governments have been very concerned to erect national fora and encourage the establishment of industrial relations institutions; a desire to which organized employers have made some response. As in France, there has therefore been some rise in high-level interactions in these countries, and attempts to establish a very loose neo-corporatism.

However, because of the weakness of institutions, none of this has been incompatible with a high level of autonomy for managers and employers at company level. Again as in France, it is often difficult to determine whether one is still witnessing traditional *patron* behaviour or modern managements using the latest HRM techniques in personnel policy; or whether casual employment contracts are a residue of the semi-rural past or new numerical flexibility. A similar uneasy coexistence between largely formal aspirations for national-level concertation and institutional development, and unilateral employer control over the workplace can also be seen as part of the democratic transition in central Europe.

Neo-corporatist systems

IV: Tense neo-corporatism

The previously highly stable neo-corporatist systems of Scandinavia came under considerable strain during the 1980s. The familiar push to shop-floor action by workers was supplemented by a decline in the proportion of the work-force in export-oriented manual employment in manufacturing which had supported the whole edifice. To an extent only recently recognized, the moderation of Scandinavian centralized wage determination had been based on an awareness by union leaders in this sector of the effect on international competitiveness of increases in unit labour costs (Crouch 1990b; Lash 1985). Over time this manual manufacturing dominance of both work-force and trade unions has become diluted by public service workers who lack exposure to competition, and white-collar workers whose unions have been less concerned with macroeconomic issues and more with their members' relative position. The theory here predicts an assault by management on high-level institutions, though because within such systems employers have strong co-ordinating power, they retain strategic control over the level at which they wish to pursue industrial relations.

The co-ordinating powers of Scandinavian organizational structures were therefore eroded from the late 1970s. At the heart of this system had been the great scope and power of the organizations on both sides of industry. While accounts usually stress the lead taken in this process in the late nineteenth and the early twentieth centuries by labour movements organizing simultaneously for industrial and political purposes (Stephens 1979), Scandinavian employers found it easier to form their own strong, disciplined organizations in response. These then often took the initiative in pressing labour to increase its own centralization.

The decentralizing challenges of the late 1960s and 1970s undermined the effectiveness of these central structures, although on both sides of industry, especially the employers, they retained considerable importance. During the 1980s union membership in Denmark and Sweden did not suffer the decline experienced elsewhere, though Norway was in line with the more general trend. (Denmark and Sweden, though not Norway, long ago developed the Belgian system of associating trade unions with the administration of unemployment benefit. This seems to provide a counter-cyclical reinforcement to membership during recessions.)

Since the 1980s these countries have seen the familiar pattern of employers producing their own powerful response to workers' earlier decentralization challenge. In each case, however, and in contrast with Britain and France, the decentralization has been supervised by the central employers' associations; observers have termed it a 'centralized decentralization' (Due et al. 1994). This much is common: the trajectory of the development has varied considerably among countries.

Most action has taken place in Denmark and Sweden, and the biggest contrast is between these two. Norwegian developments have been similar though less dramatic, and located somewhere between the others.

In both Denmark and Sweden the central employers' bodies began to say in the early 1980s that they wanted to stop central bargains and move to either branch or company level. Note that the central bodies announced that such a development would be desirable; it did not happen because they had collapsed or were in a state of internal conflict, as in the United Kingdom or Italy. Employers' organizations had not lost their strategic capacity for high-level action; they wanted to use this to privilege different levels as they saw fit. This is consistent with the theory that the present period offers employers a range of options. Particularly in Denmark, there have been years when the central bodies reasserted the desirability of recentralizing, albeit temporarily.

In Denmark employers spent much of the 1980s developing company-level industrial relations (Amoroso 1990; Scheuer 1992; Due et al. 1994: Part III). They were assisted in this by the fact that unlike most other European countries, Denmark has a 'British' system of union organization, with few genuine 'industry unions', and a large general union representing the low-skilled across several sectors. Inter-union rivalry has therefore been a continuing problem.

However, by end of the decade the central bodies of capital and labour had jointly developed a new agreed strategic model that explicitly recognized the space to be allocated to local action. At the same time both sides reorganized themselves to cope with the change in employment structure described above. Danes can be described as having reconstructed an articulated system, with considerably greater scope than in the past for company-level action under managerial leadership, yet with no collapse of higher levels. The organizations have not lost their strategic capacity to plan the outlines of the system, even if they have recognized the role of the firm. Norway has progressed likewise, with a similar associational reconstruction.

Swedish developments have so far been more conflictual (Rehn and Viklund 1990; Pestoff 1991; Kjellberg 1992). As in Denmark, there has been division among the unions, though concerning only contemporary problems of manufacturing versus services and manual versus non-manual, not the older question of skilled versus unskilled. Employers have taken advantage of this as well as growing shop-floor militancy and the growing failure of the central bargaining system to contain inflation in order to demand the dismantling of the national pay-bargaining system and the decentralizing of all industrial relations to branches and, eventually, to individual companies. A particularly aggressive role has been played in this by SAF, the central employers' body. SAF has taken the view that Sweden is being isolated by its special institutions and strong social democracy from the Anglo-American approach which it regards as superior and likely to become globally dominant (Pestoff 1991).

By the early 1990s SAF wanted to take this policy much further and demolish all aspects of the Swedish articulated industrial relations system, including labour market management and administrative neo-corporatism as well as centralized bargaining. This has implications going far beyond labour questions, for the system of formally involving functional interests in policy formation and administration is a long-established principle of Nordic government, predating the industrial age. SAF now wishes to change all Swedish characteristics that do not conform to the Anglo-American model, which means that organizations such as itself should become lobbies and pressure groups, not co-administrators. Part of SAF's reasoning is that while a formalized co-administration system necessarily includes representatives of labour, a lobbying system requires no formal rules, and the greater resources of the employers' side could reduce union influence to insignificance.

Meanwhile employers have been pressing on with company-level employment strategies, with HRM and quality circles being particularly important. It is difficult in Sweden to avoid dealing with unions, although firms have been able to take advantage of unions' slowness in responding to change. Further, Swedish unions have always been reluctant to accept workers' commitment to individual companies and are therefore likely to oppose HRM and quality circles. In 1993 the Swedish system remained locked in controversy, with no indications of an attempt at an agreed revised model.

One can account for the Danish–Swedish difference on this point in two ways. First, the countries have very different company structures, the former being dominated by small firms and the latter by large ones. In the former case, firms which already have a strong tradition of organization fear the consequences of being left without organizational cover and continue to look to associations even when wanting a shift towards company labour policy. The Swedish economy is dominated by very large companies which possess the resources to develop company-level strategies without difficulty.

Second, the political cycle has been very different. In Denmark the social democrats were out of office from 1981 to 1992, and although the government took no major steps hostile to unions, it did embark on a neo-liberal approach and considerably reduced its own relations with unions. After some years it seemed to have reached the limits of such an approach in Denmark, and began to work with unions again. In Sweden the political change did not take place until 1990. Although the bourgeois parties had been in office in the early 1980s, at that point they saw their aim as proving that the Swedish welfare system was safe in their hands. Sweden did not therefore experience a period of neo-liberal government at that time, and the right had to remain in opposition in the country with the strongest labour movement in the world throughout the neo-liberal decade of the 1980s. When it eventually came to power in 1991, it therefore embarked on an aggressively new-rightist policy, doing so at a time when organized business was also extremely militant: deregulation, because it was delayed, took a particularly explosive form.

To determine whether industrial structure or politics has been more important, we must await further political development in Sweden. Norway fits both theses (Foss 1992; Dølvik and Stokland 1992). Small firms predominate, though the average size of state-owned enterprises is higher than in Denmark, and there have been more oscillations of government than in either of its neighbours. Depending on how developments turn out in Sweden, it is possible that we shall eventually witness a readjusted rather than a collapsed Scandinavian model, with far greater autonomy for companies, although under surveillance of continuing central organizations. For unions this threatens their traditional solidaristic wage policy and presents the challenge of whether they can participate in company personnel strategies.

Finland has always diverged from the general Nordic pattern. Modernizing very late and containing a very powerful communist wing within the labour movement, neo-corporatism was always more difficult to develop. However, the employers' organization has had the typical Nordic centralized form. Unions have also tended to follow the Swedish model as they overcame their internal divisions (Lilja 1992).

Finland certainly constitutes a case of tense neo-corporatism. However, whereas the Scandinavian tension has taken the form of once highly stable systems entering a period of crisis, in Finland the neo-corporatism was successfully erected only in the 1970s. In some respects Finland is a country with an Italian legacy of disaggregated though politicized conflict, but with Scandinavian organizational structures. Of the various countries trying to achieve neo-corporatism in the 1970s or early 1980s (such as the United Kingdom, Italy, Ireland and Spain), Finland was the only one which really possessed the institutional base that was likely to succeed. In several respects it has been a strategy of Swedish imitation. Now that the Swedish model has changed, will Finnish employers seek to imitate the new Swedish pattern and seek a radical decentralization? Or will they try to build on the previous project, and perhaps take a Danish route? As Lilja remarks (1992: 215), it is not possible to predict.

V: Stable neo-corporatism

The theory predicts less challenge to supra-company institutions in cases of neo-corporatism that remained stable. This certainly seems to be confirmed by the Austrian and German cases, though for reasons more interesting to the issue of company strategies than the simple fact of stability (Traxler 1992; Jacobi and Müller-Jentsch 1990; Jacobi et al. 1992). As in Scandinavia, these countries have long possessed highly co-ordinated, disciplined employers' organizations linked to strong business associations whose continuing role in the economy has not been in doubt (Crouch 1993: chapters 7, 10). Employers have therefore not wanted to give up this capacity for co-ordination. This has been reinforced by the fact that, particularly in Germany, employers have been more comprehensively organized than labour. Austrian and German unions have been unable to develop the ambitious solidaristic strategies of Scandinavian labour, nor have they ever secured rights in law as strong as in the Nordic countries.

At least as important, however, have been the well-known works council systems in both countries. These have not only imparted a clear company level of action throughout what I have called the European Fordist period, but have also been thoroughly integrated within the general system of industrial relations. For present purposes the most important implication of this structure is that Germany and Austria did not experience the extreme disparity between developed high-level and undeveloped low-level industrial relations during the 1950s and 1960s implied by figure 8.1.

The consequences of the works council system have been ambiguous. Initially unions, especially in Germany where they have always had more difficulty securing control over works councils, resented the councils for performing, in collaboration with management, tasks that should be left to union combativeness. In time, however, they learned how to make themselves useful to works councillors, and during the 1980s came to be grateful for the protection of workers' rights and their own access to the plant which works councils afforded at a time when employers in some other countries were becoming militant in ways that have prevented labour from seizing the initiative (Jacobi and Müller-Jentsch 1990; Jacobi et al. 1992).

The shift to a company level within an otherwise co-ordinated system has been far less threatening to workers and unions, employers and employers' associations, than in the British, French or Scandinavian inherited systems. These have therefore been cases of considerable stability.

Even then there has been some strain. Some German firms wanting to introduce HRM have taken the opportunity to develop quality circles and team-leader systems that bypass works councils, while the latter have argued that they should be the basis for such ventures. The unions feel challenged by these developments and are aware that their and the works councils' style of dealing with company-level participation is threatened by the new approaches. However, because of their long connection with the works council approach, they are at least well informed about the character of the changes and are probably in a stronger position than unions elsewhere to keep track of them and develop responses.

The important question for the future is whether German unification and the associated hard-currency regime of the Bundesbank will impose too much strain on both countries' systems (Austria being fully tied to the Deutschmark) and threaten more instability in the labour market than the structures can absorb.

VI: Social promotion

The idea of a limited neo-corporatism as a form of social promotion, offered at some point in the past to help ensure that a weak unionism remained quiescent, and left in place because it had not subsequently become troublesome, seems to apply in Belgium, The Netherlands and Switzerland. However, these countries differ in their early trajectory. The Low Countries followed the typical Euro-Fordist pattern of development of high-level extra-company industrial relations and exclusion of unions from the plant (Spineux 1990; Vilrokx and van Leemput

1992; Visser 1990, 1992). Switzerland in contrast was closer to the Austro-German pattern of articulation and integration of levels, except that the emphasis was far more clearly on the lower level. Most Swiss collective bargaining has been conducted at company or plant level. This has, however, differed from the British version of that pattern by being completely though informally reconciled with wider objectives through the strong associational structures that effectively govern Switzerland (Farago and Kriesi 1986; Hotz-Hart 1992).

Belgium has differed from the other two: while their union membership has been low, Belgium's is one of the highest in Europe. However, uniquely within western Europe, the Christian component of the union movement has since 1960 been more important than the social democratic wing. While this has protected Belgian labour from attacks by the new right, it has also implied a growing passivity.

In all three countries, and especially in Switzerland, labour threatened stability less than elsewhere during the 1970s. Employers have therefore had less motive to disturb existing institutions in their search for new company-level strategies. In Belgium and The Netherlands there had been enough militancy for employers and right-wing governments to experiment with dismantling some national participative structures in the early 1980s, although this did not last long. As in Denmark, Germany and Ireland, there was a return to former patterns after some readjustment to weaken the position of organized labour (Hemerijck 1993).

The move to company policies has placed less strain on the Swiss system, though as elsewhere employers have demonstrated some restlessness with the constraints imposed by collective agreements on their pursuit of company personnel policy and flexible contract terms (Hotz-Hart 1992). The Dutch had adopted a German works council system (replacing their earlier Franco-Belgian model) in 1976. However, this had been introduced at a time of great weakness among Dutch unions and they have been far less imaginative than their Austrian and German counterparts in using it. Stability is primarily secured through employer autonomy and a continuing national norm of consensus. Belgium lacks a works council system of the German type, although, as in The Netherlands, both the deep embeddedness of industrial relations institutions in national life, and the fact that employers can usually achieve flexibility at company level when they want it, inhibit challenges to the inherited mechanisms of regulation. These systems are unlikely to experience radical alterations to existing formal structures, not because employers lack the power to enforce change, but because they can secure virtually all their needs for company autonomy without confronting them.

Conclusion: Towards New Models?

This discussion has demonstrated considerable diversity in the response of different European systems to the recent challenge of managerially determined company-level strategies. There are three explanations for this diversity.

First, the stylized historical trajectory of figure 8.1 has to be considerably amended for several countries, and differences during the Euro-Fordist period affect the encounter between the different levels in the later period. The model mainly fits the Scandinavian cases, the Low Countries, Ireland and the United Kingdom. Even within this group there are some differences. In Ireland and the United Kingdom there was a precocious rise of an autonomous shop-floor level well before the late 1960s. The Low Countries and the Scandinavians shared some characteristics with, respectively, the Franco-Italian and the Germanic models. In all these cases we should expect to find the pattern anticipated in figure 8.1: during the 1980s a crisis over the weight of different levels in the system with a subsequent shift towards company level at the expense of higher levels. While the expected rise in management-led company autonomy is found in all cases, the thesis of an associated collapse of extra-company levels fits only the United Kingdom unambiguously, and possibly Sweden if very recent trends continue.

In France and Italy (and to some extent the Low Countries) the high level differed in being heavily dependent on statutory support, the real weight of the system resting on union exclusion from the company. We should here expect management to be most able to move unambiguously to the company level. Again, while important trends of this kind are seen in all cases, it is powerful only in France – and even there it is offset by a modest rise in extra-company collective agreements.

In Germany and the Alpine countries there was a different and even more important divergence from the initial model in that the high level was already closely integrated with the low, and the high level was protected on the employers' side by powerful associations. We should therefore expect little disturbance to the overall shape of these systems by employers' pursuit of new managerial practices. This expectation is confirmed.

A slightly similar articulation had been achieved through union structures rather than the bargaining system in the Scandinavian cases, where shop-floor union representatives had a clear role within the centralized system. Business associations there too were powerful within the system, although the greater union control and greater approximation of these cases to the model should lead us to expect less stability than in Austria and Germany; the centralized decentralization found confirms expectations.

The second variable, still contained within the terms of the model, concerns the strength of workers' shop-floor challenge in the late 1960s and 1970s. The stronger this was, the more determined we should expect management to be to retake the initiative at company level. This suggests the most aggressive managerial responses to be in Italy, the United Kingdom, France, Ireland and the Scandinavian countries. The evidence confirms this expectation, although the subsequent return to more conciliatory approaches in Ireland, Denmark, Norway, to a limited extent France, and most surprisingly Italy, is unexpected.

Finally, however, the above discussion has had to leave the bounds of a theory about the development of levels in order to consider political variables. These are of two kinds. First, where new-right governments encouraged and supported employers in moves to neo-liberal policies, in macroeconomic policy, in their own relations with unions and in changing the legal framework, employers were more likely to connive at undermining central structures: the United Kingdom throughout the period; Belgium, Denmark, Germany, Ireland and The Netherlands temporarily in the early 1980s; and Sweden in the early 1990s. Second, where governments of any colour had anxieties about the stability of the social order, they were likely to reinforce rather than demolish national bodies for industrial relations conciliation, and this in turn inhibited employer militancy: primarily Italy and Spain, although to some extent also France and Germany.

It is only when this third factor is taken into account that a satisfactory explanation can be given for all countries. It enables us to make sense of the continuing search for extra-company consensus in Italy and post-unification Germany, and the continuing search for agreements despite labour's weakness in France, Spain, Portugal and Greece. It also helps explain similar attempts in small countries worried about international economic vulnerability (Ireland, Denmark, Finland and Norway), and in those where a conciliatory system of industrial relations is part of national political arrangements (Belgium, The Netherlands and Switzerland). Even when considering such a question as the growth of company-level industrial relations, we find we need recourse to political variables for a full explanation.

References

Amoroso, B. 1990: Development and crisis of the Scandinavian model in Denmark. In G. Baglioni and C. Crouch (eds), 71–96.

Auerbach, S. 1990: *Legislating for Conflict*. Oxford: Oxford University Press.

Baglioni, G. and Crouch, C. (eds) 1990: *European Industrial Relations: the challenge of flexibility*. London: Sage Publications.

Barreto, J. 1992: Portugal: industrial relations under democracy. In A. Ferner and R. Hyman (eds) 1992a, 445–81.

Bordogna, L., 1992: *Le Nuove Organizzazioni non confederali*. Turin: Giappichelli.

Crouch, C. 1977: *Class Conflict and the Industrial Relations Crisis*. London: Heinemann.

Crouch, C. 1982: *Trade Unions: the logic of collective action*. London: Fontana.

Crouch, C. 1990a: United Kingdom: the rejection of compromise. In G. Baglioni and C. Crouch (eds), 326–55.

Crouch, C. 1990b: Trade unions in the exposed sector: their influence on neo-corporatist behaviour. In R. Brunetta and C. Dell'Aringa (eds), *Labour Relations and Economic Performance*, London: Macmillan and International Economic Association, 68–91.

Crouch, C. 1993: *Industrial Relations and European State Traditions*. Oxford: Oxford University Press.

Dølvik, J.E. and Stokland, D. 1992: Norway: the 'Norwegian model' in transition. In A. Ferner and R. Hyman (eds) 1992a, 143–67.

Due, J., Madsen, J.S., Jensen, C.S., and Petersen, L.K. 1994: *The Survival of the Danish Model: A historical sociological analysis of the Danish System of collective bargaining*. Copenhagen: Jurist-og Økonomforbundets Forlag.

Edwards, P. et al. 1992: Great Britain: still muddling through. In A. Ferner and R. Hyman (eds) 1992a, 1–68.

Estivill, J. and de la Hoz, J.M. 1990: Transition and crisis: the complexity of Spanish industrial relations. In G. Baglioni and C. Crouch (eds), 265–99.

Farago, P. and Kriesi, H.-P. 1986: *Wirtschaftsverbände in der Schweiz*. Güsch: Verlag Rüegger.

Ferner, A. and Hyman, R. (eds) 1992a: *Industrial Relations in the New Europe*. Oxford: Blackwell Publishers.

Ferner, A. and Hyman, R. 1992b: Italy: between political exchange and micro-corporatism. In A. Ferner and R. Hyman (eds) 1992a, 524–600.

Foss, P. 1992: Problems of centralized collective wage bargaining and incomes policy in Norway. Unpublished DPhil thesis, University of Oxford.

Goetschy, J. and Rozenblatt, P. 1992: France: the industrial relations system at a turning point? In A. Ferner and R. Hyman (eds) 1992a, 404–44.

Hardiman, N. 1988: *Pay, Politics and Economic Performance in Ireland, 1970–1987*. Oxford: Oxford University Press.

Hemerijck, A. 1993: Origins, establishment and fragmentation of Dutch corporatism. Unpublished DPhil thesis, University of Oxford.

Hotz-Hart, B. 1992: Switzerland: still as smooth as clockwork? In A. Ferner and R. Hyman (eds) 1992a, 298–323.

Jacobi, O. and Müller-Jentsch, W. 1990: West Germany: continuity and structural change. In G. Baglioni and C. Crouch (eds), 127–53.

Jacobi, O., Keller, B. and Müller-Jentsch, W. 1992: Germany: codetermining the future. In A. Ferner and R. Hyman (eds) 1992a, 218–69.

Katzenstein, P. 1984: *Corporatism and Change: Austria, Switzerland and the politics of industry*. Ithaca: Cornell University Press.

Kjellberg, A. 1992: Sweden: can the model survive? In A. Ferner and R. Hyman (eds) 1992a, 88–142.

Kritsantonis, N.D. 1992: Greece: from state authoritarianism to modernization. In A. Ferner and R. Hyman (eds) 1992a, 601–28.

Lash, S. 1985: The end of neo-corporatism? – the breakdown of centralised bargaining in Sweden. *British Journal of Industrial Relations*, 13(3) 215–39.

Lilja, K. 1992: Finland: No longer the Nordic exception. In A. Ferner and R. Hyman (eds), 1992a, 198–217.

Martínez Lucio, M. 1992: Spain: constructing institutions and actors in a context of change. In A. Ferner and R. Hyman (eds) 1992a, 482–523.

Maurice, M., Sellier, F. and Silvestre, J.-J. 1982: *Politique d'éducation et organisation industrielle en France et en Allemande*. Paris: Presses Universitaires de France.

Millward, N., Stevens, M., Smart, D. and Hawes, W.R. 1992: *Workplace Industrial Relations in Transition*. Aldershot: Dartmouth Publishing.

Negrelli, S. and Santi, E. 1990: Industrial relations in Italy. In G. Baglioni and C. Crouch (eds), 154–99.

Offe C. and Wiesenthal, H. 1980: Two logics of collective action: theoretical notes on social class and organizational form. *Political Power and Social Theory*, 1, 67–115.

Olson, M. 1982: *The Rise and Decline of Nations: economic growth, stagflation and social rigidities*. New Haven: Yale University Press.

Pestoff, V. 1991: The demise of the Swedish model and the resurgence of organized business as a major political actor. Stockholm: Department of Business Administration, University of Stockholm.

Pinto, M. 1990: Trade union action and industrial relations in Portugal. In G. Baglioni and C. Crouch (eds), 243–64.

Purcell, J. 1987: The impact of corporate strategy on human resource management. In J. Storey (ed.), *New Perspectives on Human Resource Management*. London: Routledge.

Purcell, J. 1993: The end of institutional industrial relations. *Political Quarterly*, 64(1) 6–23.

Regalia, I. 1988: Forme della rappresentatività e democrazia nelle esperienze sindacali verso gli anni 90: problemi e questioni aperte. Milan: IRES Lombardia.

Regini, M. 1982: Changing relationships between labour and the state in Italy: towards a neo-corporatist system? In G. Lehmbruch and P.C. Schmitter (eds), *Patterns of Corporatist Policy-Making*, London: Sage Publications, 109–132.

Rehn, G. and Viklund, B. 1990: Changes in the Swedish model. In G. Baglioni and C. Crouch (eds), 300–25.

Reynaud, J.-D. 1975: *Les Syndicats en France*, Volume I. Paris: Editions du Seuil.

Scheuer, S. 1992: Denmark: return to decentralization. In A. Ferner and R. Hyman (eds) 1992a, 168–97.

Segrestin, D. 1990: Recent changes in France. In G. Baglioni and C. Crouch (eds), 97–126.

Sisson, K. 1987: *The Management of Collective Bargaining: an international comparison*. Oxford: Blackwell Publishers.

Soskice, D. 1978: Strike waves and wage explosions, 1968–1970: an economic interpretation. In C. Crouch and A. Pizzorno (eds), *The Resurgence of Class Conflict in Western Europe since 1968*. Volume 2. *Comparative Analyses*, London: Macmillan, 221–46.

Spineux, A. 1990: Trade unionism in Belgium: the difficulties of a major renovation. In G. Baglioni and C. Crouch (eds), 42–70.

Stephens, J.D. 1979: *The Transition from Capitalism to Socialism*. London: Macmillan.

Traxler, F. 1992: Austria: still the country of corporatism. In A. Ferner and R. Hyman (eds) 1992a, 270–97.

Trigilia, C. 1986: *Grandi partiti e piccole imprese*. Bologna: Il Mulino.

Vilrokx, J. and Leemput, J. van 1992: Belgium: a new stability in industrial relations? In A. Ferner and R. Hyman (eds) 1992a, 357–92.

Visser, J. 1990: Continuity and change in Dutch industrial relations. In G. Baglioni and C. Crouch (eds), 199–242.

Visser, J. 1992: The Netherlands: the end of an era and the end of a system. In A. Ferner and R. Hyman (eds) 1992a, 323–56.

von Prondzynski, F. 1992: Ireland: Between centralism and the market. In A. Ferner and R. Hyman (eds) 1992a, 69–87.

9

Workplace Unionism: Redefining Structures and Objectives

Michael Terry

Introduction

The waves of union militancy that shook several European countries during the late 1960s and the 1970s were frequently initiated, and often controlled, by shop-floor activists rather than by national union leaderships. Indeed in several countries, perhaps Italy and France in particular, key struggles were as much against what were perceived as bureaucratic, collaborationist, right-wing union leaders as against employers. Workers' control was a demand applying both to the politics of production and to trade unionism, requiring locally controlled and democratic trade union structures on the one hand, job control and *autogestion* on the other.

Many supporters of shop-floor spontaneity argued that strong workplace unionism both articulated the interests of workers and most effectively allowed them to influence and control their working environment and conditions. Conversely, centralized and bureaucratic structures, and in particular those which derived from legal rights rather then being rooted in workers' autonomous actions, were criticized as ineffective and undemocratic, designed to draw the teeth of militant mobilization. Hence, among other examples, the drive by Swedish unions for more effective forms of workplace representation in the 1970s; attempts in West Germany to develop union-based steward systems as a radical alternative to institutionalized works councils; the emergence and development of spontaneous workplace organization in Spain based on mass meetings; and criticisms of the 1970 Italian *Statuto dei Lavoratori* as legislation designed to demobilize and incorporate the spontaneously-created *consigli di fabbrica* of the 'hot autumn'.

Implicitly and explicitly, one influential 'model' for workplace union organization and behaviour was that of the British shop steward system. Directly elected stewards, accountable to their members on a day-to-day basis, often fiercely independent of union 'bureaucrats', deploying collective workers' power untrammelled by legal rights or constraints to negotiate over pay, conditions and job controls appeared to many as the apotheosis of effective, militant, workplace unionism. Indeed, during the 1970s British shop steward organization was frequently cited, in the United Kingdom and elsewhere, as the form of unionism best suited to defend and articulate workers' interests in a period of rapid technical change and work reorganization (see, for example, Degen, 1976).

As we now know, such confidence was misplaced. British workplace unionism, although still a significant presence in many private and public sector companies, has found itself increasingly pushed to the margins of workplace activity (Marchington and Parker 1990; Terry 1989; Brown 1993). In Germany, by contrast, criticism of the system that separates collective bargaining from worker representation at plant and company levels has been muted as its advantages have become 'self-evident'. 'It is now almost universally agreed that the system allows flexible adjustment to change *without weakening the representational strength of unions*' (Jacobi et al. 1992: 220, emphasis added). As will be argued below, precisely those features of autonomy and decentralization celebrated in Britain contributed to stewards' marginalization, while the greater centralization and rigidities of the German system have buttressed it against similar decline. Autonomous workplace unionism appears, despite the claims made for it during the 1960s and 1970s, to have fared less well as an agent for effective worker representation during the 1980s than its more integrated, less independent, counterparts.

It could be suggested at this point that the UK experience does nothing more than reflect the consequences of more than a decade of the weakening of unions under attack by government and employers and that it could be reversed under a more supportive regime. It will be argued, however, that such broad explanations fail both to deal adequately with the British experience and to provide a framework for the analyses of other countries. Although the retreat from the model of shop-floor autonomy can be observed in most European countries, the manner in which this has occurred and the political and economic contexts differ considerably. This chapter offers explanations for the different trajectories of workplace unionism in Europe in the 1980s. It stresses the nature of workplace organization, the institutional framework within which it operates and how these have combined to shape union responses to the challenges of the decade.

The first part examines the different forms of shop-floor unionism which emerged from the general institutional consolidation in the 1970s and identifies the different traditions of workplace unionism which confronted the novel challenges of the 1980s. The next section examines such evidence as exists concerning union responses to these challenges, both as agents for the representation of members' interests and as organizations seeking to influence employer behaviour. Finally, an account is suggested for at least some of the observed patterns.

The analysis should be of relevance to contemporary workplace union organization in general; however, given the nature of much of the literature and available research, there is an inevitable bias towards the private manufacturing sector. The issues raised by the growth of private services and the changing nature of the state sector can only be touched on from time to time.

The 1970s: Institutional Development and State Intervention

During the 1970s, in different ways in different countries, shop-floor unionism either consolidated its earlier, more tenuous, position, or emerged as a significant force for the first time. Governments attempting to establish 'corporatist' solutions to economic problems were seriously concerned by the disruptive potential of shop-floor mobilization and action. Their general approach was to provide institutional support for workplace collective representation as a partial trade-off against national union co-operation in addressing economic problems, generally with policies of wage restraint.

The implications of these developments were the subject of competing interpretations in the United Kingdom and elsewhere. Did these changes strengthen the power and representative capacity of organized labour in the workplace, or did they weaken them by incorporation and demobilization? The debates of the 1970s presented these as mutually exclusive views. Here it will be argued that it is necessary to transcend this dichotomy; to argue that there were both gains and losses, and that the key element lies in understanding the relationship between them.

Although the precise effects of the changes in government policy were varied, they generally enabled local union organization to spread beyond those sectors whose market and technological features had helped its development (engineering, and in particular the motor vehicle industry, was often cited as the *locus classicus*) into sectors where the structural environment was less favourable. This was particularly noticeable in countries with no prior legislative support for effective local representational structures (works councils): the 1970 *Statuto dei Lavoratori* in Italy and the 1974–7 Social Contract legislation in the United Kingdom provided the bases for such institutional expansion. In countries with works council systems the self-confidence of workplace unionists often found expression less in expanding sectoral coverage than in radical criticism of such systems (their formal separation from union organization and their weak or non-existent rights to bargain, mobilize and strike). In Sweden the voluntary system of works councils 'proved completely inadequate to channel workers' increasing demands' (Kjellberg 1992: 121) in the radicalized climate of the 1960s and 1970s, and, following the enactment of the 1976 co-determination legislation, the major unions withdrew from the works council agreements as a means of putting pressure on employers to reach co-determination agreements.

In Germany, particularly in the metal industry, local union representatives – *Vertrauensleute* – increasingly abandoned their traditional role and started to challenge the dominance of the established works councillors, often pressing a more radical, oppositional form of local unionism. Here the combination of increasing scope for local bargaining and the established rights of the works council led not to the abandonment of the works council systems but to their strengthening and closer integration with the unions. While the struggles for control between *Vertrauensleute* and works councils were real enough in some key sectors during the 1970s, by the late 1980s at least, 'the rivalry between *Vertrauensleute* and [works councillors] ended in victory for the works councillors, a reflection of the legally-established position of the works councils and their strategic role in recruiting union members' (Jacobi et al. 1992: 245). Or, as some might put the same point though with a marked difference in emphasis, it ended with the effective union capture of works councils. In any case it can be agreed that in both Sweden and Germany the emergence of assertive workplace unionism had both radicalized and greatly changed the existing system and had more firmly established its presence and role.

Even in Spain, where the industrial turmoils were even more marked, by the beginning of the 1980s state intervention had helped stabilize patterns of workplace representation, and, as in France and Italy, apparently also contributed to the containment of spontaneous local action and organization.

It is possible to categorize, or at least to cluster, local unionism in Europe by the late 1970s into three broad groups. First, we can identify those countries in which a form of viable workplace unionism developed during the 1970s alongside, or in opposition to, although eventually in co-ordination with, statutorily-based systems of employee representation (Germany, Austria, The Netherlands); systems of viable trade unionism in the workplace with no effective statutory supports or adjuncts (United Kingdom, Ireland); and systems with elements of statutory support in place though with weak workplace union presence (France and, to a lesser extent, Italy and Spain).

There is increasing consensus that the first group afforded the most support for workplace unions during the 1980s and that unions in that environment have been the most successful in dealing with recent challenges. Two rather different types of criteria are used for this assessment: the institutional stability of workplace unionism over the period; and more controversially, the argument, sometimes implicit, that such an environment has succeeded in fostering a form of unionism that does not threaten, and possibly even accommodates and enhances, managerial objectives. Before evaluating these claims, it is necessary to look at the challenges of the 1980s.

The Challenges for Workplace Unions in the 1980s

Unions have faced three major challenges; while none is entirely novel, each has acquired a particular emphasis in the 1980s. First, unions have had to respond to a series of production-related issues deriving from economic restructuring. These often required a qualitatively different approach from that commonly associated with 'distributive' issues such as bargaining over pay and conditions. Second, and related to this, unions faced significant and rapid changes in the composition of the work-force and hence their membership, actual and potential, with profound implications for their representative capacity. Third, there have been important changes in the institutional frameworks for bargaining, consultation and participation at workplace level, deriving from legislation, pressures to reform existing systems of bargaining and consultation, and, from the 1980s, interest among employers in new forms of direct participation.

Although all three issues are important, the dynamic of economic restructuring has driven the process and had the greatest impact on workplace unionism. In many, perhaps most, companies the extent of organizational and technological change has been markedly less than might be suggested by at least some evangelizing texts. Nevertheless, enough has happened under all three headings during the 1980s to make it worth looking at them and their implications for workplace union organization in some detail.

Issues of production and issues of distribution

Unions' stock-in-trade in dealings with employers in all European countries has been bargaining over issues of distribution, concerning the terms and conditions of employment; in few countries have unions sought to bargain over issues of production. In most countries bargaining over pay and conditions – the key union activity – has been centralized. Consultation over work-related (production) issues took place, formally and separately, at workplace and company level, frequently through statutory consultative bodies such as works councils, often with no formal union role. In practice, of course, this separation was rarely clear-cut. In Germany, the country where it formally appears most distinct, in fact the interrelationship of union and works council was and remains important. Nevertheless, the general observation remains valid. The exceptions are Ireland and the United Kingdom. In the United Kingdom, with no such formal separation, and more decentralized bargaining, employers often fiercely resisted conceding formal bargaining rights over production issues. In some industries (print, engineering, the docks) powerful shop-floor unions established, if only fleetingly, a degree of control over job content, the pace of work, and the implementation of change. However, such controls were essentially based on the defence of the status quo, and when dealing with job demarcations, frequently took as their basis a managerially-derived division of labour; rarely were they innovative.

These differences had a number of important implications for shop-floor union organization and behaviour. First, since unions directed much of their activity towards supporting collective bargaining, they tended in centralized systems to neglect workplace-based organization (Regalia 1984). Second, in those countries with centralized pay bargaining and a strong form of collective representation at local level by unions or works councillors (the latter often also union activists), workplace representatives were able to channel their ideas and interests directly into production issues and to articulate their own positions on them rather than simply accept managerial priorities. Such a process was visible in Germany and Austria, where the separation between national and company-level, and between bargaining and co-determination/consultation was most clearly codified. It also occurred in Sweden, where, despite the absence of a 'dual system', a similar situation applied during the 1960s and much of the 1970s as a consequence of union and employer emphasis on highly centralized systems of pay determination. According to some (see, for example, Kjellberg 1992: 121–4), this encouraged Swedish workplace unions in the 1970s to drive for greatly enhanced influence over work organization, often in the name of the 'humanization of work'.

In France, which also had centralized pay bargaining, but, in the 1960s and at least some of the 1970s, relatively uninstitutionalized workplace systems, union perspectives on production issues tended to be reactive and antagonistic to employers. During periods of general militancy this was reflected in union demands. In Italy, the unions' 'struggle against Taylorism' similarly began as a reaction to production issues, which evolved into a clearer political position, developing during the 1970s into an advocacy of workers' self-management. I have argued elsewhere (Terry 1993) that this phase was also important for understanding the responses of unions and workers in the 1980s to managerial pressures for greater flexibility.

Thus, even if in more general and reactive terms than in Sweden, French and Italian unions fashioned positions on production questions that were separate from traditional agendas for collective bargaining concerned with terms and conditions of employment. In Britain, by contrast, it is difficult to identify any emergent position of the unions over production issues. The decentralization of collective bargaining allowed unions to evade the problems by turning changes in technology or work organization into opportunities for reopening negotiations on the terms and conditions of employment. Employers, hostile to any suggestion of formal union participation in such issues, readily collaborated in this process. In practice, as noted above, in some industries British workplace unions did exert considerable pressure on at least some 'micro' elements of production – the pace, intensity and organization of work and hence, indirectly, the introduction of new technology. However, British unions' rhetoric of job control, although at times antagonistic to management, like those of Italian and French unions, lacked the intellectual coherence of the 'struggle against Taylorism'; it was essentially an opportunistic response, often cementing rather than challenging Tayloristic forms of work organization.

There were thus observable correlations between the structures for handling production and distribution issues and union perspectives on production questions. Where they were separated and unions, directly or indirectly, maintained a strong presence in the workplace, union energy went into developing a proactive strategy. Where local union organization was weaker, conflict over production issues often took the form of general campaigns of opposition; and where decentralized collective bargaining predominated, issues of production hardly entered unions' agendas.

The foregoing prompts two further points. The first is that proactive union policies on production issues have tended to develop in the context of 'collaborative', 'consensual' structures, whether those of Swedish local collective bargaining (union-based) or of German co-determination (union-influenced though not directly union-based). In the 1960s and 1970s, with the emphasis on autonomy and conflict, these were often criticized. Second, and this emerges more inferentially, proactive policies tend to be found where there are clear and strong linkages between local and national union systems, again tendencies that run counter to those of local autonomy. From this it may be suggested that the structures and ideologies of workplace unionism alone are insufficient to generate such a response. Production policies require workplace-level acceptance and implementation, yet the formulation of a union response other than rejection or *ad hoc* bargaining demands a capacity for strategic thought which cannot emerge only from local structures.

This discussion has sought both to identify the different starting-points from which shop-floor unions responded to the changes of the 1980s and to indicate some of the linkages between union action and institutional forms. The analysis will be further developed below.

During the 1980s the importance of production issues became much greater as 'restructuring' came to be seen as the key to competitive success in the manufacturing sector. The rapid introduction of new technology and, in particular, the reorganization of work and the intensified search for 'flexibility' heavily influenced managers' pre-occupations, with a consequent reduction in the priority accorded to the traditional agenda of union–management relations, namely, the bargaining of the terms and conditions of employment. The implications for work-forces have often been profound, and unions have come under pressure – from their members as well as employers – to attach greater weight to production issues.

Two other changes were visible in this process in all European countries. First, employers emphasized the decentralization of production issues on the grounds that they could best be implemented at the level at which work was performed, that is, the company, establishment or workplace. They were not seen as appropriate to national, sectoral, multi-employer bargaining. Second, managers increasingly questioned the suitability of any form of bargaining or consultation over such matters; competitive pressures impelled speedy and tough implementation.

Unions were thus confronted with radical change in working patterns in an environment generally less conducive to collective bargaining than in earlier decades. The problem for unions, especially at workplace level, has been to formulate an appropriate response to proposals for work-force restructuring. Unlike pay and conditions bargaining, unions cannot easily respond by demanding more, for production issues are different in kind. As indicated above, one can identify three broad sets of responses: to resist such change; to accept it and to bargain over the terms of its introduction (enhanced pay, shorter working hours, etc.); or to make an independent input into the restructuring. What has happened in practice will be discussed in the next section.

Changes in work-force composition and the representativeness of unions

Three major sub-questions arise. First, how European unions have chosen to define their interest constituency, that is those on whose behalf they seek to act. By and large unions in mainland Europe, whether or not they profess a 'class' perspective, have accepted a broad responsibility to represent all workers: members and non-members; employed and unemployed. Again the United Kingdom provides the clearest contrast: a country in which unions argue the exclusive need to represent their own members in employment. This is related to a second question; whether, in addition to such aspirations, unions operate within national legal frameworks of representation at plant and company level which require the interests of all employees to be represented. Here again, systems based on collective bargaining such as those of the United Kingdom can be contrasted with those based on works councils of other northern European states.

The third question is crucial for the 1980s: how do unions in practice define the interests of those they represent? Here, there is considerable cross-national similarity: most union organizations have sought to articulate the interests of male, full-time, manual workers. This found its clearest expression in Italy in the 1960s and 1970s, when the unions identified with the 'mass worker' whose interests were to be pursued with policies of solidarity and *egualitarismo*.

These issues become of profound concern to our understanding of unions' representative capacity. The 1980s and 1990s have seen significant changes in the organization of work under the influences of changed product and labour market pressures and new technologies of production. The managerial drive for 'flexibility' led to rapid changes in established divisions of labour, patterns of working time, new forms of contracts of employment and for services, and increasingly, what has been widely referred to as an 'individualization' of the employment relationship, as witnessed by the growing use of individual performance-related pay.

All these have worked to change the familiar terrain of union membership and membership interests as the patterns of stable, routine, mostly permanent, full-time employment have become disrupted to a greater or lesser extent.

The implications for unions are profound, though the impact has differed according to the nature of the pre-existing systems. To take one obvious example, the problems were quite different for those unions which had previously operated, structurally and ideologically, to represent the total collectivity of workers compared with those which operated on the basis of sectional representation. For the former – as in the case of the Italian mass worker – the problem was that an increasing number of workers came nowhere near the mass worker ideal, and their interests were inadequately represented on that basis. On the other hand, Italian unions (along with most others in mainland Europe), vertically structured on an industrial basis, confronted quite different problems from those encountered by British unions, based on occupational definitions and boundaries that were increasingly fluid and blurred. In Italy, companies pursuing the blend of integration and diversity held to be the hallmarks of flexible production have correspondingly emphasized the need for less monolithic patterns of representation; while in Britain, employers have called for more integrated structures of inter-union co-operation (single-unionism, or the unions' preferred alternative, 'single-table bargaining').

However, the flexibilities have changed not only the 'constituencies' of unions, but also the market and bargaining power of groups within the workplace and the interests that those constituencies look to unions to represent. In effect the impact of work restructuring may be seen as *privileging* the position and interests of certain groups, usually though not exclusively those performing (multi-)skilled, 'core' work activities, and *weakening* the position of others, increasingly those on a variety of 'non-permanent' employment contracts providing companies' 'numerical flexibility'. The challenges for any union movement basing its structures and demands on those of the notional male manual worker are obvious.

This type of argument carries even more weight when applied to the challenge facing workplace unions as a consequence of their historical failure to recognize the significance of the sexual division of labour and to identify and pursue the interests of women. These failures, which are to be found in every union movement, have taken on ever-greater importance as the influence of women in the workplace, both in their numbers and in the work they perform, increases.

This challenge to representation, while perhaps the most important, is not the only one. Other groups too have argued that pre-existing structures have failed to represent them properly: they include new white-collar professional and managerial groups (*cadres, quadri*), workers on personal contracts outside the scope of collective determination of pay and conditions, homeworkers, outworkers and subcontract workers. All, in different ways, have been denied effective representation through workplace union structures. The unions' capacity for representation has been pulled and stretched by the changes in the organization of work and production, and they have been under increasing pressure to respond to these new groups and demands while at the same time continuing to satisfy the needs of their established membership.

In short, unions whose own structures, constitutions and ideologies emphasized openness, and which operated within legal frameworks conferring collective representational rights on all employees, found it easier to accommodate the growing diversity of employee types than those whose structures reflected occupational closure and the articulation of the interests of union members exclusively. However, the differences are of degree only; few unions can claim to represent the workplace-driven interests of, for example, women and part-time employees as effectively as those of male full-timers.

Institutional change and new forms of participation

As indicated above, two broad sets of changes pose challenges for workplace unionism, though of different kinds. First, there have been changes in the institutional framework of workplace union activity; second, there have been managerial innovations loosely grouped under the heading 'human resource management', designed to facilitate employee participation and involvement, without the direct and explicit intervention of workplace unions. Both have taken place within the overall context, described above, of decentralization of management decision-taking and of bargaining and consultation structures. Looking at the first category, two broad approaches to change can be identified. First, in the United Kingdom, perhaps uniquely, there has been systematic government and employer action to weaken the few legal rights enjoyed by unions at the workplace and to marginalize workplace unions and their representatives, shop stewards. In many workplaces, local trade unions have felt themselves under institutional threat, and their leaders have feared victimization.

In stark contrast, in no other European country have there been adverse changes in legal support for workplace unionism; and in many cases there have been initiatives to strengthen workplace collective institutions, or union organization, or both. The clearest example is probably France, where the 1982 Auroux laws placed clear responsibilities on employers to bargain with unions as well as strengthening union rights at local level. In Spain, legislative intervention provided, or appeared to provide, a more stable basis for workplace unionism. In Italy, since the late 1980s, governments, employers and the union confederations have sought ways of changing the electoral base of the *rappresentanze sindacali aziendali* in order to strengthen the position of the 'most representative' unions.

There are minor exceptions, such as the establishment in Germany in the late 1980s of works committees for management staff. Nevertheless, even changes designed to strengthen rather than weaken the representation of shop-floor workers can pose challenges for their unions. In France the Auroux laws coincided with other economic and institutional factors that worked against union organization and at the same time put heavy strains on inadequate and under-resourced union administrative structures (Goetschy and Rozenblatt 1992: 417–18). In both Spain and Italy the interventions have been designed, amongst other things, to strengthen a particular form of institutional workplace presence at the expense of more 'spontaneous' local forms. Whether favouring the 'most representative' confederations at the expense of the *Cobas* in Italy or the UGT against the CCOO confederation with its origins in workplace activism in Spain, the tendency has been similar. The institutional support has simultaneously reinforced the central 'moderate' confederations and contributed to a demobilization of workplace unionism. As Martínez Lucio has argued in respect of Spain, although the implications of the argument are universal:

> State institutional support . . . may have provided a minimum basis for union action and allowed the movement to consolidate. . . . But at the same time, institutionalization may be seen to have weakened the unions' autonomous capacity to organize and mobilize workers; their recognition, legitimacy and influence derive more from the state than from their own members. (1992: 503)

Since it is increasingly clear that the effectiveness of employee representation, whether by unions or works councils, depends upon strong union organization capable of effective worker mobilization

(Visser 1991: 25–30), any intervention that reduces this will constitute a problem for workplace unions, in the long if not the short term.

The consequences of the second category of changes – the introduction of human resource management techniques of employee participation – are equally ambiguous. Their approach to the management of labour contains no explicit role for trade unions or collective bargaining. Indeed many versions of HRM reject collective bargaining as embodying antagonistic relationships, and unions as a disruptive alternative source of worker allegiance. Certainly HRM has been used, directly and indirectly, by employers seeking to deunionize or marginalize union influence. The problem of HRM for shop-floor trade unions, especially those with a developed tradition of collective bargaining, is that the new techniques threaten many of the activities of communication, information exchange, and handling of employee concerns on which the daily relationships of trust and support between unions and members have been built. Certain techniques, such as quality circles, also provide potential mechanisms for the resolution of problems that had previously been handled by local collective bargaining or consultation.

In the United Kingdom many unions fear that the changes outlined in this section will, intentionally or not, eliminate effective workplace unionism. In other countries they are seen, cumulatively, as significant, though in different ways. In Sweden, for example, it is claimed that

> the aim of new management strategies in Sweden . . . has not been to create union-free enterprises but rather to encourage the union's loyalty to the individual enterprise: a local form of corporatism. To the extent that these efforts are successful, they will erode the strong solidaristic element in Swedish unionism. . . . Fears about the emergence of a multitude of disparate models at local level led the unions to postpone negotiation on local co-determination agreements until a central settlement had been found. (Kjellberg 1992: 147)

In the United Kingdom the concern is over the elimination of workplace unionism; in Sweden it is over the creation of a form of fragmented workplace unionism. Although the concerns are different, in both cases they indicate worries over the future viability of existing forms of union organization.

The Responses of Workplace Trade Unions

The dilemmas faced by unions can be clearly seen, for example, in the British public sector where the unions had to respond to government and managerial proposals for the privatization and contracting-out of services – and hence jobs. For several years the policy of the external union was to resist the proposals, to keep the work 'in-house'. In reality this was virtually impossible to achieve and many local union organizations had to accept the managerial redefinition of work organization; instead they sought to prevent privatization by agreeing to undercut the competitive tenders. This meant accepting, on behalf of the local membership, job losses, pay cuts, and a general worsening of conditions of service. Not surprisingly this in turn contributed to a membership disillusion with the union. To achieve any influence on the terms of work reorganization, therefore, the local union had to ignore its own national policy, accept the new, managerially-imposed parameters, and take huge risks with the loyalty of its members.

This example, though clearly showing the interlinked elements involved is only one example of the problems facing workplace unions. We need to look at the evidence from different countries, although this is not always plentifully available.

Production issues

In responding to managerial proposals for the restructuring of work, unions have had to deal with a number of problems. First, they can tackle production issues effectively only at company or enterprise level rather than within the individual workplace or establishment. This is a level at which shop-floor unions in a number of countries, including France, Italy and the United Kingdom, are traditionally rather weak, while other countries (Germany, Greece) benefit from at least the formal right to works council representation here. In the United Kingdom again, attempts to establish effective company-wide organization (combine committees) have been bedevilled by rivalry between workplace-based steward bodies and the representatives of the external unions.

Second, qualitatively different problems of response are posed for occupationally-based 'craft' unions, as may be found in the United Kingdom and Greece, compared with the more vertically integrated industrial/sectoral unions of most other European countries. To put it simply, significant change in work organization threatens the stability, possibly the very existence, of unions based on the existing division of labour. There is therefore perhaps an inevitable tendency to caution and hostility not necessarily encountered in 'industrial' unions.

Third, there has been the problem of technical expertise. In many countries employers have supplied detailed information on company performance as justification for changes in production organization.

Unions wishing to contribute directly to such debates have in some cases experienced difficulties in formulating a response (see Terry 1989 for UK examples). Such expertise may be provided via external unions (requiring a degree of integration of workplace structures with external unions) or by independent experts, to whom right of access by unions or works councils is stipulated by law in several European countries including France and Germany.

Finally, production issues pose what might be best described as *ideological* problems for some unions. It has been noted that the bargaining dynamics of such issues appear to be different from those of traditional bargaining over pay and conditions. In particular, work organization is less easily negotiated through an ideology of opposition or antagonism to management. Instead it seems to require an engagement with technical managerial ideas and concepts; an acceptance of certain managerially defined parameters of problems and issues. It requires, in terms of the starting-point of this chapter, a retreat from purely autonomous, antagonistic workplace union organization.

If unions are to engage with this issue, therefore, it follows that such strategies contain inherent risks – structural, ideological, and in terms of the relationship between shop-floor unions and their members on the one hand, and management on the other. The nervousness of unions in moving away from traditional approaches can be seen in relation to the question on flexible working hours in Germany where

> trade unions' earlier fears of losing control over this sphere of labour relations have given way to the view that flexible working hours serve not only the employers *but also the unions themselves, by satisfying employee demands for individual variability of working time.* (Jacobi et al. 1992: 251, emphasis added)

This particular example illustrates not only the risks but also a 'positive-sum' outcome in which all – unions, employers and employees – gain. Nevertheless, such outcomes are by no means universal, as can be seen by comparing the differing abilities of shop-floor union movements in different countries to construct such a response. By way of illustration we can look at experience in three countries: Sweden, Britain and Italy.

In Sweden, unions have reformulated the concept of 'solidarity' away from wages and conditions alone to embrace production issues as well (Kjellberg 1992: 132–6; Sandberg 1992). The approach is linked to the concept of 'good jobs', combining both financial rewards and job satisfaction. The responsibility of the union is to increase the number of these jobs and to negotiate systems of training which improve workers' access to them. This enables the unions to pursue their objectives of fairness and 'solidarity' while allowing them to embrace the new production approaches.

A number of points need emphasizing. First, this approach is intended as a fully-fledged union alternative, embodying workers' rather than employers' interests in the new workplace dynamics. Second, it is conceived nationally, and delivered nationally and locally through bargaining at sector and workplace levels, with workplace representatives acting under national guidance. Third, it has its origins in Swedish unions' long-standing acceptance of the importance of a union view on matters of production and work organization, of which the 1960s and 1970s experiments in 'humanization' are the clearest example. Fourth, Swedish unions have been able to develop these approaches in an environment of organizational stability. Fifth, there is high union density and associated widespread support for unions among members. And finally there is a history of at least a degree of employer acceptance of the usefulness of union contributions to such debates.

Against these adventurous developments in union thinking has to be set the fact that in practice they have so far had little impact. The majority of workers never have the chance to develop their skills, never step off the bottom rung (Kjellberg 1992: 135). Kjellberg adds that recent opinion surveys show that 'most Swedish workers see little scope for influencing the actions of the local union . . . [and] a smaller but still significant proportion doubt the union's ability to influence workplace conditions'.

This also illustrates the risk that unions may be taking in developing such innovatory policies: they may emerge at the cost of democratic and effective unionism. The example may be interpreted as lending support to those who argue that 'collaborative' engagement with employer policies of restructuring compromises the autonomy and capacity for resistance of workers' organizations and inevitably reduces their capacity to act as the militant representatives of their members (for a recent forceful statement of this view see Cohen 1991). The possibility of a 'virtuous circle' of advantage for all parties suggested by the German example of working-time is by no means yet confirmed in respect of more thoroughgoing and adventurous union initiatives.

However, the argument of this chapter is that, such debates aside, British unions have not had the option of developing these approaches, despite arguments that they should do so (see Leadbeater

1987). Even if stewards and others had wanted to try a more adventurous approach, the knowledge that their organizations were vulnerable and they themselves open to criticism (or worse) from members and employers if they miscalculated, acted as a powerful inhibitor. The autonomy of British workplace unions, their occupational, 'craft' bases, and their dominant attention to local bargaining over pay and pay-related matters all combined to prevent a co-ordinated and strategic response to novel managerial initiatives in the sphere of production. Partly as a result of this, British unions at workplace level have in practice accepted not only managerial priorities but often also their proposed solutions (see Terry 1989), undermining members' confidence in the utility and influence of workplace unions. There is no evidence that British workers have a higher opinion of their unions' capacity to influence workplace affairs than their Swedish counterparts.

Other countries can be examined in the light of this combination of factors. In Italy, unions have succeeded in using the legal guarantees provided, together with their traditional acceptance of forms of workplace flexibility, to construct widespread systems of collective bargaining in the workplace. In Italy, as in Germany, working-time flexibility has become a dominant issue for local bargaining and it is seen as allowing a mutually beneficial linkage of employees', unions' and managers' interests. However, these claims need to viewed with some caution. In general, the outcomes are less integrative than this approach might suggest. Often workplace bargaining in Italy entails a trade-off between accepting employer demands on flexible working-time, for example, and an increase in formal union rights at workplace level. In other words, workers are required to accept change in their working patterns – of which they may in general approve, but which they and their unions have not been able to influence – in exchange for an improvement in *union* rights. This is a particular form of bargaining entailing a trade in two different bargaining 'currencies'. Its continued success depends in part on the assumption that workers, in unions or not, will accept as useful and in their interests an advance in union stability. Recent events in Italy, including the ballot rejection of some key agreements and, in the public sector, the influence of the informal rank-and-file *Cobas*, suggest that this is not at all clear.

These three different types of union response can be seen as appropriate and comprehensible in the context of particular national systems of industrial relations and trade unionism. Nevertheless, the question has to be asked whether they are all equally viable.

The new human resource management

We can extend this discussion by looking at local union responses to another of the challenges noted above: the introduction of 'union-free' techniques of human resource management. Since these are characteristically techniques implemented in the workplace, the differing responses of unions can best be understood in the light of the pre-existing structures there. In France, with its long-standing tradition of autocratic management and limited union strength in the workplace, quality circles have become more widespread than in any other European country (Goetschy and Rozenblatt 1992: 423). Despite some resistance to them from managers and employers who fear even the limited degree of democratization they might imply, they appear to have further weakened the (often already insubstantial) position of unions within the enterprise.

In Britain, with a much stronger union presence in the workplace, the new techniques have also been viewed by unions with undisguised suspicion as a key element of a co-ordinated policy of deunionization such as has occurred in the United States, and as a clear threat to the unions' monopoly over the channelling of managerial information and worker opinions and interests. If the overall policy of unions has been to shift away from opposition to grudging acceptance (Martínez Lucio and Weston 1992), this is partly from lack of choice and partly a recognition that in at least some workplaces quality circles allow workers to make contributions previously denied them through collective bargaining. Quality circles and the like also raise issues of the organization of production, working patterns, and so on, which British workplace unions have not been used to handling.

> [In Germany,] some unions and works councils at first rejected such participation initiatives, especially quality circles, but in most cases they have now accepted them, and some representatives of the unions and the works councils regard them as the first step towards 'codetermination at the workplace'. (Jacobi et al. 1992: 245)

Such diverse responses illustrate clearly the need to locate new initiatives within particular contexts before labelling them 'pro-' or 'anti-' union. One key point is whether or not they are perceived as a threat to the existing unions and other employee representative structures (or indeed, as in France and elsewhere, including the United Kingdom, to managerial systems). In Germany, with quality circles as with working-time, initial suspicions appear to have been turned to advantage by unions whose security is not threatened in the same way and which are more used to dealing with production issues. The second point is the degree to which quality circles are valued by employees, not only because they may find the subsequent arrangements more congenial but also because they appreciate seeing their knowledge and expertise acted upon. Hence, straightforward opposition to quality circles by unions may antagonize members. This is a dilemma for British unions, whose structures are based on bargaining and which have a suspicion of being implicated in managerial systems and logics, while it is markedly less so, for example, for Swedish and German unions.

Changing work-force and membership composition

As noted above, unions have been facing a change both in their 'constituencies' and the interests they need to represent on behalf of those constituencies. In many cases they have sought to change the latter in order to accommodate the former. To take an example already referred to, although unions in many countries were initially suspicious of the concept of flexibility, they came to see it as an issue which might actually heighten their appeal to groups of members and potential members. The specific issue of working-time flexibility has already been mentioned. In rather more sweeping terms Negrelli has argued for Italy that 'trade union action has transformed the flexibility of labour from a restriction to a resource' (Negrelli 1992: 82).

In other words, unions altered their objectives to respond to the perceived wish of their members to accept managerially introduced change. Failure to do so might have weakened unions' claims to effective interest representation. Unions have had to change their objectives considerably in many countries in order to retain members' loyalties. As will be argued below, this cuts little ice with members when the response is essentially a passive acceptance of managerial priorities and definitions; rather, as implied by the quote from Negrelli above, it works only when union-based responses can be seen to embody a specifically employee-based alternative formulation.

In practice, however, such changed objectives have rarely been pursued in a way that confers equivalent benefits on the entire work-force. Working-time flexibility, for example, may well provide benefits and attractions for certain groups of workers, primarily those in the better-protected 'core' jobs. It is more difficult to adduce evidence that workers in forms of precarious employment perceive that their interests in working-time arrangements have been effectively pursued by the union.

Following this line of argument, it has to be concluded that existing shop-floor union structures have not responded well to the challenges posed by the diversification of interests and interest groups. Part-time, casual and temporary workers (overwhelmingly women) have not been persuaded in appreciable numbers into unions. Nor is there much evidence, in the United Kingdom at least, that local union negotiators are seriously seeking to advance the interests of female workers on non-traditional contracts (Colling and Dickens 1989). Such groups, occupying a weak position in the labour market, are still outside meaningful union protection, even in those cases where unions directly, or through works councils, claim the responsibility of negotiating on behalf of the entire work-force.

Rather different, though no less important, has been the failure of unions in some countries (notably Italy and France) to retain the loyalty and commitment of groups with stronger positions in the labour market, such as certain skilled or professional groups in the public sector. The consequences of this failure can be seen in the militant, shop floor-based action undertaken by unofficial yet well-organized groupings such as the *coordinations* and *Cobas*. In taking these actions they have challenged not only existing union structures but also their objectives and ideology. Their tactics and demands are occupationally based, short-term and opportunistic, embodying a move from broad to narrow collectivities, from strategic to *ad hoc* action.

Putting these points together it can be seen that unions' claims to representativeness, and hence both their local bargaining strength and their ability to pursue co-ordinated objectives, have been seriously undermined by the tendency of new production logics to fragment and differentiate categories of workers. On the one hand, the growing numbers of workers on non-traditional contracts find themselves weakened and excluded; on the other, stronger groups able to 'go it alone' effectively have done so, thus reducing the potential for integrated collective action. In the public sector certain strategically placed groups have sought to use their bargaining leverage against both employer attempts to limit pay or impose other controls and the central solidaristic strategies of the 'official' unions.

Finally, it is clear, at least from the UK experience, that local union organizations and their activists are increasingly providing advice and support to individual employees/members rather than operating through collective action. The most obvious reason for this is that in the 1980s and 1990s shop-floor life for many workers has become tougher and more demanding – greater intensity of work, tighter control and disciplinary action by managers. In these circumstances the availability of a local supporter or advocate becomes increasingly important, and there is some circumstantial evidence to support the view that such individual relationships are increasingly underpinning employee support for trade unionism. Whether or not this is a general phenomenon, and what the long-term implications are for organizations that are conceived as essentially collectivist in nature, it is too early to say.

Accounting for the Responses

The foregoing account has been one-sided in focusing almost exclusively on *changes* in the environment within which workplace union organization operates and on union responses to those changes. It has touched only briefly on the stabilities of the system: the continuity of wages and conditions bargaining by local union representatives in at least many large manufacturing companies; the continuing work of local committees acting in the area of health and safety; the wide range of local consultative arrangements. The justification for the focus on change has been that it throws up important challenges to existing forms of collective employee representation at the workplace. This section will examine the responses to these challenges in terms of two key factors: first, the degree of guaranteed security or stability of local collective representation in the workplace; second, the nature of the relationship and the degree of historical and current integration between workplace union organization and the outside union.

Unions seeking responses to the challenges of restructuring which are meaningful both to their members and the managers with whom they may wish to negotiate incur major organizational and ideological risks. These derive from the new terrain on which they have to work, in both membership composition and bargaining or consultation subject-matter, and from the new environment of 'proactive' managerial techniques of human resource management.

The evidence suggests that the organizations most capable of developing successful strategies have been the well-organized, long-established, statutorily protected forms found in countries such as Germany and Sweden. Their institutional security allows them to take risks without endangering the viability of collective organization itself. At the other end of the spectrum are countries such as the United Kingdom. Here, the environment of government and managerial hostility, and the absence of legal institutional guarantees, have exposed the frailty and vulnerability of even long-established and well-organized workplace unions. Under these circumstances the dominant response was, unsurprisingly, cautious, conservative and antagonistic (Terry 1989).

A similar reasoning lies behind responses to new HRM techniques. Where the security of independent collective representation is provided in law, the threat of employers adopting a 'union-free' strategy is much less than where unions have no such guarantees. It is therefore to be expected that German unions appear to have embraced quality circles, for example, more enthusiastically than their UK counterparts. In between, in countries such as Italy, with a legally guaranteed right to a union presence at the workplace, if not to full recognition, unions have been able to make limited advances, especially in the area of working-time, without always engaging directly with the full agenda of restructuring.

'Organizational security' therefore facilitates the kind of union responses that employers might perceive as helpful, supportive, and likely to predispose them to grant further recognition and consultation rights. Yet what of unions' relationship with their members? Can a similar analysis be advanced? The answer here appears more complex. Although legally guaranteed union security appears to enable more risk-taking with regard to members, it does so by insulating the unions to a degree from the employee/membership responses. At its simplest and most vehement the point can be made that 'the neutralization of direct member influence on union policy is a prerequisite for the unions to perform their functions of negotiating and dealing with employers . . . in a cooperative and authoritative way' (Jacobi et al. 1992: 234).

In other words 'risky' decisions are possible in an environment in which unions derive their strength from sources other than the membership directly (for example, from legal rights) and hence may effectively ignore membership pressures. However, such an approach would be seen as highly contentious, risking the long-term viability of union organization since, as the Italian and other experiences show, well-placed workers may form their own organizations, while the weaker may drop out of union participation altogether.

During the 1980s and 1990s a common approach has been to argue that restructuring provides workplace unions, employees and managers with the opportunity to construct mutually beneficial, integrative solutions to issues of flexibility and work organization. New working arrangements are the most frequently cited example. In this view no fundamental risks are entailed, to bargaining or representative structures, since all parties appreciate the outcomes. This approach does tend to rely on a highly optimistic account of the dynamics and outcomes of restructuring.

The second and related factor is the relationship of workplace unions to the external official unions. This relationship contains a number of important elements. First, the wider union can simply be a source of expert advice, increasingly necessary in the more complex bargaining environment of the 1980s. Second, it can assist in the development of more broadly based strategic inputs to bargaining. The UK example has shown the problems encountered by autonomous shop-floor unionism in moving away from shorter-term, economistic demands; the German and Swedish examples show the contribution that the external union can make.

There is, however, at least one more important element to the relationship, namely, the tradition and ideological basis of centre–local union relationships. In the United Kingdom, again at one extreme, union practice and ideology of local 'direct' democracy and militancy contributed during the 1960s and 1970s to a dominant 'model' of unionism, shared by activists of left- and right-wing tendencies. This held that shop-floor autonomy from the official unions was an indication, even a guarantee, of effective, strong unionism. In many other European countries, despite the shop-floor challenges of the 1960s and early 1970s, that view never gained the same ascendancy.

An alternative democratic tradition, rooted in a wider, in some cases class-based, conception of union constituencies and interests, legitimized a greater degree of central control and authority. Local activists saw themselves as the local representatives of this wider organization, not, as often in the British case, in *opposition* to it. The implications for this chapter are that such unions – in France, Italy, Germany and Sweden – were ideologically and structurally better placed to develop the partnership-based unionism outlined above. In the United Kingdom, the most recent research suggests that the patterns are changing, and that stewards, under the pressures of the new demands, are increasingly turning to their external unions for support at just the time when those unions, starved of resources by membership loss, are least able to provide it.

Whatever the force of these arguments, it cannot be concluded that the existence of legal rights and such a tradition of integrated central union authority guarantee in themselves the effective collective representation of workers. It is clear that a third element is required, namely strong, independent union organization. The French experience makes clear that granting local union rights and guarantees does not automatically produce extended and strengthened unionism in the workplace. Similarly, with a rather different emphasis, the work of Visser (1991: 26–30) shows clearly that without strong organization in the workplace, works councils are effectively taken over by management, whatever the legal rights conferred on employees.

The dilemma, as seen in the French and Spanish examples, is that legal rights for collective workplace structures may themselves contribute to the demobilization of local unionism and reduce the individual and collective incentive to unionize. Moreover, to what extent is a broader co-ordinated 'strategic' union response consistent with strong organization in the workplace? Here we fall into the perennial problem of seeking to estimate union power, particularly in the workplace.

Trade unions are more than merely vehicles for the presentation of ideas. They are also structures for the mobilization of worker pressure as a countervailing power to that of employers. The developments of the 1980s suggest that increasingly the focus of such mobilization has to be the workplace if it is to be effective.

Mobilization encompasses not only overt collective action but also other manifestations of active support of workers for unions. There are no readily comparable data available. Union density, a self-evident measure in 'voluntarist' systems such as in the United Kingdom is less useful in legally based systems of works councils such as in Germany. Therefore all we can do is attempt to trace changes over time within countries. In such cases a frequently used index of union influence is their relative success in elections for works council seats.

In Germany, perhaps the most stable of our examples, the data on union successes in works council elections show that DGB unions have maintained their support, although there has also been a small increase in the success of non-union candidates. However, this latter trend has been most marked for management staff, who in 1990 elected 80 per cent of non-union delegates to their works committees. In the United Kingdom the high levels of union membership which persist in many workplaces indicate continuing support for unions. Whether this reflects merely the passive continuation of long-lasting habits may be tested when the widespread model of deducting subscriptions from pay comes under new legal rules. However, unions' failure to organize new workplaces in the face of managerial resistance suggests a gradual reduction in British unions' general representative capacity (see Millward et al. 1992: 70–7). In Spain, despite a fall in union density, unions have increased their support in works council elections. In The Netherlands the figure is stable at around 70 per cent despite a marked fall in union density. In France the 1980s saw a noticeable decline in union success in works committee elections alongside continuing falls in union membership and failure to exercise appreciable influence over the composition of the new workplace structures. This represents a long-term problem, perhaps again indicative of the continued impotence of French unions in the workplace.

If the evidence can be summarized, it is that where an effective system of representation exists in the workplace, whether based on collective bargaining or a works council, workers will appreciate the importance of the employees' point of view being represented by an effective organization – a trade union – even if they themselves are not members. Support for the maintenance of a strong union presence in the workplace persists. However, there is also evidence that workers are questioning the effectiveness of workplace unionism in ways that will continue to pose problems even for the apparently most successful unions. In Sweden workers question both the influence and democracy of their unions, although this has not yet led to declines in formal support. In France declining confidence in workplace representative structures may be reflected in the increase in abstentions in workplace elections; in Spain there is evidence of membership 'disenchantment' with unions. In Italy there is some evidence of increasing employee discontent with agreements reached by unions at company level. There is also evidence from France, Spain and Italy, most notably among particular groups in the public sector, of membership frustration with the established unions.

Conclusions

The 1980s have therefore witnessed the development of a new dominant form of workplace union in Europe: pragmatic, increasingly sophisticated in its dealings with employers, increasingly operating through works councils and their statutory rights. The United Kingdom remains the exceptional case, though no longer in a manner that others seek to emulate. One key change renders at least one element of the 1960s and 1970s UK model inappropriate. It is difficult to see how, given the internationalization and flexibility of production introduced and developed during the 1980s, *autonomous* shop-floor union organization in single plants can ever wield effective power. The new structures of capital require an integrated, company or sectoral base of organization. That, no doubt, is why many companies across Europe have spent so much time during the 1980s and 1990s trying to foster an increasingly atomized unionism in the workplace. The strengthening of integrated structures may well be a crucial issue for unions in the future.

Nevertheless, 'works council model unionism' is by no means assured of continuing success. As has been noted, it runs the risk of giving the impression that employees need not join unions, and engaging more with the immediate concerns of managers than of union members. Evidence of consequent dissatisfaction may be found in membership loss, reductions in electoral support for unions, the emergence of unofficial local structures challenging the official dominance, and the continuing inability of workplace unions to provide an effective voice for the increasing numbers of weak and precarious employees more or less everywhere.

Acknowledgements

I am very grateful to Dr Peter Leisink, of the University of Utrecht, for comments on a draft of this chapter, and to the two editors, whose contribution greatly exceeded what that description might imply.

References

Brown, W. 1993: The contraction of collective bargaining in Britain. *British Journal of Industrial Relations*, 31(2) 189–200.

Cohen, S. 1991: Us and them: business unionism in America and some implications for the UK. *Capital and Class*, 45, 95–127.

Colling, T. and Dickens, L. 1989: *Equality Bargaining: Why Not?* Equal Opportunities Commission Research Series. London: HMSO.

Degen, G.R. 1976: *Shop Stewards*. Frankfurt and Cologne: Europäische Verlagsanstadt.

Ferner, A. and Hyman, R. (eds) 1992: *Industrial Relations in the New Europe*. Oxford: Blackwell Publishers.

Goetschy, J. and Rozenblatt, R. 1992: France: the industrial relations system at a turning point? In Ferner and Hyman (eds), 404–44.

Jacobi, O., Keller, B. and Müller-Jentsch, W. 1992: Germany: codetermining the future. In Ferner and Hyman (eds), 218–69.

Kjellberg, A. 1992: Sweden: can the model survive? In Ferner and Hyman (eds), 88–142.

Leadbeater, C. 1987: In the land of the dispossessed. *Marxism Today*, April, 18–25.

Marchington, M. and Parker, P. 1990: *Changing Patterns of Employee Relations*. Hemel Hempstead: Harvester Wheatsheaf.

Martínez Lucio, M. 1992: Spain: constructing institutions and actors in a context of change. In Ferner and Hyman (eds), 445–81.

Martínez Lucio, M. and Weston, S. 1992: The politics and complexity of trade union responses to new management practices. *Human Resource Management Journal*, 2(4) 77–92.

Millward, N., Stevens, M., Smart, D. and Hawes, W. 1992: *Workplace Industrial Relations in Transition*. Aldershot: Dartmouth Publishering.

Negrelli, S. 1992: Economic flexibility and social solidarity. In T. Treu (ed.), *Participation in Public Policy-Making*, Berlin: Walter de Gruyter, 73–96.

Regalia, I. 1984: *Eletti e abbandonati*. Bologna: Il Mulino.

Sandberg, A. 1992: Changing workplace IR in Sweden: on union responses to 'new management'. Paper prepared for IREC and European Foundation Workshop, Dublin.

Terry, M. 1989: Recontextualizing shopfloor industrial relations. In S. Tailby and C. Whitston (eds), *Manufacturing Change*, Oxford: Blackwell Publishers, 192–216.

Terry, M. 1993: Workplace unions and workplace IR: the Italian experience. *Industrial Relations Journal*, 24(2) 138–50.

Visser, J. 1991: Employee representation in west European enterprises. Paper presented to Third European Regional Congress of the Industrial Relations Research Association, Naples/Bari.

10

Strikes and Industrial Conflict: Peace in Europe?

P. K. Edwards and Richard Hyman

Introduction

This chapter reviews strike patterns in Europe and examines the leading explanations for them. The key question is whether, as Shalev (1992) argues, the 1980s and 1990s mark a 'resurgence of labour quiescence' that stands in contrast to the high levels of strike activity of the two preceding decades. A central argument is that prevailing explanations of international differences tend to focus on a limited range of explanatory factors. The interactions between different forces need to be taken into account. Such an approach is developed, albeit no more than schematically, towards the end of the chapter.

The task of comparison faces many difficulties. First, countries vary in their definitions of strikes and methods of compiling data. Second, how far can strikes be taken as indicators of all forms of collective action? Britain is the only European country with detailed survey evidence on non-strike sanctions. Such sanctions, notably bans on the use of overtime, occur at least as often as strikes (Brown 1981; Milner 1993). The British system has been unusual in lacking both legal restraints on the use of industrial action and detailed substantive agreements. It is unlikely that non-strike sanctions are at all common in countries, such as Germany and Sweden, with well-established peace obligations. Strikes may well be a more complete indicator of the use of sanctions here; in any event, the absence of data on other actions limits the analysis of strikes.

Third, to what extent is a strike a homogeneous social phenomenon? Peterson (1938: 3) offered a definition which subsequent writers have frequently quoted: 'a temporary stoppage of work by a group of employees in order to express a grievance or enforce a demand'. Yet, as Durand and Dubois have argued (1975: 9), 'this classic definition conflicts with spontaneist or political interpretations': a strike may also be an expression of anger without precise bargaining objectives, or a socio-political act. The nature, purpose and meaning of strikes evolve historically and differ within countries, and even more so between countries, reflecting contrasts in industrial relations institutions and cultures.

Strikes have generally been analysed in terms of the demands and organizational capacities of workers. Though employers are evidently parties to disputes, their role, both directly in the handling of disputes and indirectly in their management of the employment relationship, has often been neglected. Even before the 1980s, their role was more important than has often been acknowledged. In France, for example, the traditional pattern of frequent short disputes certainly reflected the strategies of the unions, notably the belief in direct protest. However, it was also shaped by the autocracy of employers and their lack of interest in the careful regulation of the workplace (Gallie 1978). In Germany, a general history of industrial peace has been punctuated by massive disputes, for example in 1963 and 1978, which reflected the determination by employers to resist certain union demands (Müller-Jentsch 1981; Jacobi 1985). During the 1980s, many strikes, far from indicating labour insurgency, were defensive struggles against determined employers. Obvious examples are the Fiat strike in Italy in 1980 and the miners' strike in Britain in 1984–5.

A further little-discussed issue in international comparisons concerns the structure of employment. The greater the concentration of strike-prone industries in a country, the higher that country's position will tend to be in the international 'league table' of strike incidence. Limitations on the availability of data apart, one reason why the appropriate statistical controls have not been made is probably that any one industry displays wide variations in strike rates. The allegedly distinctively strike-prone sector of coal-mining has experienced wide differences between countries (Rimlinger 1959) and indeed within them (Church et al. 1990). There is no uniform 'industry effect' that can be isolated. Nevertheless, the relevance of the point remains. Consider for example the fact that in strike-free Switzerland the economy is dominated by small firms which are research-intensive and employ skilled technicians, the result being a 'high degree of work discipline and morale' (Hotz-Hart 1992: 299); whereas Finland, with a high strike rate, had been dominated by the timber industry (Lilja 1992: 205), whose communities conform in some respects to the 'isolated mass' of strike-prone workers identified by Kerr and Siegel (1954). These features of industrial structure are likely to affect the character of industrial relations and thus go some way towards explaining differences in strike activity.

There are three main ways in which these issues can be approached: statistical analysis of strike patterns between countries and over time; historical reconstructions of the changing dynamics of conflict (Shorter and Tilly 1974); and case studies of individual disputes or the 'micro' patterns of strikes within a workplace (Batstone et al. 1978).

The overview of strike trends in this chapter concentrates on the first, although it also draws on the historical approach to explore explanations of international patterns. Strike data are presented on eleven countries. Eight are given particular attention: four (France, Germany, Italy and the United Kingdom) for their size and also their very different strike records; and the remaining four for the ways in which they illustrate different strike patterns. These four are Austria and Sweden (low levels of strikes), Denmark (a variant of the Scandinavian model of few strikes) and Finland (high strike rates). The other three countries (Ireland, The Netherlands and Norway) are mentioned more briefly. In other cases, there are problems with the continuity of official statistics (Belgium), strikes have been so rare as to make statistical analysis redundant (Luxembourg, Switzerland), or the presence of dictatorial regimes for long periods makes time-series analysis impossible (Greece, Portugal and Spain).

International Differences in Strike Patterns

The shape of strikes

Strikes are measured in three dimensions: the number of separate disputes, the number of workers going on strike, and the total number of working days 'lost'. Each has difficulties (reviewed by Franzosi 1989b and Shalev 1978a). The number of strikes is the least reliable indicator for comparative purposes, since countries differ in the extent to which they record small, short strikes. (When Finland relaxed its criteria in 1973, the number of strikes increased almost fourfold.) Where reporting criteria remain constant, however, trends of frequency can be considered within individual countries. From what is known generally about national systems of industrial relations, some comparisons can also be made between countries; for example the rarity of strikes in Sweden compared with Britain is not a mere statistical artefact. The figures for workers involved and days lost (volume) are less sensitive to national variations, since the smallest strikes necessarily contribute little to the aggregate statistics. However, the exclusion by some countries of political or public sector disputes is a difficulty for comparability. Participation and volume, usually calculated for comparative purposes in relation to the size of the labour force, are therefore the most popular measures for cross-national comparison.

The overall 'shape' of strikes can be measured, following Shorter and Tilly (1974), by calculating from the three raw indices the frequency of strikes (number per 1,000 employees) and their average size and duration. The product of these gives the overall 'volume', or number of days lost per 1,000 workers. Table 10.1 presents calculations for the eleven countries identified above.

Italy and France have been marked by frequent, short and large strikes. In particular, the size of Italian strikes was a major contributor to the country's position at the head of the strike table. These well-known characteristics reflect the use of the strike as a weapon of protest and demonstration.

At the other extreme, Sweden has had few strikes, although when they have occurred they have been quite large and long. The result was a low overall volume of strikes. Austria and Germany probably have very similar strike shapes; however, the absence of data on frequency prevents exact calculations. Assuming that the size of strikes was the same as in Sweden, strike frequency must have been exceptionally low. The situation in Denmark was similar, though the number of strikes has been relatively high, producing a strike volume double that of Sweden. The immediate cause of the pattern in these four countries is, as Clegg (1976) shows, the extent of comprehensive national or industry agreements, together with clear peace obligations. Strikes are thus rare, yet when they occur they are large, reflecting the organizational capacities of the unions. The Danish variant would then be explained by the relative strength of craft unions in this country (Scheuer 1992: 175), which limited the authority of national confederations and made the peace obligation less all-encompassing.

Finland has had frequent and quite large and long strikes, producing an overall volume similar to Italy's. The reasons are taken up below. Finally, the United Kingdom has recorded moderate levels on all three measures. Data are given separately for the coal industry and the rest of the economy because coal exerted an overwhelming influence on the strike record during the 1950s, accounting in some years for three-quarters of all recorded disputes. The industry's role fell steeply thereafter, so that overall trends obscure the picture in the rest of the economy. Average figures on size and duration are also particularly suspect in Britain. The country has had two main forms of dispute: the small and brief stoppage at workplace level, and large and

Table 10.1 Overall shape of strikes, 1950–1990

	AUS	DK	FIN	FRA	GER	IRE	ITA	NL	N	SWE	UK All	UK Non-coal
Freq.	(1)	50	466	120	(11)	100	135	10	11	17	85	57
Size	(500)	523	256	612	(500)	267	2,042	476	705	500	564	753
Duration	1.8	5.5	4.2	2.3	5.4	11.9	1.7	4.7	9.6	8.7	5.8	5.3
Volume	19	145	343	170	30	318	478	21	73	72	275	224

'Freq' is the frequency of strikes: the number per million members of the work force.
'Size' is mean size: the number of workers taking part, divided by the number of strikes.
'Duration' is the number of days lost in strikes divided by the number of workers participating. It measures how long the 'average' striker was on strike, not the length of the average strike.
'Volume' is the number of working days lost per 1,000 employees.
If S is the number of strikes, W workers participating D days lost and E the number of employees, Freq. = S/E; Size = W/S; Duration = D/W; and Volume = D/E.
For Austria and Germany, data on the frequency of strikes are not available. The mean size of strikes has been estimated as similar to that in Sweden, and the figures for frequency calculated accordingly.

Source: Calculated from International Labour Office, *Yearbook of Labour Statistics* (Geneva: annual)

long official disputes. These patterns reflect, respectively, the workplace orientation of collective bargaining (Edwards et al. 1992: 54–6) and discontent in the public sector in particular.

Explanatory models

From the late 1970s, the leading efforts to explain these differences have drawn on the concept of corporatism. Initially, there were two main variants. The first, the mainstream corporatist model, orders countries according to the degree of centralization among unions and employer associations, the degree to which these organizations enjoy representational monopolies, and the participation of unions in public policy formulation (for example, Lehmbruch 1984). The level of conflict is expected to decline where strong corporatist arrangements exist, as in Austria, Sweden and The Netherlands. The power resource variant (Korpi 1983; Korpi and Shalev 1979) stresses the mode of incorporation of working-class movements into national political systems. Where, as in Sweden, labour has been politically powerful, workers' goals could be pursued in the political arena, and hence industrial conflict was rendered unnecessary. The key turning-points in strike patterns were associated with political change, not with institutional reforms.

This account was extended to other countries, notably Norway and Austria, which also had very low levels of strikes. In addition to this pattern of low conflict, four other cases were identified. First, there were the countries, such as Ireland, where the working class has never played a significant political role and where strikes remained economic trials of strength. Second was the case of 'alienation' from the polity, entailing not an absence of political activity but appreciable electoral support for left-wing parties combined with exclusion from the key apparatuses of the state. Unions typically used short though massive strikes as demonstrations of protest. France and Italy exemplified this type. Third, countries such as Belgium and the United Kingdom were seen in various ways as intermediate between the main types identified. Finally, there were problem cases which did not fit the theory. Switzerland, The Netherlands and Germany have all had low strike rates despite the absence of any significant working-class role in the polity. The first of these might be explained in terms of the weakness of unions; however, Germany, with its stronger union movement, remained an important anomaly. All three cases are also problems for mainstream corporatism, since they score lower on indices of corporatism than the Nordic countries, yet have comparable strike patterns.

Assessment of these theories needs to consider how far they work in general, and how far they can interpret the specific developments of the 1980s and 1990s. The former is undertaken here and the latter in the following section.

There are three general problems. First, can the anomalies be satisfactorily explained? Crouch (1985) draws on the auxiliary concept of consociation to deal with some of them. It refers to a situation where there are several parties, each with its own electorate that is largely inaccessible to others. Such parties have to form coalitions with each other, and once labour parties are drawn into governing coalitions they will moderate their demands. Crucially, employers have to recognize the inevitability of unionism and to abandon the 'fight to the finish' as either an industrial or a political strategy. This account helps to explain the Swiss and Dutch examples. Crouch admits, however, that it leaves unexplained the case of Finland (consociational yet with high levels of conflict), though he offers the additional speculation that the role of the communist party here may have worked against class compromises.

Germany has presented an even larger problem. Cameron (1984) deals with this from a different starting-point by examining the various trade-offs possible between unions, employers and the state. Using data from the 1960s and 1970s, he finds clear associations between low strike rates, low inflation rates and high levels of employment. Nevertheless, corporatist institutions are not necessary for this pattern to emerge. In the case of Germany, Cameron explains it in terms of two familiar features of the country: workplace institutions which give workers clear influence over managerial policies; and industry-level unions whose bargaining strategy is driven by the broad concerns of the industry (see Streeck 1984). Implicit within such accounts is recognition of the need to explore the dynamics of labour relations within each country. Thus some models of corporatism place Germany and Ireland in the same category, even though their patterns of conflict are very different. Single-factor and static explanations do not move the analysis very far.

The second general issue concerns the mechanisms connecting the existence of certain institutions with levels of conflict. Consider the key case of Sweden. Fulcher (1987) points out that the decline in strike activity preceded the electoral success of the social democrats in 1932, and reflected the easing of the depression and the associated wage reductions which had provoked conflict. Moreover, he claims that the institutionalized peace signalled by the Basic Agreement of 1938 did not stem from a trade union switch from the mobilization of industrial to political power, but rather a change in employer strategy. Fearing that state intervention in industrial relations might open the way to socialism, he suggests, they felt obliged to seek the regulation of conflict through a more co-operative relationship with the unions. In short, it was not a simple growth of working-class political power which was important, but a change in the management of labour relations affecting all parties.

Third, corporatist and power resource models tend to assume that conflict was not deeply embedded in capitalist workplace relations. They examined neither the roots of conflict in the workplace nor the strategies of employers and the state. Their rhetoric notwithstanding, their analytical approach had a great deal in common with that of the industrial relations institutionalists (Edwards 1983). The problem of the shop-floor was illustrated by Fulcher (1973) in the case of Sweden. Taking the example of unofficial action in a shipyard, he showed that certain elements of worker discontent could not be accommodated within corporatist institutions. Swedish shop-floor relations run counter to a model of industrial peace in other respects. The country has long been noted for high levels of absenteeism and labour turnover. Such phenomena should not be seen simply as alternative forms of conflict, although it is plain that they were seen as problems by employers and that they were among the stimuli to new forms of work organization in firms like Volvo (Gyllenhammar 1977; Berggren 1992). They may not have been direct indices of conflict, yet they showed how workers used tight labour markets and generous sick pay arrangements to negotiate the balance of effort and reward.

Fulcher (1987: 231) makes three points that stand in contrast to conventional corporatist models. These are that Swedish social democracy abandoned socialist goals and accepted capitalism; that the state, employers and unions co-operated in managing the economy; and that the 'labour movement has integrated and subordinated labour' (meaning that unions channelled and contained shop-floor action). Fulcher argues that Swedish corporatism turned on the ways in which employers and the state regulated the challenge of labour.

We thus agree with Therborn (1992) that the original corporatist models were not so much wrong as partial efforts in the right direction: the original definition of corporatism was too narrow; and there was a monocausal model in which complex phenomena such as strike patterns were linked in unsatisfactory ways to one variable (a country's score on an index of corporatism). We also agree that further efforts to define such indices and to correlate them with outcomes such as strikes are unlikely to be very productive. As Crouch (in chapter 8 of this volume) shows, the literature has been drifting towards a recognition that corporatism has different forms, and that these operate not as static structures but as part of a dynamic relationship between capital, labour and the state. For Therborn (1992) and Pekkarinen et al. (1992: 2), corporatism has two variants: the institutionalization of consensus which entails the exclusion of weak social groups, examples being Austria and The Netherlands; and the institutionalization of conflict, as in the Nordic countries, where there is an articulation between powerful interest groups. We indicate how such ideas may be developed after trends in strike rates have been discussed.

The Trend of Strikes, 1950–90

Within the broad pattern of strikes there have been substantial increases and decreases in strike rates. In this section, we examine the key trends and consider explanations for them.

Strike trends

As noted above, a popular view is that the 1980s and 1990s represent a major era of labour peace, a view most carefully developed by Shalev (1992). We first consider the same period as Shalev, 1960–90, and enter some qualifications to the picture. By placing this period in longer perspective, we then include some more fundamental objections.

The key trends

Shalev (1992) discusses 18 countries for the period 1960–89, using workers involved per thousand employees (WI) as his key indicator and comparing averages for 1968–79 with those for 1980–9. Taking his twelve European countries for which data can be calculated, six indeed show large declines of more than 25 per cent, though there were smaller declines in two, no change in a further two, and a large increase in the final two. The unweighted average for all his countries (that is, an average giving each country the same weight, regardless of its size or its strike rate) in fact shows an overall increase. There was thus no even process of pacification of European labour relations.

Moreover, to compare the 1980s with the period immediately preceding, when strike activity in most countries was the highest for several decades, is misleading. In table 10.2 data are assembled for the period back to 1950. Austria displayed the clearest long-term fall in strike rates. In France, there was a substantial fall in worker involvement and days lost during the 1980s, though strike frequency was little lower than in the 1950s. There were declines, too, in Italy, though to levels that were not particularly low by historical standards. The same is broadly true of Britain, though there was a continuing fall in strike rates in the 1990s which suggests that strike activity here may be falling to historically very low levels. In Germany, rates fluctuated: though figures were very low at the end of the 1980s, there was a very similar period two decades earlier. Substantial disputes in the public sector in 1992 suggested that the potential for strikes had not disappeared. In Finland, by contrast, there was a broad stability of strike rates, while Sweden and Denmark were both marked by long-term increases. In Sweden in particular, the 1980s proved to be more strike-prone than preceding periods by a considerable margin.

Such points become even more significant when post-war experience is placed in a long-term context. Strikes have displayed a strong tendency to occur in waves (Shorter and Tilly 1974; Cronin 1979). For example, major upsurges occurred in many countries at the end of the first world war. Some analyses relate these waves to cycles of accumulation in capitalist economies (Screpanti 1987; Silver 1991). The upsurge of conflict in the 1960s would then be seen as just one long wave, with the implication that subsequent decline may be a downswing and not a secular trend.

Commonalities and divergences

These conclusions based on examining raw data can be made more precise. Is there any statistical evidence of a clear upward or downward trend in the extent of strike action, and how far has the movement of strikes been common across countries? The most straightforward way to assess this is to correlate strike data with a variable representing time. It is also possible to examine whole decades: is there any evidence that the 1980s as a whole were less strike-prone than other decades?

Numbers of strikes and workers involved are considered here, days lost tending to fluctuate too wildly for useful analysis. For strike numbers, data from nine European countries are examined; for workers involved, ten countries are considered. Over the whole period 1950–90, the number of strikes tended to rise in Denmark and Sweden and to fall in The Netherlands and the United Kingdom (the last being mainly due to the special features of the coal industry). Results for workers involved (which used the logarithm of the number to smooth wide year-to-year fluctuations) showed no overall trend in Germany, Sweden or the United Kingdom, a long-run decline in Austria, and increases in Denmark, France and Italy.

Table 10.2   Strike trends: annual averages, 1950–1991

	AUS	DK	FIN	FRA	GER	IRE	ITA	NL	N	SWE	UK All	UK Non-coal
Frequency: strikes per million employees												
1950–4	7.3		31.5	117.0		83.5	82.1	18.3	25.2	9.7	73.1	23.1
1955–9	17.7		29.5	114.0		56.1	103	15.4	14.2	4.4	105.0	28.1
1960–4	18.8		27.0	107.0		69.0	175	17.2	8.9	5.3	104.0	52.5
1965–9	13.0		41.3	64.7		102.0	162	5.8	4.4	4.3	94.0	79.2
1970–4	41.0		445.0	175.0		152.0	251	7.3	7.9	19.3	118.0	112.0
1975–9	95.3		836.0	172.0		142.0	150	6.4	11.2	24.6	94.7	84.3
1980–4	69.2		728.0	115.0		127.0	92.6	2.7	9.8	29.5	53.3	42.4
1985–9	115.0		373.0	84.7		74.3	67.2	6.7	6.6	27.4	36.6	27.8
1990–1	81.5		145.0	64.7		44.7	50.9[a]	4.7	4.7	16.5	18.6	16.5
Workers participating per 1,000 employees												
1950–4	9.1	1.6	16.7	87.5	4.8	11.6	154	3.4	3.2	3.5	25.0	17.7
1955–9	16.2	9.8	57.4	78.6	7.2	7.4	81.8	3.7	11.8	0.5	30.5	20.4
1960–4	29.9	18.4	19.4	111.0	3.4	16.0	148.0	6.0	5.1	0.6	61.8	55.6
1965–9	25.3	8.8	19.4	126.0	2.8	40.1	198.0	2.4	0.5	2.1	48.0	46.1
1970–4	6.9	46.7	178.0	106.0	9.0	32.4	278.0	7.4	4.2	6.1	64.6	58.7
1975–9	0.6	34.2	166.0	71.7	6.2	35.4	591.0	4.6	4.0	4.2	67.4	66.1
1980–4	3.0	22.1	173.0	20.9	7.2	27.1	452.0	5.7	8.3	42.0	51.2	45.3
1985–9	3.1	56.5	96.3	12.3	3.2	48.0	190.0	2.8	19.4	15.3	32.0	28.4
1990–1	14.3	14.1	67.3	10.2	7.9	12.5	76[a]	5.3	15.0	8.4	8.7	8.5

Volume: days lost per 1,000 employees

1950–4	24.0	3.8	500.0	501.0	60.9	227.0	300.0	18.0	48.6	82.6	81.7	64.1
1955–9	35.1	122.0	784.0	130.0	34.1	111.0	303.0	20.8	170.0	15.7	190.0	171.0
1960–4	80.7	227.0	154.0	150.0	18.6	255.0	625.0	29.0	106.0	4.9	131.0	117.0
1965–9	22.7	31.7	83.1	127.0	5.5	540.0	812.0	5.0	7.6	19.7	155.0	145.0
1970–4	14.2	360.0	597.0	169.0	47.8	428.0	1,049	47.7	53.4	55.8	578.0	441.0
1975–9	1.3	72.2	385.0	177.0	43.4	678.0	1,140	24.8	28.7	26.8	474.0	477.0
1980–4	1.6	96.9	400.0	75.3	43.6	348.0	633.0	17.8	54.8	225.0	414.0	244.0
1985–9	2.1	204.0	282.0	34.9	1.8	219.0	183.0	8.5	113.0	112.0	161.0	123.0
1990–1	9.8	31.4	280.0	27.3	8.8	136.0	211[a]	23.8	35.0	87.8	48.5	48.2

[a] 1990 only.

For Austria, there are no data for 1950–52.

For Finland, until 1971 stoppages lasting less than four hours were excluded unless at least 100 days were lost. This seriously affects the frequency and worker participation series, though the volume series to a much smaller extent.

For France, data are missing for 1968, and also for frequency (1982) and workers participating (1969). From 1983 onwards, workers participating are given as monthly averages; these figures have been multiplied by 12.

Source: As for table 10.1

A more detailed exercise takes eight countries and, as discussed below, includes unemployment as an explanatory variable. Is there any evidence that, once the effects of unemployment have been controlled, strikes have displayed long-term trends? The question is considered by looking at correlations with time and also including variables for the decades of the 1960s and 1970s, to assess whether there was some special feature of these periods encouraging strikes. Looking at strike frequency, there was, when the effects of unemployment were controlled, a long-term trend to rising numbers in Denmark, France, Italy and Sweden, and no marked trend in Britain. Comparisons of the 1950s, 1960s and 1970s with the 1980s showed: in Denmark, a low level of strikes in the 1950s, though no other variations; in France, no difference between decades; in Italy, not only much higher strike rates in the 1970s than the 1980s, but also lower rates in the 1950s and 1960s than the 1980s; in Sweden, lower rates for all three earlier decades; and in Britain higher rates for the 1960s and 1970s. Thus only in Britain did the 1980s stand out as having a particularly low strike rate, and even there, as shown above, the statistics marked a decline to the levels of the 1950s and not a complete disappearance of the strike.

Shalev (1992) remarks that the 1980s have seen a breakdown of previous patterns and a fragmentation of different national experiences. One way to consider this is the correlation between strike indices in different countries. In fact, there never was a very strong association. In the 1950–70 period for example, almost half the correlation coefficients between the numbers of strikes in different countries were 0.25 or smaller. The movements in worker involvement were even more weakly related to each other. If anything, there was an increase in diversity during the second period. It was not so much that there was a common pattern up to 1970 which then fragmented, but rather there were several types of strike movement whose differences became even more marked.

Explanatory factors

Strikes and economic conditions

Perhaps the most obvious explanation of declining strike rates is economic recession. The leading theoretical models were developed in North America (for example, Ashenfelter and Johnson 1969). Their key argument was that the frequency of strikes increases as unemployment falls (because tight labour markets raise workers' bargaining power), yet is reduced by rising real wages (because such rises take the edge off workers' discontents). Apart from serious deficiencies in their own terms (see Shalev 1980), these models perform poorly in Europe. Some writers claim to detect uniformity (Hibbs 1976; Paldam and Pedersen 1980). Hibbs pooled data on days lost in strikes from a range of countries and argued that fluctuations reflected common forces. More careful consideration questions these findings. Shalev (1978b) has exposed deep flaws in Hibbs's methodology. As for Paldam and Pedersen, examination of their country-by-country results points to similar technical problems.[1]

Davies (1981) conducted a more careful analysis in which models were specified for each country in turn and the fit with actual strike trends was explored. There were two key empirical findings. First, the level of unemployment was, at least until the mid-1970s, directly and not inversely related to strike levels in some countries, notably Belgium, The Netherlands and Sweden. Second, real wages displayed a variety of links with strikes, including a positive association in Germany, an inverse link in The Netherlands and Italy, and no association in France. Davies explained these results in terms of the institutions of collective bargaining. In countries like Germany, Sweden and Belgium, unions do not rely on the business cycle for their bargaining power but instead engage in industry- or national-level negotiations that contain strikes during booms. It thus appears that not only the level of strikes but also the trend over time varies according to institutional structures.

As for trends in the 1980s, very little work has been done to test whether models developed earlier still apply. In particular, can the decline in strikes in countries like the United Kingdom and France be explained by rising unemployment, or was there a qualitative shift in the determinants of strikes? As noted above, there is little evidence of the latter. As for unemployment, an examination of data for eight countries shows mixed results. There are the expected inverse links between strike frequency and unemployment in Italy and Britain but positive links in Denmark and France and no clear associations in the other four countries. There are virtually no significant relationships with the measure of worker involvement.

Evidence that economic conditions have had a clear and uniform effect on strike levels is thus very limited. This is not to dismiss the role of economic conditions, but to argue that they seem to operate differently in different countries and that their effects are not automatic. There is little close correspondence between unemployment levels and strike rates, although unemployment can shape the bargaining policies of unions and managements. Its effects are mediated by industrial relations and political institutions, as other approaches to conflict stress.

Sectoral distribution: decline of the mass production strike?

In addition to short-term economic conditions, longer-term changes in the composition of the labour force have been seen as causes of changing strike levels. In particular, the decline of large-scale mass production in many countries has led to suggestions that the strike has been disappearing along with it. Closely associated are the increased feminization of the labour force, the reversal of the century-old trend towards ever larger production units, the decentralization of managerial control and the spread of subcontracting arrangements in large corporations, and the expansion of 'atypical' forms of employment relationship. There are two issues here: How far has there been a sectoral shift? And, more generally, what can be said about the character of industrial militancy?

In relation to the first, two sorts of calculation are possible: What percentage of strikes occur in a given sector? And how strike-prone is a sector in relation to the national average? For present purposes, broad classifications into mining, manufacturing and services (which includes both public and private services) are sufficient. The four largest countries are considered; data are presented in table 10.3.

Italy shows the greatest extent of strikes in the tertiary sector. The proportion of strikes and days lost accounted for by services rose steadily from the 1960s. By the end of the period, the sector's proneness to strikes was virtually the same as the national average. Though manufacturing declined in its contribution to the number of strikes, workers here continued to be about twice as strike-prone as the national average. The extent of a shift towards the tertiary sector should not, however, be exaggerated. Its share of strikes has been substantial since the 1960s, and its growing share in the 1980s reflects less a growth in militancy here than a decline in aggregate strike levels in the economy generally (Ferner and Hyman 1992a: 582; Regalia et al. 1978).

Britain displays a rapid rise in the role of the service sector, from being virtually strike-free in the early 1960s to producing a quarter of strikes and days lost by the late 1980s. Private services were responsible for part of the rise, with bank employees, for example, using industrial action on a wide scale for the first time (Heritage 1983). However, much of it was concentrated in the public services, in which a series of notable disputes affecting nurses, local authority workers and teachers began to develop from the 1970s (Edwards et al. 1992: 49–50). Falling strike levels in manufacturing during the 1980s contrast with rates in the public sector, which were more or less steady (Millward et al. 1992: 281). The continuing major role of the coal industry is also evident: though the number of strikes fell during the 1960s and 1970s, in the 1980s coal accounted for a quarter of all stoppages. The massive national strikes of the 1970s and 1980s are reflected in the figures on days lost. The continuing decline of the industry in the 1990s suggests, however, that its role in strikes will fall; in 1990, for example, there were twice as many strikes in public administration and education as there were in coal-mining. Finally, and in contrast to Italy, the strike-proneness of manufacturing workers fell during the 1980s: the overall decline in strikes reflects both the declining size of the sector and the tendency of workers within it to reduce their use of the strike at a rate greater than that of other workers.

Trends in France and Germany, however, suggest no clear rise in the role of services. In France (where suitable data on the number of strikes by sector are not available), manufacturing increased its share of days lost. Moreover, and in contrast to Britain, the overall decline in strikes during the 1980s was not due to any special decline in manufacturing, which in fact increased its relative strike-proneness. There was little clear overall trend in services. There was, however, a substantial increase in the relative strike-proneness of the public sector, often marked by new rank-and-file co-ordinating groups (Goetschy and Rozenblatt 1992: 438). In Germany, manufacturing dominated the strike picture throughout the period. In both countries, there was a steep fall in strike activity in the coal industry.

These differing experiences suggest that there has been no general trend towards a growing role of the service sector in strikes. As Ferner's chapter 3 in this volume shows, however, there have been common pressures on the state as employer, and the resulting attempts to control labour costs no doubt underpinned a more conflictual atmosphere in industrial relations, as public sector strikes in France and Britain testify. Yet the precise way in which these forces have operated has plainly been different. As Ferner also stresses, there has been a variety of national responses. Just how these responses have affected strikes, so that trends in services in Italy and France, for example, have been so different, is an issue for future research. What is clear is that the decline of formerly heavily strike-prone industries, like coal and the docks, will tend to reduce overall levels of strike activity. Although public sector workers seem to have become more militant, their use of the strike has not counteracted its reduced role elsewhere.

Such findings are relevant to debates on the new working class which in the 1960s challenged the conventional view, expressed in particular by Lockwood (1958), that such workers are inherently undisposed to collective action because of their closeness to manage-

Table 10.3 Sectoral distribution of strike activity

FRANCE

	Distrib. of days lost by sector			Days lost per head as % national average		
	Mining	Mfg.	Serv.	Mining	Mfg.	Serv.
1960–4	33	29	7	1,800	104	4
1965–9	7	49	2	437	173	8
1970–4	3	50	9	223	179	37
1975–9	1	63	4	34	227	16
1980–4	–	72	5	53	284	15
1985–9	–	74	6	92	326	17

GERMANY

	Distrib. of days lost by sector			Days lost per head as % national average		
	Mining	Mfg.	Serv.	Mining	Mfg.	Serv.
1960–4	12	87	–	421	234	–
1965–9	8	54	–	316	137	2
1970–4	–	91	4	32	232	16
1975–9	–	95	1	22	266	3
1980–4	0	98	–	0	287	–
1985–9	0	74	5	0	230	15

Table 10.3 Continued

ITALY

	Distrib. by sector				As % national average			
	Strikes		Days lost		Strikes per head		Days lost per head	
	Mfg.	Serv.	Mfg.	Serv.	Mfg.	Serv.	Mfg.	Serv.
1960–4	53	17	52	13	202	63	198	47
1965–9	56	18	59	13	197	64	208	46
1970–4	55	21	57	19	176	65	181	60
1975–9	53	23	48	23	191	82	170	80
1980–4	53	22	60	16	201	89	228	64
1985–9	45	28	39	29	195	92	170	98

UNITED KINGDOM

	Distribution by sector						As % National average					
	Strikes			Days lost			Strikes per head			Days lost per head		
	Mining	Mfg.	Serv.	Mining	Mfg.	Serv.	Mining	Mfg.	Serv.	Mining	Mfg.	Serv.
1960–4	51	30	1	14	66	1	1,600	83	4	432	182	4
1965–9	18	54	2	9	64	1	718	152	6	357	181	5
1970–4	7	66	3	25	49	2	426	191	10	1,490	140	7
1975–9	12	61	5	1	78	11	857	197	16	67	208	34
1980–4	22	49	10	45	37	7	1,520	174	31	3,190	133	22
1985–9	25	36	19	24	25	27	2,140	156	48	2,090	111	70

- = less than 0.5 per cent but not zero.

Source: As for table 10.1.

ment and their distinctive labour market position. The notion that a scientifically trained salariat would have the knowledge to challenge traditional definitions of managerial authority and would be in the lead in developing new collective demands was supported by evidence from France (Touraine 1971) and Italy (Low-Beer 1978). However, subsequent assessments (Hyman 1983) showed that these cases were exceptional and that much of the new militancy was short-lived.

If the original 'new working class' theories were based upon developments in the private sector, the subsequent focus has switched to the public. The 1970s saw a rapid expansion of collective organization – whether in established trade unions or in professional associations and quasi-unions – among white-collar employees in public services and administration in most European countries. These groups took an increasing part in industrial action during the 1980s (Baglioni 1990: 17). In Sweden, for example, the willingness of the non-manual workers to challenge the egalitarian wage policies of LO exploded in a series of major conflicts in the public sector. In Italy, the 1980s were marked by the emergence of the *Cobas* (*comitati di base*) as unofficial organizations of public sector groups (in many cases white-collar) rejecting the moderate policies of the official confederations and at times organizing very effective strike action (Bordogna 1989; Fiorai 1989; Negrelli and Santi 1990).

Such developments may be placed in a longer-term perspective. The character of strikes has evolved during the development of modern industry. Shorter and Tilly (1974: 11–18), followed by many other writers, identify a four-stage evolution. Small, local stoppages by skilled artisans during the early nineteenth century became overshadowed during the period 1880–1930 by large, often industry-wide, confrontations. The next 30 years saw the rise to prominence of semi-skilled workers. Finally, science sector and professional workers led new demands from the 1960s. The most recent evolution seems to point to a weakening of the lead role of this last group and the emergence of public sector workers as the new lead group.

Several qualifications must be underlined. First, models of transition can be too strong if they imply that all workers in a group become strike-prone. A study of an exceptionally strike-prone and supposedly homogeneous industry, British coal-mining, shows that strike rates have varied widely between individual mines and that within any one mine they fluctuate dramatically (Church et al. 1990). Any model of strikes which sees them purely as the product of the structural characteristics of an occupation must be rejected. Second, just as not all miners or mass production workers struck in the past, so there is likely to be wide variation among the new lead groups. Third, the links between structural position and striking are complex. Accounts such as Bordogna's (1989), which identify general forces affecting public sector workers and which presume that these forces will lead to strikes, are heavily reliant on the example of one country, in this case Italy. Although the forces making public sector workers more subject to rationalization and work pressure may be broadly common, the links with strikes depend on how these forces are mediated by different national institutions.

Corporatism and the management of conflict

Trends in the 1980s posed several problems for corporatist models (Shalev 1992: 111). For example, there was a sharp decline in strike levels in France without any evidence of increased participation in the polity. (The possible explanation of the accession to power of a Socialist government is rejected, on the grounds that this did not in fact mark any great change in labour's political influence: Kesselman 1983.) Most seriously, there were large increases in strike rates in the two key exemplars of corporatism, Sweden and Norway.

As suggested above, the solution is not to abandon the whole approach of corporatism but to recognize that corporatist structures were means of regulating capital–labour conflicts which could come under strain. The breakdown of the Swedish model is discussed below. As for France, as is again indicated below, the declining rate of strikes was the result of new approaches to the management of conflict among unions, employers and the state. These reflected, though were not determined by, economic conditions. The country's long-established pattern of frequent, large demonstrations was thus altered.

The Dynamics of Conflict

How, then, can an integrated view be developed? Franzosi (1989a), taking Italy as his illustrative case, argues that economic and political economy accounts both fail to offer adequate explanations. The former can explain the growth of strikes during the 1950s and 1960s as the consequence of tightening labour market conditions following a period of rapid growth. However, they cannot account for specific strike explosions such as those of 1959 and 1962. More fundamentally, whereas economists treat the business cycle as an external force, it should be seen as 'the byproduct of employers' and state actions aimed at curbing labor militancy by thwarting workers' bargaining power in the labor market' (p. 467). That is, economic trends are not asocial phenomena, but are used by employers and the state to manage militancy. Political accounts fail in two respects. First, political crises in Italy have followed, and not led, strike waves. Second, if strike waves reflect activity in the political centres of nation-states, why do these waves occur at similar times in different countries?

Rather, strikes have to be seen in terms of the dynamic relationship between labour, capital and the state. On the behaviour of employers, Franzosi cites several reactions to strikes. In the short term, these included sacking union militants and capital flight. In the longer term, there were attempts to replace labour with machinery and to move towards smaller plants. The state promoted small-scale industry in an attempt to develop a more pluralistic class structure, and at times it aided employers in outright repression.

Franzosi calls his account a mode-of-production view. He does not develop the model at length. For example, he does not answer the question of the joint timing of strike waves in different countries. In the following discussion, we use a broadly similar account which may be called, less grandly, a view of labour regulation. By this we mean not such specific theories as French *régulation* analyses of social structures of accumulation, but the ways in which the ever-present possibility of conflict is organized, expressed and controlled (Edwards 1992: 372).

There are four levels at which work is regulated: the workplace, the enterprise, the industry and the state. Workers can challenge the approaches of employers and governments at each level. Key issues in the workplace include systems of discipline and the handling of grievances, rules on the allocation of work, and the behaviour of managers and supervisors. At the level of the enterprise or the industry lie questions of wages policy, in particular the degree to which wage-bargaining is co-ordinated. The state can also be concerned with co-ordination, through corporatist mechanisms, and is important in its role as employer and in its management of the economy as a whole.

The following discussion begins with the case of Sweden; it then sketches an account of other countries.

The heyday of the centralized structure in Sweden was the 1950s and early 1960s. How did it induce labour peace? At workplace level, industrial unionism and a legal apparatus making strikes unlawful during the term of a collective agreement inhibited unofficial strikes (Fulcher 1991: 197–9). This point is worth stressing. Though the law may actually be used rarely, in a country like Sweden where industrial relations institutions are well established and in particular where there is a strong tradition of organized unionism which is responsive to the demands of workers, the desire to use unofficial action to pursue grievances is likely to be restrained.

As numerous accounts (for example, Lash 1985; Kjellberg 1992) show, the 'Swedish model' then came under pressure from workers (notably in unofficial strikes at the end of the 1960s), unions (in demands for new forms of economic democracy and in challenges to the wage leadership of manual unions from white-collar and public sector organizations), and employers (with growing demands for flexibility). The state came to play a new role as the social democrats lost their monopoly on power and as they and their conservative opponents strove to reorganize the economy. The resultant strains underlay a rise in the use of strikes. The Swedish model was not a permanent solution to conflicts in the employment relationship, but was the outcome of historically specific attempts to manage its tensions. As the tensions increased, the model began to have difficulties.

A similar analysis can be applied to other countries. At the *workplace level*, countries with low strike rates often have externally prescribed institutions of representation. In Germany and Austria, workers have legally guaranteed rights of co-determination within the workplace; rather weaker, and not legally mandated, institutions exist in Switzerland (Hotz-Hart 1992: 310); in The Netherlands, though works councils have been historically weak, legislation restricted employers' freedom in certain key areas such as dismissals (Visser 1992: 340, 327).

The sharpest contrast is with Britain, where the tradition of works councils is absent. Unlike their counterparts in much of Europe, who had developed comprehensive national or industry-level agreements, and those in North America, whose single-employer agreements were backed up by a legally defined right to manage, British employers lacked any comprehensive approach to managing the shop-floor. In large parts of industry where union power was weak, employers remained free to run the shop-floor largely as they wished. Where there was a union challenge, notably in engineering, employers swung between toughness and compromise. Like their Italian counterparts, they were capable of a tough line against union activists, particularly in the early 1950s. However, this went along with acquiescence in worker involvement in the organization of work. A cycle of distrust developed, as workers tried to use their bargaining power to gain concessions. Workplace relations were resolved on a day-to-day basis, with the strike being an ever-present possibility (Batstone et al. 1978). In many respects, Ireland shared this tradition, though the relatively small size of its manufacturing sector and the smallness of plants within the sector meant that the problem of workplace-level strikes was not as severe as in Britain.

This environment allowed strikes to become a normal feature of industrial relations in many plants: there were few institutional constraints, and managerial acts of omission or commission led workers to use stoppages as normal bargaining weapons. However, this system also rendered shop-floor union organizations particularly vulnerable to managerial counterattack. In the political and economic circumstances of the 1980s, unionists who wanted to sustain shop-floor militancy found it hard to do so, while others came to question its relevance. As noted above, industrial action became very uncommon in private manufacturing industry during the 1980s.

The importance of the workplace is also clear in the case of France. The issue here is why strike rates fell so fast during the 1980s. Shalev (1992) points to the rapid decline in union membership as a potential loss of capacity to organize industrial action. However, since French unions have in the past been able to sustain high levels of strike activity with little formal organization, this may be only part of the explanation. An additional factor may be the modernization of French employers. From the late 1970s, the national association, the Conseil National du Patronat Français, developed from a loose federation to become a more powerful organization, and individual employers turned their attention to the organization of work and means of work-force expression such as quality circles at plant level (Sellier 1985: 193–8). These developments may have reduced the sense of distance between management and workers which was so apparent in earlier comparative analysis (Gallie 1978).

In another high-conflict country, Finland, the workplace was also important. As noted above, the country's economic structure promoted confrontations between employers and masses of workers. Participative structures at workplace level were introduced only from the late 1970s. There were thus few institutions to regulate conflict at this level. The fragmentation of the union movement and political struggles within it exacerbated the tendency towards weak institutionalization. The role of the communist party was not the free-floating factor suggested by Crouch, for a militant union movement reflected a specific material context.

The general relevance of *enterprise* and *industry* levels is evident. In Germany, industry-level bargaining has co-ordinated wage demands and has prevented workers in individual firms from pursuing their own wage claims. In Britain, by contrast, the weakness of industry-level regulation helped to encourage a lack of normative consensus about wage levels (Goldthorpe 1978) and made it very difficult for incomes policies to function for any length of time. This did not mean that workers would necessarily strike over every pay claim. However, it certainly permitted them to do so when other conditions were appropriate. This approach shaped the public as much as the private sector. Periods of pay policies raised issues of relativities in a sharp manner, for workers discovered that in a fragmented system, wage restraint was unlikely to bring long-term rewards.

Finland further illustrates this theme. Employers here long stood out against the corporatist arrangements of Scandinavia. Their hostility to centralized wage agreements added to the existing sources of conflict at workplace level. Attempts at wage restraint have broken down in the face of competitive struggles between different union groups in a manner reminiscent of Britain.

In the case of Germany, strong institutions at workplace, enterprise and industry level help to explain the rarity of strikes. Elsewhere the *national level* has been more important. The case of Sweden has been discussed above. Variations between Sweden and Denmark are evident here. In the latter country, it has proved more difficult to contain wage drift with centralized agreements. Unionists have had more freedom at industry and local level to pursue their demands, a freedom that is likely to have contributed to the higher level of strike activity.

The United Kingdom illustrates a more complex role for the state. Throughout the post-war period, governments have tried to control inflation. Evidence showed that although such policies reduced the frequency of strikes while they were in operation, there was often a resurgence of activity once a policy collapsed (Davies 1979). Although state efforts to regulate the economy shaped strike activity in the private sector only indirectly, the public sector from the 1970s saw the emergence of a series of large national strikes among hitherto largely quiescent groups such as teachers, postal workers, and health workers. These strikes reflected not only discontent at pay restraint but also, as mentioned above, the growing organization of public sector workers as unions instituted systems of local representation.

Ireland offers a variant on the British picture. Its system of industrial relations has its roots in the voluntarist approach, so that industrial action at shop-floor level was constrained neither by law nor collective agreement. During the 1970s, however, a series of national agreements sought consensus between employers, unions and the state on rates of wage increase. In contrast to the views of labour movement theory, these agreements were not the result of political power on the part of unions but reflected efforts by the state to deal with economic problems. During the 1980s further institutionalization combined with recession to reduce the level of strikes (von Prondzynski 1992: 84; Hardiman 1988).

The centralization of bargaining in Finland would be expected to produce a similar result. As table 10.2 shows, the level of strike activity in the 1980s was certainly lower than that in the 1970s. As the country moves further towards a Scandinavian model, a further reduction in strike levels would be expected, no doubt assisted by the declining relevance of traditional communist politics.

These sketches suggest how the approach of writers like Franzosi can be developed. Corporatist analyses tended to be static and to assume that the workplace level ceased to be an issue more or less automatically once national-level institutions were in place. These institutions have to be seen, rather, as part of a continuing relationship between unions, employers and the state. The management of conflict is likely to be as important in the future as it was in the past, indeed possibly more so. Though overt disputes may be less frequent, employers in many countries are giving increased attention to the control of the workplace in their efforts to compete internationally (Edwards 1992). In the past, buoyant demand may have made it possible to tolerate some disputes. Growing competition may make this more difficult. The control of the workplace may take on a new salience, even though the traditional expression of conflict over relations of control and subordination – the strike – may be declining in significance.

Conclusions

Up to the 1970s, there were three main patterns of strikes in Europe. The first was the infrequent, large-scale industry-wide dispute. As noted above, this pattern reflected a strong role for unions in some countries (Sweden, Norway and Denmark) and a consocial model in others (The Netherlands and Switzerland), with other countries reflecting a mix of the two (Germany, and more problematically Belgium). Where collective bargaining was institutionalized though more decentralized – Britain, and to a lesser extent Ireland – strikes were more frequent yet more fragmented, and hence smaller and shorter. Here, the second type prevailed: the more frequent, workplace stoppage, often functioning as a brief token demonstration within company-level collective bargaining. In the Mediterranean countries (France, Italy, and – after the fall of the dictatorships – Spain, Portugal and Greece) collective bargaining was far less firmly institutionalized, and trade unions with a weak membership base were more closely tied to party-political priorities. Here, two types of strike prevailed. One was the plant-level symbolic protest, designed to pressurize management within the complex dynamics of 'arms-length bargaining' (Batstone 1978); the other, the industry-wide or more often economy-wide token action to influence government decision-making. While serving the agenda of (in particular communist) union-linked political parties, such actions also made pragmatic sense in national contexts where the state had a key role in defining minimum wages and other employment-related benefits, though where labour had no direct representation in government.

By the 1970s, strike patterns were altering in significant respects. First, relative peace in the public sector was under increasing strain, from both employer attempts to economize (or government attempts to impose exemplary wage restraint) and growing trade union consciousness among employees. The result was a diverse pattern of conflict types: national token stoppages; more protracted industry- (or service-) level strikes; and more localized, usually short disputes, particularly in 'strategic' services such as public transport or refuse disposal. Second, the much discussed 'new demands' of 'new' groups of industrial workers which had helped fire the explosions of the late 1960s (Kirchlechner 1978) reached the official industrial relations agenda. After the pattern of stoppages between 1968 and 1970, which were commonly fragmented and often unofficial (even anti-official), there developed across much of Europe a pattern of more centralized disputes over issues on the 'qualitative' agenda, most importantly shorter working-time. Third, growing competitive pressures led employers (with increasing state encouragement) to restructure and economize, a process linked to technological innovation which challenged established systems of organizing work and employment; here the consequence was often company-level disputes.

The 1980s saw a further qualitative shift. The last change noted above became increasingly provocative in the early 1980s; the Fiat strike of 1980 symbolizes the type of company-level struggle against restructuring and redundancy which became common across Europe. However, as the decade progressed, this type of dispute seems to have become less frequent (though re-emerging, most recently, in the German *neue Länder*). It could be argued that in firms which survived the pressures of intensified competition, management and unions recognized a common interest in containing disruptive conflict, and thus developed forms of microcorporatism. At industry level, the 'qualitative demands' of the previous decade assumed an increasingly defensive role: a means of reshaping and mitigating the restructuring which could not be frontally resisted. Hence the 35-hour week was now pressed, less as a means of enhancing workers' leisure than as a mechanism of job-sharing; or collective regulation of technological innovation as a means of employment protection rather than industrial democracy. The shift from new initiatives to defensive struggles is also apparent in the public sector: many of the key conflicts in the 1980s or early 1990s consisted of resistance against job loss, work intensification, or declining relative pay. Also important were economy-wide protest stoppages reflecting tensions in the process of national political exchange. This might be characterized as a 'don't push us too far' response to the delicate process of sharing the costs of recession and economic restructuring: a signal that union consent has its limits. Here, the exemplary cases are in southern Europe: the Spanish general strike of 1988 and the series of Italian analogues in the 1980s. In contrast to these various defensive reactions, there are signs of a new type of more aggressive action by groups with a more secure and advantaged labour market situation seeking to escape the more generalized restraints on collective bargaining. The actions of the Italian *Cobas* are the prime example, and the *co-ordinations* in France and Belgium, or the actions of public transport workers in Spain, present parallels. A key question for European industrial relations in the remainder of the 1990s is whether the suppression of generalized conflict by adverse economic and political circumstances may encourage a proliferation of such fragmented militancy.

Looking more generally, the strikes which enter national statistics may become less satisfactory indicators of overt disputes. Treu (1987: 114), for example, points to the rise of small-scale 'micro conflicts' in Italy. And beneath these conflicts – which are still strikes in the sense of being collective work stoppages to enforce a demand or express a protest, even if they do not enter official figures – may be many other changes in the organization of work. The smaller size of firms, new production technologies and new forms of payment and of labour utilization all affect the ability to engage in strikes and, more fundamentally, the perceived need for strike action. Little research has been done on these topics, not least because the research traditions in many countries have not made the negotiation of consent at workplace level a central issue. As other chapters in this volume demonstrate, however, many employers are giving increased attention to the workplace in considering more flexible uses of labour and new devices such as quality circles.

Running against any tendency towards the increased emphasis on the organization of co-operation among manual workers are some counter-trends. These include the growing rationalization of the work of clerical and managerial staff (Dopson and Stewart 1990). Though such workers are unlikely to engage in strike action to the extent practised by manual workers in the past, they are subject to the effects of job loss and closer measurement of their behaviour. How they respond to these pressures will reflect the ways in which the conflictual aspects of work relations are defined and negotiated.

Research in the future needs to address such issues. There will also be a need to turn attention away from the developed world. It is indeed conceivable that the strike will wither away here. Overall rates of activity seem to have peaked around the time of the two world wars, so that in a country like Germany post-1945 levels have been historically low. The weapon of the strike may have a particular relevance to manual workers at particular stages of industrialization. However, as other countries industrialize, and as the former Soviet bloc moves towards free market models, they may experience further explosions of overt militancy, following an industrial and political dynamic quite different from that in developed countries.

Note

1 Multicollinearity (a high level of association between independent variables resulting in unreliable coefficients) seems to be a substantial problem in 13 of 17 cases, while autocorrelation as indexed by the Durbin–Watson statistic is a problem in 8. The model seems to pass all relevant tests only in the case of France.

References

Ashenfelter, O. and Johnson, G.E. 1969: Bargaining theory, trade unions and industrial strike activity. *American Economic Review*, 59(1) 35–49.

Baglioni, G. 1990: European industrial relations in the 1980s. In Baglioni and Crouch, 1990, 1–41.

Baglioni, G. and Crouch, C. (eds) 1990: *European Industrial Relations*. London: Sage Publications.

Batstone, E. 1978: Arms'-length bargaining: industrial relations in a French company. Mimeo, Industrial Relations Research Unit, University of Warwick.

Batstone, E., Boraston, I. and Frenkel, S. 1978: *The Social Organization of Strikes*. Oxford: Blackwell Publishers.

Berggren, C. 1992: *Alternatives to Lean Production: work organization in the Swedish auto industry*. Ithaca: ILR Press.

Bordogna, L. 1989: Il pubblico impiego alimenta i Cobas. *Lavoro 80*, 8, 69–73.

Brown, W. (ed.) 1981: *The Changing Contours of British Industrial Relations*. Oxford: Blackwell Publishers.

Cameron, D.R. 1984: Social democracy, corporatism, labour quiescence and the representation of economic interest in advanced capitalist society. In J.H. Goldthorpe 1984, 143–78.

Church, R., Outram, Q. and Smith, D.N. 1990: British coal mining strikes 1893–

1940. *British Journal of Industrial Relations*, 28(3) 329–50.

Clegg, H.A. 1976: *Trade Unionism under Collective Bargaining*. Oxford: Blackwell Publishers.

Cronin, J.E. 1979: *Industrial Conflict in Modern Britain*. London: Croom Helm.

Crouch, C. 1985: Conditions for trade union wage restraint. In L.N. Lindberg and C.S. Maier (eds), *The Politics of Inflation and Economic Stagnation*, Washington, DC: Brookings Institution, 105–39.

Crouch, C. and Pizzorno, A. 1978: *The Resurgence of Class Conflict in Western Europe since 1968*. 2 vols. London: Macmillan.

Davies, R.J. 1979: Economic analysis, incomes policy and strikes. *British Journal of Industrial Relations*, 17(2) 205–23.

Davies, R.J. 1981: The political economy of distributive conflict. PhD thesis, University of Warwick.

Dopson, S. and Stewart, R. 1990: What *is* happening to middle management? *British Journal of Management*, 1(1) 3–16.

Durand, C. and Dubois, P. 1975: *La grève*. Paris: Armand Colin. Edwards, P.K. 1983: The political economy of industrial conflict.

Economic and Industrial Democracy, 4(4) 461–500.

Edwards, P.K. 1992: Industrial conflict: themes and issues in recent research. *British Journal of Industrial Relations*, 30(3) 361–404.

Edwards, P.K., Hall, M., Hyman, R., Marginson, P., Sisson, K., Waddington, J. and Winchester, D. 1992: Great Britain. In Ferner and Hyman, 1992b, 1–68.

Ferner, A. and Hyman, R. 1992a: Italy. In Ferner and Hyman 1992b, 524–600.

Ferner, A. and Hyman, R. 1992b: *Industrial Relations in the New Europe*. Oxford: Blackwell Publishers.

Fiorai, B. 1989: Casi di dissento tra sindicali e lavoratori o tra sindacati. *Lavoro 80*, 8, 131–47.

Franzosi, R. 1989a: Strike data in search of a theory: the Italian case in the postwar period. *Politics and Society*, 17(4) 453–87.

Franzosi, R. 1989b: One hundred years of strike statistics. *Industrial and Labor Relations Review*, 42(3) 348–62.

Fulcher, J. 1973: Discontent in a Swedish shipyard. *British Journal of Industrial Relations*, 11(2) 242–58.

Fulcher, J. 1987: Labour movement theory versus corporatism. *Sociology*, 21(2) 231–52.

Fulcher, J. 1991: *Labour Movements, Employers and the State: conflict and co-operation in Britain and Sweden*. Oxford: Clarendon Press.

Gallie, D. 1978: *In Search of the New Working Class*. Cambridge: Cambridge University Press.

Goetschy, J. and Rozenblatt, P. 1992: France. In Ferner and Hyman, 1992b, 404–44.

Goldthorpe, J.H. 1978: The current inflation. In F. Hirsch and J.H. Goldthorpe (eds), *The Political Economy of Inflation*. London: Martin Robertson, 178–205.

Goldthorpe, J.H. 1984: *Order and Conflict in Contemporary Capitalism*. Oxford: Clarendon Press.

Gyllenhammar, P.G. 1977: *People at Work*. Reading, Mass.: Addison-Wesley.

Hardiman, N. 1988: *Pay, Politics and Economic Performance in Ireland, 1970–87*. Oxford: Clarendon Press.

Heritage, J. 1983: Feminisation and unionisation: a case study from banking. In E. Gamarnikow et al. (eds), *Gender, Class and Work*. London: Heinemann, 131–48.

Hotz-Hart, B. 1992: Switzerland. In Ferner and Hyman, 1992b, 298–322.

Hibbs, D.A. 1976: Industrial conflict in advanced industrial societies. *American*

Political Science Review, 70(4) 1033–58.

Hyman, R. 1983: White-collar workers and theories of class. In R. Hyman and R. Price (eds), *The New Working Class?* London: Macmillan, 3–45.

Jacobi, O. 1985: World economic changes and industrial relations in the Federal Republic of Germany. In Juris et al. 1985, 211–46.

Juris, H., Thompson, M. and Daniels, W. (eds) 1985: *Industrial Relations in a Decade of Economic Change*. Madison: Industrial Relations Research Association.

Kesselman, M. 1983: Socialism without the workers: the case of France. *Kapitalistate*, 10/11, 11–41.

Kerr, C. and Siegel, A. 1954: The interindustry propensity to strike. In A. Kornhauser et al. (eds), *Industrial Conflict*, New York: McGraw-Hill Book Company, 189–212.

Kjellberg, A. 1992: Sweden. In Ferner and Hyman, 1992b, 88–142.

Kirchlechner, B. 1978: New demands or demands of new groups? In Crouch and Pizzorno, 1978, Volume 2, 161–76.

Korpi, W. 1983: *The Working Class in Welfare Capitalism*. London: Routledge and Kegan Paul.

Korpi, W. and Shalev, M. 1979: Strikes, industrial relations and class conflict in capitalist societies. *British Journal of Sociology*, 30(2) 164–87.

Lash, S. 1985: The end of neo-corporatism? The breakdown of centralised bargaining in Sweden. *British Journal of Industrial Relations*, 23(2) 215–39.

Lehmbruch, G. 1984: Concertation and the structure of corporatist networks. In Goldthorpe, 1984, 60–80.

Lilja, K. 1992: Finland. In Ferner and Hyman, 1992b, 198–217.

Lockwood, D. 1958: *The Blackcoated Worker*. London: George Allen and Unwin.

Low-Beer, J.R. 1978: *Protest and Participation: the new working class in Italy*. Cambridge: Cambridge University Press.

Millward, N., Stevens, M., Smart, D. and Hawes, W.R. 1992: *Workplace Industrial Relations in Transition*. Aldershot: Dartmouth Publishing.

Milner, S. 1993: Overtime bans and strikes. *Industrial Relations Journal*, 24(3) 201–10.

Müller-Jentsch, W. 1981: Strikes and strike trends in West Germany, 1950–78. *Industrial Relations Journal*, 12(4) 36–57.

Negrelli, S. and Santi, E. 1990: Industrial relations in Italy. In Baglioni and Crouch, 1990, 154–98.

Paldam, M. and Pedersen, P.J. 1980: The macro-model explaining industrial conflict. Memo 1980–6, Institute of Economics, University of Aarhus.

Pekkarinen, J., Pohjola, M. and Rowthorn, B. 1992: Social corporatism and economic performance. In J. Pekkarinen, M. Pohjola and B. Rowthorn (eds), *Social Corporatism*, Oxford: Clarendon Press, 1–23.

Peterson, F. 1938: *Strikes in the United States, 1880–1936*. Washington, DC: US Department of Labor Bulletin 651.

Regalia, I., Regini, M. and Regneri, E. 1978: Labour conflicts and industrial relations in Italy. In Crouch and Pizzorno, 1978, Volume 1, 101–58.

Rimlinger, G.V. 1959: International differences in strike propensity of coal miners. *Industrial and Labor Relations Review*, 12(3) 389–405.

Scheuer, S. 1992: Denmark. In Ferner and Hyman, 1992b, 168–97.

Screpanti, E. 1987: Long cycles in strike activity. *British Journal of Industrial Relations*, 25(1) 99–124.

Sellier, F. 1985: Economic change and industrial relations in France. In Juris et al., 1985, 177–210.

Shalev, M. 1978a: Lies, damned lies and strike statistics. In Crouch and Pizzorno, 1978, Volume 1, 1–19.

Shalev, M. 1978b: Strikers and the state. *British Journal of Political Science*, 8(4) 479–92.

Shalev, M. 1980: Trade unionism and economic analysis. *Journal of Labor Research*, 1(1) 133–74.

Shalev, M. 1992: The resurgence of labour quiescence. In M. Regini (ed.), *The Future of Labour Movements*, London: Sage Publications, 102–32.

Shorter, E. and Tilly, C. 1974: *Strikes in France, 1830–1968*. Cambridge: Cambridge University Press.

Silver, B. 1991: World-scale patterns of labour–capital conflict. In I. Brandell (ed.), *Workers in Third-world Industrialization*, London: Macmillan, 217–33.

Streeck, W. 1984: *Industrial Relations in West Germany*. London: Heinemann.

Therborn, G. 1992: Lessons from 'corporatist' theorizations. In J. Pekkarinen, M. Pohjola and B. Rowthorn (eds), *Social Corporatism*, Oxford: Clarendon Press, 24–43.

Touraine, A. 1971: *The Post-industrial Society*. New York: Random House.

Treu, T. 1987: Labour relations in the public service in Italy. In T. Treu (ed.), *Public Service Labour Relations*, Geneva: ILO, 111–44.

Visser, J. 1992: The Netherlands. In Ferner and Hyman, 1992b, 323–56.

von Prondzynski, F. 1992: Ireland. In Ferner and Hyman, 1992b, 69–87.

11

Industrial Relations and the Social Dimension of European Integration: Before and After Maastricht

Mark Hall

Introduction

Renewed impetus towards European integration since the mid-1980s, particularly the completion of the single European market and the prospect of economic and monetary union, has generated pressure for developing the 'social dimension' of the European Community[1], including the extension of the EC's regulatory role in industrial relations matters. Such proposals have proved highly controversial. Years of fierce debate culminated in the decision at the Maastricht EC summit in December 1991 to include in the Treaty on European Union a social policy protocol enabling more extensive EC intervention in this field than hitherto. The political divisions over the social dimension are most starkly illustrated by the decision of the government of a major member state – the United Kingdom – to opt out of the new treaty's social policy provisions, having previously refused to sign the 1989 EC social charter. However, there is also a more general lack of consensus among key parties to the debate about the extent to which Community-wide labour standards are necessary in a single market or in the context of economic and monetary union. Consequently, the practical impact of the new procedures established by the Maastricht social policy protocol remains uncertain.

To date, the evolution of the EC's social policy role has been uneven and limited. The Treaty of Rome did not establish a clear Community competence in this sphere, and the scope for and momentum behind EC social policy initiatives have been highly sensitive to shifts in the prevailing political and economic context. Prior to the social policy initiatives dating from the late 1980s, the impact of the EC's intervention in the industrial relations field had essentially been confined to a number of narrow though important areas such as equal opportunities and employment protection legislation.

The subsequent debate can best be understood in terms of competing conceptions of the social dimension on the part of member states, EC institutions and employer and trade union organizations. These reflect both alternative responses to intensified economic pressures and the wider debate about the future direction of European integration. The argument that the development of a single market would encourage 'social dumping' (that is, multinational companies establishing or relocating their operations in countries with cheaper labour costs and less stringent employment legislation, thus generating downward pressure on the higher labour standards that exist in countries such as Germany) has been central to the European trade union case for a comprehensive, Community-wide employment law framework and has been emphasized by several member states, notably France. Another concern is that the single market will exacerbate the existing regional 'division of labour' within the Community and reinforce the competitive disadvantages (in infrastructure, technology, productivity, labour force skills, etc.) of the least developed countries and regions (Mosley 1990: 161); the increased 'cohesion funding' won at Maastricht by the 'peripheral' member states led by Spain was to reduce the 'economic differentials' within the Community (Leibfried and Pierson 1992: 340). Arguably the most developed notion of the social dimension concerns the promotion of a 'European model of production' (Lange 1992: 227) – based on high skills, high quality, high technology and high productivity, including a high degree of co-operation ('social partnership') between management and labour – throughout the EC and Europe more generally, as an alternative to the US model of the highly deregulated labour market with its 'hire and fire', low-wage employment growth strategy.

Politically, the European Commission and most member states have seen the development of the social dimension as an important vehicle for securing the support of the European labour movement for the single market project and for enhancing the 'social acceptability' of the consequent economic restructuring. The Commission presents the social dimension as the 'human face' of the EC (Shanks 1977a: 5; Flynn 1993). The expansion of the Community's competence in the social policy field has also been a central element, at least symbolically, of the 'political union' espoused by most member state governments.

However, for the UK Conservative government and UNICE, the European employers' confederation, an expansive and interventionist conception of the EC's social dimension is inimical to the deregulatory thrust of the single market and threatens the competitiveness of European industry and job creation. They have generally opposed the EC-level regulation of employment conditions and industrial relations practices, arguing that EC intervention should essentially be confined to issues such as the mobility of labour and the recognition of professional qualifications which are essential to the operation of the single market. The UK government's concern to avoid EC regulation undermining its deregulatory strategy for the domestic labour market has been reinforced by its anti-federalist stance in debates about the EC's general development. While strongly supporting the establishment of the single market, the government has fought against the erosion of inter-governmentalism and the principle of unanimity in Council decision-making in areas of the EC's activities other than market integration.

As a result of these divergent views, and the complex political processes of EC decision-making, the nature and extent of the social dimension remain ambiguous and contested. On the one hand, the proponents of an expansive EC social policy have been broadly successful in setting the agenda (in the form of the social charter and the accompanying action programme) and achieving treaty revisions at Maastricht which should facilitate future EC intervention in important areas of social policy. On the other hand, some of the key legislative elements of the social charter action programme remain blocked, because of successful rearguard action by the UK government and UNICE or reservations on the part of a wider range of member states. Those measures which *have* been passed have generally had only limited practical implications for most member states, reflecting the tendency towards a 'lowest common denominator' approach in the Council of Ministers' negotiations.

Moreover, member states' policy responses to Europe's slide into recession will also have important implications for the social dimension. Current EC concerns about unemployment and competitiveness are again focusing increasingly on 'Eurosclerosis' – the view that European economic performance is being undermined by excessive regulation and labour market inflexibility compared with the United States and Japan. Despite attempts to challenge this analysis (see TUC 1993), it seems to be increasingly influential within the European Commission (*Financial Times* 9 September 1993) as well as the Council, and inevitably calls into question member states' willingness to pursue further EC employment legislation, notwithstanding the new possibilities offered by the Maastricht social policy protocol.

Against this background, the aims of this chapter are to chart the evolution of EC industrial relations policy, to examine why attempts to establish an effective regulatory role for the EC in this sphere have to date proved largely unsuccessful, and to assess whether the Maastricht treaty is indeed likely to be a watershed in the development of the EC's industrial relations role. The chapter falls into three main sections. The first identifies the effects of the changing political and economic context and a range of institutional constraints on the historical development of EC social policy. The second discusses the key features of the social policy strategy of the Delors Commission prior to Maastricht. The third part explores the likely future trajectories of EC industrial relations regulation post-Maastricht. The central argument is that, despite the attempts made at Maastricht to ease the institutional constraints on EC intervention in the employment and industrial relations sphere, the ambiguities of the social policy protocol and the uncertainties stemming from the coexistence of two regulatory procedures (one covering all twelve member states, and the other excluding the United Kingdom) are likely to limit the impact of the treaty's social policy innovations. More fundamentally, significant progress in the area of EC social policy will continue to depend on economic and political circumstances. The current recession in Europe and concern about relative employment costs and competitiveness may undermine member states' political will to press ahead with an extensive programme of further social measures at European Community level.

The Evolution of EC Industrial Relations Policy

Historically, the main instigator of extending the Community's social policy role has been the European Commission itself. The development of an integrated 'European industrial relations system' (CEC 1988: 65) has consisted of two main elements: the adoption of 'substantive', regulatory measures at Community level, usually in the form of EC directives, to 'harmonize' (that is, align more closely) the national laws and practices of member states or to regulate transnational industrial relations matters; and 'procedural' initiatives such as the promotion of 'social dialogue' between European-level employer and trade union organizations and their inclusion in a network of sectoral or advisory bodies which feed into the Commission's policy development work. The balance between these elements, as well as the details of the policies pursued by the Commission, have varied over time, reflecting changing circumstances and the personal agendas of influential actors such as Commission President Jacques Delors and successive social affairs commissioners. However, although the Commission has the right of initiative and can exercise a high degree of 'relative autonomy', this is essentially confined to setting the Community's agenda. Actual decision-making rests, of course, with the Council of Ministers, which has frequently restrained the Commission's ambitions in the social policy field (as in others), particularly once debate moves beyond the establishment of broad principles to the enactment of specific proposals. On occasion, the member state government holding the presidency of the Council of Ministers has had a major influence on the overall direction of EC social policy. In short, the Commission does not operate in a political and economic vacuum. Social policy options are conditioned and restricted by broad political and economic factors, and by the views of key member states (particularly France, Germany and the United Kingdom), Community institutions such as the European Parliament and the Economic and Social Committee, and the 'social partners'. Moreover, the terms of the social policy debate have also been shaped by a series of specific institutional constraints, as discussed below.

The changing political and economic context

At certain stages, the conjuncture of particular political and economic conditions has created 'windows of opportunity' (Leibfried and Pierson 1992: 334) for the enlargement of the EC's social policy activities, resulting in two key periods of social policy activism during the Community's history: 1974–80 and 1989 to the present. Proposals from Community institutions and member states for extending the EC's regulatory role in the social policy area have tended to arise in response to changing competitive conditions associated with key transitional stages of European integration. Thus, with the completion of the Community's initial stage of development – the establishment of a customs union by the end of 1969 – discussions about economic and monetary union and the enlargement of the Community provided the context for a new emphasis on social policy matters which culminated in the adoption of the first EC social action programme in 1974. Similarly, in the late 1980s the central EC project of completing the single market was the catalyst for wider moves towards European integration including the development of the social dimension. The broader economic climate is also part of the equation. The 1974 social action programme was seen by its authors explicitly in terms of tackling the 'social consequences of growth' (Shanks 1977a: 5; cf. Hepple 1987). Conversely, member states' commitment to its full implementation was dissipated by the onset of recession (Shanks 1977b: 382). The more recent proposals for expanding the EC's social dimension were also developed against a background of economic growth in the second half of the 1980s and the optimism generated by the '1992' single market initiative. Again, the indications are that adverse economic developments may undermine member states' willingness to carry through the current programme.

The political complexion of the governments of key member states is also of obvious relevance. The coming to power of the social democrats in West Germany in 1969 was influential in raising the priority of the EC's social policy role. Prompted by the Brandt government and by the Commission, which had at various stages during the 1960s attempted to win the support of the Council of Ministers for a more active social policy, the Hague summit of 1969 stressed the need for greater concentration on social policy matters. Willy Brandt's argument that 'social justice should no longer be considered by the Community as an appendage of economic growth and that an effective social policy would enable people to identify more readily with the European organization' (Collins 1975: 216) found a response at the 1972 Paris summit. This declared that member states 'attached as much importance to vigorous action in the social field as to the achievement of economic union' and backed Brandt's call for an action programme. In the 1980s, the French socialist government's policy of promoting *l'espace social européen* provided the initial impetus and framework for social policy developments under the Commission presidency of Jacques Delors, formerly a French Socialist government minister.

Similarly, political and economic developments in the early 1980s led to a general 'impasse' over EC labour law initiatives. The UK Conservative government elected in 1979 played a leading role in blocking a range of proposed directives within the Council. By the early 1980s, centre-right, mainly Christian Democrat-led governments had assumed office in several member states (Belgium, The Netherlands, Denmark and, most importantly, Germany) and the Socialist government in France had adopted a conservative economic strategy. Christian democratic political philosophies, influenced by a doctrine of social responsibility and links with Catholic trade union organizations, have generally involved a positive view of social policy: the same governments were prepared to give at least symbolic support to the development of the EC's social dimension later in the 1980s in the context of the single market programme. However, the scope for the United Kingdom's strategy was widened by the general political immobilism within the Community which characterized the first half of the 1980s (Noel 1989: 4), and by member states' domestic policy responses to recession: a number of EC governments pursued 'moderately' deregulatory labour law policies with which the Commission's regulatory proposals were seen as inconsistent (see below).

Institutional constraints

Intra-Community institutional factors – most notably the lack of a clear treaty basis and the paralysis stemming from the requirement for unanimity in decision-making, the crisis of the EC's 'upward harmonization' strategy, and the limited development of 'social partnership' at European level – have also tended to constrain the development of the EC's social policy role.

Market integration and social policy intervention

From its inception, the European Community's primary focus has been on economic integration, albeit as the means of achieving wider political integration. A consequence was that, under the terms of the Treaty of Rome, EC intervention in social policy issues could be justified only in terms of its contribution to market integration. In other words, social policy issues were dealt with not in their own right but in terms of their effect on the relative economic positions of member states (Collins 1975: 4). Moreover, in the view of the Community's founders, the economic impact of social policy questions was likely to be very limited. Prior to the establishment of the Community, there was considerable debate about whether disparities between the labour and social costs of employers in different member states would have the general effect of distorting competition, necessitating extensive Community-level intervention. The French government favoured the general alignment of labour and social standards, fearing that existing French labour laws might put the country at a competitive disadvantage. Nevertheless, the predominant view put forward in the Spaak report and by the ILO committee of experts was that differences in the general levels of wages and social costs were a function of differences in productivity; exchange rate adjustments remained a possible corrective measure if costs and productivity moved out of line. Although certain specific distortions might need remedying, the need for intervention would be strictly limited (Davies 1992). Indeed, the general harmonization of social conditions was seen as the outcome of, not the precondition for, the effective operation of the common market.

This approach – essentially economic liberalism – was largely though not unequivocally adopted in the social policy section of the Treaty of Rome. In response to French concerns, the treaty included specific references to the need to ensure equal pay between men and women and the maintenance of paid holidays. However, the central ambiguity of the treaty's social policy provisions lay in Article 117, in which member states agreed on the general objective of improving and harmonizing workers' living and working conditions: it was stated that this would result not only from the functioning of the common market but also from the procedures of the Treaty and the approximation of regulations. Thus the Treaty fudged the central issue of whether the harmonization of social policy should be left to the market or whether Community intervention would be necessary. It also failed to provide any specific mechanism for such intervention: under Article 118, the Commission was allotted only the very general task of 'promoting close co-operation' between member states in the social policy field.

The absence of a specific treaty basis on which the Commission could propose Community legislation on employment and labour law matters did not emerge as a major problem during the Community's initial stage of integration: the main focus of EC social policy over this period was on facilitating the free movement of labour (for measures on which a specific treaty base *did* exist) and the establishment of the European Social Fund to promote the regional and occupational mobility of workers. However, in 1974, to enable the implementation of the social action programme, political agreement was necessary within the Council of Ministers to sanction the use of Article 100 of the Treaty as the legal basis for labour law directives (Crijns 1987: 55). This enables the 'approximation' of provisions in the member states which 'directly affect the establishment or functioning of the common market'. A number of labour law directives adopted over the 1970s – on collective redundancies (1975), equal pay (1975), business transfers (1977) and business insolvencies (1980) – were based on Article 100. Thus their implicit rationale was that

> the disparity between the labour costs imposed upon employers by national legislation in the different member states as regards, for example, reducing the size of the labour force or taking over another employer's business had the effect of distorting competition between employers in different member states. (O'Higgins 1986: 586)

However, if variations in, for example, statutory redundancy procedures are accepted as distorting competition, it is difficult to see why a similar argument does not apply to many other aspects of employment law (Wedderburn 1990: 67). In practice, as the then director-general for social affairs at the Commission made clear, the content of the 1974 social action programme 'reflected a political judgement of what was thought to be both desirable and possible, rather than a juridical judgement of what were thought to be the social policy implications of the Rome Treaty' (Shanks 1977a: 13).

More recent debates have confirmed the Community's reluctance to accept a general economic logic for social policy intervention. Notwithstanding the Commission's use of the rhetoric of 'social dumping' in pressing the case for the development of the social dimension, internal Commission assessments suggest that the actual dangers of social dumping are limited (CEC 1988: 67). Moreover, only once has the Commission proposed using Article 100A of the Treaty as the legal basis for a social policy proposal – and even then this appears to have been a political gesture made in the expectation of its almost certain failure. Article 100A, introduced by the Single European Act, enables qualified majority voting[2] by the Council in respect of measures 'which have as their object the establishment and functioning of the internal market', but excludes provisions 'relating to the rights and interests of employed persons'. Some commentators have argued that a radical interpretation of Article 100A could and should be the legal basis for a wide range of social policy measures because they affect competition within the internal market and not just 'the rights and interests of employed persons' (Vogel-Polsky 1990). The Commission's 1990 proposal for a directive to harmonize part-time and temporary workers' entitlements in respect of statutory and occupational social security schemes, annual holidays, 'dismissal allowances and seniority allowances' was based on Article 100A on the grounds that differential provision in these areas might give rise to distortions of competition (Hall 1991: 148; Davies 1992: 346). This approach was strongly criticized within the Council of Ministers and the proposal itself has made no progress. Nevertheless, this move in the 'treaty base game' (Wedderburn 1990: 52) served to highlight once again the limits placed on the EC's potential role in social policy role by social policy's secondary status under the terms of the treaty, and to reinforce the Commission's case for treaty revisions to provide a clear, direct and free-standing legal basis for Community labour law measures.

It also highlighted the limited scope for qualified majority voting in respect of social policy issues. The principle of unanimous decision-making by the Council of Ministers emerged as an important constraint on EC intervention in industrial relations matters during the 1980s when a range of proposed labour law measures was blocked, often single-handedly by the United Kingdom. Limited innovations were introduced in the social policy field by the Single European Act. The new Article 118A enabled qualified majority voting for the adoption of directives aimed at 'encouraging improvements, especially in the working environment, as regards the health and safety of workers'. However, as noted above, employment issues were expressly excluded – at the behest of the UK government – from the more general provision enabling majority voting for internal market measures. Whether or not a particular proposal is subject to qualified majority voting or unanimity can have considerable implications for its prospects of adoption. The Commission has therefore interpreted Article 118A broadly and has used it as the legal basis for a number of directives proposed under the social charter action programme, including those concerning maternity rights and working-time, to enable their adoption by qualified majority voting. The UK government has criticized this approach and has threatened to challenge the legal basis of the working-time directive in the European Court of Justice. More generally, the extension of qualified majority voting to a wider range of social policy issues emerged as a key demand in the treaty revision debate in the run-up to Maastricht.

Problems of harmonization

In addition to the limits on Community competence in the social policy field, the harmonization process itself has been problematic. Commission labour law proposals have frequently failed to reach the EC statute book, and the general impasse over this area of Community legislation during the 1980s led to a reassessment of the Commission's approach to harmonization.

Differing regulatory traditions among member states condition their perceptions of what is the most appropriate 'style' and content of EC industrial relations and labour law policy. The diversity between member states in this respect has grown with the enlargement of the Community. The European Commission's own analysis divides member states into three broad categories: the 'Roman–Germanic system', which is found in the majority of member states (including the original six) and in which the statutory regulation of individual and collective employment relations is extensive; the 'Anglo-Irish system' with its voluntarist tradition and more limited role of statutory regulation; and the 'Nordic system', in which collective agreements are the central element of the system of regulation (CEC 1989: 8–12). In general terms, EC proposals have tended to reflect the dominant 'Roman–Germanic' or continental tradition with its emphasis on legal regulation. Even though there are wide variations in the level of statutory provision between the countries in the 'Roman–Germanic' category, particularly between the southern Mediterranean countries and the original six EC member states, the more general, structural incompatibilities with EC social policy proposals are more likely to arise in the Anglo-Irish and Nordic systems.

Moreover, collective labour law issues have traditionally been regarded as less susceptible to harmonization – or 'transplantation' (Kahn-Freund 1974: 21) – than individual rights or substantive provisions. This is because collective institutions and procedures are seen as integral to national political and social power relations and so member states will normally be anxious to prevent their disruption. The fate of a range of EC proposals for employee participation over more than two decades is ample testimony to the intractability of the problems associated with the harmonization of member states' employee representation or participation arrangements (Hall 1992). Only EC measures which require information, consultation or participation *procedures* in respect of certain specific 'social' issues, and which accommodate member states' existing employee representation arrangements rather than specifying particular institutional forms, have gained acceptance by the Council of Ministers. These are the 1975 collective redundancies directive (amended in 1992), the 1977 business transfers directive, and the 1989 health and safety 'framework' directive. So while a limited degree of procedural harmonization has been achieved in the collective labour law field, the more far-reaching proposals affecting the *institutions* of employee representation – or, in the case of the proposed 'Vredeling' directive, requiring a formal consultation procedure on a range of key company decisions affecting employees' interests – have consistently failed to be adopted. Indeed, the focus of the Commission's current proposals for employee participation is confined to *transnational* information and consultation procedures: neither the European company statute nor the European Works Councils directive would harmonize national company-level employee representative structures. The draft fifth company law directive – which would – is to all intents and purposes moribund.

However, experience during the 1980s, as well as under the current social charter action programme, suggests that Commission proposals of an individual or substantive nature which have significant implications in terms of increasing labour costs *also* tend to be resisted by member states. The Europe-wide preoccupation with labour market flexibility and deregulation which developed over the 1980s appears to have undermined any clear-cut distinction between the prospects of legislative proposals on individual or substantive issues and those on collective matters. Indeed, the implications of EC social policy harmonization for the international competitiveness of European business emerged in the 1980s as a major issue.

The leading proponent of the view that an extensive EC social policy would damage competitiveness has been the UK Conservative government. On its election in 1979, it began to oppose systematically all EC labour law initiative which it saw as raising employment costs and reducing labour market flexibility, including 'Vredeling' and proposed directives to regulate part-time work, temporary work, and parental and family leave. The United Kingdom also prevented the adoption of a (non-binding) recommendation on the reduction and reorganization of working-time which was supported by all other member states. Although two supplementary equal treatment directives and several health and safety directives were adopted, the overall trend during most of the 1980s was clearly against further labour law harmonization. The UK government's approach reflected its own particular domestic labour market agenda and its determination to restrict EC social policy intervention. The more general policy shift towards labour market flexibility and deregulation discernible in, for instance, Germany, France and Belgium (Vranken 1986) took place within much more detailed regulatory regimes than the United Kingdom's and without the direct restriction of trade union influence which characterized the UK government's approach. Against this background, when the United Kingdom held the presidency of the EC in the second half of 1986, it was able to secure the adoption by the Council of an 'action programme on employment growth' which emphasized the removal of labour market rigidities and the promotion of flexible employment patterns and was intended to reorientate EC labour market policy towards deregulation. However, accounts of the 1986 UK presidency (Welsh 1988; Matthews 1993) suggest that the 'action programme' was little more than an empty diplomatic coup, generating little real commitment to its aims among the United Kingdom's EC partners and resistance from the Commission. It certainly failed to make a lasting impact on the direction of EC social policy, being superseded, in effect, by a counter-initiative by the subsequent Belgian presidency, designed to ensure that labour market flexibility should not undermine workers' essential legal protections. Indeed, the Belgian presidency's proposal to establish a Community-wide platform of guaranteed social rights paved the way towards the social charter strategy.

More generally, member states' attitudes to particular EC labour law proposals are likely to be strongly influenced by whether such proposals are compatible with existing national regulatory frameworks and policies and whether they will help or hinder the competitiveness of their national industries and services. Member states with the lowest standards tend to want to avoid 'upward harmonization', while the states with more advanced provision are likely to press for alignment for defensive reasons. Moreover, successive enlargements of the Community have resulted in greater social and economic heterogeneity among the member states, making a strategy of upward harmonization more difficult to sustain.

Against this background, the aims and methods of labour law harmonization, in particular the appropriateness of the 'normative' (CEC 1988: 62) or 'monolithic' (Brewster and Teague 1989: 281) model of upward harmonization used by the Commission during the 1970s and early 1980s, came increasingly to be questioned – even though in practice EC measures had usually stopped well short of specifying the alignment of member states' provision in a particular policy area with that of the most advanced member state, certainly by the time a negotiated settlement had been reached by the Council of Ministers. In the light of the impasse reached within the Council during the 1980s, it was accepted within the Commission that 'a more flexible and pragmatic approach' to harmonization was necessary. Rejecting, on the one hand, the established 'normative' approach and, on the other, a fully 'decentralized' approach (meaning a minimal role for EC regulation, as proposed by the United Kingdom), the Commission proposed a new balance between Community-level and national action and between legislation and collective bargaining (CEC 1988: 68), under which considerable discretion would be left to member states over how to apply broadly framed EC minimum standards in ways consistent with national traditions and practice. This approach dovetailed with the more general emphasis on 'subsidiarity' developing within the EC at the time. The 1989 social charter emerged as the main vehicle for this new strategy. It was envisaged that the charter would be implemented by a combination of EC legislation, measures by member states and collective agreements.

The limited development of 'social partnership' at EC level

A key element in the integrated European system of industrial relations the Commission has sought to foster is the participation of supra-national interest groups in EC policy-making. In the early years of the Community the main forum for trade union and employer representation in the development of EC policy was the Economic and Social Committee (ESC) – the EC's consultative forum established by the Treaty of Rome. However, the members of the ESC are from a range of national interest groups, nominated by national governments, and accordingly the ESC did not provide an appropriate vehicle for the formal inclusion of international trade union and employer bodies in EC policy-making. During the 1960s, informal Commission contacts with such bodies sometimes occasioned suspicion and criticism on the part of member state governments (Collins 1975: 206), though a number of EC-level joint sectoral bodies were set up.

In the early 1970s, however, the Council's acceptance of a more extensive social policy role for the Community saw the establishment of new quasi-corporatist institutions to promote consultation between European-level trade union and employers' organizations and Council and Commission representatives – and indeed the establishment of the European Trade Union Confederation (ETUC). A series of tripartite conferences was held between 1970 and 1978 on a range of macroeconomic and social policy issues. In addition a Standing Committee on Employment was established to enable direct consultation between representatives of the bodies concerned. However, while UNICE, the European employers' confederation, participated in such exercises, it remained unwilling to be party to binding decisions on behalf of its constituents, therefore avoiding giving any legitimacy to the development of a centralized European social policy (Schmitter and Streeck 1992: 207). As a consequence, the ETUC became increasingly frustrated at the lack of concrete progress and in 1978 'threatened to reconsider its participation in future meetings [of the tripartite conference] unless proposals were put forward to give a new impetus to the conference's activities' (CEC 1988: 109). No further conferences were held.

Despite the limited impact of the initiatives of the 1970s, the promotion of the 'social dialogue' between European-level trade union and employers' bodies became the incoming Delors Commission's initial strategy for breaking the 1980s impasse over EC social policy legislation. This approach was embodied in treaty revisions affected by the Single European Act. The new Article 118B gave the Commission the task of developing 'the dialogue between management and labour at European level which could, if the two sides consider it desirable, lead to relations based on agreement'. The intention was that discussions between the 'social partners' should be the precursor to EC legislation, in the hope that legislative proposals based on an agreed approach between the two sides of industry would have a stronger chance of being accepted by the Council of Ministers. 'European-level collective bargaining' has long been an objective of the ETUC (ETUC 1988a). UNICE, however, was unwilling to take part in the social dialogue on this basis, insisting that the outcome of the so-called 'Val Duchesse' talks, initiated by the Commission in 1985 and attended by the ETUC, UNICE and CEEP (the public employers' organization), should be restricted to non-binding 'joint opinions' (not even agreements) without any legislative follow-up. Thus, although the Val Duchesse initiative proceeded, yielding a series of joint opinions, it did not represent the breakthrough hoped for by the Commission in the social policy sphere. For UNICE, the consistent ability of employer interests to secure sufficient opposition within the Council of Ministers under the unanimity principle to block key legislative proposals has always been a disincentive to co-operate wholeheartedly with such initiatives (Schmitter and Streeck 1992). By 1991, however, faced with the prospect of treaty revisions enabling extensive use of qualified majority voting for social policy legislation, UNICE changed its traditional approach and agreed to a procedure, incorporated almost in its entirety in the Maastricht social policy protocol, enabling European-level agreements. The implications of this are explored later in the chapter.

EC Social Policy under Delors: Preparing the Ground for Maastricht

The institutional constraints on an expansive EC social policy identified in the preceding analysis have each been addressed in the social policy debates and initiatives launched by the Commission under Delors since 1985. Overcoming the social policy impasse of the early 1980s was an important personal objective of Delors and the notion of the 'social dimension of the internal market' was intended to link the social policy agenda to the Delors Commission's central economic and political project – the establishment of the single European market. Prior to the social charter initiative, however, the Delors Commission's social policy strategy evolved in an uncertain fashion. The 1985 'white paper' was virtually silent about the social policy implications of the single European market, with the reintroduction of the European company statute the only proposal directly affecting workers' rights. As outlined earlier, the Single European Act made only limited changes to the EC's social policy treaty provisions, and the objective of the Delors Commission's initial emphasis on social dialogue was effectively thwarted by the position adopted by UNICE. Moreover, the 1986 UK presidency's 'action programme on employment growth' ran counter to an expansion of EC social policy regulation. It was the 1987 Belgian presidency of the Council which marked the turning-point in the EC social policy debate and effectively re-established the political basis for an active EC role in industrial relations. As well as providing an alternative to the UK presidency's 'action programme', the Belgian presidency's advocacy of a Community-wide platform of guaranteed

social rights also signalled a modification of the Community's established – though increasingly unviable – approach to labour law harmonization, with the emphasis now explicitly on the development of
a floor of minimum rights.

Subsequent developments illustrate the complex dynamics of social
policy development within the Community. The Belgian presidency's
proposal was elaborated by other EC institutions, notably the Economic and Social Committee (ESC 1987; 1989) and the Commission
itself (CEC 1988), and by the ETUC (1988b). From this process, in
which a network of French socialist/CFDT officials in the various
institutions concerned played an important co-ordinating role, the
proposal for an EC charter of fundamental social rights emerged.
Delors committed the Commission to proposing the establishment of
a platform of guaranteed social rights at the ETUC Congress in May
1988 (a pledge repeated to the TUC in September 1988). A crucial area
of ambiguity within the Commission, however, was whether such a
charter would be an end in itself, that is, a general political statement
with only moral force, or the basis for a legislative programme. The
evidence suggests that Delors's initial inclination was the former.
Writing in 1988, Patrick Venturini, a senior Delors aide, argued that a
social charter '[had] the advantage of not recommending Community
laws' which he saw as 'unrealistic at the present time' (Venturini 1989:
70). The ETUC, however, campaigned hard for legislative backing,
and the appointment of Vasso Papandreou in 1989 as commissioner
responsible for social affairs proved to be an important development:
unlike her predecessor, Manuel Marín, Papandreou was convinced of
the need for substantial social safeguards to accompany the single
market. Thus, when the Commission adopted a preliminary draft of
the charter in May 1989, it included a commitment to the preparation
of an action programme and associated legislative proposals.

Within the Council of Ministers, the most significant outcome of
negotiations over the charter was the heavy emphasis on subsidiarity.
The final version, agreed under the French presidency of the second
half of 1989, reflected member states' concern to underline the constitutional limits of the Community's competence and to stress the
importance of respecting national practice. This was reinforced by
amendments weakening many of the individual provisions of the
charter (Bercusson 1990; Hall 1990). These changes were partly an
unsuccessful attempt to accommodate the United Kingdom's objections to the charter but also reflected tacit support for some of the
United Kingdom's concerns among the peripheral member states.

The Commission's action programme of 47 proposed measures was
also strongly influenced by subsidiarity and the limited treaty bases

available. No legislative commitments were made in respect of some of the central principles of the charter. This was the case, for example, in respect of the right to fair remuneration and the right to freedom of association – aspects of the charter which the action programme specifically stated were the responsibility of member states. In the sphere of industrial relations and labour law, the two most notable themes of the action programme concerned the establishment of minimum standards in respect of a range of working conditions (to guard against 'social dumping') and the desirability of giving employee information and consultation procedures a transnational dimension. In the former category, key proposals included directives regulating the conditions of 'atypical' workers and workers posted to other EC countries, working-time, maternity rights and contractual information. In the latter were the revision of the existing collective redundancies directive and the introduction of an (unspecified) instrument on employee information and consultation in Community-scale companies. In addition the action programme included an extensive range of technical health and safety proposals, for which there was general political and industrial support and a clear, qualified majority voting legal basis, and a number of vocational training initiatives.

The action programme did not, therefore, venture very far beyond the Commission's long-standing social policy agenda. Several proposals (for example, on 'atypical' work and working-time) represented a repackaging of earlier Commission measures which had failed to win Council backing. For the most part, however, the objectives of the proposals in the action programme were less ambitious than their antecedents. Nevertheless, the action programme was intended as a 'transitional demand': within the Commission it was calculated that the expected difficulties in securing the adoption of key elements of the programme in the face of UK opposition would emphasize the inadequacies of the existing treaty bases for EC social policy, particularly the limited scope for qualified majority voting, and thus increase the pressure among other member states for treaty revisions. Moreover, once the two inter-governmental conferences – on 'economic and monetary union' and 'political union' – had begun in December 1990, there was, inevitably, a close relationship between the progress of the social charter action programme and the discussions on possible treaty revisions, including more qualified majority voting in the social policy area. Tactical considerations dictated a cautious approach, in both their content and legal basis, to Commission proposals during late 1990 and 1991 for directives on contractual information, European Works Councils and collective redundancies, in order to bolster the Commission's case for significant treaty revisions to extend the

Community's industrial relations role. Over-ambitious proposals at this stage on questionable legal bases could have seriously undermined member states' support for more qualified majority voting on labour law matters.

By the end of 1993, four years after the adoption of the social charter, the bulk of the proposals in the Commission's action programme had been adopted, although those proposals involving binding legislative measures often fared less well. In the area of minimum working conditions and industrial relations procedures, the directives adopted – on contractual information (Clark and Hall 1992), the revision of the collective redundancies directive (Dolding 1992), workers' maternity rights (EIRR 1992) and working-time – each represented a dilution of the Commission's original proposals, particularly in the case of the maternity rights directive. Member states are generally concerned to minimize the impact of EC legislation on their current national arrangements. While this has not resulted literally in 'lowest common denominator' outcomes, member states have been prepared to agree only to relatively minor amendments to existing national provision. However, a number of key proposals have encountered more intractable problems within the Council, namely those concerning European Works Councils, 'atypical' work and the minimum terms and conditions of workers assigned to another EC member state, and have not yet reached the EC statute book. Significantly, in some cases this is in spite of having a legal basis enabling their adoption by qualified majority voting. Their difficulties within the Council reflect opposition or important reservations on the part of a range of member states. For example, the Commission's proposed Article 100A directive on the rights of 'atypical' workers was opposed by Denmark, Germany, Ireland, Luxemburg and Spain as well as the United Kingdom (Lange 1992: 251). Notwithstanding the United Kingdom's opposition, the adoption of the working-time directive was delayed for a considerable time by disagreements between France and Germany (about the length of the 'reference period' over which hours worked may be averaged for the purposes of meeting the directive's maxima, and the level at which collective agreements derogating from the directive's provisions may be concluded). In any case, in practice, there is an 'overwhelming bias [in] the EC system towards compromise and consensus, even when in principle ministers can resort to majority voting' (Ludlow 1993: 249).

In the case of the proposed directive on European Works Councils – which is based on Article 100 of the Treaty and therefore needs unanimity within the Council for adoption – only the United Kingdom is opposed to the legislation in principle, though other member states have had reservations about aspects of the Commission's proposal and it is strongly opposed by UNICE. The background to and provisions of the directive have been extensively analysed elsewhere (see Gold and Hall 1992; Hall 1992; Hall et al. 1992; Marginson 1992). It is arguably the most far-reaching component of the social charter action programme, in that it would lay the basis for transnational industrial relations procedures within multinational companies operating across the Community. Neither the Portuguese nor UK governments made any attempt to progress the proposal during their presidencies of the Council of Ministers in 1992. However, in 1993, discussion of the directive within the Council was restarted by the Danish presidency and continued under the subsequent Belgian presidency. The UK government is maintaining its opposition to the directive and will therefore prevent its adoption under the normal treaty provisions. Nevertheless, there now appears to be broad agreement among the other eleven member states on the directive. It therefore seems likely that now that the Maastricht treaty has finally been ratified by Germany, the eleven will move to adopt the directive under the Maastricht social policy protocol, thus circumventing the United Kingdom's veto.

The Significance of the Maastricht Social Policy Protocol

The social policy agenda of the inter-governmental conference on political union was set by the Commission's proposals for extensive treaty revisions (CEC 1991). Emphasizing the wide gap between the existing treaty powers and the ambitions set out in the social charter, the Commission argued for the establishment of explicit Community competence to legislate on a range of employment and industrial relations issues and for the extension of qualified majority voting. In addition, the Commission sought to boost the role of the social partners in the Community-level regulation of industrial relations matters by suggesting that, before presenting legislative proposals, the Commission should consult the social partners about the scope for achieving particular objectives through framework agreements between them, with the possibility of legal backing for such agreements by the Community institutions. This latter proposal was reinforced by a memorandum from the Belgian government proposing an EC-level procedure paralleling the Belgian system of 'law by agreement', whereby agreements reached between the parties represented in the tripartite Conseil National du Travail can be consolidated by royal decree (Vilrokx and van Leemput 1992: 374). The establishment of an equivalent European-level body was canvassed in the Commission's proposals to the inter-governmental conference, subject to the outcome of discussions in an *ad hoc* social dialogue working group. In the event, the social partners' agreement on proposed treaty revisions of 31 October 1991 recommended that the treaty should provide for the conclusion and extension of Community-level agreements though without creating a new joint institution on the Belgian model. The social partners' agreement was subsequently included, almost in its entirety, in the proposed Maastricht social chapter.

Although the social partners' agreement was consistent with the ETUC's objective of establishing a negotiating role at EC level as well as a framework of EC social legislation, it marked a major change in UNICE policy. As we have seen, UNICE had previously insisted on a 'weak' form of social dialogue with non-binding joint opinions the only outcome. This change was motivated by the widespread expectation during 1991, despite the United Kingdom's stated opposition, that the extension of qualified majority voting in the social policy area was a likely result of the treaty revision process. Under both the Luxemburg and Dutch presidencies, successive working drafts of the proposed new treaty included a social chapter establishing a direct, free-standing Community competence in the social policy field and earmarking a range of issues for qualified majority voting. Throughout the negotiations, the United Kingdom remained strongly opposed to any extension of the EC's social policy role, although, given the scope for linkages to be made with other issues of importance to the United Kingdom, a compromise on the social chapter seemed at least a possibility. In this context, pressure within UNICE from the Belgian, French and Italian employers' organizations resulted in a change in UNICE's policy of opposing European-level agreements (Goetschy 1993: 151). Even though UNICE's policy shift caused considerable misgivings on the part of the CBI, it was essentially for defensive reasons – to enable UNICE to fend off or at least delay proposals for EC legislation under the new treaty provisions by opting to explore the scope for framework agreements, the implementation of which would be likely in practice to be largely voluntary.

At the Maastricht summit, however, the UK government refused to accept even a watered-down version of the social chapter, put forward by the Dutch prime minister Ruud Lubbers as a possible compromise, whereas the French government in particular was not prepared to accept a treaty which failed to extend qualified majority voting on social policy issues. The eleventh-hour outcome, brokered by the

Germans and the Dutch presidency (*Financial Times* 12 December 1991), was the social policy protocol to the treaty. This allowed the other eleven member states, without UK participation, to adopt directives in the social policy field on the basis of what had been proposed as the social chapter of the Maastricht treaty. These will not apply to the United Kingdom. This procedure will operate alongside the existing social policy provisions of the Treaty of Rome, to which the United Kingdom remains a party.

The agreement between the eleven provides the Community with direct and extensive legal competence in the social policy field, subject to 'the need to maintain the competitiveness of the Community economy', and the more general requirements of the Maastricht treaty in respect of 'subsidiarity'. It enables the Council, without UK participation, to adopt directives by qualified majority voting on a range of matters including health and safety, working conditions, information and consultation, and equal opportunities. Unanimity is required for measures on certain other matters including social security, the termination of employment, and the collective representation of workers and employers, including co-determination. A third category of issues – pay, the right of association, the right to strike and the right to impose lock-outs – is excluded altogether from the scope of legislative intervention under the protocol. The other key innovation is the potential role of the social partners in the formulation of EC labour law. The Commission is required to consult the social partners on both the principle and content of proposed social policy directives. In the course of this process, the social partners may jointly opt to attempt to deal with the issue in question by means of a Community-level agreement. In this case a period of up to nine months is allowed for the negotiation of an agreement (though the social partners and the Commission may jointly decide to extend this time limit). Where such agreements are concluded, two implementation routes are envisaged. The first is 'in accordance with the procedures and practices specific to management and labour and the Member States'. The second implementation route, available at the joint request of the signatory parties and on a proposal from the Commission, is by a Council decision, on the basis of qualified majority voting if appropriate.

For some commentators, the Maastricht social policy protocol marks a fundamental change in the Community's hitherto underdeveloped social policy role (Bercusson 1992; Fitzpatrick 1992). Certainly, on paper, the extended legal competence for EC social policy intervention, the wider scope for qualified majority voting and the inclusion of the 'social partners' in the legislative process are all

changes with profound implications. Yet the procedural ambiguities of the social policy protocol and the United Kingdom's exclusion from its scope may well limit its actual impact.

The 'optimistic' scenario arising from Maastricht revolves around
the extended scope for qualified majority voting injecting a new dynamism into EC social policy developments. The United Kingdom's
exclusion from the social policy protocol procedure means that a
'qualified majority' in the Council will be 44 out of 66 votes rather than
54 out of 76 votes. A social policy directive could therefore potentially
be adopted with the support of as few as six member states. In theory,
this development should facilitate the adoption of a more extensive
EC regulatory framework affecting employment and industrial relations. It would enable the preparation of a more strategic social
action programme which addresses more directly the central employment issues raised by economic integration, whereas at present the
need to identify measures which can be dealt with by qualified majority voting has resulted in a 'false ordering of priorities' (Coldrick
1991: 37). The threat of more systematic legislative intervention by
the EC ought to induce UNICE to participate in negotiations over
possible Community-level agreements. Either way, new impetus
would be given by the protocol to the development of the EC's social
policy role.

A more pessimistic view plays down the likely impact in practice of
qualified majority voting on social policy issues. As already noted, the
requirement for unanimity and the stridency and predictability with
which the United Kingdom has opposed the Commission's key social
policy proposals over many years may have enabled certain other
member states to pull their punches, at least in public, in respect of
their own reservations about particular measures (Teague 1989: 317;
Lange 1992: 242). To the extent that this has been true, more qualified
majority voting may serve to bring the reservations of other member
states out into the open, but it will not translate automatically into
more EC directives being adopted by the Council. In any case, the fact
that the United Kingdom stands outside the scope of directives
adopted under the protocol may well deter the extensive use of
the new procedure. The Commission, the eleven and even the ETUC
are likely to be generally predisposed to use the 'normal' twelve-
member-state procedure for social policy proposals as far as is possible
in order to avoid too much 'variable geometry' within the Community. Moreover, in the context of deepening recession elsewhere in
the EC and developments such as Hoover's highly publicized relocation of production from France to Britain on grounds of labour costs
and work-force flexibility (*EIRR* 1993), the other member states are

likely to be reluctant to adopt potentially costly employment measures under the protocol which might be perceived as working to the United Kingdom competitive advantage. The European Works Councils directive may not fall into this category: it would have no direct impact upon labour costs and, as well as providing some procedural check on 'social dumping' moves of the Hoover type, its provisions would in any event apply to UK-based multinationals with substantial operations elsewhere in the EC and are in practice likely to have important repercussions in the United Kingdom's (Hall 1992). More generally, however, while there will be political pressure from the trade unions and others for at least some use to be made of the social policy protocol, the *legislative* output may well be limited. Certainly Padraig Flynn, Papandreou's more conservative successor as EC social affairs commissioner, prefers to emphasize the potential role of the social partners (*The Guardian* 27 February 1993), echoing German CDU minister of labour Norbert Blum (*Rheinischer Merkur* 30 October 1992).

A corollary of this is that the legislative threat which induced UNICE to concede the framework for European-level agreements with the ETUC enshrined in the Maastricht social policy protocol may now be much less potent. Without the prospect of extensive new EC employment legislation, UNICE's motivation for participating in discussions about possible agreements would be considerably weakened. Only on issues on which there is a serious possibility that the eleven would agree to legislate is UNICE likely to perceive any advantage in opting to activate the social partners' negotiating procedure under the protocol.

This more pessimistic – and almost certainly more realistic – scenario is reinforced by a range of procedural and legal difficulties associated with the operation of the protocol (see Bercusson 1992; Fitzpatrick 1992; ETUI 1992; UNICE 1992). These suggest not only that the protocol is unlikely to generate early results in the shape of directives or agreements between the social partners, but also that the practical impact of the latter is highly uncertain. For instance, it would not be possible, in the case of a proposed directive currently under discussion within the Council of Ministers though likely to be blocked by the United Kingdom, simply to switch from the existing legislative procedure for the twelve member states to the social policy protocol and adopt the proposal without UK participation. The Commission would have to initiate the full procedure provided for by the protocol, including the necessary consultations with the European Parliament and the Economic and Social Committee, irrespective of the advanced stage that may have been reached under the existing legislative process. If the social partners then opted to deal with the issue through the 'social dialogue' route envisaged by the protocol, this would pre-empt or at least delay the legislative process.

Perhaps the major area of uncertainty, however, concerns the implementation of agreements concluded between the social partners under the protocol. Clearly, much will depend on the actual content of any such agreement. They would need to be more specific than the texts of existing joint opinions which offer only the most general guidelines to national negotiators. However, the protocol makes it clear that the first of the potential methods of implementation envisaged (that is, 'in accordance with the procedures and practices specific to management and labour and the Member States') means 'developing, by collective bargaining according to the rules of each Member State, the content of the agreements'. It 'implies no obligation on the Member States to apply the agreements directly or to work out rules for their transposition, nor any obligation to amend national legislation in force to facilitate their implementation'. Thus, with the exception of any scope within national industrial relations systems (for example, Belgium, France and The Netherlands) for using an extension procedure for collective agreements which 'develop' the contents of Community-level agreements, this method of implementing Community-level agreements relies essentially on voluntary means within each member state. Their impact would therefore be indirect and almost inevitably patchy.

However, the second, quasi-legislative method of implementing Community-level agreements under the protocol (that is, 'by a Council decision') also raises major difficulties. Under Article 189 of the Treaty of Rome, a decision taken by the Council 'shall be binding in its entirety upon those to whom it is addressed'. Council decisions have not hitherto been used in an industrial relations context and a key question concerns the identity of the potential addressees of a Council decision purporting to give legal force to a Community-level agreement between the social partners. In any case, even assuming that the content and wording of such an agreement is clear and capable of being enforced in this way and that the appropriate social partner organizations and the Commission all agree to initiate the 'Council decision' method of implementation, it is questionable how often the governments of the member states, notwithstanding the availability of qualified majority voting, will be prepared to give legal backing on a 'take it or leave it' basis (Fitzpatrick 1992: 206) to regulatory instruments which they will have played no part in shaping. From a British perspective, it is hardly surprising that the prospect of binding

EC-wide collective agreements was seen as unacceptable 'Euro-corporatism' by the UK Employment Secretary and emerged as the United Kingdom's main grounds for rejecting the Dutch presidency's watered-down, social chapter compromise which was tabled at Maastricht (*Financial Times* 28 February 1992).

There are also uncertainties among the 'social partners' themselves. UNICE has adopted a restrictive attitude to the possibilities of European-level agreements under the social policy protocol, insisting that negotiations about such agreements will only follow a formal initiative of the Commission, and minimizing the scope for sectoral as opposed to 'inter-professional' (economy-wide) agreements. On the union side, a difficult post-Maastricht debate has been taking place within the ETUC about the prospects of 'European collective bargaining'. In particular, German unions have differentiated between the type of negotiations envisaged under the protocol (that is, 'social dialogue' in response to a legislative proposal by the Commission) and traditional collective bargaining, and have tended to advocate a more autonomous trade union approach to European bargaining on a sectoral basis. This may reflect an unwillingness to risk disturbing the constitutional relationship within the German trade union movement under which the DGB has no collective bargaining role. More-over, the substantive terms of European agreements would often be below German standards and could have the effect of undermining German unions' future bargaining position. Nordic trade unions also have reservations about the implications of European-level agreements for national collective bargaining and seem to view a legislative approach to establishing European-wide minimum standards as more realistic (Dølvik 1993: 369). For the most part, however, the national trade union centres within the ETUC – including the TUC – have a positive view of the possibilities of European-level agreements as envisaged in the Maastricht social policy protocol, notwithstanding the uncertainties already identified. The ETUC's (1993) position paper reflects German union concerns about the need for strict control over the remit of the European-level bargaining units and proper evaluation of the outcomes. It also appears to give priority to the sectoral as opposed to 'inter-professional' level as the site for European collective bargaining. UNICE, however, intends to resist sectoral negotiations: as already noted, its post-Maastricht strategy is to confine its participation in European-level negotiations to those issues which are the subject of a Commission initiative under the social policy protocol, and these are seldom likely to be sector-specific (Tyszkiewicz 1992: 12).

Conclusion

In the two decades since the member states agreed on the need for a more active EC social policy, actual progress has been limited and faltering. Political enthusiasm for EC social measures has waxed and waned according to economic circumstances and the pace of European integration. In addition, institutional factors such as the lack of a clear treaty basis for EC intervention have meant that in the face of differing national agendas, the diversity of national industrial relations practice and employer opposition, the Commission's social policy proposals have frequently been blocked. Some of the most important legislative elements of the 1989 social charter action programme in the area of working conditions and industrial relations have yet to reach the EC statute book. Although those which have been adopted may be important symbolically, in most cases they are of limited practical significance for member states' national provisions.[3]

However, the recent phase of accelerated progress towards European integration has resulted in the easing of the institutional constraints stunting the development of the EC's social dimension which were identified earlier in the chapter. The Maastricht social policy protocol has established – for the first time outside the area of health and safety – direct Community competence to legislate on a range of key employment and industrial relations issues. The availability of qualified majority voting on such issues has been extended. Reflecting the debate about 'subsidiarity', there has been general agreement between the Commission and the member states on the desirability of a lighter regulatory framework, based on minimum standards rather than 'upward harmonization', with the aim of ensuring greater compatibility with existing national practice. The European employers' confederation UNICE has for the first time, however reluctantly, accepted the possibility of entering into European-level collective agreements with the ETUC, and a legal framework for the negotiation and implementation of such agreements has been written into the Maastricht social policy protocol. These are significant developments which should, on paper at least, facilitate the implementation of a more extensive, coherent and effective EC industrial relations policy. Indeed, Maastricht has the potential to be a watershed in the evolution of the EC's social policy role.

Yet whether the Maastricht social policy protocol will result in a new era of EC social policy activism will crucially depend, as before, on wider political and economic developments – at national and European level. In the longer term, the dynamics of the single

European market and planned monetary union may eventually generate renewed pressure for a more integrated EC industrial relations
policy, the implementation of which would be facilitated by the
Maastricht social policy settlement. In the short term, however, the
stalling of progress towards monetary union, the onset of recession in
Europe and the United Kingdom's self-exclusion from the social
policy agreement signed by the other eleven member states may
mean that its potential for giving a new impetus and coherence to EC
industrial relations policy will remain largely unrealized.

The sharpening focus of current EC discussions about growth, competitiveness and employment on the issue of labour market flexibility
and the implications of EC employers' social costs for the level of
employment may result in the scaling down – or even the implicit
abandonment – of the Commission's social policy agenda. The Commission's November 1993 'green paper' on European social policy
options avoided specific policy commitments. The outcome of the
December 1993 Brussels summit, especially its emphasis on deregulation as a means to promote employment, prompted UK ministers
to claim that the EC social policy debate was going their way. The
Commission's 'white paper' on the future of EC social policy, due in
mid 1994, will be an important indicator in this respect.

In any case, the recession in Europe is prompting renewed moves to
make existing national employment regulations more flexible in key
member states such as Germany and France (under its new conserva-
tive-led government). This reduces the chances of an extensive new
programme of social policy measures at EC level. The recession will
also reinforce the other eleven member states' concern not to damage
their competitive position *vis-à-vis* the United Kingdom. The eleven
may well be inhibited by the United Kingdom's opt-out from making
extensive use of the social policy protocol – at least in the case of
proposed measures which would add substantially to the cost of employment – when the resulting directives would not apply in the
United Kingdom. (The proposed European Works Councils directive
is the most likely proposal to be taken up under the social policy
protocol.) The same considerations are likely to strengthen the determination of the other EC member states to bring the United Kingdom
within a common EC social policy framework in the course of the next
treaty revision exercise in 1996. Without a change of government, the
United Kingdom is unlikely to agree simply to 'opt back in' to the
provisions of the Maastricht social chapter. However, the recognition
that UK companies cannot be fully insulated from the effects of
measures adopted under the social policy protocol – at least in respect
of their operations elsewhere in the EC – may lead to pressure for the

United Kingdom to resume a full role in EC social policy matters. One possibility may be a settlement based on the 'Lubbers compromise' rejected by the United Kingdom at Maastricht. In the meantime, the social policy protocol is likely to yield few regulatory measures of real substance. At present, therefore, the most that can be said is that Maastricht represents the high watermark of as yet unrealized EC social policy aspirations.

Acknowledgements

I would like to thank Jon Clark, Jon Erik Dølvik, David Foden, Deborah France, Michael Gold, David Lea, Paul Marginson, Bill McCarthy, Cherry Mill, Keith Sisson, Simon Wilson and the editors for their helpful comments on an earlier draft of this chapter.

Notes

1   To avoid the complications arising from periodic changes in nomenclature, the term 'European Community' is used throughout the chapter, except where reference to the Treaty on European Union is necessary.
2   Where qualified majority voting applies, the votes allocated to the various member states are weighted to reflect the size of their populations, with France, Germany, Italy and the UK having 10 votes each and the other, smaller countries having between two and eight votes. A qualified majority is 54 votes out of a possible 76.
3   A notable exception is the potential impact on the UK of the November 1993 EC directive on working time. In the UK, working time has largely been a matter for voluntary regulation by employers and unions. However, subject to the outcome of the UK government's threatened challenge in the European Court of Justice to the directive's legal basis, the new directive will mean the UK has to legislate on key working time questions, including maximum weekly working hours and minimum annual holiday entitlement.

References

Bercusson, B. 1990: The European Community's Charter of Fundamental Social Rights of Workers. *Modern Law Review*, 53(5) 624–42.
Bercusson, B. 1992: Maastricht: a fundamental change in European labour law. *Industrial Relations Journal*, 23(3) 177–90.
Brewster, C. and Teague, P. 1989: *European Community Social Policy: its impact on the UK*. London: Institute of Personnel Management/Academic Press.
Clark, J. and Hall, M. 1992: The Cinderella directive? Employee rights to information about conditions applicable to their contract or employment relationship. *Industrial Law Journal*, 21(2) 106–18.
Coldrick, P. 1991: The protection of workers' rights in Europe: a trade union perspective. In S. Milner and L. Hantrais (eds), Workers' rights in Europe, *Cross-National Research Papers*, 5, Aston University, 33–42.

Collins, D. 1975: *The European Communities: the social policy of the first phase*, Volume 2. London: Martin Robertson.

Commission of the European Communities (CEC) 1988: The social dimension of the internal market. *Social Europe*, special edition.

Commission of the European Communities 1989: *Comparative Study on Rules Governing Working Conditions in the Member States*. SEC (89) 1137.

Commission of the European Communities 1991: The social dimension and the development of human resources. In Trades Union Congress, *Reshaping the European Community*, London: TUC Publications.

Crijns, L. 1987: The social policy of the European Community. *Social Europe*, 1/87, 51–62.

Davies, P. 1992: The emergence of European labour law. In W. McCarthy (ed.), *Legal Intervention in Industrial Relations: gains and losses*, Oxford: Blackwell Publishers, 313–59.

Dolding, L. 1992: Collective redundancies and Community law. *Industrial Law Journal*, 21(4) 310–15.

Dølvik, J. 1993: The Nordic trade unions and the dilemmas of European integration. In J. Fagerberg and L. Lundsberg (eds), *European Economic Integration: a Nordic perspective*, Aldershot: Avebury, 353–79.

Economic and Social Committee (ESC) 1987: Opinion on the social aspects of the internal market (European social area). *Official Journal of the European Communities*, C356, 31–4.

Economic and Social Committee 1989: Opinion of the Economic and Social Committee on basic Community social rights. *Official Journal of the European Communities*, C126, 4–14.

European Industrial Relations Review (EIRR) 1992: Pregnant workers directive adopted. *EIRR*, 226, 16–18.

EIRR 1993: The Hoover affair and social dumping. *EIRR*, 230, 14–20.

European Trade Union Confederation (ETUC) 1988a: Creating the European social dimension in the internal market: European social programme. In ETUC 1991, *VIIth Statutory Congress: Supplement to Report on Activities 88/90*, Brussels: ETUC, 40–55.

European Trade Union Confederation 1988b: Community charter of social rights. In ETUC 1991, *VIIth Statutory Congress: Supplement to Report on Activities 88/90*, Brussels: ETUC, 58–64.

European Trade Union Confederation 1993: European collective bargaining – ETUC strategy. Brussels: ETUC (mimeo).

European Trade Union Institute (ETUI) 1992: *The European Dimensions of Collective Bargaining after Maastricht*. Brussels: ETUI.

Fitzpatrick, B. 1992: Community social law after Maastricht. *Industrial Law Journal*, 21(3) 199–213.

Flynn, P. 1993: The EC needs a human face. *The European*, 4 March, 9.

Goetschy, J. 1993: L'Europe sociale à la croisée des chemins: choix, incertitudes et atavismes de l'accord social de Maastricht. *Sociologie du Travail*, 2/93, 147–62.

Gold, M. and Hall, M. 1992: *European-Level Information and Consultation in Multinational Companies: an evaluation of practice*. Luxembourg: Office for Official Publications of the European Communities/European Foundation for the Improvement of Living and Working Conditions.

Hall, M. 1990: UK employment practices after the social charter. *Personnel Management*, 22(3) 32–5.

Hall, M. 1991: The social charter action programme: progress and prospects.

Industrial Law Journal, 20(2) 147–52.

Hall, M. 1992: Behind the European Works Councils directive: the Commission's legislative strategy. *British Journal of Industrial Relations*, 30(4) 547–66.

Hall, M., Marginson, P. and Sisson, K. 1992: The European Works Council: setting the research agenda. *Warwick Papers in Industrial Relations*, 41. Coventry: Industrial Relations Research Unit.

Hepple, B. 1987: The crisis in EEC labour law. *Industrial Law Journal*, 16(2) 77–87.

Kahn-Freund, O. 1974: On uses and misuses of comparative law. *Modern Law Review*, 37(1) 1–27.

Lange, P. 1992: The politics of the social dimension. In A. Sbragia (ed.), *Euro-Politics: institutions and policymaking in the 'new' European Community*, Washington: The Brookings Institution, 225–56.

Leibfried, S. and Pierson, P. 1992: Prospects for social Europe. *Politics and Society*, 20(3) 333–66.

Ludlow, P. 1993: The UK presidency: a view from Brussels. *Journal of Common Market Studies*, 31(2) 246–60.

Marginson, P. 1992: European integration and transnational management–union relations in the enterprise. *British Journal of Industrial Relations*, 30(4) 529–45.

Matthews, D. 1993: The 1986 UK presidency: an assessment of its impact on social policy initiatives. *ESRC Single European Market Initiative Working Papers*, 10. London: National Institute of Economic and Social Research.

Mosley, H. 1990: The social dimension of European integration. *International Labour Review*, 129(2) 147–64.

Noel, E. 1989: The Single European Act. *Government and Opposition*, 24(1) 3–14.

O'Higgins, P. 1986: International standards and British labour law. In R. Lewis (ed.), *Labour Law in Britain*, Oxford: Blackwell Publishers, 572–94.

Schmitter, P. and Streeck, W. 1992: From national corporatism to transnational pluralism: organised interests in the single European market. In W. Streeck, *Social Institutions and Economic Performance*, London: Sage Publications, 197–231.

Shanks, M. 1977a: *European Social Policy, Today and Tomorrow*. Oxford: Pergammon Press.

Shanks, M. 1977b: The social policy of the European Communities. *Common Market Law Review*, 14, 375–83.

Teague, P. 1989: Constitution or regime? the social dimension to the 1992 project. *British Journal of Industrial Relations*, 27(3) 310–29.

Trades Union Congress (TUC) 1993: *The Next Phase in Europe: report to the 1993 Congress*. London: TUC Publications.

Tyszkiewicz, Z. 1992: Social policy after Maastricht: the point of view of European employers. Brussels: Union of Industrial and Employers' Confederations of Europe (mimeo).

Union of Industrial and Employers' Confederations of Europe (UNICE) 1992: The social chapter of the Maastricht Treaty. Brussels: UNICE (mimeo).

Venturini, P. 1989: *1992: The European Social Dimension*. Luxemburg: Office for Official Publications of the European Communities.

Vilrokx, J. and van Leemput, J. 1992: Belgium: a new stability in industrial relations? In A. Ferner and R. Hyman (eds), *Industrial Relations in the New Europe*, Oxford: Blackwell Publishers, 357–92.

Vogel-Polsky, E. 1990: What future is there for a social Europe following the Strasbourg summit? *Industrial Law Journal*, 19(2) 65–80.

Vranken, M. 1986: Deregulating the employment relationship: current trends in Europe. *Comparative Labor Law Journal*, 7(2) 143–65.

Wedderburn, Lord 1990: *The Social Charter, European Company and Employment Rights: an outline agenda.* London: Institute of Employment Rights.

Welsh, M. 1988: Labour market policy in the European Community: the British presidency of 1986. *RIIA Discussion Papers*, 4. London: Royal Institute of International Affairs.

12

Tripartism in Eastern Europe

Lajos Héthy

Introduction

In the context of profound political and economic change, eastern Europe has witnessed the emergence of national tripartite institutions. High-level negotiations between the state and representatives of employers and labour have played a significant role in the transition to liberal-democratic regimes. Such practices may be considered as variants of 'neo-corporatism', in the sense defined by Cawson (1985: 8) as

> a specific socio-political process in which organizations representing monopolistic functional interests engage in political exchange with state agencies over public policy outputs which involves those organizations in a role that combines interest representation and policy implementation through delegated self enforcement.

Tripartist arrangements of this kind first appeared in Hungary: the Németh government established a tripartite National Council for the Reconciliation of Interests (NCRI) in 1988. The example was followed elsewhere in eastern Europe. In Bulgaria, a National Commission for Co-ordination of Interests (NCCI) was set up in 1990, its name echoing the similarly euphemistic formulations of the 1970s, which evaded the use of politically and ideologically less acceptable terms such as 'conflict' and 'bargaining' (see Héthy 1988). In post-revolution Czechoslovakia, tripartite Councils of Economic and Social Agreement were convened at both federal and republican levels and a tripartite General Agreement was concluded in early 1991. In Poland, a tripartite State Enterprise Pact was negotiated in 1992, and a tripartite National Negotiating Commission was proposed.

This chapter is a preliminary attempt at comparative analysis of this phenomenon, concentrating on Poland, Hungary, Czechoslovakia and Bulgaria in the period 1988–92. Inevitably, the analysis is constrained by the relative novelty of the phenomenon and the scarcity of reliable information about it. Within these limitations, the chapter explores the developments that go under the label of tripartism in these countries, analysing the political and economic constraints within which national-level institutionalized tripartism has emerged and operates. It asks how far the preconditions exist for effective tripartite structures and how they fit into the fabric of the emerging political and economic systems. Finally it considers whether tripartism is a transitory phenomenon or has a long-term future.

The Economic and Social Context

The stage was set for tripartism by a common process of political and economic change that, within a broadly similar pattern, assumed differing forms in the individual countries. In 1989–90 new political regimes took over in eastern Europe. In the Czechoslovak 'velvet revolution' of 1989, people took to the streets to overthrow the old regime; in Poland the gradual transition of 1989–90 was based on a negotiated compromise between General Jaruzelski's regime and Solidarity; while in Hungary the Round Table agreements of 1989 between the Reform communists and the opposition led to elections the following year (Bruszt 1992). In Bulgaria the socialists (ex-communists) participated in the government until as late as autumn 1991. Only in Poland had a strong, organized opposition been built up against the communist party state prior to the fall of communism. Solidarity was both a social movement and a trade union, deeply rooted in society and enjoying the support of the strong Polish Catholic Church. It was forced to operate underground during the period of martial law (1981–9), losing part of its popular support as a result. In Czechoslovakia, Hungary and Bulgaria, by contrast, the new political forces were unorganized and unprepared for power, lacking clear political programmes and economic strategies (Róna-Tas 1991). The revolution in Czechoslovakia swept away existing social actors and institutions including the trade unions, while in Hungary, Poland and Bulgaria most remained in place, including the already reformed trade unions.

From this ferment emerged a collection of predominantly right-wing and conservative governments in eastern Europe. Following the split in Solidarity in Poland, right-wing governments relying on multiparty coalitions were in office between the 1991 and 1993 elections. In the Czech part of former Czechoslovakia, the right-wing alliance ODS–KDS (civic democratic party – Christian democratic party) did well in elections, while in Slovakia HZDS (the Movement for a Democratic Slovakia), regarded as left-wing, received most votes. In Hungary, the conservative centre-right Antall government, elected to power for a four-year period in 1990, was based on a three-party coalition whose backbone was the Hungarian Democratic Forum.

The new political regimes faced immense problems of economic management. In the task of stabilizing and transforming their economies through privatization, deregulation and the establishment of the institutions of the market economy, their options were severely limited. They appeared to have room for strategic manoeuvre only with regard to the speed of implementation. It was this which primarily differentiated the neo-liberalist 'shock therapy' of the Mazowiecki government (bearing the name of finance minister Balcerowicz) in Poland in 1990 from the 'gradual reforms' adopted by both the Németh (1988–90) and Antall governments (1990–3) in Hungary.

Both approaches had social and political risks and both held the prospect of rewards. The first exposed the population to a sudden 'shock' and envisaged a quick recovery, although the process could well drag on for a lengthy period of time. The second strategy, while sparing the population this 'shock', implied a gradual increase in burdens – although these would be eased somewhat by a 'social safety net' – and carried the risk that continued reforms might not be wholly successful (Héthy 1991a). Although Czechoslovakia's strategy for economic transformation was conceived under the influence of neo-liberalist economists such as the then finance minister Klaus, in practice (taken together with the so-called Scenario for Social Reform) it came close to the Hungarian gradualist approach (Musil 1992). In the rest of the region, including Bulgaria, the old 'command systems' withered away in 1990, but little was done in the immediate aftermath to construct a strategy for the new economic order.

While economic strategies have been present in most of the region, political and social strategies aimed at mobilizing support for (or at least securing acquiescence in) economic changes and their social consequences have been painfully absent. Western experts and politicians offered ready-made formulae for stabilizing national economies and establishing the institutions of the market economy, and the region's governments accepted them with varying degrees of hesitation. Strategies for economic stabilization and transformation, while they have improved some economic indicators and helped control inflation, have led to large falls in GDP and industrial output, declining real wages and consumption, increasing poverty and rapidly rising unemployment (Ferge 1991). Although the economic changes were probably unavoidable and promised improvements for the population in the long run, in the short term they put an end to security and meant further belt-tightening for most people.

Political stability and social unrest thus appear to be issues of major concern. However, few efforts were made to ensure wider political legitimation; public support has been taken for granted. Some governments, as in Czechoslovakia and Poland, gestured towards the need for social support by a populist approach to privatization, a strategy in part dictated by the lack of suitable private investors (Stark 1992). Despite the potential emergence of a strong middle class as the major social pillar of the new political regimes, the majority of society still comprises the traditional working class, and most of the middle class, narrowly defined, live on the verge of poverty. In short, governments are being forced, often desperately, to try to bridge the widening gap between their formal legitimacy and eroding public support (Héthy 1991a).

The Emergence of Tripartism

Social dialogue, primarily between government and labour for reasons to be discussed below, has appeared to be a promising means of achieving political legitimation and social tolerance. Changes taking place in labour relations (Héthy 1993; Thirkell et al. 1993) opened up space to establish new bipartite and tripartite contacts among the social partners.

There were strong arguments for national-level institutionalized tripartism. First, tripartite dialogue and co-operation at national level had been important in reducing social tensions in western market economies in the period after the second world war and especially in the 1960s and 1970s (Streeck 1993). Tripartist arrangements had also helped ease the pain of political and economic transformation following the end of Francoism in Spain, a transition in some ways similar to the process in eastern Europe. Tripartism could therefore be seen, potentially at least, as similarly beneficial in eastern European countries, despite its current eclipse in western Europe.

Second, tripartite arrangements were encouraged by the long experience of corporatist traditions of forced tripartite (or, rather, in the absence of employer associations, bipartite) co-operation under the previous communist regimes.

Third, there was a degree of pressure from international organizations, including the ILO, the World Bank and the European Community, to establish tripartism. In Hungary, for example, the World Bank's Human Resources Development Programme promoted the establishment of a number of regional retraining centres to be run by a national-level tripartite body, the National Training Council. The G24's assistance programme, PHARE, managed by the EEC, has just launched a project to support the development of 'social dialogue'. In Bulgaria the 1991 extension of tripartism was closely linked to negotiations with the International Monetary Fund (IMF) (Thirkell and Tseneva 1991).

Finally, national-level institutionalized tripartism provided a potential mechanism for the mutual reinforcement of the legitimacy of the social partners: a field in which all were faced with considerable deficits. Trade unions, despite their rather low prestige, appear to have a double significance in the new industrial relations and in the economic and political context. First, their membership includes social groups which bear the brunt of economic stabilization and transformation; second, they have a high degree of public support. Trade unions have managed to remain mass organizations (for membership figures, see MacShane's chapter 13 in this volume), while the new political parties, in contrast to the former ruling communist parties, do not have a mass base (Thirkell et al. 1993).

The situation of trade unions varies considerably from country to country. On the one hand, independent or alternative unions, following the prototype of Polish Solidarity, were established in most countries prior to the fall of communism: these included the unions that were later to form the Democratic League of Independent Trade Unions in Hungary and Podkrepa in Bulgaria. On the other hand, with the exception of Czechoslovakia, where the former communist unions were dissolved, the trade unions of the party–state have survived. They redefined their role to give top priority to the representation of workers' interests, declared their independence of the then ruling communist parties, decentralized and democratized their organizational structures and often themselves became pluralized.

These complex changes have led to similarly complex outcomes. In Hungary, there are seven major trade union confederations, of which six participate in the NCRI. The most important is MSzOSz. In Poland the stage is dominated by the now divided Solidarity and the 'successor' Polish Trade Union Alliance (OPZZ). In Bulgaria, Podkrepa (Support) and the 'successor' Confederation of Independent Trade Unions of Bulgaria, CITUB, are in a similar position. In Czechoslovakia the large new Czech and Slovak Federation of Trade Unions,

CSKOS, and the smaller Confederation of Arts and Culture were established.

The coexistence of old and newly formed unions has led, in addition to the creation of a pluralist union structure, to division and confrontation. In Poland the two major confederations did not talk to each other for years; in Hungary the relations of the large 'successor' MSzOSz, the League and the Workers Councils (another newly formed confederation) in 1990–2 were heavily burdened with conflicts over legitimacy and representativeness. Behind these divisions lay the thorny problem of the redistribution of existing trade union assets; only in Czechoslovakia could the issue be successfully settled at an early stage, under an agreement reached in 1990. In Hungary six of the confederations arrived at a settlement on the redistribution of a proportion of the assets in 1992, following controversial government intervention the year before which had provoked the bitter hostility of the traditional unions. Solidarity's efforts to recover its confiscated assets handed over to OPZZ under martial law in 1981 led to similar confrontations in Poland.

Employers' organizations in the region faced difficulties in some ways similar to those of the unions: both had to prove their legitimacy and representativeness, secure their membership and mobilize its support. The activities of employers' organizations in the industrial relations area have also been hindered by the fact that employers' organizations, even where they existed in the past, had few, if any, industrial relations functions.

Economic transformation involving privatization and the emergence of a new private sector, particularly of small and medium-sized enterprises (SMEs), is leading to a profound reshaping of employers. Large state-owned enterprises are being broken up and privatized, while genuine new private employers are appearing on the scene. However, this process has not yet resulted in the consolidation of a new 'class' of employers. For example, the interim solution to the problem of privatization adopted in Hungary – that of institutional cross-ownership whereby other state-owned corporations acquired state property (Stark 1992) – created a great number of 'quasi-private' companies whose behaviour retained important traits inherited from their past in the state sector. Multinational companies, such as GM, Suzuki, Ford and Nestlé, have appeared on the scene only very recently. General Electric-Tungsram, one of the few exceptions to become established before 1990, dates from 1988.

In this context, the work of the national umbrella organizations for employers such as MAOSz in Hungary and the Polish Employers' Confederation is complicated by the fact that they are attempting to play a dual role. They represent both the employers of the shrinking state sector and those of the emerging private sector, themselves differentiated between 'home-grown' entrepreneurs, largely in SMEs, and big international companies. In what may be a sign of a new consolidation of employer interests, the Hungarian MOASz and HAIC – the Hungarian Association of International Companies – arrived at an agreement in summer 1993 to initiate jointly a revision of the new Labour Code, aimed at curtailing the rights of labour. MAOSz also appears to have ambitions to represent multinational companies in the NCRI, of which the HAIC is not a member.

Given the unstable and ill-defined nature of interest representation in the region, therefore, tripartism had the potential to help newly emerging organizations of both labour and capital define themselves as sets of collective interests and also to achieve greater institutional consolidation. In the words of Touraine (1991: 469), while

> the main problem in the Western-style countries has been that of moving from economic actors to labour and social relations, in these systems [of eastern Europe] . . . the problem is how to move from political and national mobilisation towards the creation of social actors.

The various pressures described above were felt in different ways in the countries of the region. The Antall government in Hungary and the government of the Union of Democratic Forces in Bulgaria (1991) were left a legacy of tripartite structures and practices. They were faced with the dilemma of whether to retain and reinforce them, or to limit or even eliminate them. The pragmatic Hungarian answer has been to accept an incremental growth of tripartism since 1990 (Héthy 1992b) while the Bulgarian political response was to restrict tripartite arrangements, having toyed with the idea of abolishing them. In Czechoslovakia, the idea of tripartism was conceived by social democratic elements within the new government in the context of an unexpected confrontation between the new parties and parliament and the new labour organizations. The Polish case, in which tripartism was initially absent, may be explained by the dual role of Solidarity, dominating parliament and government in 1989–90 while remaining one of the two main labour confederations; tripartism did not appear to offer any advantages in this phase (although the idea of a social pact was floated). Subsequently, with Solidarity gradually disintegrating (Morawski 1992) and right-wing coalitions taking over the government, the notion of tripartism was to emerge as an alternative.

Developments in labour relations opened the way for new types of bipartite and tripartite contacts. First, even though political change was accompanied, in Poland and Bulgaria, by new kinds of transitional linkages between unions and the state (Thirkell and Tseneva 1991), political reform generally entailed the clear separation of the state and political parties from the organizations of workers and employers. Second, legitimacy and representativeness became issues of critical importance for workers' and employers' organizations which could survive and function only as autonomous actors relying on the support of their membership, rather than on state sponsorship. Third, while industrial relations structures are still in a state of flux and fragmentation (Fischer and Standing 1991), legislative changes have removed obstacles to genuinely free collective bargaining and promoted its development at sector or enterprise level; the existence of collective labour disputes has been recognized and mechanisms for dispute settlement have been introduced. Finally, trade union rights and forms of workers' participation have been adapted to the new conditions of emerging private ownership and the market economy. In general, this involved the curtailment of existing rights of unions and of separate institutions of workers' participation (Thirkell et al. 1993).

Tripartite Bodies and their Functions

This section describes the growth of tripartite institutions in the different eastern Europe countries before identifying the broad strands of their work.

In Hungary, tripartism has gradually evolved from its beginnings in 1988 as a form of national wage-bargaining. In 1990 the scope of the National Council for the Reconciliation of Interests (NCRI) was widened to include a consultative role in public policy formulation, and participation was extended to include all seven trade union confederations and nine employers' associations. The government has left it to the workers' and employers' 'sides' of the NCRI to determine their own representation. Both have remained largely unchanged, although in 1993 the small labour confederation, Solidarity, was expelled from the workers' side for its extremist approach. Until 1990, the NCRI was limited to plenary sessions; subsequently, specialized committees and an administrative secretariat were added and regional organs developed. Its committee structure covers areas such as wages and labour, health and safety, economic issues, privatization, social affairs, the labour market, dispute resolution, training (through the tripartite National Training Council), and social security. A separate Council for the Reconciliation of Interests in Public Services (CRIPS) was established in 1990 with the participation of central and local government, public service unions and employers.

The NCRI has rights of information and consultation concerning government policies. In 1990–1, for example, it discussed issues such as the re-election of Enterprise Councils (the institutions of workers' self-management), the economic programme, and the government's plans of the envisaged World Expo. It also has the power to reach agreements on draft legislation. In 1991, it came to agreements on social aspects of the 1992 budget, wage regulations for 1992, and compensation for increases in energy prices. The NCRI may make recommendations to the social partners, for example on wage-bargaining; and takes decisions about the guaranteed minimum wage (Herczog 1991).

In Czechoslovakia the federal Council of Economic and Social Agreement had four major functions: to reach general agreements on major issues of employment and pay (mainly the minimum wage); to co-ordinate approaches to legislation on labour and social security issues; to comment on measures in the fields of employment, pay, and social and economic policies; and to intervene in large-scale conflicts related to collective bargaining and the implementation of collective agreements. Similar councils were established at the level of the Czech and Slovak states, and regional economic and social councils were set up in such crisis areas as northern Moravia (Musil 1991). After the division of Czechoslovakia the federal council ceased to exist, although the republican councils continued to function (Cziria 1993).

Tripartism in Bulgaria has gone somewhat further than in Hungary and Czechoslovakia, extending into economic strategy formulation (Thirkell and Tseneva 1991). The National Commission for Co-ordination of Interests (NCCI) was set up in April 1990 by the government, the Confederation of Independent Trade Unions of Bulgaria (CITUB) and the National Union of Economic Managers (NUEM). It was joined somewhat later by the Podkrepa Labour Confederation. Subcommissions were established to deal with areas such as credit policy and banking, employment, redundancies and retraining, pay and the minimum wage, industrial conflict, privatization, social insurance, and labour and social legislation. Decisions were taken by consensus. Tripartism was also developed at sectoral and regional levels (Atanassova-Tseneva 1992).

Despite the relatively tardy development of similar arrangements in Poland, for reasons explained above, tripartite dealings have assumed greater importance since 1992, with employers, represented by the Polish Employers Confederation, and unions, represented by both

Solidarity and OPZZ, participating in talks leading to the 1992 State Enterprise Pact (Tyszkiewicz 1992).

Within these bodies, three broad areas seem to have opened up for national tripartite negotiations in the countries examined. First, they have dealt with developments in the field of industrial relations and labour legislation, for example the 'deregulation' of pay determination and the consolidation of collective bargaining. Second, tripartite bodies have participated in public policy formulation in areas such as incomes policy, social wage measures, and employment policies. Third, they have had a role in the prevention and settlement of industrial disputes and wider social conflicts.

The three areas are closely interrelated, for the impact of tripartism is realized in part through new labour relations institutions and procedures and negotiated public policies, which, in turn, may be instrumental in the prevention and alleviation of labour and social tensions and conflicts. Tripartite actions in these areas, however, differ considerably in both their importance and their time horizon. Those related to the transformation of labour relations have a long-term relevance; public policy measures have shorter-term implications (usually having time horizons of a year or so); while conflict settlement is sporadic, depending on the actual occurrence of conflict.

These roles are considered in turn in the following sections.

Shaping Collective Bargaining

There is now a general conviction in eastern Europe that the employment relationship should be based on genuine 'free collective bargaining' between workers and employers. All four of the countries covered have already enacted laws regulating industrial relations actors and collective bargaining procedures. The major pieces of legislation include Hungary's Strike Act (1989) and Labour Code (1992), Czechoslovakia's Act on Collective Bargaining (1990), the Polish Acts on Trade Unions and Collective Dispute Settlement (1991), and Bulgaria's Labour Code (1993). However, legislation was often adopted hurriedly, before substantial issues of bargaining had been fully defined and the conditions for effective bargaining established. As a result, there are several unresolved issues: How much space can be left to wage-bargaining, given government stabilization policies? Is centralized wage-bargaining to be preferred to decentralized bargaining, as implied by tripartite initiatives? Doubts also persist about the representativeness and organizational effectiveness of both unions and employers at enterprise, sectoral and national levels, and in the public and emerging private sectors. Thus 'it is difficult empirically to assess [the] workability and acceptability' (OECD 1993) of the legislative framework that has been established.

Legislation on collective bargaining was born out of new types of relationships between governments and parliaments on the one hand and labour organizations on the other. The unions were often included in preparing legislation, even when formal tripartite institutions did not yet exist. In Poland, Solidarity was already active in the preparation of the first strike legislation of the region, the Trade Union Act of 1982, and it once again took part in the legislative process in the new political context of the early 1990s. In Hungary, the Strike Act (1989) and the NCRI were conceived in the same spirit of tripartism, and the preparation of the Labour Code (1991–2) was subject to exhaustive negotiations among the social partners. Tripartite procedural agreements were concluded in Bulgaria prior to the enactment of the 1993 Labour Code; they covered issues such as trade union rights in the enterprise, the role of unions and other worker representatives in collective bargaining, workers' participation, limitations on the right to strike, and individual employers' rights (Atanassova-Tseneva 1992).

The involvement of labour in industrial relations legislation has often provoked conflict. In Czechoslovakia, for example, the unions 'opted for a policy of confrontation' in the period leading up to the Collective Bargaining Act (December 1990) and the General Agreement (January 1991), threatening strike action in support of their arguments (Musil 1991).

Tripartite institutions have played a role in the gradual substitution of administrative intervention in industrial relations, particularly in wage determination. The NCRI in Hungary was originally created, as noted above, as an institution of national-level wage-bargaining. It took decisions on the guaranteed minimum wage and made recommendations on average, maximum and minimum enterprise-level wage increases. Between 1988 and 1992 the government retained its right to issue regulations to limit wage increases. This reflected fears about the inflationary impact of pay rises and the need to keep consumption under control. However, there were grounds for thinking that deregulated wages would have little impact on prices, given the financial crisis of state enterprises, the determination of private entrepreneurs to resist wage demands, and labour's weak bargaining position.

Administrative wage determination, which in 1988 permitted only 2 per cent nominal wage increase in the national economy, was gradually relaxed. A more flexible system was introduced in 1989–91 (Héthy 1991b), under which enterprises were free to raise wages beyond the recommended level if they were in the position to pay the taxes on them (that is, a general 50 per cent entrepreneurial 'profit' tax and a 43 per cent social security contribution); even then, several categories of enterprises (such as those with foreign stakeholding) were exempt. In 1992, an agreement in the NCRI 'suspended' wage regulation by the government. An average 23 per cent nominal wage growth was envisaged for 1992, slightly above the forecast rise in consumer prices. The body recommended a minimum of 13 per cent and a maximum of 28 per cent for enterprises. It was also agreed that organizations exceeding the recommended maximum would be obliged to pay taxes only if wage growth went beyond the negotiated level in the national economy as a whole (Tájékoztató 1992). The NCRI also took steps to promote collective bargaining at industry level as a way of enforcing the provisions of the national agreement (Berki 1992). Finally, a 1992 agreement of the NCRI completely abolished administrative wage determination (Tóth 1993).

The guaranteed minimum wage has been repeatedly raised in Hungary by the NCRI since 1988. The unions have constantly urged increases in response to increases in the cost of living (regardless of the possible adverse effects of higher wage costs on employment). Employers, especially in recent years, have opposed increases in the minimum wage because of its impact on production costs, particularly in low-wage industries and agriculture. They have made unsuccessful attempts to push such decisions down to enterprise-level collective bargaining where they have been in a much stronger position relative to their employees than at national level (Garzó 1991). The government has also made efforts to limit minimum wage growth, given its position as employer in the traditionally low-wage public services sector.

In Czechoslovakia and Poland there has likewise been a trend to the deregulation of pay determination. Governments in both countries have maintained their restrictive wage policies in the state sector, although greater flexibility for state enterprises to bargain within the limits set by the law was introduced in Czechoslovakia in 1992 (Hradecka 1992); while in the tripartite State Enterprise Pact, the Polish government envisaged a certain liberalization in the state sector, suggesting the establishment of a National Negotiating Commission and proposing a partial substitution of the unpopular *popiwek* or payroll tax with a system of negotiated wage levels (Tyszkiewicz 1992). Outside the state sector, the Polish government refrained from direct intervention, while the Czechoslovaks lifted directive wage control in private firms and joint ventures with more than 30 per cent foreign capital in 1992.

In addition to the direct participation of tripartite bodies such as the NCRI in the liberalization of wage determination, there appears to be a close relationship between pay deregulation, collective bargaining and national-level institutionalized tripartism. Deregulation of pay determination (and of the labour market generally) is a requirement of the transformation towards the market economy. The willingness of governments to do away (albeit reluctantly and gradually) with direct controls over wage growth opens up both the possibility and the need for collective bargaining and potential tripartite co-operation in this field. In the past the development of collective bargaining has been paralysed, and tripartite co-operation seriously constrained, by the government's adherence to direct intervention in pay determination.

Negotiating Public Policies

In the context of macroeconomic stabilization and transformation, policies on incomes, employment and social welfare have become central to the relationship between governments, unions and employers. Each of the countries has seen tripartite discussions in some or all of these areas.

In Bulgaria, negotiations between the government, CITUB, Podkrepa and NUEM led to a series of agreements in 1990–1 covering a wide range of matters of concern to workers: employment, wages, inflation, living standards, health and safety, social benefits, etc. The implementation of these agreements was accompanied by repeated confrontations between government and unions (Atanassova-Tseneva 1992; Thirkell and Tseneva 1991).

In Czechoslovakia a tripartite General Agreement on public policy measures was signed in January 1991. It established improved unemployment benefits and redundancy compensation, and obliged the government to spend 25 per cent of the employment budget on 'active employment policy' measures promoting entrepreneurship and retraining. It also covered pay determination, allowing partial compensation for increases in the cost of living and regulating the minimum wage (Musil 1991). Negotiations in 1991–2 concentrated on the same issues. They were accompanied by often sharp differences between the government and the trade unions, particularly over the question of the guaranteed minimum wage. Arguments centred on the true extent of the fall in real wages, in relation to the productivity of Czech workers.

Such claims were seen as exaggerated by some experts; moreover, 'legislation on the minimum wage enforced in tripartite negotiations by trade unions backed by the employers' body [at that time chiefly representing former state enterprise managers] runs counter to efforts to achieve greater wage differentiation' (Hradecka 1992). Following the separation of the Czech and Slovak Republics, such tensions continued. In March 1993, for example, the Slovak trade unions walked out of the Republic's Council in response to the government's failure to consult it on an important piece of social security legislation (Cziria 1993).

Similar conflicts over the role of tripartite bodies in government policy-making have arisen in Hungary. Despite formal provisions under Labour Code 1992 for consultations in the NCRI on 'issues of national importance affecting employment', the government has frequently adopted major pieces of economic legislation without consultation, provoking sharp protests from the NCRI partners.

Nevertheless, an important agreement on income, employment and social policy measures in relation to the 1993 state budget was concluded in the NCRI at the end of November 1992. In addition to regulating the guaranteed minimum wage and abolishing state regulation of wages as mentioned above, the agreement obliged the government to prepare and present to the NCRI an employment strategy, with special provisions for large-scale redundancies. It fixed the size of the Employment Fund, which finances active employment policy measures and is paid for primarily out of revenues from privatization; and laid down employers' and employees' contributions to the 'Solidarity Fund' (which finances unemployment benefit) and set the duration and level of benefits. Other measures dealt with the age of retirement, the growth of pensions for 1993, and pay determination in public services. In addition, the agreement's provisions covered broader areas of public policy such as taxation: it established exemptions from value-added tax for personal medicine and domestic energy consumption. Finally, the agreement required the government to submit to the NCRI its strategy on budgetary, social security, fiscal, industrial and agricultural policies.

In Poland, tripartite intervention in public policy emerged later than elsewhere. By 1991–2, however, government attitudes were veering away from the neo-liberalism of the beginning of the decade. Kuron, the minister of labour and social affairs, spoke in 1992 of the intention to create a 'social market economy, which on the one hand protects the weaker members of society, whilst on the other draws wide social groups of employees and others into responsible activity' (Tyszkiewicz 1992: 31). The 'Social Dialogue' programme initiated by the labour ministry sought ways of creating 'efficient machinery of tripartite consultation at national level, and the inclusion of workers' and employers' organizations in the process of creation of socio-economic policy, in particular in the labour relations sphere' (Baczkowski 1992).

Tripartism has assumed new functions within the emerging systems of labour relations. In Hungary, for example, with the consolidation of new labour market institutions, the NCRI acquired new powers. One of its specialized committees, dealing with the labour market, was given the right under the Employment Promotion Act 1991 to determine the broad principles governing the utilization of the Employment Fund and to monitor the Fund's use. The National Training Council – another committee of the NCRI – has been given similar functions in the field of vocational training and retraining. The Council runs the regional retraining centres established under a World Bank programme and controls the Vocational Training Fund, financed by obligatory employer contributions.

The tripartite agreements which have been concluded in the region are mostly limited to policy formulation on incomes, employment and social issues. In general, they are short-term measures valid for periods of a year or less. By their nature, such agreements have little impact on long-term policies and strategies. They can be instrumental in their implementation, but have little influence on their architecture. For example, in Czechoslovakia the 1991 General Agreement may be looked upon as an annexe to the broader programme, the so-called scenarios of economic and social reform. In Hungary the 1992 agreement was simply an annexe to the 1993 state budget.

The Settlement of Conflicts

In the period 1989–92 there was a general fear in the region of strikes, social unrest and even of a more generalized 'social explosion' in response to the hardships imposed by government policies. This has raised the question of the role of tripartite bodies in conflict management.

Statutory regulation of collective disputes of labour generally includes procedures for conflict resolution. Legislation on strikes (Poland 1982, 1991; Hungary 1989; Czechoslovakia 1990; Bulgaria 1990) lays down limitations on industrial action to protect the public interest. In Hungary, for example, strikes are illegal if deemed 'anti-constitutional', or 'related to purposes other than achieving workers' social and economic interests'; in Czechoslovakia solidarity strikes are unlawful; warning strikes are allowed in Hungary and Poland. In most of the countries strikes are illegal or restricted in certain essential services (state administration, the military and police, fire brigade, public transport, health service, etc.). Restrictions include the obligation to provide 'sufficient level of services' (Hungary).

In practice, however, strike legislation has often failed to contain explosions of workers' unrest, since most measures affecting workers' interests – such as austerity measures in economic policy – are taken by government, and the state is still the major employer in the economy and will remain so in the future. Moreover, legal provisions are not enforced and violations rarely sanctioned.

Poland and Bulgaria have suffered a great number of strikes, while industrial action has been limited in Czechoslovakia and Hungary since 1989–90. Political strike action has been fairly frequent, despite legal restrictions. In Poland, for example, over a ten-month period in 1991–2, illegal action resulting in work stoppages amounted to between one-third and one-sixth of total recorded conflicts; in Czechoslovakia such illegal action was estimated to amount to 15 per cent of all cases (OECD 1993).

Strikes have been sporadic and insignificant in Hungary since the Strike Act 1989, probably because the country's vast informal economy provides some compensation to important groups in the work-force for losses caused by governmental policies (Ladó et al. 1991). None the less, the interrelationship of public policy formulation and national outbreaks of conflict is well illustrated by developments in Hungary in the period 1989–92, in particular by the 1990 taxi- and lorry-drivers' blockade – an example of an illegal 'demonstration of public disobedience'. The blockade was preceded by a series of national conflicts, such as the trade unions' call for a half-hour general warning strike in protest against planned meat price rises in 1989, and more generalized industrial action by miners, airport employees, judges and others in July–September 1990.

The taxi-drivers' blockade which paralysed Budapest and the country for three days in October 1990 was in protest against an average 65 per cent increase in the administered price of petrol. It followed the government's point-blank refusal of the drivers' demands. The blockade led to two days of direct negotiations between the government and the drivers. The government's offer of 'special' compensation was refused, and it threatened police intervention. Finally the government convened the NCRI. The body spent the whole day in televised session while demonstrators for and against the taxi-drivers attempted to influence its deliberations. The government finally gave in and suspended the price increase for the short period until the liberalization of the price of petrol (Ladó 1991). It is interesting that the NCRI's intervention took place despite the fact that it had no formal functions of conflict resolution. Moreover, the mostly private taxi-drivers and lorry-drivers were self-employed, with only loose contacts with unions or employer associations. They none the less accepted the NCRI's role.

The blockade held lessons for all the partners. Beyond increasing the prestige of some of the union and employer organizations and their leaders, and influencing the attitudes of the government on industrial relations matters, it proved the practical use of the NCRI in dispute settlement. In general, it certainly contributed to the reinforcement of tripartite structures and practices. None the less, the pattern of conflict continued to follow its own dynamic. In June 1991, for example, MSzOSz proposed a social policy package including an increase in the guaranteed minimum wage, redundancy payments for the unemployed, workers' participation in privatization, social compensation for rises in the administered price of energy, etc. Its demands were backed up by the threat of a warning strike which was suspended when negotiations with the government proved (at least partially) successful. In December 1991, MSzOSz again called a warning strike as the NCRI failed to achieve agreement on the guaranteed minimum wage.

In Poland, as mentioned, no progress was achieved on national-level tripartism before 1992, despite serious outbreaks of strike action on several occasions after 1989. Subsequently, however, the Polish government did move to create procedures for the resolution of conflicts in the state sector, and an agreement was reached between government and the National Committee of Solidarity. At the same time the government consulted unions and (although not obliged to by law) the Polish Employers' Confederation on drawing up a list of mediators (under the 1991 Act on the Settlement of Labour Disputes). The ministry of labour and social affairs sponsored a series of tripartite meetings and launched a programme on 'Social Dialogue' (see above), with the co-operation of the ILO. The aims included the creation of institutions to promote the peaceful settlement of social conflicts, and of tripartite national machinery covering socio-economic policy and the labour relations sphere more generally (Baczkowski 1992).

Thus fears of large-scale social conflicts, and political efforts to find mechanisms for dealing with them, have provided a major motive for the development of national-level tripartite institutions and negotiations across the region. Even in Czechoslovakia, with a relatively low level of social conflict, the tensions and debates of autumn 1990 (as well as news of the Hungarian taxi- and lorry-drivers' blockade) speeded up developments leading to the establishment of the Councils of Economic and Social Agreement (Musil 1991); their functions included decision-making 'in large-scale collective disagreements related to collective bargaining and the implementation of collective contracts', although such eventualities had not yet arisen in the country.

Tripartism: Prospects and Limits

The effective functioning of tripartism in the region is dependent on several interrelated preconditions. First, within the constraints of the emerging political structures and economic system, a sufficient 'space' must be available for tripartite agreements in the economic and social policy field. Second, the actors – governments, labour organizations and employer bodies – must have the capacity to make and adhere to such agreements. Third, all the actors must be sufficiently imbued with philosophies of co-operation and take a pragmatic approach to the possibilities for agreement. They must also to a degree share political objectives and ideological values concerning the functioning of the emergent economic system. Finally, formal tripartite institutions must be established as a site for negotiation between the actors.

Economic crisis, with failing performance and competitiveness and plummeting per capita incomes, narrows the scope for alternative policies. Tripartite negotiations have taken place and agreements been reached against a backdrop of declining real wages, growing unemployment and deteriorating social benefits. The situation is often aggravated by pressures to address growing budget deficits and to cut hefty international debt. The increased taxes levied to make good the shortfalls in state budgets have been resisted not only by the unions, but also by employers in both the state and private sectors. None the less, the achievement of the agreements described above shows that there is still some space, however limited, for seeking the 'least worst', socially most acceptable, options. The danger for the trade unions, however, is that their approval of such public policies may undermine the social prestige and support which they had lost in the past and have only partly regained.

Following the phase of 'pluralization', workers' organizations in Bulgaria, Hungary and Poland have been severely divided. At the same time the successor unions of the old regime have been looked upon with suspicion, even hostility, by the new governments and political parties. The major issue of political debate has been the unions' legitimacy and representativeness (see MacShane's chapter 13 in this volume). In Hungary, for example, union representativeness has been repeatedly tested by legislation (in 1991–3), despite the fact that the government accepted *de facto* the legitimacy and representativeness of the seven confederations through their participation in the NCRI. Nevertheless, while divisions and conflicts have weakened the unions' position, and their public reputation is relatively low in all the eastern European countries, they have remained large and powerful by comparison with their counterparts in western Europe. In 1991 the estimated level of unionization was about 40 per cent in Poland, 60 per cent in Hungary, and 75 per cent in Bulgaria. In Czechoslovakia density was also high and no divisions occurred.

As suggested earlier, employers' organizations are in a much less consolidated state than trade unions. Their constituency is subject to constant changes owing to the collapse of state industry, privatization, the development of SMEs and so on. They are extremely heterogeneous and the status of their membership is open to considerable debate. In Hungary, the nine employers' associations in the NCRI represent state-owned enterprises, private undertakings, industrial, agricultural and consumer co-operatives, small craftsmen and retail traders, etc. In Bulgaria the National Union of Economic Managers – a major participant in tripartite negotiations – was founded in 1990, not as 'a real employers' association, but rather a trade union to defend the specific interests of state directors' (Atanassova-Tseneva 1992). Elsewhere in the region, however, the pattern is for employers to be represented in tripartite forums by a single umbrella organization, as with the Co-ordination Councils of Entrepreneur Unions and Associations of the Czech and Slovak Republics, and the Confederations of Polish Employers.

The policies and attitudes of both governments and unions have fluctuated between pragmatic co-operation and confrontation. Most unions have accepted the inevitability of transformation and its social consequences (including unemployment and falling real wages); nevertheless, by their very nature as workers' representatives, and given their socialist orientation and in many cases their communist roots, they have been opposed to the neo-liberal or conservative political and economic philosophies of the mostly right-wing governments in power. Those unions which cherished hopes of a renaissance of workers' self-management, which had deep historical roots in the region, were profoundly disappointed by privatization policies, particularly in Czechoslovakia and Hungary. In addition, the relationship between government and trade unions has often been clouded by short-term political rivalry. Government strategy has tended to oscillate between inclusive policies, aimed at building compromise and consensus, and exclusive ones, aimed at the marginalization of political opponents (Bruszt 1992).

What emerges from the history of tripartism in the region is the transience of the conditions for stable relationships. Most of the pre-conditions were present in Hungary in 1988, the year of the establishment of the NCRI: the unions were still united, the state sector was still predominant, and all three partners had reformist communist leaderships advocating a 'socialist market economy' based on the ideology of the 'third way'. Within a couple of years, however, none of these conditions still held.

The boundaries of tripartism have been somewhat vague. Governments have seen it as a means of securing approval and support for their short-term policy measures, especially austerity programmes; while the social partners, particularly the unions, have attempted to use tripartism to influence longer-term government policies and strategies. Issues of crucial importance for the future of social co-operation and harmony, notably privatization, have been carefully evaded in most tripartite negotiations. In Hungary, the social partners complained that the government had failed to submit its privatization strategy to the NCRI in 1991; nor was it touched upon in the November 1992 agreements. However, in Bulgaria, the tripartite negotiations of 1991 addressed the problem of privatization. In Poland it was a major item in tripartite talks leading to the State Enterprise Pact in 1992; the agreement covered the role of the unions during privatization, worker share ownership, and the scope for worker buy-outs (Tyszkiewicz 1992).

Tripartite agreements are not in themselves legally binding; to be implemented by governments they have to be followed up by legislation. The Czechoslovak General Agreement, for example, explicitly imposed such an obligation on government, and in Hungary the November 1992 NCRI Agreement was pushed through parliament in the debate on the 1993 budget.

However, implementation through legislation has resulted in modifications to tripartite agreements. For example, in the 1992 Hungarian agreement, the average 14 per cent growth of pensions was amended in parliament so that increases were paid in two instalments, reducing the actual increase to below 10 per cent. Such changes reflect the often loose and unregulated relationship between tripartite bodies and parliament, with the latter often regarding the former as impinging on its legislative prerogatives. Again in the Hungarian case, parliamentary committees evaluating draft legislation are not obliged to invite NCRI representatives to their sessions (Herczog 1991); nor is there a specialist committee dealing with issues of industrial relations, employment, and so on. Another relevant factor in the modification of tripartite agreements is the presence in parliament of deputies with a labour movement background. In Hungary, there are very few trade unionists in parliament, in contrast to Poland or Bulgaria where appreciable numbers of Solidarity and Podkrepa representatives were, in certain periods, members of parliament.

The fact that government decisions are not automatically converted into legislation provides governments with room for manoeuvre with respect to their tripartite commitments. In Hungary, for example, the government's draft of the new Labour Code of 1992 was submitted to parliament after thorough-going discussions and agreements in the NCRI. In parliament, however, more than 500 suggestions for amendment were made, many of them by MPs of the governing coalition. Thus in effect the government tacitly retained its right to modify its part of the NCRI agreements with reference to its 'limited influence' over legislation.

There is as yet little reliable empirical evidence of whether, and to what extent, tripartite agreements have been implemented in practice; nor how far the workers' and employers' sides have been able to carry through their own commitments and impose them on lower echelons within their respective organizations.

There is currently much talk in central Europe of 'social contracts' or 'social pacts' (Musil 1991; Agh 1993). Political change in Hungary and Poland was based on negotiated political agreements between the previous communist regimes and their opponents; trade unions participated in the round table talks in both countries. However, such negotiations have not been followed up by comprehensive social contracts between the major political forces setting out the economic and social strategies of transformation. The economic programme of the Mazowiecki government in Poland, the 'scenarios' for economic and social reform in Czechoslovakia and the Antall government's 'programme for national recovery' in Hungary were worked out by narrow groups of experts and subsequently endorsed by legislation. In this sense, despite Solidarity's decisive role in the formulation of economic strategy in Poland in 1989–90, the frequent political references to 'social consensus' in Czechoslovakia, and the long record of the NCRI in Hungary, tripartism has (except for a brief period in Bulgaria) had no role in global strategy formulation, outside the specific sphere of industrial relations.

Conclusions

The major current challenge for eastern Europe is to accomplish economic stabilization and transformation while maintaining social and political stability. The economic programmes of 1990–2 have precipitated falling GDP and industrial output, declining real wages and living standards, and growing unemployment and poverty. Most of the new governments, despite their undeniable democratic legitimacy, face serious and growing deficits in public support for their programmes of change. While some countries, such as the Czech Republic and Hungary, appear to have established a new political stability, others are riven by permanent political conflicts. There is a general fear, whether justified or not, of a 'social explosion'. Governments, cornered by economic crisis and pressures to cut social expenditure, have very limited means of defusing the tensions. It is within this economic, social and political context that institutionalized national-level tripartism has come to play such a significant role in the region in recent years. The social dialogue that it implies seems to be an element of a pragmatic political response to the challenges facing the region.

Tripartism is, however, unstable and fragile, as are the emerging political and economic systems. Governments, still predominant in labour relations and in the management of the economy, faced large though often divided labour organizations. The employer groups of the old regimes are in a phase of disintegration while new ones are as yet hard to define.

The fluctuating fortunes of national tripartite bodies will depend above all on political change and on the related structures of interests and power, as well as on the philosophies of the major actors, particularly of governments. The often febrile fluctuations witnessed to date, together with the absence of global 'social pacts', underline tripartism's acute political vulnerability. Old political forces attempting to secure their survival and new ones looking to establish a foothold tend to look upon tripartism as an interim solution, providing scope for short-lived and narrow political compromises as well as for a mutual reinforcement of legitimacy, representativeness and public support. Tripartite bodies offer information (about the governments' political intentions) and are a focus for press and media coverage.

Thus tripartism is based on the pragmatism of the social partners, and its existence has very little to do with the essential political and economic philosophies of the new regimes in the region. If at present it is maintained by such pragmatism, its future consolidation will depend on the construction of stable political, economic and industrial relations systems in the individual countries.

Acronyms and Abbreviations

CITUB	Confederation of Independent Trade Unions of Bulgaria
CRIPS	Council for the Reconciliation of Interests in Public Services (Hungary)
CSKOS	Czech and Slovak Confederation of Trade Unions
HAIC	Hungarian Association of International Companies
League	Democratic League of Independent Trade Unions (Hungary)
MAOSz	National Association of Hungarian Employers
MSzOSz	National Confederation of Hungarian Trade Unions
NCCI	National Commission for Co-ordination of Interests (Bulgaria)
NCRI	National Council for the Reconciliation of Interests (Hungary)
NUEM	National Union of Economic Managers (Bulgaria)
OPZZ	Polish Trade Union Alliance
Podkrepa	Podkrepa (Support) Confederation of Labour (Bulgaria)
Solidarity	NSZZ Solidarnosc – National Trade Union Alliance 'Solidarity' (Poland)

References

Atanassova-Tzeneva, E. 1992: The reconstruction of industrial relations in Bulgaria in a transition period to a market economy. In Hoof et al. (eds), 49–72.

Agh, A. 1993: Az elsö szociális paktum. (The first social pact.) *Népszabadság*, Budapest, 30 January.

Baczkowski, A. 1992: Preventing and resolving industrial conflict (in Poland). OECD Seminar on Industrial Conflict Settlement, Warsaw, 18–20 May.

Berki, E. 1992: A bérszabályozástól a béralkuig. Bérmegállapodások 1992 elsö felében. (From wage regulation to wage-bargaining. Wage agreements in the first half of 1992.) *Munkaügyi Szemle*, Budapest, 11 (November), 21–28.

Bruszt, L. 1992: Transformative politics: social costs and social peace in East Europe. *East European Politics and Societies*, 6(1) 55–71.

Cawson, A. 1985: Introduction. In A. Cawson (ed.), *Organized Interests and the State*, London: Sage Publications, 1–21.

Cziria, L. 1993: Labour relations in the CSFR/Slovakia. Workshop of the Project Privatization, Restructuring and Labour Relations, Canterbury, 3–6 April.

Ferge, Z. 1991: Marginalisation, poverty and social institutions. *Labour and Society*, 16(4) 417–37.

Fischer, G. and Standing, G. 1991: Restructuring in eastern and central Europe: labour market and social policy issues. ILO–OECD–CEET Conference. Paris, 11–13 September.

Florek, L. 1992: The impact of industrial relations and political transformation in Poland. *IIRA 9th World Congress, Sydney, 30 August – 3 September: Proceedings*, Volume 4, 50–7.

Garzó, L. 1991: Kollektiv alku a munkahelyen. (Collective bargaining at the enterprise.) *Munkaügyi Szemle*, Budapest, 6 (June), 1–3.

Góra, M. 1991: Shock therapy for the Polish labour market. *International Labour Review*, 130(2) 145–63.

Herczog, L. 1991: Az Érdekegyeztetö Tanács elsö esztendeje. (The first year of NCRI.) *Munkaügyi Szemle*, 9, September, 3–6.

Héthy, L. 1988: *Organisational Conflict and Cooperation*. Budapest: Akadémiai Kiadó.

Héthy, L. 1991a: Towards social peace or explosion? Challenges for labour relations in central and eastern Europe. *Labour and Society*, 16(4) 345–58.

Héthy, L. 1991b: Structural adjustment and changes in income distribution in the 1980s in Hungary. WEP Working Paper No. 32. International Labour Office, Geneva, December.

Héthy, L. 1992a: Hungary's changing labour relations system. In G. Széll (ed.) *Labour Relations in Transition in Eastern Europe*, Berlin/New York: De Gruyter, 175–82.

Héthy, L. 1992b: Political changes and the transformation of industrial relations in Hungary. *IIRA 9th World Congress, Sydney, 30 August – 3 September, Proceedings*, Volume 4, 58–67.

Héthy, L. 1993: Changing labour relations in eastern (central) Europe. In *Economic and Political Changes in Europe*, 3rd European Regional Congress of IIRA, Bari/Naples, 23–6 September 1991. Bari: Cacucci Editore, 63–83.

Héthy, L. and Csuhaj, V.I. 1990: *Labour Relations in Hungary*. Budapest: Institute of Labour Research.

Hoof, J.V., Slomp, H. and Verrips, K. (eds) 1992: *Westbound? Changing industrial relations in eastern Europe*. Amsterdam: SISWO.

Hradecka, J. 1992: Economic changes in today's Czechoslovakia. IVth International Meeting of Work Sociology. Bologna/Forli, 10–17 November.

Jones, D.C. 1992: The transformation of labour relations in eastern Europe: the case of Bulgaria. *Industrial and Labor Relations Review*, 45(3) (April), 452–70.

Ladó, M. 1991: The losers' victory – the winners' defeat? Contribution to the conference on 'Social Conflicts', Institute of Labour Research, Budapest, and Luigi Sturzo Institute, Rome, 29–30 May (manuscript).

Ladó, M., Szalai, J. and Sziráczky, G. 1991: Recent labour market trends and labour policy in transition in Hungary. ILO–OECD–CEET Conference, Paris, 11–13 September.

Morawski, W. 1992: Trade unions in Poland: dilemmas of dependence. Independence and relative autonomy (manuscript).

Musil, J. 1991: New social contracts. Responses of the state and the social partners to the challenges of restructuring and privatization. *Labour and Society*, 16(4) 381–99.

Musil, J. 1992: Czechoslovakia in the middle of transition. *Czechoslovak Sociological Review*, Special Issue, Prague, 28 (August), 5–21.

OECD 1993: Preventing and resolving industrial conflict. *Labour Market and Social Policy Occasional Papers*, 22. Paris.

Róna-Tas, A. 1991: The selected and the elected: the making of the New Parliamentary Elite in Hungary. *East European Politics and Societies*, 5(3) (Fall), 357–393.

Stark, D. 1992: Path dependence and privatization strategies in East Central Europe. *East European Politics and Societies*, 6(1) (Winter), 17–53.

Streeck, W. 1993: The rise and decline of neo-corporatism. In *Economic and Political Changes in Europe*, 3rd European Regional Congress of IIRA. Bari/Naples, 23–6 September 1991, Bari: Cacucci Editore, 27–62.

Tájékoztató a bérmeghatározás 1992: évi változásairól. (Changes in wage determination in 1992.) *Munkaügyi Szemle*, 2 (February), 1–11.

Thirkell, J. and Tseneva, E.A. 1991: Bulgarian labour relations in transition. Tripartism and collective bargaining. *International Labour Review*, 130(2) 355–66.

Thirkell, J., Scase, R. and Vickerstaff, S. 1993: Transitional models of labour relations in eastern Europe: Bulgaria, the Czech and Slovak Republics, Hungary and Poland. Paper presented to Annual Conference of British Universities Industrial Relations Association, York, 2–4, July.

Touraine, A. 1991: Economic reform and democracy: a new social contract? *Labour and Society*, 16(4) 467–77.

Tóth, G. 1993: Bérmeghatározási rendszer '93. (Wage determination '93.) *Munkaügyi Szemle*, 6 (June), 1–8.

Tyszkiewicz, M. 1992: Jacek Kuron's new economic policy. *Labour Focus on Eastern Europe*, 43, 31–3.

13

The Changing Contours of Trade Unionism in Eastern Europe and the CIS

Denis MacShane

Introduction

The changes in eastern Europe and the former Soviet Union are un-precedented in the history of employment and labour organization anywhere in the world. In the space of two years, a huge world region with a centrally planned and closely interlinked economic system largely cut off from the capitalist world was turned upside down. The communist economic and political system was based on the world of work. Ownership, management, employment, pay, housing, social security, industrial relations and the political or representative role of the union were utterly different from the capitalist world. Trade unions in the former Soviet Union and in the communist states of central and eastern European were giant organizations fully inte-grated into the 'democratic centralist' system of command and control shaped by Lenin and Trotsky and polished by Stalin.

Thus official trade unions under communism were not trade unions in any western sense of the word. They have been seen, rather, either as administrative branches of enterprise management responsible for social and welfare duties or as command and control mechanisms for the ruling party apparatus. At moments of revolt such as in Berlin in 1953, Budapest in 1956, or Gdansk in 1980, workers quit the official unions in droves and sought to set up more independent worker organizations. In short, seeking models that correspond to existing western structures usually leads to confusion rather than enlightenment.

Up to 1980 the monolithic nature of the system served to disguise clear social tensions arising from the rapid industrialization of mainly agricultural economies despite sporadic upsurges of worker-based revolt such as those already mentioned, as well as Czechoslovakia in 1968, and Romania in 1977. In Russia and the Ukraine, some workers had raised the banner of independent trade unionism and found themselves in psychiatric prison hospitals for their pains.

The arrival of the Polish union, Solidarity (*Solidarnosc*), in 1980 dramatically challenged the monopoly of communist trade unionism. In addition to raising worker demands connected to pay and conditions, the revolt by Polish workers was based on workplace organization and took the institutional form of trade unionism (MacShane 1981). Despite the repression of Solidarity in December 1981, notice had been served that the authority of communist trade unionism was no longer unquestioned in eastern Europe. In the course of the 1980s, some unions sought to adapt, as in Hungary, and other resisters to communist control such as the Podkrepa union in Bulgaria decked themselves in the Solidarity mantle.

Though most official unions in eastern Europe and the Soviet Union scorned Solidarity and continued, at least in their public pronouncements, as if nothing needed to change, the various events of 1989 swiftly buried such complacency. From the legalization of Solidarity to the execution of the Romanian leader, Ceauçescu, the workers of the Soviet bloc played their part. However, though the changes of 1989 were enormous they were not quite a revolution such as swiftly ushers in a new set of social institutions based on a new ideology and driven by popular pressure which sweeps all before it. Nor were they analogous to the 1945 upheavals when an external occupying force (the Allies in western Europe and Japan, the USSR in eastern Europe and North Korea) imposed a new political and economic system. Although at the beginning of the 1990s there was the opportunity to create new forms of trade unionism, employment and industrial relations, there was no clear vision of what the new model should be. The process is still under way, and each country is seeking its own path to a new world of work, welfare, industrial relations and worker organization. The ex-Comecon countries have to be considered and treated separately: the differences between Slovenia and the Ukraine are as big as the differences between Denmark and Turkey.

The nine communist states of USSR, Poland, Hungary, Czechoslovakia, German Democratic Republic (DDR), Yugoslavia, Romania, Bulgaria and Albania which existed prior to 1989 have been replaced with 29 independent states, each with its own government and legislature. Russia, in addition, has 30 autonomous republics, some of which are claiming independence and all of which are organizing units for trade unions. The DDR has been absorbed into Germany and its union representation taken over by the West German unions. However, although the former communist monolith appears to have disintegrated into a many-pieced mosaic, there are certain common trends that enable a picture to be drawn of the development of and prospects for trade unions.

The biggest difference is between the ex-Soviet Union, now the different republics of the Commonwealth of Independent States (CIS) and the other European lands that fell to communist rule only after 1945. Within the CIS, the predominance of Russia, whose economy is three and half times that of the Ukraine (its nearest rival in GDP), and which is forty to fifty times the size of states such as Latvia or Tajikistan, places it in a category apart. In addition, whereas the European ex-communist states orient themselves principally to the west, seeking in particular membership of the European Community, Russia is a self-sufficient continental economy, with large areas of its territory in Asia and thus interacting with Japanese and Chinese influences. Ex-Yugoslavia and Albania are also cases apart, for obvious reasons, although Slovenia's avoidance of the political-military struggles between Serbs, Croats and Bosnian Muslims has allowed a more settled development of the labour market.

Geographical propinquity and history are important determinants of trade union development in eastern Europe. The Slovak capital, Bratislava, is thirty minutes' drive from Vienna. Frankfurt is as close to Prague as it is to Berlin. Finnish trade unionists can talk to their counterparts in Estonia without need of interpreters for their language. When Volkswagen workers set up a European Works Council they included representatives from the Skoda company in the Czech Republic, now 70 per cent owned by VW, to sit alongside VW workers from its subsidiaries in Spain (Seat) and Belgium. Unions in Austria, with four ex-Comecon countries on its border (Hungary, Slovakia, the Czech Republic and Slovenia) moved swiftly to provide material help and advice so that the post-1989 unions in southern central Europe could move in the direction of the carefully modulated social partnership policies that have helped sustain prosperity, full(ish) employment and union influence in Austria.

Certain union traditions appear to have survived successive dictatorships in central Europe. In 1928, in the steel town of Henningsdorf near Berlin, a communist-led strike against wage cuts lasted for 100 days before it was broken. In 1953, the town's workers marched to Berlin in the June uprising. In 1993, the metalworkers of Henningsdorf joined the strike to defend the commitment to the gradual equalization of East and West German wages.

Thus it is not accurate to depict the entire trade union movement in central Europe as having been born or reborn in 1989. The powerful Hungarian metalworkers' federation occupies the same handsome building in Budapest since the union was founded in 1887. The Czech lands were home to one of Europe's most powerful social democratic and trade union movements between the wars. Igor Pleskott, who in 1989 emerged from a metal factory in Prague to head the newly democratized 1.5 million-strong Czechoslovak metal union, had taken part in the workers' councils movement of the Prague Spring in 1968, and his parents, prominent pre-war social democratic politicians, had been executed by the Nazis. In Hungary, an extraordinary twentieth-century trade unionist, Pal Forgacs, emerged late in the 1980s to guide the Democratic League of Independent Unions (Liga) in opposition to the communist union organization. Forgacs, an active trade unionist since the late 1930s, had sought to sustain a social democratic political presence in the Hungarian trade unions after 1945: a forlorn effort which earned him spells in prison.

Economic Context

Reading the literature on economic and social changes, including labour movement and political developments, published since the fall of the Berlin Wall, the sense of apocalyptic prediction that failed to come true is overwhelming. The end of Soviet communism marked by the events of late 1989 was such a shattering historical event that many expected a period of spectacular and total transformation to follow. However, the grand designs for total economic liberalism proposed by western free market ideologues have had to confront the complex political pressures of 'actual existing democracy' in post-communist societies. The outcome has entailed confused and untidy compromises.

Despite these complexities and the obvious differences between countries, it is still possible to note common trends. All the post-communist states undertook economic reforms aimed at moves towards a market economy. First, price controls were liberalized and currencies made convertible. Centrally planned production was abolished. Second, money supply was controlled (except in Russia) and governments sought to balance their budgets. Third, privatization programmes were launched by selling state property (mainly to the managers of enterprises, or in Russia to labour collectives) with employee participation in share ownership. Shops and small companies were sold outright to individuals, and foreign corporations bought into privatized enterprises or launched their own operations. Fourth, foreign investment was encouraged and advisers from international institutions such as the International Monetary Fund, the European Community and various consultancies set up operations in eastern Europe.

The move towards market relationships was much more evident in trade and distribution and some service sectors than in manufacturing where the bulk of unionized workers were to be found. In addition, the large number of public employees working directly for ministries, regional and local government, and para-statal organizations constituted an important block of employees who remained unionized.

The increase in economic activity noted by visitors to the eastern European capitals, who saw shiny new shops filled with goods and an emerging economy based on service and import companies, could not compensate for the massive slump in industrial output, the collapse in trade with the Soviet Union and between the former Comecon states, and the impact of the recession in western Europe which led the European Community to impose protectionist quotas on textile, steel and agriculture exports from eastern Europe. National fragmentation contributed to economic collapse; for example, after the break-up of Czechoslovakia, trade between the two new republics dropped by 30 per cent in the first half of 1993 and hopes of a marked growth in Czech GDP were shattered.

As the OECD noted in 1992,

> there is growing concern about the social costs of market-oriented reforms in Central and Eastern Europe. The fall in living standards associated with the rapid growth in unemployment and declining real wages has dampened the initial enthusiasm that accompanied the first steps in the transition process. (OECD 1992: 239)

Table 13.1 Percentage change in industrial output, 1990–1992

	1990	1991	1992
Poland	−24.2	−12.9	−7.6
Hungary	−10.5	−19.1	−18.9
Czechoslovakia	−4.0	−21.0	−22.0
Romania	−17.4	−18.7	−17.6
Bulgaria	−16.3	−27.5	−17.5

Source: European Commission

In 1993, the ILO said, 'there are reasons to believe that in some regions 50 per cent of the population live in poverty' (ILO 1993: 2).

A trade union official visiting Croatia in December 1992 noted conditions which, though exacerbated by military action in ex-Yugoslavia, paralleled those observed throughout much of eastern Europe, the Balkans and Russia.

> Real wages have fallen dramatically (estimates suggest by over 40 per cent in 1992) and unemployment is running at over 20 per cent. In addition many employees are forced onto *cekanje*, a system of compulsory leave, where employees receive only part of their salary. Whilst many products in Croatia are sold at world prices (shoes and clothes, for example), the average monthly wage for October 1992 was £40. The minimum wage in November 1992 was £18. A casual examination of prices in Zagreb suggests it would be almost impossible to survive on this amount of money. Thus informal and *trade union distribution networks will have assumed a huge importance at this present time.*[1] (emphasis added)

Some increase in output generated by private firms was noted in Poland in 1993, although starting from the much reduced base of the decline in the Polish economy after 1989, but the overall picture remained gloomy. The United Nations Conference on Trade and Development forecast a further 12 per cent slump in output in central and eastern European countries in 1993 (following reductions of 15 and 16 per cent in 1991 and 1992, respectively) and said that these countries found themselves in 'a twilight zone where there is neither plan nor market' (UNCTAD 1993).

Union Structures

Early in 1990, it was possible to identify four main categories of trade union in addition to the unified German trade union movement. First, there are newly created unions defining themselves by strident anti-communism and supporting a nationalist, free-market politics. Examples are Solidarity in Poland, Fratia in Romania, Podkrepa in Bulgaria, Sotsprof in Russia, and the Liga in Hungary. A second group comprises former communist unions that were taken over lock, stock and barrel in 1989 by a post-communist leadership. This is notably the case in the KOS confederation in Czechoslovakia (which in 1993 split into its Czech and Slovak components). Third is a group of reformed communist unions that had already accepted the need for change in the 1980s and accelerated this process after 1989 by electing new leaders, reforming constitutions, renewing membership on the basis of a post-communist platform and generally accepting and functioning according to 'western' pluralist norms. The MSzOSz confederation in Hungary and the Confederation of Independent Trade Unions of Bulgaria (CITUB) fit into this category. Finally, there are the inheritors of the old communist trade unions such as the OPZZ in Poland, the Federation of Independent Unions in Russia, and smaller communist-run unions in the Czech Republic (see table 13.2).

The extent to which so-called 'reformed unions' are linked to their communist past is to some degree a subjective judgement. In the case of Czechoslovakia, the leadership at national, regional and often local level was swept aside in the velvet revolution of November 1989 to be replaced with democratically chosen leaders. However, the union's structures and institutions remained in place. In Hungary, reform had been under way since the mid-1980s, and to demonstrate their 'newness', the 'reformed' MSzOSz unions asked all their members to apply for new membership cards in the course of 1992.

Any tabulation inevitably imposes a static picture on an evolving set of relations. Two contradictory tendencies can be distinguished. First, in the 1990s many union movements have been further sub-divided by splits, some political, some based on personalities and the growing nationalism and separatism in the region. But second, in many countries where unions initially denounced their rivals as stooges, they have begun to come to terms with the fact that they are condemned to pluralism. By 1993, the impact of unemployment, cuts in living standards, the struggle for enterprise survival and the hostility towards unions of any sort from imported free market ideologues and advisers combined to oblige some teeth-gritting co-operation between 'old' and 'new' unions. In Lithuania, where unions were split between the reformed Centre for Free Trade Unions, inheritors of the old Soviet union movement and the Lithuanian Workers' Union (linked to the nationalist Sajudis movement), signs of greater cohesion are emerging at factory level. In Kaunas, for instance, Lithuania's three main groups have formed a co-operative body to defend 'common interests' (ICFTU 1993).

Political and International Affiliations

Co-operation faces many obstacles, however. The defining criterion for the category of 'post/anti-communist unions' remains a strong opposition to co-operation with reformed communist unions. Inter-union rivalries are especially strong in Russia where the alliance

Table 13.2   Main unions in eastern Europe and CIS*

	Unions operating under pre-1989 communist structures	Unions reconstituted after 1989	Post-/ anti-communist unions
Albania	KSL		BSPSH
Belarus	FTUB		NPG (B) Confederation of Free Trade Unions of Belarus TU
Bulgaria		CITUB	Podkrepa
Croatia		SSSH	HUS KNSH
Czech Republic		Czech-Moravian Trade Union Chamber	
Estonia		EAKL	
Hungary		MSzOSz ASzOK	Liga SzEF MOSz ESzT
Latvia		FTUFL	Latvian Labour Confederation
Lithuania	LCFTU	Unification of Lithuanian Trade Unions	LWU
Poland	OPZZ		Solidarity Solidarity 80
Romania**		CNSLR	Fratia Alfa Cartel BNS
Russia	VKP	FNPR	Sotsprof NPG
Serbia	SSSS		Nezavisnost BSKP (Kosovo)
Slovakia		KOZ-SR	
Slovenia		ZSSS	Neodvisnost
Ukraine	FPU		VOST Sotsprof (U)

*The initials chosen are those by which the unions are commonly known in the literature, sometimes English-language acronyms, sometimes vernacular acronyms. The Czech and Slovak unions split up in the course of 1993 following the sundering of Czechoslovakia.

** Fratia and the CNSLR announced a merger in mid-1993 after Fratia decided that the reformed former official union had been 'purged' of its communist leaders.

between the former official unions and enterprise directors creates powerful barriers to the organizing activities of the post/anti-communist unions (see chapter 14 in this volume). In this area, relations with unions outside the region, notably those from western Europe and the United States, play an important role.

The three main existing components of the world labour movement reacted differently to the breakup of the communist trade union structure after 1989. The International Confederation of Free Trade Unions (ICFTU) and their associated International Trade Secretariats (ITSs) moved swiftly to implant themselves in eastern Europe. The Catholic World Confederation of Labour (WCL) also sent envoys; however, other than with Solidarity in Poland, the confessional tradition of trade unionism had little appeal. The Soviet-run World Federation of Trade Unions (WFTU) faded as unions all over the region withdrew from membership, though the Polish OPZZ hosted, in October 1993, a leadership meeting of WFTU unions from Vietnam, Cuba, Middle East Arab States and the Communist Confédération Générale du Travail from France.

International and European federations sent scores of missions to eastern Europe and the CIS. ICFTU leaders were able to meet presidents of the post-communist states to argue for union rights and more social protection during transition. The question of affiliation remained sensitive, however.

ICFTU accepted into membership only unions which had been created in a specifically anti- or post-communist mould. Polish Solidarity became an ICFTU member in 1986, Podkrepa in 1990. The Brussels international maintained contacts with other unions that had reformed themselves; however, opposition from the American Federation of Labor-Congress of Industrial Organizations (AFL-CIO) or Force Ouvrière of France initially prevented the affiliation of unions such as MSzOSz in Hungary. The ICFTU accepted the double affiliation of Hungary's MSzOSz and the Democratic League in December 1993. MSzOSz's metal union federation, as well as the Bulgarian ex-communist metal union, had already been accepted as members of the International Metalworkers Federation, the biggest of the western international trade secretariats. Other ITSs also affiliated many reformed unions from eastern Europe with the endorsement of American industrial unions. As US multinationals entered eastern Europe in search of new markets and low-wage production, the economic logic for American and western European industrial unions to support organizing and wage demands was stronger than adherence to any cold-war litmus test laid down by their national centre (Seideneck 1993).

Although the AFL–CIO devoted considerable resources to supporting anti-communist unions in the region, it was outweighed by the
activity of western European unions which were more catholic in their
approach to unions in the region. Germany's social democratic
Friedrich Ebert Foundation had programmes and offices in Russia and
other countries; the Austrian labour movement was extremely active
in the Czech Republic and Slovakia; and the wealthy Swiss unions also
acted from pragmatic self-interest to prevent the creation of a permanent low-wage economy in central Europe. The French government
funded a foundation run by French metal unions to help steelworkers
with conversion programmes in eastern Europe. Even the anti-labour
British government provided resources to the engineering union,
AEEU, to send officials and shop stewards for two weeks to help
Romanian metalworkers as they adapted to the new order. Other
western European countries had similar programmes, channelled
through national trade unions, for bilateral support work with eastern
European unions. The ILO also set up a ten-person team in Budapest
in 1993 to help labour and social security ministries, unions, and
fledgling employer organizations.

The major exceptions to the wave of affiliation to the western internationals were the unions which still were active in the leftover networks of the WFTU. Although Russian unions and Poland's OPZZ
formally left the WFTU, old networks and activities remained.
The OPZZ hosted WFTU executive meetings in Warsaw and the
Russian Federation of Independent Unions continued to operate at
ILO gatherings with former allies of the WFTU.

The entire question of the Russian trade unions remained one of the
unresolved problems four years after the fall of the Berlin Wall and
two years after the defeat of the Moscow *putsch*. Their leaders and
much of their *modus operandi* were so little changed from the old
centralist order that it was difficult to categorize them wholly as trade
unions recognizable by western European norms. Unlike the reformed
eastern European unions which had dramatically changed structures,
leaders and language, many of the Russian unions, while proclaiming
themselves democratic and reconstituted, still gave the impression of
hoping for a return to the old monolithic way of working. The anti-
communist unions in Russia such as Sotsprof or the NPG, as well as
the ultra-nationalist unions in the secession republics, were also vehement in their condemnation of the 'old' federations. Two key
questions remain to be answered about the reconstituted Russian
unions: first, which direction will they take or which alliances will they
seek if Russia reverts to an authoritarian, possibly nationalist, political
model; and, second, whether the large number of union members is a

wholly passive, paper membership which could evaporate quickly once mechanisms of ownership, management, and social payments are fundamentally altered.

For the western internationals there was another question to be considered before rushing to affiliate the old Russian unions. Even in their reduced size, the Russian unions were giant organizations which, by weight of membership, would swamp all but the biggest of the western national centres in the international bodies. Affiliating Russian unions on the basis of a vote per member would dramatically alter the balance of power in the western internationals. At the same time, the Russian unions, at least up to 1993, did not seek formal membership of the western internationals. Unlike eastern/central Europe, where a fairly clear, if turbulent, political settlement had been achieved, the political and economic problems of Russia and the CIS were still unresolved. Until the picture is clearer in the former Soviet Union, its trade unions are likely to remain isolated – at least by comparison with the integration of the eastern European unions into international labour activity – with only sporadic contacts with unions in the West.

Internal Organization

Internal union structure also shows many variations. The classic divide between general unions incorporating all workers and autonomous industrial or craft federations is widespread. Unions born out of anti-communist struggle such as Polish Solidarity and Podkrepa have organized as general unions, in both cases under a charismatic, populist leader (at least until Lech Walesa was elected president of Poland). The union leadership has opposed the creation of independent industrial or 'branch' federations for workers in sectors such as metalworking, public service, transport, and so forth. A Podkrepa spokesperson denounced the 'infiltration of certain persons into the branch structure [and] the unfeigned careerism and marked "branch" egotism which is generating countless problems within the organization'.[2] Successor unions which were taken over by democratic leadership after 1989 have tended to organize on an industrial basis. The main way of distancing themselves from central control under communism was simply to declare independence and autonomy from the old federation. Nevertheless, in Prague and Moscow, all the unions remain housed in the old central union headquarters, and in the regions the enterprise unions remain the dominant form of organization.

Russia has by far the most complex of trade union structures. In addition to the successors of the old unions, important professional groupings such as the Federation of Air Traffic Controllers have emerged as independent bodies. There has been a marked development of independent craft unions in key sectors such as mining and in journalism. An independent Metal, Foundry and Mining Workers Union was created in 1991. A co-ordinating council, VKP, acts as a link between the unions in the CIS republics.

There is in many countries a visible gap between the activities at the enterprise level which are local and particularist, often with little reference to the national centre, and the interventions with ministries and the media by national leaders in capital cities.

The leadership of the post-1989 unions shared one characteristic with the previous unions: few if any of the new presidents and general secretaries were workers. As in western Europe, there was a marked shift to graduate union functionaries. In Bulgaria, for example, *Doctor* Konstantin Trenchev heads the anti-communist Podkrepa union and confronts *Professor* Krastyu Petkov, chair of the Council of Independent Unions of Bulgaria (inheritor of the old communist federation). Petkov's background in social science is shared by Marian Krzaklewski, an academic who was elected president of Solidarity in 1992; this is in contrast to the Solidarity of 1980–1, where, despite the strong presence of intellectual advisers, the leadership was in the hands of workers. Krzaklewski's opponent who heads the communist-created OPZZ union is Ewa Spychalska, a political scientist. In the Czech Republic and Slovakia, the majority of the executive board of the metal unions are professional engineers. It is important to remember that unions under communism always included directors, managers, technicians and professional staff who would not normally be union members in the West.

Enterprise unions also tend to be led by officials with managerial or technical qualifications, notably engineers. A common pattern is an alliance between the management and the union of an enterprise in a common struggle to keep it alive. Privatization led by local managers has usually been carried out with the support of enterprise union leaders. Burawoy and Krotov (1993: 61), in their study of the changes in the Vorkuta coal complex of northern Russia, noted that the strike leaders who had organized the strikes of 1989 had now gone into business:

one of the most successful and controversial of the ex-leaders bragged about how he now employs 1,000 workers. He had washed his hands of the workers' movements and without batting an eyelid embraced business as the only worthwhile way of promoting the welfare of all.

The main reason for the arrival of this graduate leadership is a further reflection of the peculiar top–down revolution that took place. Leaders were hurriedly replaced as part of a renewal or democratization of existing unions. Research institutions were often the places where experienced knowledgeable executives unconnected with communist party excesses in the 1980s could be found. Alternatively, anti-communist activists – also drawn from an educated political elite – went out to form new unions as organizations that would undermine communist rule. In Hungary in 1988, the first independent union in eastern Europe since Solidarity was launched among scientists and technicians and other workers in research institutions. The absence of a widespread workplace-based movement (with the exception of the miners' movement in Russia and the Ukraine) in 1989 meant there was no springboard for leaders from among rank-and-file workers. The leadership of the post-1989 unions is anomalous in that it is divorced by education and work experience (though not by social origin) from the social categories it purports to represent. Thus the unions in eastern Europe should be seen as socio-political groupings in addition to their function of defending workers' employment conditions. They constitute a key component of the primitive civil society painfully being created on the rubble of pre-1989 state systems.

Collective Bargaining and Organization

In traditional terms, unions are meant first to organize, then to bargain, and finally to take part in politics. In eastern Europe and Russia, in traditional sectors such as heavy industry or the public sector, the unions have little need to organize and their bargaining partner remains the state. In contrast, in the new privatized sectors of the economy – notably services and distribution – union presence is minimal. However, while the ex-Soviet and eastern European labour markets remain in limbo – neither wholly privatized nor wholly state-owned – the majority of employed workers remain union members. Although membership is often passive, the level of unionization remains relatively high, because unions continue to provide social goods (see table 12.3). Although the cradle-to-grave welfare and social role of unions under communism has been much reduced, they continue to offer access to holiday centres, clinics, and, in Russia, food and goods sold at the workplace. Holding a union card for a nominal membership payment thus makes sense even if a sense of identity with the union is low. This is particularly the case in Russia.

> As long as the 'Profkom' [works trade unions committee] confines itself to allocating that which is assigned to allocate, it should not have anything to fear from company management. The allocative function represents the trade unions' right to exist in company plants. As the workforce does not associate trade unions with the genuine representation of their interests, that is all that is expected of them. Where trade unions do stand up or speak out against the director, the latter can then quickly withdraw this function from them without their having any chance of regaining it through mobilizing the workforce. (Hoffer 1993: 11)

There are contests for organization between rival unions although there is also evidence that workers may hold two union cards: one of the old-established union that provides access to goods, the other of a new union to show a personal political commitment to a more democratic organization. For the time being, union membership remains high in eastern Europe (see table 12.3). Unemployment and the removing of pensioners and other non-active workers from union membership rolls reduces actual numbers. Yet in Bulgaria, for example, the ILO estimates 75 per cent of the work-force still to be unionized in 1993. In Romania, the CNSLR–Fratia confederation has 3.7 million members, one-third of the Romanian work-force. Even in Poland, where privatization has gone the furthest and disillusionment over the effectiveness of the unions is high, there are still four million members in OPZZ and two million in Solidarity, representing a density higher than in most western European countries. The new or anti-communist unions have stronger representation amongst white-collar and technical grades of employees, while older unions such as OPZZ in Poland, MSzOSz in Hungary and CITUB in Bulgaria have the bulk of their membership amongst manual workers. Union membership is at its highest in the publicly-owned enterprises.

These surprisingly high figures of union membership do not betoken strong pro-union engagement, however. For example, of those Russian workers replying to a poll in 1992, only 5.1 per cent regarded the unions' protection of workers' rights and interests as good or very good, compared with 72.9 per cent who voted it poor or very poor (Hoffer 1993).

One unresolved question is whether the levels of union membership are wholly linked to the communist system of social and economic organization and therefore will decline as capitalist relations

Table 13.3 Trade union membership in eastern Europe ('000s), 1991–1992

Hungary	
Democratic League of Independent Trade Unions (Liga)	130
MOSz (National Alliance of Workers' Councils)	160
'Solidarity' Trade Union Workers' Alliance	75
ASzOK (Autonomous Trade Unions' Confederation)	345
ESzT (Intellectual Workers' Trade Union Assoc.)	63
SzEF (Trade Unions' Co-operation Forum)	557
MSzOSz (National Confed. of Hungarian Trade Unions)	2,682
Poland	
OPZZ (Polish Trade Union Alliance)	5,000
NSZZ Solidarnosc (Solidarity)	2,500
Czech Lands and Slovakia	
CSKOS (Czech and Slovak Confederation of Trade Unions)	7,000
Bulgaria	
CITUB	1,700
Podkrepa	500

gradually take over; or whether workers, while acknowledging the faults of the former trade unions, are sensitive to the need for some collective organization in order to protect themselves both in the transition period and under the new economic order. An important test of trade union popularity in Hungary in 1993 yielded results very different from those indicated in the Russian survey. In line with the French system, the Hungarian government decided that social security (that is, health and pension insurance schemes) should be managed jointly by employers and workers. Elections for union representatives on the management boards were held amongst all Hungarian employees. Before the election there was a widespread feeling that disenchantment with the unions – there are eight rival union federations in Hungary – would lead to a low turnout. Participation generally in municipal and other elections in Hungary had dropped to below 20 per cent. Anti-union politicians insisted that a 25 per cent participation rate should be achieved for the unions to have the right to nominate their representatives in line with the ballots, expecting that they would fail to reach this level and thus be discredited as representative organizations. In fact, the turn-out was rather high with 39 per cent of employees casting a vote. The results showed a strong preference for the reformed MSzOSz federation (see table 13.4).

Organizing for such elections or mobilizing for or against government decisions represents the main area of activity by unions. Collective bargaining with employers at industrial or enterprise level has not yet become a focal point. The main reason has simply been the absence

Table 13.4   Pension fund election in Hungary, 1993

Union	Votes (%)
MSzOSz	50.1
Works Council Federation	10.9
Co-operation Forum	10.6
Liga	10.1
Christian Social Union	8.4
Intellectual Union Congregation	6.2
Autonomous Unions	4.8

Source: MSzOSz Statement 21 May 1993

of employers. 'The employer side is the weakest in the [region's] tripartite structure . . . and the principles on which employer organizations are based are not yet clear,' stated the ILO (1993: 2; see also chapter 12 in this volume). By mid-1993, only four organizations, from Poland, Hungary, the Czech Republic and Slovakia had been granted recognition by the International Organization of Employers. Tapiola (1992: 4–5) has written of a 'Bermuda Triangle' between the three functions of the

> owner (still mainly state), manager and trade union(s). Confusion between the role of these three poles of industrial relations is a serious obstacle to tripartism in practice. It is equally clear that labour–management relations work only if the division of labour is established at the basic level. Currently the manager does not always know where her or his powers start i.e. what is the relationship to the owner. Incomplete or non-existent legislation does nothing to alleviate this problem. As to the union, the manager does not know what should be negotiated with it – and with whom, one or several union bodies, or works councils encompassing the whole personnel and being formally separate from the unions?

Collective bargaining often takes the form of making demands and threatening protest action if they are not met. Whether directed at enterprise management or at ministries, demands are often couched in the form of a political appeal rather than a researched set of proposed adjustments forming the opening claim in a process of compromise and resolution in the traditional sense of collective bargaining in capitalist societies. The Sotsprof union inside the AZLK car factory near Moscow distributed leaflets in the summer of 1993 making the following demands:

1 Increase wages by 45 per cent and compensate for the amount still due for February–May 1993 according to the indexation of wages, as provided for in the collective agreement.
2 Continue to index wages regardless of the financial activities of the factory.
3 The immediate transformation of the factory into a joint-stock company, according to the decision of the work collective. (The shares should belong to the workers, and we propose to create a General Fund of Shares so that those who want to sell their shares can sell them only to other workers of the factory and not to outsiders.) Distribution of stocks to the AZLK bank among the factory's employees.
4 Introduce hourly wages in routine-flow work to ensure the quality of the product. Introduce a 30 per cent bonus for quality and a 20 per cent supplement for brigades who conclude agreements on defectless production.
5 Sale to factory employees of cars on credit at a 20 per cent discount.

AZLK Workers! We call on you to support these demands and to respond with a strike if they are rejected by management.

The Joint Union Committee, Sotsprof.[3]

The tone of this appeal conveys a recruiting purpose in the efforts of the independent Sotsprof union to dislodge the official carworkers' union. However, in Belarus, it was the carworkers' union itself that called for an 80 per cent increase in its members' wages to cover the rise in food prices following their liberalization in June 1993. The union's demands were addressed 'to the Council of Ministers, as owner of the enterprise, and to the administration of the enterprises, as employer',[4] the bodies which in Belarus, as still elsewhere in the region, are considered to be the collective bargaining partners for the unions.

Although industries taken over by private foreign interests with no experience of unions (for example, Turkish or Greek investors in shipping or textiles) may be crudely and cruelly de-unionized, the larger multinationals in the manufacturing sector will seek some union accommodation by searching generally for a pliant, enterprise-centred union structure.

Conversely, it is in the interests of the new states to have a certain degree of union representation and hand over to unions responsibility for negotiating pay and conditions. Where union membership sinks below 20 per cent, as for example in France or the United States, the government takes over a far wider responsibility for legislating social protection, from minimum pay to the protection of the disabled or minorities at work. As it is, the new governments face a difficult legislative burden without having to negotiate or control in detail every operation of the labour market.

Strikes

All the states in the region have seen significant political protest strikes initiated by the unions. Strikes or the threat of strikes have led to the fall of governments in Poland and Bulgaria. The miners' strikes in Russia in 1989 and 1991 fatally undermined Gorbachev, and worker unrest remains a continuing concern for Yeltsin. Action by transport workers in Hungary (though in this case, mainly self-employed taxi- and lorry-drivers) which brought Budapest to a halt, or the occupation by Romanian miners of Bucharest, were crucial events in forcing changes in government policy. Although the motives and methods vary, industrial action has had far more impact on political developments in the eastern half of Europe in the 1990s than in the western half.

Theoreticians enjoy drawing distinctions between economic and political strikes, and eastern Europe provides rich new evidence for this age-old debate. The idea of a 'transition from one model of industrial conflict, characteristic of the preceding epoch, to an entirely new model, deriving from the market economy [wherein] political strikes must be replaced by economic ones' appears far removed from the evidence. Although many strikes are over pay, the underlying conflict is over 'the distribution of costs of the economic transformation [and] the question of the division of assets remaining from the preceding epoch, in the context of the new organization of the economic system' (Kloc 1993: 36). Even what appear on the surface to be purely economic strikes are in fact political. The dispute in 1992 between workers and management at a car factory in Poland taken over by Fiat centred on the strikers' demand for a share of the profits and pay to be raised gradually to Italian levels. This demand threatened the core model of foreign investment-led development in Poland, by situating the workers as employees of a multinational corporation whose reference for pay should be their fellow employees in western Europe. General Motors workers in Hungary raised similar demands after they returned from training in a GM plant in Austria, and found that although they were doing precisely the same work as Austrian GM employees, they received only one-sixth of their pay. In Hungary workers have grumbled but have taken no action – so far. In Poland, the Fiat dispute swiftly moved from a local union–management pay fight to a struggle with the prime minister, who flatly rejected any deal along the lines sought by the strikers. The two unions concerned were the communist OPZZ and the right-wing though wage-militant Solidarity 80 – at opposite political ends of the old–new, communist–anti-communist spectrum, yet united in this instance in seeking to resist Poland's becoming a new low-wage area of exploitation.

Although the strike was lost, the lesson was learnt that industrial action over pay unavoidably became political. For some unions, including those led by former *apparatchiks* of the communist trade union movement, the answer is privatization, which will create a class of employers with whom they can negotiate.

> We want private owners to take over the means of production becuase we want to bargain with partners who can actually fulfil what they negotiated with us. Our employer, the State, never fulfilled its contract with us and now is so bankrupt that it has nothing left to give

is how one Russian trade union official in St Petersburg puts it (Field 1992: 51). Yet the unions' support for privatization is also ambiguous. In Russia,

> workers have a very clear idea of what they want from the privatization of their own enterprise. On the one hand, they want the profits which have always been taken from the enterprise to be used to increase wages and social expenditure. On the other hand, they see privatisation as a way of curbing the power and cutting the privileges of the enterprise administration. (Clarke 1992: 26)

Thus strikes can be both for higher wages and in favour of privatization programmes, the former being seen as being dependent on the latter. The lack of a clear political-economic programme leaves strike action as a disconnected, sporadic series of work stoppages, workplace occupations, and street protests carried out by often competing unions or by spontaneously gathered groups of workers whose strike committees rarely transform themselves into enduring organizations. There are small groups of left-wing activists hoping and proselytizing for a new surge of worker action which would transform politics and usher in a new revolutionary era. Although Boris Kagarlitsky's many writings portray this tendency, Clarke (1992: 27), writing about privatization, is right to observe that

> it would be naive to see the struggle over privatization as one which necessarily unifies the working class. Privatization can also be the basis of divisions among workers. Entitlements linked to length of service

discriminate against women, young and temporary workers. Privatization to the labour collective leaves out all those not attached to state
enterprises as employees or pensioners. Sale to the labour collective at
knock-down prices benefits workers in profitable enterprises, while
burdening the unprofitable. Like all struggles, the struggle over privatization is one in which workers have to construct a unity, which is
extremely difficult in the absence of effective organizations within
which differences of interest can be democratically resolved.

The absence of a dominant party to which most workers would give
their allegiance adds to the political-economic uncertainty about the
meaning and purpose of strike action in post-communist eastern
Europe and the CIS. Strikes can easily be depicted as sectional. In a
long-running dispute with the independent Federation of Air Traffic
Controllers, the Russian government has justified its attacks on the
union by claiming that other groups of workers in the air trans-
portation industry resented the special wage increases and other
'privileges' obtained by the Air Traffic Controllers as a result of the
strike action by their post-communist union. Yet in this dispute, as
in many others, threats by the government to criminalize industrial
action and imprison strikers – following the example of President
Reagan against air traffic controllers in 1980 – have not yet been
implemented. The right to strike is still seen as a defining difference
between the old communist and the new post-communist regimes.

Some sense of self-limitation may also be present in the minds of all
unions since, irrespective of their views, none wishes to push use of
the strike weapon to a showdown with the state, leading to direct
repression of strikers and a ban on the right to strike itself. The weight
of history denies the use of strike action to achieve socialist ends,
because socialism (in the communist totalitarian sense of the word) is
what the 1989 revolution overthrew. What cannot be fully estimated is
the extent of the social pressure building up as unemployment, social
welfare cuts and increased poverty take their toll. Gavril Popov (1990),
when mayor of Moscow, conjured up the spectre of the authorities
being

> attacked by waves of workers fighting for their own interests. . . . The
> masses long for fairness and economic equality. The further the process
> of transformation goes, the more acute and glaring the will be the gap
> between those aspiration and economic realities.

Popov's alarmism dating from 1990 has not yet come true. Perhaps he
and other commentators are wrong, and although Russia and eastern
Europe will limp through a longer and more painful adjustment, they

will do so without great upheavals such as are expressed, triggered or resolved by giant strikes. Instead, strikes will continue as they have been in the first years of the post-communism: a means to press home demands and express discontent though not a system-changing means of action. In that sense, strikes will have been normalized and become part of a process of dialogue rather than an all-or-nothing mechanism for total upheaval.

Political Role of Unions

In general, both old and new unions are barely aware of their power and have yet to define a political role. They often feel they can hardly keep their heads above water and cannot match the resources and 'sophistication' of their new comrades from western Europe and North America who arrive with hard currency and much advice. Yet many eastern European unions publish a daily newspaper, a tool of worker communication long dead in the west. In Prague and Bratislava, the unions occupy handsome city-centre offices, from where fleets of chauffeur-driven cars carry officials to meetings with ministers or to airports for high-profile international consultations and conferences.

Certainly, the unions lack the power they once enjoyed under communism, and their reduced resources do not match the demands made upon them. Moreover, they neither have an overarching political vision, nor mobilize around anti-capitalist rhetoric – the occasional reference to Nordic social democracy represents the height of leftist oratory. Nevertheless, despite the lack of outward signs of traditional western trade unionism – militant or corporatist – the unions in the ex-Comecon lands are important social organizations in the construction of a post-communist society.

As Héthy shows (chapter 12), most countries have set up tripartite national commissions which often have a national political profile as high as individual ministries or parliamentary committees. Considerable preparation is required in moving away from a planned economy. The economic and social analyses of the unions, while they cannot counter the ideology of the free market enthusiasts, at least provide coherent arguments for introducing capitalism which either provides rights for employees or allocates resources for social provision. Unlike the financial consultants who either know little of the language of the country, or, if they do, are concentrated in the capital cities, the unions are adept at manoeuvring with deputies, ministers and civil servants, and have the political weight of support in workplaces and the regions.

> The trade unions' economic demands are expected to be voiced not so much on a 'mass scale' as in a 'hidden way' – in talks between function-aries and ministries. . . . The corridors of power will continue to be the epicentre [of union activity]

wrote Bychkova about the need to distinguish between the impact of strikes in Russia and the effective power relations concerned (*Moscow News*, 37, 1992). Although the IMF may be the single most important individual player in the politics of eastern Europe, no one at its Washington office actually votes in Poland, Hungary or Russia. While the eastern European societies remain democracies, their unions of millions of members will continue to play an important political role.

Indeed, the creation of a trade union was seen as necessary for each new national entity called into being. In Belarus, the independent trade union organization in Minsk was linked to the Belarus national-ist party. The breakup of Yugoslavia, in particular, gave rise to the large number of trade unions based on the new states and new politi-cal formations that came into being in the 1990s. The anti-Soviet, anti-communist nationalism of Polish Solidarity provided a role model for unions such as Podkrepa in Bulgaria, or Vost in the Ukraine.

Although the division between reformed and new unions remains important, the socio-economic issues which underpin all union work have reasserted themselves. The enthusiastic commitment to neo-lib-eral policies proposed by the IMF, which in the first period of post-communist rule had been adopted by the new anti-communist unions, has given way to a more prudent assessment as the impact of these policies makes itself felt. The Polish union, Solidarnosc, organized a parliamentary vote against its own government in May 1993 to protest at the cuts in wages of teachers and public employees which were carried out by the Warsaw government in line with IMF dictates. What began as a protest turned into a parliamentary vote of confidence and the government was defeated as Solidarity deputies made common cause with the parliamentary group of the former communist party to defeat a Solidarity-backed government. A new election was called in September 1993 as a result of the parliamentary defeat; that the former communists now regrouped in the Polish social democratic and peasants parties were the main beneficiaries was hardly the desired outcome of Solidarity's political manoeuvring. However, what the election showed was that under the conditions of democracy there was strong support for a socially-oriented labour-based politics.

The political–parliamentary imbroglio in which Solidarity found itself could be seen in other eastern European countries and in the Soviet Union, where trade unions had to seek new political relationships. It proved to be an extremely difficult task. The heritage of political control by communist parties made the organic party–union links of traditional European labour movement politics impossible to reproduce. The traditional language of the labour movement – from the word 'socialism' to the appellations 'brother' or 'comrade' – was taboo. Former communist parties renamed themselves social democratic parties, while the tiny genuine social democratic parties which came into existence after 1989 with the help of western European social democratic money and the return of exiles were unable to make a parliamentary breakthrough. Although Lajos Föcze, president of the Hungarian Chemical Workers union, describes himself as a social democrat, he is contemptuous of the 1990 parliamentary election campaign of the reconstituted Hungarian social democratic party:

> That they went into the elections on an anti-communist platform was perhaps understandable at that time. That they championed liberal economic policies was rather less so. And that they campaigned under an anti-trade union slogan was wholly unacceptable. Workers are not impressed by people who run around factories trying to lecture workers about who was a good social democrat and who was a bad social democrat in the 1950s. The average voter has other things to worry about. (ICEF 1993)

In Russia, both Sotsprof and the independent miners' union, NPG, were unconditional supporters of Yeltsin, seeing in the success of his policies the defeat of the traditional trade union structures and a weakening of the FNPR, the inheritor of the old Soviet unions. The FNPR refused to advise its members how to vote in the constitutional referendum called by Yeltsin in 1993. It created links with the Civic Union group in the Russian parliament which united the anti-Yeltsin forces. In September 1993, Igor Klochkov, the FNPR's president, threatened a general strike in response to Yeltsin's dissolution of parliament. However, at the time of the armed confrontation between the army and the supporters of Rutskoi two weeks later, Klochkov went on television to express his full support for the Yeltsin's efforts to restore 'law and order'. This not only reflected a prudent assessment of the likely outcome of the violent confrontation that shook Moscow for two days, but also indicated that the FNPR had no power to mobilize its nominal seventy million members in favour of insurrectionary politics. Surprisingly, the FNPR appears to have emerged unscathed from the Moscow events, although Klochkov was dismissed by the federation in an apparent gesture of loyalty to Yeltsin. By contrast, the independent unions seem to have suffered, despite their pro-Yeltsin stand, with the closure of their Moscow offices.

The OPZZ union in Poland formed part of the SLD (Democratic Left Alliance) which emerged as the largest single party after the Polish election of 1993. However, the leading party within the SLD, the Polish social democrats (ex-communist), supported a continuation of privatization policies to which the OPZZ was opposed. Thus a post-communist political bloc between the formerly united union and party wings of communism was unlikely to be sustained beyond the temporary alliances of an election.

Merely to list the names of the new parties and their tentative trade union links can lead to a sense of bewilderment, although the underlying pattern is clearer. The linkage between party and politics and trade unions is facing as great a challenge in the post-communist economies east of the Oder as it is in the western European states. Parties search for unions to deliver votes and unions look for parties that can win power and deliver jobs and pay. However, neither partner is capable of delivering its side of the contract. Unions are no longer able to direct the votes of their members while parties in government find themselves so constrained by sectoral demands and international economic pressure that cutting pay and payrolls rather than raising wages or social benefits is the order of the day.

One of the first moves by the post-communist governments was to remove the automatic political privileges of the unions. From then on they would have to survive either by entering into political alliances with parties or by withdrawing from direct political representative activity altogether. Responses varied. The leader of the anti-communist Podkrepa union in Bulgaria, Konstantin Trenchev, made clear his political alliance with the Union of Democratic Forces, and, to the dismay of some of his French advisers who advocated a non-political role for the union, threw himself into party and parliamentary politics with vigour.

One obvious core for left-wing or worker-centred politics are the ex-communist parties now accepting parliamentary democracy. Although Lazslo Pasternak, president of the MSzOSz metal federation in Hungary, was elected to parliament nominally as an independent, he sat with the Hungarian socialist party, the inheritor of the former ruling communist party. The Hungarian socialists have now been accepted as a member party by the Socialist International, and an intense debate is taking place among European social democratic parties over the admission of ex-communist parties such as Poland's social democrats. Obtaining between 10 and 20 per cent of the vote – and in the case of Poland, Bulgaria and Lithuania, holding government office – the former communists are seen as the main defenders of industrial worker interests in a political spectrum that is otherwise economically and socially regressive.

In general, all the unions in the region, whether pro- or anti-communist in origin, have an interest in using strong political connections for maintaining discipline in their ranks. For example, in the state-owned enterprises connected to the arms industry, which are now making a new entry as competitive low-cost producers on the world arms market, the unions, enterprise and government department concerned will sustain a triple alliance to keep exports, jobs, and hard currency cash flow alive. Similar deals may be arranged in the raw material extractive sector of metal ores, coal and petrochemicals.

Legal Changes

New constitutions and laws affect trade unions in two distinct ways. Legal changes to underpin the free market, such as privatization and the abolition of laws protecting workers from dismissal, placed pressures on unions as they sought to adapt to the new economic system. In some cases, the unions were able to negotiate legal protection for employees during privatization. The 'Accord on the Reorganization of State-Owned Enterprises' signed between the Polish government and the unions in 1993 provided for workers to elect representatives to the board of directors and to be allocated 10 per cent of the shares of privatized enterprises. Most Russian privatization has been in the form of sales of shares to the works collective.

Also important were specific laws altering the institutional rights and privileges of the unions. In addition to their political role under communism as part of the ruling front organizations, which meant that union leaders automatically sat in national and regional legislatures as well as forming part of the party leadership, unions had been important social institutions with a legal responsibility for the provision of workplace-based services. Although union membership was never formally compulsory under communism, every employee belonged to a union to obtain access to the social benefits it administered. Of the entire pay roll 1 per cent was transferred to the unions as membership dues. This enormous sum allowed the unions to become giant property owners in their own right in addition to the buildings and lands they administered as the social managers of the workplace. Union-owned property in the workplace constituted an important part of the fixed assets of many enterprises. The Russian trade unions, for example, were housed in an imposing group of buildings taking up almost an entire block in the Lenin Prospect in Moscow. In each Russian city and town the union presence was marked by a large, handsome building on a prime real-estate site. This property portfolio is both an important capital resource for the union and the cause of great conflict.

The 'new' unions were operating from tiny offices, dependent on equipment donated by their friends in the west. They often had difficulty in penetrating workplaces as a local alliance of 'old' union leaders and managers did not want to disturb existing patterns of co-operation. To obtain a government or judicial award granting property belonging to the 'old' union would not only mean the instant creation of a network of regional and local offices, it would also send a powerful signal to enterprise directors and workers that the 'new' unions were installing themselves in place of the 'old'. Disputes over the allocation of union property have been one of the biggest sources of conflict between 'new' and 'old' unions.

On the whole, governments have stayed out of inter-union fights over property rights, thus reinforcing the view that eastern European governments are not seeking direct confrontation with the unions, nor trying to reduce their status or field of operations as might be expected in societies hoping to clear away all obstructions to undiluted free market capitalism. Unions in most countries are still able to collect dues by means of deducting 1 per cent of the wage bill – a sum far in excess of union revenue in Britain or France, for example.

There is often an ambiguity about the legal changes affecting workers in the region. While laws are passed which weaken or abolish union rights as they existed under communism, and there are even direct attacks on unions themselves, most governments are struggling to develop employment and workplace laws that protect citizens and the independent national interest. There are several laws which limit the extent of foreign ownership. Hungary adopted an Employment Law in 1991 which obliged employers to give three months' notice before laying off more than 25 per cent of staff in enterprises with more than 30 workers. Moreover, the employer is obliged to consult workplace committees, usually controlled by the union, and 'workers' representatives are to determine the principles and phasing of lay-offs, and to determine workers' benefits in addition to those required by law' (Plant 1993: 22).

A common union complaint was that while some new laws appeared to give unions a say in the elaboration of national policy, or to provide for workplace rights and guarantee wages and conditions, such appearances were belied by their actual application and by union weakness *vis-à-vis* government, employers and local administrators.

This sense of weakness and frustration stems from the underlying economic fragility of the post-communist societies. Unions had to assert their claims against a shrinking national economy and there were ferocious disputes over how the assets and wealth that did exist should be distributed. No country had a settled administrative structure, and while democratic institutions appeared vigorous, half a decade was a short time to sink deep democratic roots.

Although the complaint about the shallowness or inapplicability of legal change was fair, the hunt for a settled rule of law, compromise and arbitration covering all institutions concerned with social-economic transactions in eastern Europe will continue for years to come. This note of caution is necessary, for the hunt for a descriptive (or prescriptive) theory to explain trade union development in eastern Europe and the CIS may be leading many western investigators astray. The assumption that all trade union relationships have to revolve around a dichotomy that is either class-adversarial or co-opted-collaborationist is common to those nurtured on the adversarial dialectics of (mainly) Anglo-American trade union writing. However, there are other models stretching from the Japanese to the Indian, or indeed, closer to the region, from the Austrian or Nordic labour movements, in which collaboration or coalition at the enterprise level can coexist with autonomy of representation and action at government level or in other spheres such as electoral politics. Just as the development of trade unionism in Asia, for example, has not followed any particular model from Europe or North America, it would be wrong to assume that the apparent frailty or dependence of Russian or eastern European unions betoken their demise. Certainly, although unions in many enterprises depend on the goodwill of their managers, the future survival of the enterprise may also depend on the goodwill of the work-force. As long as political democracy obtains, the governments, new and old employers, and workers will all, in their different ways, need trade unions for some, possibly a good part, of the employed work-force.

Conclusion

Some writers have argued that 'the introduction of market relations may well accentuate class struggle and the development of independent working class organizations in Eastern Europe' (Kilmister 1993: 48). Although it is true that in other parts of the world experiencing economic transformation (South Africa, Brazil, or industrializing Asia) independent working-class organization has developed, in eastern

Europe and the CIS, the economic process is the reverse. De-industralization or struggles for employment survival (in the arms industry, notably) are not conducive to militant class-centred organization. The new employment in services will create a new class of employees though in categories which traditional twentieth-century and proletarian-centred labour movements have either patronized or been unable to organize.

The problem with the mechanical transfer of formulae appropriate to societies that move from agriculture to industry, from colonialism to industrialization, from low to high levels of education, is that in eastern Europe and the CIS, few if any of the factors apply. An utterly new era of world history opened in 1989 for which new categories of analysis are needed to describe and predict worker organization. As John Lloyd has written (about Russia),

> A union between managers and workers against the government well expresses the realities of the post-Soviet industrial order. There is as yet no real differentiation of interest; at the top, Mr Volsky [Chair of the Russian Union of Industrialists and Entrepreneurs] does team up with the trade union leadership to make vague but real threats: at plant level, managers see themselves as slightly better paid members of the work collective, with little experience of firing staff and no desire to do so. (*Financial Times* 12 June 1992)

To graduates of Anglo-Saxon business schools such management may appear inimical to modern industrial capitalism, yet the description of 'a union between managers and workers', low pay differentials and a reluctance to fire workers evokes workplace relations in leading firms in Japan. I am not arguing that Russian enterprise alliances between union and managers are equivalent to Japanese structures, but cautioning against an simple extrapolation of European and Atlantic economic and labour models and categories eastwards.

In classic twentieth-century scenarios of revolution, workers' movements have lain at the heart of the process of change. To the outside world, the role of workers and their organizations has not been much in evidence since 1989. Polish workers, having signalled the end of communism with the formation of Solidarity in 1980, no longer command the front-page international attention they enjoyed in those heady days. However, the changes in train since 1989 are almost entirely to do with the world of work, in particular, the question of ownership and management. In the mammoth task of reshaping the economy, the role of worker organizations, whatever form they take, remains central.

The Soviet Union used to be scorned as 'Upper Volta with rockets'; however, post-Soviet Russia and other ex-Comecon countries show how stupid that epithet was. Unlike the third world, where the constant labour movement struggle is to build up trade unions from a very narrow base, the workers in eastern Europe and the CIS already have mass worker organizations whose membership densities compare favourably with most western unions. Unlike countries moving painfully away from primitive, socially backward forms of agricultural or raw material economies, eastern Europe and the CIS have a large industrial capacity capable of satisfying the material require- ments of their population. In contrast to the low education levels of third world countries, workers and union leaders in eastern Europe and the CIS are highly skilled, indeed over-qualified by comparison with many of their western counterparts. In short, the unions, old and new, constitute a key component of civil society whose participation in change – often taking the form of political and economic alliances – alters considerably the nature and direction of that process.

Nevertheless, first, the unions in eastern Europe need to carry out

> more decisively the job of assessing their own needs. Some of the recent developments are unique – either because they have never occurred before or their order of magnitude is such that new, innovative ap- proaches and solutions are needed. To what degree should (transitional) changes [i.e. privatization, wage and social cuts] be supported by the unions? Few have a straightforward answer to these questions. This dilemma is even more difficult for trade union activists in the Central and Eastern European countries because of lingering memories of the past system where people were told to tighten their belts and accept a miserable life for the sake of a 'bright future' which failed to materialize. (IFBWW, 1993)

Although this advice from a supportive western international labour federation is well meant, it poses the question of whether western unions themselves are analysing with sufficient clarity and depth the accelerating changes through which global capitalism is passing. When each western country has different models of trade unions which refuse to unite, merge or reform themselves to create effective transfrontier units, why should the workers of eastern Europe prove superior in wisdom or organization? Which model should they adopt: Anglo-Saxon adversarial unions, the corporatist co-determina- tion of German–Nordic systems, or Japanese–Confucian enterprise unionism?

The October Revolution of 1917 proved that communism can be established neither by revolution nor by decree. The years 1989 and after have so far shown that neither can a capitalist market economy be introduced by decree alone', write the Agenda group from Vienna (Kregeé et al. 1992: 109). The developments in eastern Europe and the CIS have thrown into relief the problem of what kind of political economy the labour movement(s) of the world would wish to have. Placed again on the agenda is the need for unions to initiate change and to undertake their own interventions in economic development, rather than be passive economic subjects. As memories of 1989 fade, it is difficult not to agree with Rupez's conclusion that the various unions seeking to find a foot in the post-communist world are 'ideologically split, disconnected and possess no definite political programme' (Rupez 1993: 38). However, the dilemma facing trade unionists in eastern Europe and the CIS is not peculiar to their region. It is the problem of the working class in every part of the world on the eve of the twenty-first century.

Notes

1   Report of ICFTU Mission to Croatia and Slovenia 3–6 December 1992.
2   R. Nenov, Podkrepa, Autumn 1992.
3   Sotsprof statement, E-Mail, 25 June 1993.
4   Union of Auto and Agricultural Implement Workers, Belarus, Resolution, 9 June 1993, Protocol No. 32/21.

References

Burawoy, M. and Krotov, P. 1993: The economic basis of Russia's political crisis. *New Left Review*, 198, March, 49–69.

Clarke, S. 1992: Privatization and the development of capitalism in Russia. *New Left Review*, 196, November, 3–27.

European Trade Union Institute (ETUI) 1993: *Social Aspects of the Assistance Programmes to Central and Eastern Europe and the CIS*. Brussels: ETUI.

Field, G. 1992: The market: soul of Russian redemption. *New Politics*, 12, Winter, 50–60.

Hoffer, F. 1993: *Conditions for Development and Prospects for Trade Unions in Russia*. Bonn: Friedrich Ebert Stiftung.

International Chemical and Energy Workers Federation (ICEF) 1993: *ICEF Info*, 1, Brussels.

International Confederation of Free Trade Unions (ICFTU) 1993: *Free Labour World*, July, Brussels.

International Federation of Building and Woodworkers (IFBWW) 1993: *IFBWW Bulletin*, April, Geneva, 1993.

International Labour Organisation (ILO) 1993: *Central and East European Team Newsletter*, 2, Budapest.

Kilmister, A. 1993: Political change in eastern Europe. *Labour Focus on Eastern Europe*, 44, 47–8.

Kloc, K. 1993: Industrial conflicts in Poland 1991–1992. *Labour Focus on Eastern Europe*, 36, 35–40.

Kregreé, J., Matzner, E. and Grabher, G. (eds) 1992: *The Market Shock: an agenda for the economic and social reconstruction of central and eastern Europe*. Vienna: Austrian Academy of Sciences.

MacShane, D. 1981: *Solidarity – Poland's independent union*. Nottingham: Spokesman.

Organization for Economic Development and Cooperation (OECD) 1992: *Economic Outlook*, Paris.

Plant, R. 1993: Labour standards and structural adjustment in Hungary. Occasional Paper 7, Interdepartmental Project on Structural Adjustment. Geneva: ILO.

Popov, G. 1990: The dangers of democracy. *New York Review of Books*, 16 August.

Rupez, V. 1993: Privatization in Russia: the position of the trade unions. *Russian Labour Review*, 1, 38–44.

Schneider, E. 1993: Gewerkschaften und Arbeitsbeziehungen in Russland, der Ukraine and Belarus. *Osteuropa*, 4/5, 473–80.

Seideneck, P. 1993: Vertiefung oder Erweiterung? Zu aktuellen Problemen der europäischen Gewerkschaftpolitik. *Gewerkshaftliche Monatshefte*, 9, September, 532–52.

Tapiola, K. 1992: *Trade Unions in Central and Eastern Europe*. Helsinki: Finnish Trade Union Confederation.

United Nations Conference on Trade and Development (UNCTAD), 1993: *Trade and Development Report*. Geneva.

14

Post-Communism and the Emergence of Industrial Relations in the Workplace

Simon Clarke and Peter Fairbrother

This chapter is concerned with the character and direction of changes in the system of workplace industrial relations which have followed the collapse of the Soviet system. It draws primarily on the Russian case, though emphasizing those aspects which have a wider application.[1]

The first section summarizes the role of trade unions and the form of industrial relations in the former Soviet system. In the second section we examine the growth of industrial conflict and the rise of the independent workers' movement in Russia between 1987 and 1991. The third section looks more closely at enterprise paternalism and 'social partnership' in the transition to the market economy, as the basis for an examination of the development of tripartism and collective agreements in the fourth section. In the fifth section we explore the limits of paternalism, followed in the sixth and seventh sections with a consideration of new patterns of workplace industrial relations, looking on the one hand at the attempts of trade unions to develop effective forms of collective bargaining, negotiation and conciliation, and on the other hand at managerial initiatives to transform labour relations by replacing collectivism with individual contracts. The argument is then drawn together in the final section noting developments elsewhere, across the former Soviet bloc, and concluding that workplace trade unionism remains central to change.

The disintegration of the administrative-command system, the collapse of the communist party, the transition to a market economy and large-scale privatization have led to profound changes in the external economic and political environment within which enterprises operate, and in the rhetoric of the former official trade union movement. Such external changes undoubtedly have a major impact on trade union organization and industrial relations in the workplace. Unfortunately, however, there has been very little research on this crucial aspect of the transition, just as there had been very little opportunity to conduct workplace studies under the old regime.[2] The collapse of the old order has created new opportunities to carry out workplace research, and has opened up access to western researchers for the first time.

Although we should expect similar patterns of development to mark the whole of the former Soviet bloc, the absence of data makes it difficult to draw firm comparative conclusions. Most of the direct evidence from other countries is limited to journalistic reports, with a few case studies based on short field trips. There is also a certain amount of impressionistic and indirect evidence based on hearsay or interpellation from various kinds of survey data, much of which is dubious on methodological and/or substantive grounds. This more superficial evidence tends to focus on the new rhetoric of the trade union leadership, and so gives an exaggerated impression of the extent and pace of change. Our own view is that although change has gone further in most of eastern Europe than in Russia, similar patterns of change can be identified, to different degrees and at different rates, throughout the former Soviet bloc, with changes within the enterprise being much slower and less dramatic than changes in the external environment. The most radical changes in workplace industrial relations in eastern Europe are associated with new investment, particularly by foreign companies and joint ventures, which is almost non-existent in Russia.[3]

Trade Unions and Industrial Relations in the Soviet System

The distinctive character of trade unionism in the Soviet system was most evident in the workplace, where the primary role of the union was not to represent its members but support to management in the drive to increase productivity, while monitoring and implementing the social and welfare policies of the communist party. Industrial relations, meanwhile, were handled informally through managerial structures, with conflict displaced and diffused through the system as a whole.

The trade unions, as the 'transmission belt' between the communist party and the masses, were constructed on strictly hierarchical lines and subordinated at every level to the communist party. Since the unions represented the interests of the working class as a whole, as against sectional interests, the principle of occupational unionism was rejected in favour of industrial unionism, with all those working in a particular branch of production being members of the same union.

Under Stalin the unions were moribund, although they acquired a progressively more important role as the regime sought to provide material and moral incentives to stimulate the growth of productivity, in place of purely repressive forms of control of labour. The primary role of the trade unions in promoting productivity, for example through socialist competition, never succeeded in mobilizing more than the core of party and union activists and was regarded with scorn by the majority of workers. In practice their main function was the distribution of social and welfare benefits, including the allocation of places in vacation centres and sanatoria, kindergartens and pioneer camps, the allocation of housing, and the administration of the bulk of the state social security system.

In the words of the present deputy director of the official Russian trade union federation (FNPR), the unions were 'not trade unions at all, but the social and welfare department of the central committee of the CPSU [Communist Party of the Soviet Union]'. Within the enterprise the trade union was universally identified with the communist party and the enterprise administration, performing its welfare and distributive functions to provide a paternalistic reinforcement of their authority.

Soviet trade unions collaborated with the enterprise administration in preparing social development plans, and signed annual collective agreements with the administration. However, their role was at best an advisory one, and more often was merely to rubber-stamp proposals drawn up unilaterally by the administration. Trade unions also had a nominal obligation to defend the considerable legal rights of workers in the face of management violation in such areas as health and safety, disciplinary violations, dismissal, illegal overtime working, and underpayment of wages and bonuses. The union had to approve any revision of norms, and no worker could be dismissed without the approval of the union. However, in practice grievance procedures were rarely used and it was very rare for the union to do anything but endorse management decisions.

Industrial relations were handled not by the trade unions, but through the management structures. Wage payments were nominally determined according to a piece-rate system, in which wage rates and norms were determined by centrally defined scales. From the 1970s there was a rapid shift from individual piecework to the brigade system of payment which was based on a collective piece-rate. Although the allocation of individual payments was nominally in the hands of the brigade itself, this led to so much conflict within brigades that an equal distribution of wages became almost universal. In practice line managers had a certain amount of discretion in the grading of workers and payment of bonuses, and a great deal of discretion in the allocation of tasks, which they would use to negotiate informally with individual workers to ensure that their shop or section met its plan targets. However, the endemic labour shortage and the extremely uneven rhythm of work meant that the wages system played little role in motivating workers, who were eventually guaranteed a regular wage more or less regardless of performance, provided that the shop met its plan targets. The piece-rate system was in practice a discretionary payment system, through which individual workers could be penalized or favoured, though it could not be used to regulate the collective effort.

Conflict at shop level was endemic, and centred on such issues as the calculation of wages and bonuses, the allocation of overtime, work allocation, the provision of supplies of parts and raw materials, disciplinary infractions, and the distribution of social and welfare benefits. However, in the absence of any means of collective expression of workers' grievances, conflicts were handled on an individual and discretionary basis by foremen and line managers, normally at the level of the primary work group, and it was very rare for conflicts to be referred beyond the level of the shop. Informal bargaining at the level of the primary work group was normal, although it was confined within strict limits, which varied considerably from one enterprise, and even from one shop, to another. Overt conflict was minimized and any attempt on the part of workers to organize independently was ruthlessly suppressed.

Short work stoppages were not uncommon under the old system, but would usually involve only a handful of workers, and would be rigorously hushed up for fear of repercussions from above. Only rarely would a stoppage involve a whole shop, and quite exceptionally a whole factory. In the event of a work stoppage (usually called a 'meeting' before 1987), senior managers and/or party officials would arrive at once, reassure the workers, and meet their demands immediately. Worker activists might be tolerated if they kept within the limits of the system and retained the confidence of their fellow-workers, although they could be ruthlessly victimized if they overstepped the bounds (Lampert 1985; McAuley 1969).

The main reason for the very low level of overt conflict was the fact that the Soviet system of production was not marked by any clear lines of class division, so that conflict tended to be displaced and diffused. The enterprise director represented the interests of the enterprise as a whole in the battle for the plan, the shop chief represented the interests of the shop in the division of enterprise resources, and the foreman and brigadier represented the interests of the primary work group in the allocation of work and wages.

Line managers would press workers' interests by reference not to the workers' demands, but to such 'scientific' indicators of morale as levels of turnover and absenteeism or plan non-fulfilment, backed up by reports from the trade union and party secretaries, which gave the line manager some protection against allegations that the failings derived from his or her own incompetence. Thus conflict between managers and workers tended to be displaced into the struggle for resources within the administrative-command system as a whole. Workers appealed to their managers to solve individual problems, looked to their managers to represent them collectively, and attributed their relative well-being to the personal qualities of their managers. Surveys regularly showed that while workers expressed very low levels of confidence in their trade unions, they had very high levels of confidence in their line managers.

The displacement and diffusion of conflict was also linked to the marked divisions within the working class. The competition for resources set workers of different brigades, shops and enterprises against one another. The Soviet working class was clearly differentiated along a number of different dimensions, although both Soviet and Western literature has largely underplayed these divisions. The occupational divisions between mental and manual workers and between (skilled) production and (unskilled) auxiliary workers, were and are much sharper in Soviet enterprises than in the West, and these divisions were systematically exploited to fragment and to maintain control over the working class in both the workplace and the wider society.

Relative pay and working conditions were important means of reinforcing these divisions. Although workers were well paid compared with the lower levels of management and intelligentsia, the latter enjoyed superior working conditions, status and power. While the intelligentsia resented the higher wages of manual workers, the latter regarded the intelligentsia as unproductive lackeys of the ruling stratum. Among the workers, egalitarianism, or 'levelling', was a means by which the allegiance of the mass of auxiliary and unskilled workers was secured, to balance the potential power enjoyed by the skilled workers as a result of their control over production. These occupational divisions were cross-cut by age and gender divisions, and by moral and political evaluations of individuals, resulting in a complex status and occupational hierarchy in the workplace in which personal qualities could play a decisive role.

There was also a clear hierarchy between enterprises, with those in the military-industrial complex paying substantially higher wages and offering markedly better working conditions than consumer industries and the service sector (the military-industrial complex is much wider than the defence sector, producing a large proportion of consumer durables and electrical and electronic goods, for example). A marked differentiation of the labour force within and between enterprises gave line managers an important lever of control: light industry and the service sector provided a 'reserve army of labour' for the military-industrial complex, and auxiliary services provided an 'internal reserve army' for the core production workers (Clarke et al. 1993: chapter 1).

Ideologically the system was wrappped up in a rhetoric which became increasingly paternalistic as standards of living gradually rose and as the enterprise provided its workers with a growing range of social and welfare benefits and scarce consumption goods. The distribution of such goods and benefits provided a very powerful lever of management control at all levels. Although this control was exercised primarily through the trade union, it was also a means of controlling the union. Management could, and did, immediately penalize any display of independence on the part of trade union officials by withdrawing goods and benefits from the appropriate shop or section. This sanction became increasingly important during the disintegration of the economy from 1989, for the enterprise often became the primary source of basic subsistence goods, acquired through barter.

The Growth of Industrial Conflict and Independent Workers' Organization

The first independent workers' organizations developed during 1987, in response to Gorbachev's attempt to mobilize shop-floor pressure in support of 'perestroika from below'. The first strikes were organized by small groups of activists at shop level over wages and working conditions. The early independent workers' organizations developing out of such conflicts were typically led by long-standing activists, with primarily political motives, many of whom had been released from prison or psychiatric hospital in the 1987 amnesty.

The independent workers' movement made only limited progress between 1987 and 1989, and strikes remained sporadic, small-scale, and were usually settled rapidly with the workers winning their demands, helped in the case of skilled workers, who were the most active, by the labour shortages which had been intensified by the growth of the co-operative sector.

Independent workers' organization grew more rapidly in response to the political polarization during 1989, as both 'democrats' and 'conservatives' sought to mobilize support among workers. Local democratic groups were formed to contest the elections of 1989 in most cities, and looked to workers for support. The United Workers Front (OFT), with its roots in the conservative elements of the trade union and communist party industrial apparatus, was formed to mobilize workers in opposition to the 'democrats'.

The most rapid and dramatic development of the workers' movement was in response to the miners' strikes of the summer of 1989, when workers' committees were set up in many enterprises, and in the coal-mining regions at city and regional level. The miners had broken through a fundamental barrier, by showing that it was possible for workers to achieve their aims by organizing independently and taking strike action, so the victory of the miners gave courage to activists everywhere. In the coal-mining regions the activists initially adopted the strategy of taking over the official structures. However, it had become clear by the spring of 1990 that this strategy was having little success, and in the autumn of 1990 the miners set up their own Independent Miners' Union (NPG).

The independent workers' movement grew in strength between 1989 and 1991, although it owed its position more to political patronage than to the development of an organizational base within the enterprise. The NPG and miners' Workers' Committees had close links with the democratic movement, and with the Interregional Group of People's Deputies, which gave them political protection and material resources. Sotsprof, which had been formed as the Association of Socialist Trade Unions in 1989, initially enjoyed the tacit protection of official structures, and then became closely linked to the Social Democratic Party, with which it signed an agreement, and to Gavril Popov, the Mayor of Moscow; Moscow City Council provided it with facilities. A number of other independent trade union federations were primarily commercial organizations, enjoying the tax advantages accorded to trade unions.

At the level of the enterprise, even in the coal mines, the official union remained dominant, using its powers of patronage to exclude competing organizations. Independent workers' organization remained very small, usually confined to one or two shops. They had only very loose connections with any wider organizations, which were mainly important in providing legal services and political contacts. Independent organization was kept weak by management's strategy of immediate concession to workers' economic demands and victimization of independent activists. It was only where activists enjoyed strong support from workers and the patronage of locally powerful political structures, or support from a faction of the enterprise administration, that they were able to survive. In every case of conflict between the official trade union and enterprise director which we have been able to examine, the union turned out to be representing an opposition faction in management. This has been a common finding throughout eastern Europe (compare Tóth 1993a: 2; 1993b: 52).

Enterprise Paternalism in the Transition to the Market Economy

The collapse of the administrative-command system was associated with a steady increase in the independence of enterprise management from higher authorities, although at the same time it deprived the enterprise director of the external support which had protected him (occasionally her) from internal challenges to his autocratic power. The removal of the communist party in the wake of the coup and counter-coup of August 1991 made it clear that the collapse of the old system was irreversible, while the liberalization of prices at the beginning of 1992 was intended to subject enterprises to the discipline of the market. However, these dramatic economic and political changes were not at first matched by marked changes in workplace industrial relations. Indeed the initial tendency was if anything towards a strengthening of the traditional system of paternalism, with the enterprise taking over what had formerly been the responsibilities of the state.

The principal reason for the attempt to strengthen traditional relationships was the relative insecurity of enterprise directors. Once their external supports had been removed, it became essential to strengthen the internal basis of their power by reinforcing the traditional paternalistic structures.

The immediate response of enterprise directors to the collapse of the administrative-command system was to present themselves as the representatives of the 'labour collective', attempting to exploit commercial opportunities, make political representations on behalf of the work-force, and legitimate their autocratic rule on the basis of the benefits provided for the workers. These benefits did not take the form of higher wages as much as the distribution of a growing range of goods and benefits, on the one hand, and the promise of security of employment, on the other. Until the liberalization of prices at the beginning of 1992, wages in private companies were typically three times those paid by state enterprises.

Although the growth of the private sector and the breakdown of wage controls meant that the labour market became increasingly competitive, state enterprises could not immediately compete with the private sector in the payment of monetary wages; instead they sought to recruit and retain labour on the basis of the paternalistic system of distribution. This development was reinforced by inflation and growing shortages, which meant that workers increasingly looked to such distribution to meet even their basic subsistence needs. In the latter half of 1991 workers were already moving back towards the security of the state enterprise, a movement which accelerated with the destabilizing impact of 'shock therapy'. In order to meet their workers' needs, enterprises sought to acquire consumer and subsistence goods by barter. Large industrial enterprises even purchased collective farms, construction companies, and food-processing, clothing and footwear companies in order to guarantee such supplies.

In the face of the disintegration of the economy, from late 1991 directors claimed that their principal priority was 'to preserve the labour collective', and declared that they would do all in their power to avoid mass lay-offs. The main priority of the economic strategy of every enterprise was to acquire sufficient cash to meet the wage bill. When there was not enough work to keep the labour force fully employed, workers were redirected to supplementary work, doing cleaning or maintenance and repair at reduced wages, put on short-time working, or sent on 'administrative vacation'. This gave rise to frequent disputes over the distribution of work and levels of payment for short-time, vacation and supplementary work. Lay-offs, meanwhile, were largely confined to 'peripheral' workers (that is, workers over pension age, workers with a poor disciplinary record, and predominantly female clerical and administrative workers), and trouble-makers.

Although management had largely lost the support of outside political bodies and repressive agencies in preventing the workers from organizing independently, this was compensated by the workers' growing fear of unemployment and economic insecurity in the face of high inflation, as well as by their increased dependence on goods and benefits distributed through the enterprise. Since the beginning of 1992, management has also shown itself increasingly willing to make use of Gorbachev's 1989 strike law, which banned strikes in strategic sectors and laid out a procedural obstacle course which had to be negotiated for strikes to be legal elsewhere, although it had hitherto been largely ignored. Meanwhile managers did their best to avoid confrontation by responding to workers' grievances within the limits of the existing system.

The attempt to preserve the internal power relations of the enterprise by no means precludes quite radical change in external relations and even in management structures. Even the more conservative enterprises have shown themselves to be very courageous in seeking new markets and developing new products with existing resources of technology and labour. However, such adaptation has not been driven by any long-term economic logic but by the need to have goods to barter and to generate a cash income to pay wages. Thus it typically entails small batch production using quite inappropriate labour, raw materials and means of production.

There has been a strong tendency to the devolution of responsibility to the level of the component plants and shops of the enterprise, shops often being made into self-financing units, with shop chiefs being given responsibility to find new markets, secure sources of supply and even to collect enterprise debt. In many enterprises even ordinary workers are offered a commission to secure orders, and in some cases have been given their own products to sell in local markets in lieu of wages. This has not been so much a positive strategy of decentraliz-ation to encourage flexible adaptation to market opportunities, as an attempt on the part of senior management to shuffle off some of the responsibility for ensuring the survival of the enterprise. Such frag-mentation was a very effective way of deflecting attacks on senior management by opening up the divisions between workers of differ-ent shops, although it carried the risk that successful plants and shops would try to break away and form independent enterprises in their own right.

Paternalism, Tripartism and Collective Agreements

The reconstitution of the traditional system of state paternalism on the basis of the enterprise was represented ideologically in the rhetoric of 'social partnership', which was associated with an increased promi-nence for the annual collective agreement within a framework of tripartism. However, tripartism was meaningless when the three par-ties were not clearly distinct. The overwhelming majority of enter-prises remained in state ownership, while the trade unions remained representatives of management, not of the workers. The Tripartite Commission, established by the government at the end of 1991, was effectively a forum in which the enterprise directorate, represented by the official trade unions, negotiated with the government over social and wages policies.

To the extent that enterprises were able to insulate the internal social relations of the enterprise from the impact of external changes, the traditional system of industrial relations was reproduced almost unchanged. The old scales of norms, wages and staffing were retained, and informal shop-floor negotiation continued to take place within the framework of managerial autocracy and within the limits of the wage fund. Production organization similarly changed little; shops and brigades still worked to weekly and monthly plan targets, now determined by the marketing and commercial departments on the basis of contracted deliveries and/or a judgement of future demand. Most enterprises retained the traditional system of collective piece-rates, with plan fulfilment bonuses and penalties for under-ful-filment. Industrial conflict was still handled primarily through the management structure, although line managers more readily referred disputes 'upstairs' than in the past.

Enterprise managers sought to maintain the subservience of the official union,[4] and to suppress any attempts at independent workers' organization, using the traditional methods of repression alongside the paternalistic rhetoric of conciliation. Management tried to show its concern by 'going to the people', visiting shops, holding meetings, providing channels of worker representation and drawing active workers into various commissions, replacing party structures (and the use of sociologists), which had previously been the principal means of assimilating active workers and the principal source of information on workers' attitudes.

There was some evolution during 1992 in the role of the trade union within the enterprise. First, the trade union was ill-adapted to the handling of issues in which there was potential for conflict. For this reason there was a tendency to create *ad hoc* commissions, or to reactivate the Labour Collective Council (STK), as a forum for resolving such matters as pay, levels of employment, and privatization. Second, from the autumn of 1992 there was a clear tendency for management to take over some of the union's welfare and distribution functions, often by simply absorbing union personnel into its own apparatus, leaving the union as an empty shell. Management's motive seems to have been the desire to take credit for the benefits provided through the union, giving more substance to its rhetoric of 'social partnership'. However, it deprives management of one of the most important levers of control over the union, making it easier for radicals to take control in the event of serious conflict. Third, on the other hand, management attempted in some cases to transfer responsibility for some of its more unpopular decisions (for example, over short-time working and lay-offs) to the union, although more typically management tended to delegate such responsibility to shop level.

One of the few changes in the legal framework of industrial relations in 1992 gave legally constituted trade unions the right to propose draft collective agreements, which would be presented for the approval of the labour collective. However, in the overwhelming majority of enterprises both union and management rejected the adversarial implications of collective bargaining contained in the legislation. They held instead to the traditional process whereby a commission of the enterprise, comprising representatives of the appropriate specialist management departments, including the trade union, would insert new sets of figures into the previous year's collective agreement. Ratification of the agreement by the director and trade union president was then a formality.

The collective agreement is in theory legally binding on management, although in the past it has included few substantive commitments of any significance, and it has been rare for there to be any effective monitoring of its implementation. With the disintegration of the administrative-command system the agreement became more important, because commitments on such matters as wages, employment and levels of social and welfare expenditure, which had previously been a part of the framework of central planning, were now commitments made by the enterprise management itself. In the conditions of extreme economic instability in 1992 the management of a high proportion of enterprises in Moscow did not sign collective agreements, on the grounds that they could not guarantee to implement them. Elsewhere, where agreements were reached, they continued to be violated and revoked by management with impunity, and the trade union remained subordinate to management. The rhetoric of 'social partnership' was no more consistent with independent forms of workers' organization than had been the rhetoric of 'socialism' before it.

In 1992 sectoral 'tariff agreements' were established in a number of industries, providing the framework within which wages were determined at enterprise level. The precedent for such tariff agreements was set by the agreement which settled the 1989 miners' strike, although in practice the first effective agreements were those introduced in aviation, education, and health in 1992, under the Law on Collective Agreements passed in March. These tariff agreements link new pay scales, which typically increase differentials in favour of higher grade workers, to industry coefficients which usually tie the scale to the legal minimum wage, a pattern which is sometimes reproduced in collective agreements at the enterprise level (this gives the minimum wage a pivotal significance in the determination of wage scales, and in the inflationary process). However, although the government has signed all these tariff agreements, it has not committed itself to providing resources to meet the implied levels of wages, so that in practice the provisions of the tariff agreements have been ignored by individual employers, with wages continuing to be determined at enterprise level.

From the end of 1991 the removal of wage controls and the escalation of inflation made it possible and necessary for enterprises to adjust pay to provide some compensation for inflation. Although such increases were formally based on agreement with the trade union, in practice the initiative always came from the enterprise's department of labour and wages, not least because the union did not have its own apparatus to provide it with the information and expertise to negotiate over wages. Thus the union continued to play a minimal role in the determination of pay scales, and most trade union officials did not even regard wages as falling within their area of responsibility. Thus pay scales and norms were generally set unilaterally by the enterprise administration, nominally on the basis of a comparison with wages paid by comparable employers and/or the official minimum wage, though in reality on the basis of labour shortages, levels of social tension and industrial conflict, and the resources available to the enterprise. Meanwhile, actual wages continued to be determined by informal shop-floor bargaining within the limits of the wage fund available to the shop chief.

Statistics on wages are completely unreliable, primarily because the system of payments is so complex, and because workers receive so many benefits in kind. However, during 1990 and 1991, regular and repeated observations confirmed that many workers in the private sector were receiving wages three times those of workers in comparable state enterprises. After the liberalization of prices in January 1992 these differentials were rapidly eroded, to be replaced with differentials between regions and branches of production which grew to the most extraordinary levels; a tenfold difference in average wage between different branches of production was not atypical, and even local enterprises in the same branch of production often paid wages which differed by a factor of two.

The general assumption has been that these pay differentials were a reflection of the monopoly power of enterprises, particularly in the energy sector, which were willing to meet pay demands because they were able to pass on increases in the form of higher prices. However, the evidence would suggest that it is primarily labour market factors which are pushing up wages in particular branches of production and particular regions. Although up to half the labour force was on short-time or temporarily laid off in the first half of 1993, there were still acute labour shortages, particularly in the strategic energy and mining industries located in the more remote and inhospitable regions, and in Moscow, where there are so many other opportunities to make money. According to this interpretation, the very high wage differentials required to induce labour mobility would be an index of the relative immobility of labour resulting from the system of paternalistic distribution which ties the worker to the enterprise, reinforced by the premium placed by workers on security in a period of instability.

The coexistence of labour shortages with massive overstaffing, covered by short-time working and temporary lay-offs, is not a paradox, but a characteristic feature of the Soviet system of production, in which chronic labour shortage always coexisted with the enormous 'internal reserve army' of auxiliary workers carrying out unmechanized manual labour and unproductive clerical work. The shortage has been one of skilled and motivated workers, who could be trusted to handle expensive plant and equipment and show the initiative necessary to maintain production and meet plan targets. The economic changes associated with the collapse of the military-industrial complex have led to a substantial increase in the relative shortage of such *kadrovye* ('cadre') workers as the private sector, and formerly underprivileged branches of production, compete for their services. Thus, although 700,000 workers left the engineering industry in 1992 (7 per cent of the industry's labour force), there were over 36,000 vacancies in engineering at the end of the year (*Trud* 21 May 1993). Large wage differentials are therefore also an index of the rapid restructuring of the labour force, as *kadrovye* workers move out of declining industries into occupations which, at least currently, are able to pay substantially higher wages.

Although enterprise managers showed themselves to be extremely flexible and imaginative in responding to the challenges and opportunities presented by the transition to the market economy, they exploited such opportunities primarily to maintain the internal power structure of the enterprise, and this defined both the form and the limits of change. The transition to the market economy initially proved no more subversive of the traditional social relations of production and forms of industrial relations than had the rise of the independent workers' movement, as the system of state paternalism was transformed into a system of enterprise paternalism. However, although there appeared at first to be little change at the level of the enterprise, the transformation of paternalism to an enterprise basis had removed the system of redistribution between enterprises which had been the stabilizing element of the old system. The success or failure of an enterprise was now determined by the fickle judgement of the market, leading to a differentiation of enterprises, according to their success or failure, which in either case made it increasingly difficult for paternalism to be sustained.

The Limits of Paternalism

The ability of the enterprise to maintain a paternalistic strategy depends primarily on its economic success, which may be a result of commercial activity or of political connections. The more successful enterprises were able to offer high wages, a good supply of subsidized food and consumer goods, and extensive social and welfare benefits. Those which were less successful struggled merely to maintain their commitment to protecting employment and avoiding lay-offs. However, paternalism proved difficult to sustain for both the most and the least successful enterprises.

In order to understand the possibilities and limits of change in workplace industrial relations, it is important to clarify the character of Soviet paternalism. Some have seen it as the expression of a kind of 'social contract' between the working class and the ruling stratum, in which the working class passively accepted its exclusion from power in exchange for the security of guaranteed employment and the gradual improvement in living standards (Ruble 1981; Hauslohner 1987). However, this is misleading: Soviet paternalism was not based on an exchange relationship, but was fundamentally a means of fragmenting the working class in order to subordinate the mass of the population to a hierarchical system of autocratic power (Conquest 1967; Schapiro and Godson 1981). Thus the preservation of the system of paternalism by enterprise management should not be seen as a response to the aspirations and anxieties of the working class, but as an attempt to preserve the existing structures of power. Thus the most paternalistic enterprises are simultaneously the most authoritarian.

The benefits that accrued to the working class from paternalism were distributed primarily through channels in the enterprise which linked entitlement and provision to pervasive systems of monitoring, inspection, regulation and control. The system of administrative distribution was, as we have seen, an essential means of maintaining the dependence of the worker on the enterprise through access to benefits in kind as well as money wages. The discretionary allocation of such benefits provided a powerful instrument of disciplinary control within a particular enterprise, and was an important aspect of the hierarchical structuring of the labour force within and between enterprises. Thus far from being the basis of a social contract with the working class, the system of distribution, allied to the autocratic structure of power, was a powerful means of individualizing workers and deterring collective responses to the crisis of the system.

The failure of paternalism

Workers certainly expect to be provided with benefits, and they judge their managers by their ability to exploit the system in order to deliver the goods. For this reason, if management is unable to deliver the benefits expected by the workers, the latter judge management to be a failure. The limits of paternalism therefore appear in the unsuccessful enterprise as the authority of management is gradually undermined.

It is striking that as managers lose authority they progressively abandon the attempt to manage. The pattern that we have observed is for labour discipline and productivity to decline and levels of conflict to increase, with frequent disputes and brief stoppages. However, dissatisfaction tends to be individualistic and conflict tends to be personalized and confined within the system. The *kadrovye* workers find jobs elsewhere, while others devote more time to secondary employment or to cultivating their allotments. Workers make demands not through the union or independent workers' organizations, but directly through or against their line managers, demanding that the foreman, shop chief, director or even the Russian president should solve their problems. Workers may throw out their shop chiefs or enterprise directors if the latter attempt to assert their authority, often to elect replacements who are known for complacency rather than dynamism. Meanwhile management raises prices in order to try to cover its escalating costs, only to find that sales dry up and production declines.

As the enterprise becomes less competitive, and both production and real wages fall, divisions begin to open up within management, between 'modernizers' and 'conservatives'. These two factions may each try to mobilize support within the work-force, exploiting divisions which are simultaneously opening up in the labour collective between mental and manual workers on the one hand, and between production and auxiliary workers on the other. This factional conflict may be expressed through existing organs of worker representation, such as the trade union or STK, which may be mobilized by either side.

In principle there is the basis for an alliance between core production workers and modernizing managers around a strategy of mass lay-offs of 'surplus' engineering and technical workers (ITR) and auxiliary workers to cut costs and to raise the wages of those who remain. Core production workers resent the burden of supporting a mass of unproductive workers and reject the egalitarian ideology of 'levelling', demanding that payment correspond to labour contribution. Many also support the reduction or commercialization of the welfare apparatus, partly because they would prefer to receive high enough wages to be able to choose to pay for higher standards of provision.

However, in practice such a reforming alliance tends to be very weak in the less successful enterprises. On the one hand, the potential losers would tend considerably to outnumber the winners, so that such a strategy could be pushed through only by authoritarian means in a situation in which management has lost its authority. On the other hand, in a situation of extreme economic and political instability there is no point in attempting a radical restructuring which would divide the labour collective, particularly when the government is pursuing an unstable and inconsistent economic policy, as the Russian government did during 1992–3. In the short term it makes much more sense for management to maintain internal unity and to look for external political support, and in the longer term, if that fails, to bail out.

The result is that unsuccessful enterprises tend to disintegration rather than transformation. Senior management tries to bring political pressure to bear on regional and national government to provide orders, subsidies and credit to enable the enterprise to survive, and may well encourage a degree of militancy on the part of the workforce, to the extent of strike action, to back up its political demands. Senior managers simultaneously prepare a bridgehead for themselves in commercial structures, often using the enterprise's resources in their own name, for which privatization provides unprecedented opportunities. Although pressure was building up to dangerous levels in many large enterprises in the military-industrial complex by the autumn of 1992, the government provided massive injections of credit, under the guise of conversion loans, which postponed the crisis.

Success and the limits of paternalism

While the paternalistic structures in many of the previously privileged enterprises of the military-industrial complex approached disintegration, many enterprises producing consumer and intermediate goods in relatively high demand were much better placed to maintain production and to provide barter goods and higher wages for their workers, especially if they were monopolists and/or had opportunities to export. The prospects of an enterprise were not determined by economic factors alone. Political connections, as well as the personality of the management team, were also important.

The successful enterprises tended to develop a strongly paternalistic management style, with a low level of overt conflict apart from small-scale and sporadic disputes over the distribution of consumer goods between different groups of workers. The union in such enterprises retained its traditional role as the agent of the administration, preoccupied with its distributional function. The paternalistic management style tended to preclude confrontation with the workers, so that there was very little fundamental restructuring of production, the main emphasis being on developing commercial and financial opportunities and diversifying production.

These more successful enterprises appeared to be locked in a virtuous circle, in which prosperity and paternalism are mutually reinforcing. However, in the most advanced enterprises we find that success created new opportunities and ambition generated new pressures for change. It was at this point that workers' deep resentment at the repressive form within which the system provided them with its meagre benefits tended to come to the fore. As goods and services became freely available on the market, workers began to demand their pay entirely in cash, so that they could buy goods and services of a better quality than those being offered through the enterprise. Skilled workers in particular demanded the opportunity to earn wages corresponding to their labour contributions.

The rejection by workers of authoritarian paternalism has coincided with the desire of managers of restructure the labour force in order to take advantage of new economic opportunities. This possibility was opened up for many enterprises by the transition to a market economy which had led to fundamental changes in the relative fortunes of enterprises in different branches of production. Enterprises which were able to sell in the market economy were able to pay much higher wages and to provide better benefits than the previously favoured military-industrial enterprises. This enabled them to attract more highly skilled and more experienced workers from the latter, transferring their existing workers to less-skilled work or encouraging them to leave on disciplinary grounds. This has left formerly privileged enterprises with acute labour shortages.

However, these changes in the composition of the labour force have not been accompanied by any more fundamental restructuring of the labour force within the enterprises. Traditional forms of labour recruitment remain. Managers routinely say that they would never choose to recruit workers from employment centres, 'because we would not know who they were'. Since 1990 enterprise directors have been announcing their intentions to lay off surplus workers. However, in practice lay-offs have been at most proportionate to the fall in production; in the two enterprises that we are studying which have carried out deep cuts in the labour force, managers were still estimating in the spring of 1993 that they could cut a further 40 per cent without loss of production, and were claiming that they would do so in the summer. The typical managerial estimate of the size of the labour 'surplus' is 40 per cent, in the sense of the proportion of workers which could be cut without loss of production. Managers in an average enterprise typically estimate that about 25 per cent of the labour force are reliable *kadrovye* workers, and this is the minimum level required to maintain production discipline.

The reluctance of successful enterprises to undertake any fundamental restructuring of the labour force suggests that 'surplus' workers do play an important role in maintaining managerial authority in the Soviet system, as argued above. A substantial restructuring would threaten to remove the foundations of managerial authority, fracturing any potential alliance between production workers and modernizing managers. Such an alliance is necessarily a shaky one in any case, given the interest of modernizing managers in appropriating a controlling stake in the enterprise, and production workers' continuing perception of managerial labour as unproductive.

This brings us back to the fundamental dilemma faced by managers. The economic pressures of the transition to the market economy dictate the transformation of the social relations of production if Russian enterprises are to have a chance of competing in world markets. However, managerially inspired attempts to restructure workplace industrial relations have aimed in the first instance primarily to strengthen managerial authority: there is no point in reducing potential costs if management loses control. This tendency has been strongly reinforced by economic instability, with enterprises very vulnerable to a loss of supplies or a sudden collapse of the market, however much they cut their costs.

Trade Unions and Collective Bargaining in the Transition to the Market Economy

In the last section we noted that the more highly paid workers have begun to reject the system of paternalism, and to demand cash wages according to their labour contribution, looking to the trade unions to represent them as wage labourers. This is the principal impetus underlying the development of independent trade unionism in Russia, which has emerged within a neo-liberal rhetoric to challenge the authoritarian paternalism of the existing system of industrial relations. This raises the possibility of the reform of the official unions, or the development of new independent unions, to provide the basis for the collective regulation of workplace industrial relations.

Official unions

In 1990, the official unions declared their independence of the communist party and the state, and the separation of their trade union from their political functions. However, the removal of their political functions left the official unions with only their role for welfare and distribution, and with the very considerable financial and property resources which had been allocated to them to fulfil this role. Following the collapse of the Soviet system, the main concern of the official unions has been to retain control of these resources, which they have frequently invested in various kinds of commercial activity. The dependence of the unions on state patronage to retain their privileged status considerably moderated their opposition to the Yeltsin government, enabling them to retain most of their property as well as control of the social insurance funds, although a minority faction pressed for a more active opposition.

At regional and sectoral levels the official unions were heavily involved in commercial activity, but were also active in promoting the development of planning structures linking the major industrial enterprises, and in pressing for state subsidies for industry on a regional and sectoral basis. The unions were the principal support for the employers' Union of Industrialists and Entrepreneurs, and the main promoters of the ideology of 'social partnership' embraced by Volsky. They were also integrated into the government's Tripartite Commission, whose main purpose was in effect to neutralize the official unions by incorporating their opposition into a bureaucratic state structure.

In our view there is little realistic prospect of a reform of the official unions. They have been largely discredited, and their activity within the enterprise is confined to welfare and distribution. Even these responsibilities of the union have been reduced since the middle of 1992, for many of the social and welfare functions of the enterprise have begun to be privatized and/or set on a commercial footing. An unpublished survey of presidents of enterprise trade union committees in the spring of 1993 found that 95 per cent considered themselves to be part of the senior management of the enterprise, and none believed that trade unionism had a future.

Although successive waves of worker activists have sought to reform the trade unions within the enterprise over the past six years, they have uniformly failed to do so, and have either been absorbed into the bureaucracy or have given up in despair or disgust. Since union powers and resources, apart from social insurance funds, derive from the administration, the administration has very close control over the activity of the union, and can simply withdraw resources from a recalcitrant union and encourage or compel workers to leave. For this reason directors prefer to keep the union, if only as an empty shell, for fear of what might take its place. The distribution of consumer goods through the enterprise has increased the scope for management control. Although we have met a handful of radical union officials, we have been unable to find a single case in which the official trade union has in practice opposed the management of the enterprise on behalf of the workers, rather than as representative of the communist party or of an oppositional faction in the administration (Tóth 1993b: 54 reports a similar impression in the case of Hungary).

Independent unionism

The alternative independent trade union federations remain very weak, with almost no rank-and-file base. Russian workers share the disillusion with unions common to other eastern European countries (MacShane's chapter 13 in this volume; Kloc 1993); the majority see no need for a trade union at all. Only a minority of workers who leave the official unions join alternative unions. The absence of such a base means that the independent unions continue to rely primarily on political support and commercial activity to maintain their existence. Nevertheless, new possibilities have been opened up by the aspirations of better-paid workers.

Since 1992 the independent unions have concentrated their efforts on negotiating industry-wide framework agreements and enterprise-level collective agreements. Independent workers' organizations were present in the commissions which drew up the first tariff agreements, in the mining and aviation industries, although the process was still dominated by the official unions and it proved difficult to enforce agreements at enterprise level.

Sotsprof launched a collective agreement campaign in 1992, following the example of the Sotsprof group in a military enterprise in Novosibirsk which had achieved an alternative collective agreement in 1991. The organization was successful in a handful of enterprises in which Sotsprof groups were able to mobilize support for their collective agreement, and on that basis to secure representation alongside the official union on the commission responsible for drawing up the agreement. Primary groups of the Independent Miners' Union also managed to include their demands in collective agreements in those mines in which they had an effective organization.

As elsewhere in the former Soviet bloc (for example, Tóth 1993b for Hungary), the independent unions have primarily organized the privileged skilled male workers, who have a high degree of independence at work. This raises the possibility of the development of an occupational unionism through which such groups of workers might consolidate their position as a labour aristocracy. However, there are serious barriers to such a development, particularly at the level of the enterprise, where it threatens to disrupt the established occupational and political hierarchy.

This is very clear in the aviation industry, which has been marked by a struggle between the air traffic controllers' union and the pilots' union. These unions both broke away from the official union and declared their independence. The attempt of the independent pilots to raise their relative pay and status has not challenged this hierarchy, since they had always constituted a privileged stratum, with a career structure closely integrated with that of management. The pilots' union soon reached a peaceful settlement of their demands, and began moves to reintegrate with the official union. The air traffic controllers, although highly skilled, did not enjoy any such privilege. Their attempt to improve their position with threats of militant industrial action was treated as a fundamental threat to the industry, and was crushed by management and the Russian government in the wake of two strikes in August and December 1992 (Borisov et al. 1993).

More generally it has proved as difficult to establish independent unionism in the workplace as to transform the official unions, for management reactions to challenges to its authority serve to reinforce the social relations of authoritarian paternalism. Management has shown itself determined to prevent the emergence of independent organization, and has sought to neutralize initiatives by a judicious combination of conciliation and repression. Most primary groups of the independent unions are not able to establish a permanent organization, or recruit an adequate number of members, although they can enjoy wider support on occasion. Where independent unions have been able to establish an effective organization, most notably the pilots and the Independent Miners' Union, this has only been by abandoning their militancy and accommodating to the hierarchical structure of paternalistic authoritarianism, working closely with management and using their political contacts to represent the interests of their respective industries in Moscow.

To sum up, the official trade unions at enterprise level have at best retained their traditional structure and functions, and at worst have been marginalized. Although independent workers' organizations have proliferated, they remain very small, are subject to severe management pressure, and do not play any significant role in industrial relations, which continue to be handled through management structures. It is very unlikely that the official union will provide an effective channel for workers' grievances, while independent unions remain very weak.

Privatization and the Transformation of Industrial Relations

The official trade unions have long argued that only after privatization can they become proper trade unions, because only then will they be confronted with an owner. Although privatization raises new issues, it does not in itself lead to fundamental changes in the social relations of production (Clarke 1992). However, following the collapse of the administrative-command system, management in the more successful enterprises has come to see paternalism as a barrier to its ambition to transform the enterprise to take advantage of market opportunities, and privatization as an element in a strategy allowing a more fundamental transformation of the enterprise. In this section we examine the possibility of such a transformation of the system from above.

The relationship between privatization and the imposition of managerial authority is complex, because those industrial enterprises already privatized have tended to be the most prosperous, with the most dynamic management, enjoying a high degree of authority usually based on a strong paternalist policy. Most of the first wave of privatizers had previously converted to a leasehold or co-operative form, which enabled them to raise wages, and privatization entailed the transfer of the majority of shares to the labour collective, sometimes in form of a closed shareholding company ('people's enterprise'). This does not mean that the workers have taken control of any of these enterprises, for Russian managers have a great deal of experience in manipulating representative bodies. However, it does mean that management has to have some concern for the workers' interests, particularly if there are divisions within management itself, and this in itself constitutes a barrier to the dismantling of paternalism.

Privatization of these enterprises has tended to be a two-stage process, the first based on the rhetoric of collective ownership and profit-sharing, and the second, beginning in 1992, consisting of the assertion of managerial authority and the transformation of the labour force into wage labourers.

Many enterprises used the promise of the dividends that would accrue with privatization as a means of holding down wages, and embraced the rhetoric of profit-sharing as the means of tying payment more closely to effort. However, this soon came into conflict with their other priorities. The attempt of management to concentrate shareholding in its own hands led it to play down the advantages of share ownership to induce workers to sell shares cheaply. This meant that shares soon came to be very unevenly distributed within the labour force, undermining the attempt to use share ownership as the basis for any kind of profit-sharing arrangement, since a growing proportion of workers had no shares. This in turn undermined attempts to restructure the labour force, since low wages meant that workers left for better-paid jobs elsewhere, or took early retirement though holding on to their shares. Low wages also made it difficult to recruit new workers. It therefore soon became apparent to such enterprises that they had to separate workers from shareholders (ideally by separating workers from their shares), and dividend policy from wages policy.

Once management has secured firm control of the enterprise through the election of the shareholders' council and board of directors, it becomes possible to try to move away from paternalism towards a system of wage labour. One element has been the formalization of the payments system, including the introduction of individual contracts. Such contracts were typical of small private enterprises, and began to be extended to privatized state enterprises during 1992. They would typically include a clear definition of the rights (few) and duties (many) of every worker. Rates of pay are related closely to duties, and include various kinds of incentive bonuses for loyalty, length of service, etc. Pay is defined individually by private negotiation between the worker and his or her immediate manager (compare a similar example from Czechoslovakia in Pollert and Hradecka 1994). Individual contracts were introduced for senior managers in the first instance, making it possible to increase their pay substantially without such increases being publicized, and then extended to ordinary workers.

A central demand of the independent trade unions has been the transfer to time wages, on the grounds that piece-work is divisive and leads to deterioration in quality and in safety standards. The demand for a guaranteed basic wage became increasingly popular as wages fell with the collapse of production in 1992. Although a few enterprises moved to such a guaranteed basic wage with production-related bonuses, however, in the two of which we have detailed knowledge this seriously undermined the authority of shop chiefs and foremen, who complained of a sharp fall in labour discipline, and the enterprise soon reverted to a piece-work system.

Although the introduction of individual contracts is only at an early stage, the attempt to extend the contract system to the shop-floor has created the potential for serious conflict, primarily because it removes the discretion of the shop chief and the foreman in using the payment system as the means of motivating and controlling the labour force. Senior management's attempt to dismantle paternalism at enterprise level, and to impose its authority on the shop-floor with a formalized payment system, comes into conflict with the continued existence of paternalistic forms of control at shop-floor level. The immediate result is that shop chiefs and foremen collude with workers in undermining the new system in order to preserve the traditional forms of informal regulation.

The attempt to strengthen managerial authority in privatized enterprises has not been conspicuously successful for a number of reasons. Workers' antagonism has been aroused by management attempts to widen pay differentials and concentrate share ownership in their own hands. This antagonism has been compounded by the secrecy surrounding privatization, leading to wild rumours about the dealings of senior management, and by the restructuring of senior management, which means, for example, that the enterprise director is rarely seen on the shop-floor. This practical rejection of collectivism and paternalism on the part of senior management became more marked in the course of 1992 as even the more prosperous privatized enterprises had to lay off workers and hold wage increases below the rate of inflation.

Although social tension in these more dynamic enterprises grew in 1992 and 1993, this was not usually expressed in direct conflict between workers and managers, but more commonly in conflict within management, between those who favoured a radical strategy of transition to capitalism and those who favoured the retention of traditional paternalistic enterprise relations. Growing social tension was shifting the internal balance of power in favour of the latter. This division was partly within the ranks of specialists, between those whose power was enhanced by the new system, and those whose functions were becoming redundant. However, much more significant was the division that opened up between senior specialists and line management, and above all the shop chiefs, who were pivotal in translating the plans of senior management into reality by securing the necessary supplies and inducing the workers to meet production targets.

The shop chief was at the focal point of a growing contradiction between the old Soviet and the new proto-capitalist systems. The power and status of shop chiefs within the enterprise was being eroded, at the same time as their responsibilities were sharply increasing. Shop chiefs were being required to increase productivity, to develop new products and new methods of production, without being given the financial or material means to enable them to induce the workers to achieve those tasks. They were then expected to resolve the industrial conflicts that arose, and take the blame if they escalated out of control.

Shop chiefs traditionally faced both ways within the Soviet system. Although as agents of managerial control they were responsible for delivering the plan, as paternalistic representatives of their shop they were expected to fight for a realizable plan and the resources to implement it. As the shop chiefs come under growing pressure from above and below, the question of where their fundamental loyalties lie becomes critical. When it comes to the crunch the shop chief has little choice except to defend his or her workers against unrealizable demands from senior management, and to represent their aspirations for job security and a minimum standard of living. This is why the main barrier to the dismantling of the paternalistic system from above comes not directly from workers' resistance, but from the resistance of line managers, which then alters the balance of forces within the managerial corpus as a whole (Soulsby and Clark 1993: 21 report the same response of shop chiefs in two enterprises in the Czech Republic).

Conclusion

It is our impression that the tendencies observed in Russia are general throughout the former Soviet bloc (compare Thirkell et al. 1993), the main difference being that the forces of change are stronger and the process more advanced in eastern Europe than in Russia (and more advanced in Russia than in countries such as the Ukraine and Kazakhstan). However, the transition from one form of social production to another is only at an early stage, even in a country such as Hungary, let alone the former Soviet Union. In general, changes in the political role and ideological rhetoric of trade unions, and in their staffing and organization at national level (Héthy and McShane in chapters 12 and 13 respectively of this volume), are much greater than changes in the workplace.

It should not be surprising to find a common pattern in developments throughout the former Soviet bloc. Although the countries of eastern Europe have their own traditions of independent labour organization to which to appeal, the old structures were systematically destroyed in the Soviet period and replaced with the distinctive forms of social organization and control which had been established in the Soviet Union. The transformation of industrial relations in the workplace in the former Soviet bloc is, in the last analysis, the transformation of the basis of class power in the social organization of production. This will be a long drawn-out process, stirring up often acute conflicts, and its destination cannot be anticipated. The subordination of the direct process of production to the imperatives of capital accumulation in the advanced capitalist countries is still not complete after over two hundred years, and has been achieved in distinctive forms in different countries.

The outcome of these conflicts will be determined not only in the workplace, but also by political struggles to secure control over state power and its extension. The pressures to maintain traditional paternalism in Russia are especially strong because of the particular vulnerability of senior management to challenges to its authority from below which are provoked by attempts to press fundamental change. This vulnerability is considerably increased by the failure to replace the communist party and the ministerial system with the institution of private ownership as the foundation of the authority of the manager. This is not simply a matter of establishing a juridical owner of the enterprise. It is also necessary for ownership to be legitimated in the eyes of the work-force, and for the claims of ownership to be endorsed and enforced juridically and politically. In the latter respect privatization has barely begun in Russia (although formally it has been more rapid than elsewhere), primarily because the state itself has lost legitimacy and effectiveness, while the judiciary has never acquired it. By contrast, in eastern Europe the rights of private property are (other than in Poland) endorsed by a more effective state power.

The struggle for state power is by no means independent of the struggle for power within the enterprise. In Russia the continued dominance of authoritarian paternalism in the enterprise has meant that, for all his liberal rhetoric, Yeltsin has in practice had to rely on conservative forces in the sphere of production. As a result, the power of the industrial *nomenklatura* has been left unchallenged, while the official unions have retained the bulk of their vast property, their check-off rights, their commanding majority on the Tripartite Commission, and their control of social security funds. At the same time, the independent unions have been marginalized and attacked by the government which they helped to bring to power.

It is important not to exaggerate the distinctiveness of Russia in these respects. The new ruling class is still undergoing formation in all of the countries of the former Soviet bloc, and it is by no means united or secure in its rule. In Poland, and to a lesser extent in Romania, as in Russia, the working class played a leading role in the destruction of the old system, and its aspirations remain a barrier to the consolidation of class rule both in the political sphere and in the sphere of production. However, even in Hungary or the Czech Republic, where the working class played a much less active role, workers' aspirations have to be contained. It is this which ultimately underlies the common patterns of development of trade unionism and workplace industrial relations across the former Soviet bloc.

The traditional pattern of trade unionism and workplace industrial relations proved an extremely powerful and effective means of limiting workers' needs and containing their aspirations. Whatever the role of the workers in the overthrow of the old system, the 'revolutions' in the former Soviet bloc were driven more by the desire of the intelligentsia and a large part of the ruling stratum to restrict the workers' new-found ambitions than to provide the workers with democratic channels through which to articulate them. For this reason the independent workers' organizations which sprang up in the first days of rebellion have proved an embarrassment to the new regimes which they helped to place in power, and they often face marginalization or slipping back into a traditional mould. Meanwhile, there has been a steady strengthening of a *de facto* alliance between the former official trade unions and supposedly liberal regimes throughout the former Soviet bloc, based on the reproduction of the traditional accommodating role of the trade union within the workplace.

This is not to argue that there are no forces of change; only that change will be slow. The threat of the emergence of an effective independent working-class organization has proved to be one of the main factors holding back the transformation of production relations within the workplace. The longer effective change is postponed the more dramatic it may eventually turn out to be. The failure to develop appropriate forms of industrial conflict resolution allows tensions to build up within enterprises. This results in the accumulation of barriers to even the smallest of changes, on the one hand, and in the politicization of conflicts which do erupt, on the other. This gives rise to the pattern of conflict which we have observed over the 1980s, in which periods of apparent worker passivity are interspersed with eruptions of spontaneous militancy. While sections of the left have hailed such spontaneous outbursts as authentic expressions of workers' aspirations, the experience of the 1980s is that in the absence of a stable institutional framework they can develop in unpredictable and uncomfortable political directions. The establishment of effective forms of workplace trade unionism is a matter of importance not only for the development of a stable system of industrial relations, but also for the effective stabilization of the nascent democracies of the former Soviet bloc, in providing a basis for the institutionalized articulation of the hopes and aspirations of the working class. This is hardly a new conclusion: it was precisely this consideration that lay behind the initiative to reconstitute democratic trade unionism in Europe and Japan in the first phase of post-war reconstruction in the 1940s.

Notes

1 The chapter draws on research funded by the University of Warwick Research and Innovations Fund, the East–West Initiative of the ESRC (Grant No. Y309253049) and the Nuffield Foundation. It is based primarily on intensive fieldwork in Russian workplaces in 1992–3, and additional information from a large number of other enterprises. The project has been carried out by a total of 32 researchers; we are very grateful to all our Russian collaborators.
2 Workplace research under the old regime was almost entirely confined within the limits of a rather narrow empiricist industrial sociology, using surveys to investigate 'labour motivation' within a social psychological framework, and was strictly controlled by the KGB. The most important exceptions were the case studies carried out in Hungary by Makó and Héthy; however these, like those of Michael Burawoy, focused on labour organization with little reference to industrial relations, which was too sensitive a matter for scientific investigation (Héthy and Makó 1989; Burawoy and Lukács 1992). The closest to an insight into workplace industrial relations under the old regime is provided by McAuley (1969) and Lampert (1985). We have discussed the development of trade unionism and workers' organization in Russia more fully in Clarke et al. (1993).
3 We have greatly benefited from discussions with a number of Eastern European colleagues, including Mária Ladó, András Tóth, Csaba Makó, Tamás Krausz, Tamás Réti (Hungary), Kazimierz Kloc, Witold Morawski (Poland), Zdenek Zboril (Czech Lands), Georgi Karasimeonov, Boyko Atanasov (Bulgaria).
4 We use the term 'official union' to refer to the continuation or successors of the former state-sanctioned unions.

References

Borisov, V., Fairbrother, P. and Clarke, S. 1993: Is there room for an independent union in Russia: the case of the Federation of Air Traffic Controllers' Unions. Eleventh International Labour Process Conference, Blackpool.

Burawoy, M. and Lukács, J. 1992: *The Radiant Past: ideology and reality in Hungary's road to capitalism*. Chicago: University of Chicago Press.

Clarke, S. 1992: Privatization and the development of capitalism Russia. *New Left Review*, 196, November–December, 3–27.

Clarke, S., Fairbrother, P., Burawoy, M. and Krotov, P. 1993: *What About the Workers?* London: Verso.

Conquest, R. (ed.) 1967: *Industrial Workers in the USSR*. London: Bodley Head.

Hauslohner, P. 1987: Gorbachev's Social Contract. *Soviet Economy* 3(1) 54–89.

Héthy, L. and Makó, C. 1989: *Patterns of Workers' Behaviour and the Business Enterprise*. Budapest: Institute of Sociology.

Kloc, K. 1993: Polish trade unions and economic transformation in Poland. (Mimeo.)

Lampert, N. 1985: *Whistleblowing in the Soviet Union*. London: Macmillan.

McAuley, M. 1969: *Labour Disputes in Soviet Russia 1957–65*. Oxford: Clarendon Press.

Pollert, A. and Hradecka, I. 1994: Privatization in transition: the Czech experience. *Industrial Relations Journal*, 25(1) 52–63.

Ruble, B. 1981: *Soviet Trade Unions*. Cambridge: Cambridge University Press.

Schapiro, L. and Godson, J. (eds) 1981: *The Soviet Worker: from Lenin to Andropov*. Basingstoke: Macmillan.

Soulsby, A. and Clark, E. 1993: Organizational restructuring in the Czech Republic. Eleventh International Labour Process Conference, Blackpool.

Thirkell, J., Scase, R. and Vickerstaff, S. 1993: Transitional models of labour relations in eastern Europe. BUIRA Conference, York.

Tóth, A. 1993a: Trade union pluralism and legal regulation of industrial relations. (Mimeo.)

Tóth, A. 1993b: Trade unions and civil society. (Mimeo.)

Index

3439